Austin Remembers

How could the Friends of the Austin Public Library celebrate Austin's sesquicentennial and the ten-year anniversary of our Austin Public Library building? The most appropriate answer seemed obvious. Publish a book of stories about Austin and its people written by the people who lived those stories.

The Friends of the Library financed *Austin Remembers* and provided the help necessary to bring it to press. Librarian, Ann Hokanson, and the library staff helped by encouraging writers to submit material, and by typing and proofreading stories. Jeanne Steinbrink, whose mother is pictured on the cover of the book, was indispensable and incredibly efficient as the project manager, a task she took on in addition to her regular job responsibilities. Many volunteers gave their time and talents to help type, proofread, collect photos, and even sell the book. We could not have completed the project without them. Of course, we could never have published a book without the knowledge and enthusiasm of our editor, Joan Claire Graham of Albert Lea.

The response from the community was overwhelming. People submitted marvelous stories as they remembered growing up in Austin and other Mower County towns, Austin's buildings, history, events and people. So the idea of *Austin Remembers*, a book of memories, has become a reality and a gift to the community, celebrating our past and our future. Happy 150th Anniversary, Austin! Happy Anniversary, Austin's beautiful public library building!

Carmen Tribbett

President, Friends of the
Austin Public Library

Thanks to our contributors,
who graciously shared their memories for all to enjoy.
And if there are those who remember things differently,
take time to consider that memory is often like a painting,
whose hard edges soften as you step back.

Success
By Ralph Waldo Emerson

To laugh often and much;
to win the respect of intelligent people
and affection of children;
to earn the appreciation of honest critics
and endure the betrayal of false friends;
to appreciate beauty, to find the best in others;
to leave the world a bit better,
whether by a healthy child,
a garden patch or a redeemed social condition;
to know even one life has breathed easier because you have lived.
This is to have succeeded.

Some photographs were reprinted with permission from
the *Austin Daily Herald*.
Others were donated by contributors.

ISBN: 0971-1971-72

Contributors and Story Pages

Richard Hall, the first person to submit material,
earned a place of honor at the front of the book
as Grand Marshal of this parade of remembrances.
All other contributors are listed in alphabetical order...more or less.

Contributors and Story Pages Continued

Contributors and Story Pages Continued

Contributors and Story Pages Continued

My Home Town
By Richard Hall

Whenever someone talks about his old hometown, those nostalgic words bring back childhood memories of a drowsy little packinghouse town located in the rich farming country of southern Minnesota. When I was a child, hometown meant Austin, Minnesota. The northwest side of town where I lived also included the countryside on the edge of town that stretched out as far as my bare feet would take me on a warm summer day.

From my point of view, hometown will always mean the people I knew who influenced my formative years, and they included my family, relatives, friends, neighbors and teachers. I believe everyone's life story is their adventure through time, and I'm reminded of an old Jewish proverb: "My family are the people I live with in time, the people whose lives prepare for mine, whose lives parallel mine, and whose lives mine prepares."

I have many pleasant memories of the Austin of my childhood, and deep down inside I have a secret longing to go back and see everything just one more time the way it used to be. So many things have changed with people, places and buildings that were so much a part of my little world of yesterday and which vanished with time. I recall in my childhood that there were so many young couples, and it was a youthful town with a lot of families with several children and very few old people. Families spent much more time outdoors.

In the 1930s, our country was going through many industrial changes from the end of the horse and buggy age to the automobile age. This transition changed almost every aspect of the American way of life. Today everything moves at a much faster pace, and progress has given us a much better standard of living. Still, I cherish many of my precious memories of the small country town of my childhood.

My yesterdays began when I walked out my back door and saw wet dew on the grass and heard the faint crowing of a rooster on the edge of town, then another one from a different direction. The distant sound of the train whistle as it made its way across the farm country blended with other morning sounds of barking dogs and singing birds.

My long-ago Austin features fathers putting in their back yard gardens on an early spring morning before hurrying off to work. Kids fishing for blue gills along the bank of the Cedar River with bamboo poles and worms listen for the 4 o'clock whistle of the Hormel plant that means their fathers will soon be home. Men in chambray shirts and bib overalls emerge from the plant after a hard day's work, carrying their black lunch pails and whistling as they walk home.

A postcard arrives in the mail telling us that my grandparents are planning to drive all the way from St. Paul to visit, and they will take me along when they visit friends and relatives. I hop onto the Jitney bus and ride all over town for a nickel, and at the end of the line the driver tells me I can stay on for another trip free if I want.

Crowds of people travel by car or on foot to stand on the Water Street bridge during a spring flood and watch water go over the dam. I sit close to the radio, straining to hear Chief Wolf Paw and send him gum wrappers so I can become a member of the Lone Tribe. At a Bible School picnic at Todd Park, I receive a double-dip ice cream cone and observe that they keep pop and watermelons cold in galvanized tubs filled with ice and cold water.

In my little Austin, I sit alone through a spooky Halloween movie after midnight, then run lickety-split home on a cold, black night. When winter weather settles in, I walk up on Main Street, where all the beautiful lights mark the arrival of Christmas season, and shoppers bustle about as the bells of St. Augustine Church chime in the distance.

I guess I can go back to those days in a way. The Austin of my childhood was a different time, long ago, when most of my happiness and many of my pleasures came from life's simple things that live on in my memory.

Cowboy Movies
By Richard Hall

Among my favorite childhood memories are the cowboy movies that I looked forward to seeing all week. Austin's Park Theatre was destroyed by a tornado shortly before they started making good talking movies, but it was replaced with a new Paramount Theatre on old Water Street. Across the street and a little to the west of the Paramount was the State Theatre, and they showed cowboy movies with cliffhanger serials almost always on Friday nights and Saturday and Sunday afternoons. If you walked east on Water Street a few blocks, you would come to the Eagle Theatre on the north side of old Water Street. Later in the 1930s, they built the Austin Theatre on the east side of the north end of Main Street.

Before I turned 12 years old, cowboy movies and serials on Friday nights were my greatest pleasures in life. I recall how I would walk blocks out of my way to see the colorful posters in front of different theatres, and I remember the newspaper advertisements of the upcoming movies.

Money was scarce, and there wasn't enough for life's necessities, let alone for entertainment. I had a hard time getting a ten cent allowance and had to beg and make promises to get a dime. I loved the excitement and suspense of the serial cliffhangers and always had to see the next week's installment to find out what happened. One summer I got hooked on a serial at the State Theatre and another one with Tim McCoy about a circus at the Eagle Theatre. For three months, until the serial had concluded, I would walk all the way from our house to the Eagle Theatre on the east side to see Saturday's matinee for a nickel.

Sometimes we would get to the State Theatre a half hour before Friday night's show, and there would still be kids in line ahead of us. Once in awhile some kids would try to break into the line ahead of us, and a scuffle would ensue. Everything would get out of control, and occasionally it would result in a fist fight. I vividly recall all the excitement and yelling.

We went to the movies in every kind of weather. In the dead of winter we'd stomp our feet to try to stay warm. The 7 o'clock show filled up fast, and the first ones in would race to get seats way down in front or save seats for their friends.

Before the movie started, there would be a lot of excitement with kids talking and yelling and running up and down the aisles. Excitement increased when the houselights dimmed, the big white movie screen lit up, and kids shuffled to get back to their seats in the dark. Some kids carried cap guns in holsters, just in case the guys on the screen needed any help, and as the first image appeared on the screen, we clapped, stomped our feet, whistled and cheered.

Everything was in black and white. A newsreel led the show, followed by a cartoon and a serial. By the time the main feature started, the kids were all worked up. We all had our favorite cowboy, horse and sidekick, and there was some kind of magic in all their names. Even the smallest children knew all the cowboys. Buck Jones, Ken Maynard, Hopalong Cassidy, Hoot Gibson, Bob Steel, Lash LaRue, Johnny Mack Brown, Bill Elliot and Monte Hale were among our favorites. Production time for cowboy movies took a little more than a week, budgets were low, and there was a never-ending supply. They generally lasted a little over an hour, with dramatic plots and lots of action.

Tom Mix was a little ahead of our time so I saw very few of his movies. Ken Maynard, who starred in films like *Lightning Strikes West*, *Six-Shootin' Sheriff*, and *Hell Fire Austin,* had a brother Kermit who was also in a number of movies. Kermit was a rodeo rider who sometimes doubled as a stunt man for his brother, but he also got top billing in several mid-'30s films such as *Trails of the Wild*, *Timber War,* and *Song of the Trail*. At one time Kermit Maynard lived in the northwest part of Austin and worked at Hormel.

Austin's Kermit Maynard 1937

I cherish those happy memories of when I was a small boy and my imagination would run wild. I lived in a cowboy world with other boys. We would run around the open field, vacant lots and school grounds with cap guns or rubber guns playing cowboys and Indians. We were so psyched to be cowboy gun fighters, and we spent sleepless nights reliving some of the dangers and shootouts we saw in the movies. Our cowboy world was a make believe world that helped us escape some of the hard times that were going on in our real world during those Depression times.

Turtle Creek
By Richard Hall

Like most folks during the Great Depression, we could only afford life's bare essentials. Children learned to make do with what they had and do without most things they wanted. Parents were reluctant to help kids out, and I never even heard of a weekly allowance, so even an 8-year-old learned to be self-reliant. I always needed money for something, but I never had any.

One of our neighbors, feeling sorry for me, rummaged through his fishing tackle and fixed me up with a small cane pole. Of course my father wouldn't let me go fishing by myself, but if the older boys agreed to let me tag along, then I got to fish Turtle Creek. I thought I was big enough to go fishing by myself, and I wanted to save enough money to buy a new cane pole. I nearly pestered my father to death, trying to figure out something to do that would earn me a little money.

Finally I got the idea that selling apples might bring in some cash, but the trouble with that plan was that by the time apples ripened enough to sell, fishing season would be almost over. My father said I could have any money that I got from selling crab apples from our tree, the only crab apple tree in our part of town. Housewives liked to make jelly from crab apples, so there was a chance I could sell a few.

Every day that summer, from the time of the blossoms, I checked those little green apples. Whenever I got the chance, I would run uptown to Decker's Hardware Store to price, admire and count their large selection of fishing poles they had leaning against the wall.

My father finally told me that the big day had arrived when I could sell crab apples. I climbed the tree and shook and shook the branches until the ground was red from all the fruit. I picked up all the best apples, put them in an orange crate in my Red Ranger wagon, and went from door to door selling a large lard pail of crab apples for ten cents.

As soon as I had enough money to buy a pole, I quit my business, ran back to my yard to park my wagon, which still had quite a few apples in it, and ran to Decker's Hardware. After studying all their poles, I found the one that I thought was the best. My boyish thinking told me that I would catch bigger fish if I had a stronger fighting line, so I bought their thickest green fish line and also a thick wire leader.

There are those who can't understand the charm of creek fishing, but for boys who never got a chance to go lake fishing, Turtle Creek was special. It wasn't until my ninth birthday in October that my father said I could go fishing by myself, and I was a happy boy. With my new pole over my shoulder, a can of worms in my hand, and full confidence that I would catch a big fish, I started out on my first solo fishing trip, walking out to my favorite deep hole at Turtle Creek.

Two old fishermen already were fishing in my favorite spot, and although they pleasantly admired my new pole, they made it perfectly clear that they didn't want a kid fishing with them. I moved upstream, baited my hook with a big gob of worms and threw in my line. The wind kept blowing my cork into shore, and I wasn't having any luck. I was thirsty and wanted a drink of spring water, so I placed a large rock on the end of my pole and took off for Seven Springs.

On my way back, I heard the old excited fishermen calling me. I came running as fast as I could, and when I got to where I had left my pole, I saw that it was way out in the water and that it was being rapidly pulled to the other side of the creek. I jerked off my shirt and jumped into the creek, and was able to grab my pole and give it a big yank. When I yanked the pole, the creature on the end of the line made a vigorous attempt to gain its freedom. The line sliced through the water and became so tense that I thought it would break. I kept yelling, "I've got a fish! I've got a big fish!"

A crowd soon gathered on the creek bank, laughing and giving advice and issuing threats, "I'm gonna tell your father on you," and "You're going to catch your death of a cold." When I heard a neighbor woman yell, "It's that Hall kid, and he can't swim," I hoped someone might jump in and help me because I was afraid. No help arrived, however, because the water was cold and dirty. I didn't care about the fish; I just wanted to get my new pole back. All of a sudden there was a violent jerk on the line, and my arm felt like it was pulled out. There was electricity in the air as the attention of the crowd was attracted to a rise in the water and someone gasped, "It's no fish; it's an alligator."

Out of the swirling water came the biggest monster I had ever seen, and it was coming right at me with its jaw set. I thought I'd be eaten alive, and didn't realize that this creature hadn't seen me and probably was just as scared as I was. In self-defense, I brought my pole down hard on its back, and I heard someone yell, "It's a snapper, and its head is as big as a lard pail."

Before I knew what was happening, the turtle made a deep dive and started pulling me, kicking and screaming, towards a deep hole. I could hear people in the crowd yelling at me to let go and forget about the fishing pole, but the water was up to my armpits, and the pole was the only thing I could hold on to. The turtle's bull-like strength had dragged me to the edge of the drop-off, and I was trembling with excitement and fatigue. I braced my feet, and with all my strength I pulled on my pole. The pole bent almost double, but I was able to bring the turtle's head to the surface, where I could see its mean eyes and open mouth.

The line stretched tight, and the pole snapped and splintered about two feet from my hand. This gave the turtle the slack and leverage it needed. There was a big splash as I went over the drop off into the deep creek water. A few seconds seemed like an eternity as the turtle dragged me across the deepest part of the pond. At this point it seemed as if the turtle had caught a boy instead of a boy catching a turtle.

Finally my head popped out of the water. Coughing and choking, with water in my eyes and lungs, I found myself standing in shallow water and mud. I still had my glasses, but I had lost my pole. Someone who has never been in soft mud doesn't have an idea of the awful feeling of being sucked into the muck, so I ran to escape until I was on a sandbar. I was sick to my stomach and distraught about my irreparable broken fishing pole. In front of all those people I had made a fool of myself, but I mustered a sense of determination and decided I was not going to quit. My parents always said I had a temper twice my size, and that's what took over as I decided to catch the turtle.

I thought the turtle had gotten away, but when I went to get my broken pole and tangled line that were still lying downstream against the creek bank, the turtle came alive again and began dragging my pole downstream. Every time I grabbed for it, he managed to keep it out of my reach. My strength was waning, and I was crazy with rage as I made one desperate grab and got hold of the pole.

Managing to stay in shallow water, I battled my way toward shore. The turtle's head kept popping out of the water, and I could see its broad back and great size as it rolled from side to side, skimmed on its side and floated and bumped along the rocks. As we reached the shallows near the shoreline, one of the old fishermen took off his shoes, rolled up his pants, and came in to help me. The turtle struggled feebly as it reached a footing on shore, then made one last vigorous stab for freedom by kicking its flippers and striking violently.

The crowd cheered as we dragged it on to the shore. The turtle tried to run away, but I ran after it, determined not to let it escape. I grabbed the shell in desperation to try to turn him over, like I had seen the fisherman do, but he was too fast and too strong. A loud and excited voice above me said, "Look out kid, you're going to get hurt," as the fisherman reached over me and flipped the turtle on its back.

Apparently this turtle had a lot of stories to tell because it had two hooks in its mouth and one in its legs. The man used my fish line to tie a stick to the turtle so it couldn't turn back over. My stomach felt like it was tied in knots, and I was quivering and blue from the cold October air. I found my shirt and put it back on as I sat down to rest and reflect on this first solo fishing trip. The fisherman said he would guard the turtle while I went home to get my wagon. He helped me load the turtle and warned me to keep my distance from the snapper. Some boys from the west side of town came to help me pull the wagon, and all the way home people stopped to look, and I related the whole story.

After all that I had gone through that day, the worst was still to come because I had to tell my dad what had happened. Putting it off as long as I could, I hid the wagon in a shed in the back of our house. When Dad came home for supper, he wanted to know where my pole was. I didn't know that someone had already told him the whole story as I reluctantly unfolded my adventure, trying to edit parts that I thought would upset him.

When I finished my tale, I think Dad felt sorry for me because he got help, and they put the turtle in a big washtub with a board and rock on top. They guessed that the turtle weighed over 25 pounds.

I was so sad and sick to think that I had waited all summer and now I didn't have my fishing pole or anything to show for it. I would go out and poke the old turtle with a broom and say, "I'm going to eat you!" When I asked my dad when we were going to eat the turtle, he said he wasn't much for eating turtles, let alone cleaning them.

A few days later my turtle was gone. My first thought was that it had escaped, and I looked all over the neighborhood for it. When I came to supper, there was a new fishing pole where I had kept mine. Dad said that he had given the turtle away, and that the new pole was mine.

Richard Hall has written several books about Austin, and they are available at the Mower County and Adams Historical Societies.

Coming to Austin…and Staying
By Wallace Alcorn

Why I came to Austin may not be as significant as why, having come, I stay. I am, in fact, no less an Austinite than one who was born here. Just as adopted children are reassured by having been chosen rather than just having happened, I stake my claim alongside the native-born by asserting I chose Austin, and Austin continues to be my choice.

Having been born and reared in the next state east, I heard of Minnesota early. However, no one gave me reason to think much about it. At the end of a college summer while working for the U.S. Forest Service in Idaho, I hitchhiked home and passed through the state for the first time. I didn't pass through Austin or see any sign of it.

From Illinois, I moved to Kansas and then to Indiana, and then back to Milwaukee and to Wheaton again for graduate school. There I met a nursing student by the name of Ann Carmichael, who had been born in England but, with her family, had escaped to Michigan just prior to the German bombing. Then she lived in Africa. I went to New York and then Grand Rapids, where I caught up with Ann, and we wed while she was teaching in a school of nursing. Together we went to Detroit and then New Jersey. I earned a Masters at Princeton and a Ph.D., driving daily from the North Jersey shore to New York University.

We returned to Wheaton so I could teach college in Chicago. I was offered the New Testament chair in a graduate seminary in Tacoma, Washington, and I drove my family, now of five, west. While on the West Coast, our national denomination office asked me to consider returning to the pastorate and taking our church in Austin. By then I had learned about the city from a friend who had been pastor of this church for over twenty years. He encouraged me to go, because he maintained serious concern for the church and community.

In March, 1976, I boarded a plane at Seattle-Tacoma to fly here to meet people. Settled in my seat, I opened the *Wall Street Journal*. Front page, above the fold: a news account reported that George A. Hormel Company might move out of Austin and construct a new packing plant somewhere else. "There goes my congregation," I thought.

From the Rochester airport I was driven to Austin through farmland such as I had never before noticed. Rich, black soil covering every field was sold around Puget Sound by the bushel; here it was taken for granted. After the weekend I flew on to Grand Rapids, Michigan to preach at a church interested in my going there. I declined to be interviewed until after the Austin church had made a decision. They invited me back for a formal interview, and Ann came with me this time.

If we were to move here, it would be by far the smallest community in which either of us had lived. We recognized it as a radically different kind of community from Milwaukee, Chicago, Detroit, New York, or Seattle. It had none of the convenient facilities and cultural events of metropolitan areas, and I was especially concerned about being distant from a university with its research library. Nonetheless, we liked what we saw. "This is a good place to raise a family," people kept assuring us. When we visited the high school to inquire into its curriculum and extracurricular opportunities for our children, we found some students sitting at the door smoking. They surprised us with polite greetings. We were to learn later from our kids that these were typed "burnies," which is to say they were presumed to be the lowest level of high school society. So, even the "burnies" were nice to us.

As we drove around town, we noticed not one property in deteriorated condition. People took pride in where they lived, and they took care of it. They left their houses unlocked and looked at me suspiciously when I locked my vehicle. People felt safe here. A sign in front of Sterling Shopping Center did make me nervous in respect to what I had heard about the Hormel situation: "Welcome to Austin, where the good life is here to stay!" Someone had ingeniously substituted a question mark.

I saw an opportunity here to practice in ministry what I had been learning through years of college and seminary research and teaching. As I weighed the considerable advantages of ministering in a small town, those of a big city began to lose some significance. I recognized the value of a daily newspaper, two radio stations, two television channels, as well as easy accessibility to public schools and city-county governments.

We piled into our station wagon and headed east, exiting and re-entering the uncompleted I-90. Austin was our destination, yet it never occurred to me we might stay long. Mark would enter Austin High School in ninth grade, Allison would enter eighth grade at Ellis, and Stephen was headed for Banfield's fourth grade. Though they attended schools in Wheaton and Tacoma, it was Austin schools that gave them the base for college and grad school. Their teachers became our friends.

As we approached from the west, I connived with the youngest to climb out when I stopped on the shoulder and run to the Austin limits sign to be the first of the children to arrive. This was now home.

Austin received us with open arms. Business in Austin, I was to learn, is more than commercial—it's also social. You don't walk in, do your business, and then walk out. Such is disappointing because only business is transacted. A social exchange is also expected. To some Austinites, meeting people is as important as having the job, and in fact, meeting people is why some take jobs. If you want to do business successfully in Austin, you first make a friend of the businessperson. Then you do business with your new friend.

The people respected (or feared) in metropolitan areas are those who demand and threaten. They get what they want, of course, but there is more to it than this, and they never learn what it is. Threatening people isn't the way to go about it in Austin. And don't try to tell people what to do, because they might do the opposite just to spite you. We must be Minnesota-nice, e.g., "You might want to…" or "Most people would.."

The people who open businesses in Austin generally recognize their side. There is no such thing as cheating someone in business and getting away with it. You just won't stay in business long in this community if you pull things like this. The word gets around, and it gets around quickly. On the other hand, good word also gets around. When a retailer pleases one customer, he acquires without salary a publicity agent who spreads the word. And his friends will take his word even when they ignore paid advertising.

Not long after arrival, everyone said we had to visit the Mower County Fair, and the family thoroughly enjoyed it. Still big-city naïve, I felt too busy in "church work" to be distracted by something so personal and fun. I quickly learned, however, I could make more pastoral contacts on the midway than in homes and that one cannot experience Austin without the fair. Moreover, I watched for other opportunities and found them in Crazy Days. I could roam the scene and meet a large portion of the population.

Our first harvest in a rural area became instructive. Initially, they thought I was trying to be funny about how little I knew of farming—until they realized I really did not know, and then they thought I was funny. They had a funny way of pronouncing *manure*, a word used often. What I found most ironic about farmers is that, on the one hand, they were universally certain no city boy could ever know anything about farming and, on the other, they were equally convinced none of the other farmers did either. Of all the people in the congregation, I found I could most rely on farmers to do what they said they would do. The other thing I learned is that it's not wise to try to tell them how to do it.

I found the plant workers to have their own peculiarities, and I had to learn a new way of listening to them. When they gripe about how hard things are, they brag. When they talk among themselves, the plant is the worst place in the world to work and you have to be crazy to seek a job there. In talking to outsiders, Hormel is the best employer in the country, and it takes a smart cookie to get a job there. They like to retire to places like McAllen, because of all the former plant workers there with whom to exchange gripes.

As much a culture shock as it was getting used to farmers and plant workers, adjustment to Minnesota winters I found horrendous. This was thirty years ago when we had real, old-fashioned winters. Early in the first winter, I drove west of town to make a call at a farm. I had to detour, because the county had given up keeping one road open. I couldn't get into the farm's lane, because it offered only tractor ruts, which I wasn't about to risk. I pushed through a snow bank up to my chest and then waded in knee-high snow to the farmhouse. I stopped for breath about half way and thought, "What in the world am I doing in a place like this?" Inside, with hot coffee and warm muffins, I remembered.

My journal records that on the last three January weekends of 1982, the wind chill reached below -100. Unbelievable. In New Jersey we cancelled schools and church services with two inches of snow on the ground and just waited for it to melt. But we held our morning services here. And people came, not as many as usual, but what we lacked in numbers we gained in spirit. These were some of the most rewarding services, and the people were unusually responsive. My guess is we were so proud of just getting to church we made sure it became worthwhile.

It isn't quite true, as the cliché claims, that "everyone in Austin knows everyone" or "everyone knows everybody else's business," but it does seem this way at times. A community organization on whose board I was serving held a reception for the Chief Justice of the State Supreme Court. Although the community was invited, no one was surprised it was the lawyers who showed up en masse. I was given the task, in the reception line, of introducing a representative of the McKnight Foundation to those passing through. Being able to name everyone and their associations, the man from the Cities asked, "Small town?" No, I corrected, it is just that it is a smaller number within town who get involved in community affairs, and we just keep bumping into each other.

As to knowing other people's business, we do sustain something of a problem. While it seems futile to try to hold things secret or get away with something underhanded, we encounter a problem with a lack of confidentiality. People, for the most part, truly care about others and are interested in them. Some non-professional employees of some professional agencies talk too openly about sensitive things that are clearly privileged communication, and we need to respect the difference between pointless curiosity and helpful concern.

While we heard that Austin is a good place to rear a family, we soon heard complaints that it's not a very good place for young adults. This, I fear, is simply one of the limitations of a small, rural community. All our children found careers elsewhere, and this makes sense. One of the nicer occurrences in recent years is a larger number of Austin-reared young adults who have returned to practice their professions in health, law, and teaching. I delight in meeting competent professionals whom I knew as stumbling kids.

As we think together about being reared in Austin or coming here and staying here, I make this observation: Austin people tend to presume what we think we hold common with other communities is actually peculiar to us. What we presume to be unique is quite common all over. It makes good sense to stay in Austin, but not all the time. The more and the farther we travel and become knowledgeable of other cultures, the more likely we are to understand ourselves. The better we understand ourselves, the more likely we are to remain by choice.

I came here in the nation's bicentennial year, and I write this for Austin's sesquicentennial. Not only is Austin the smallest community in which either of us has lived, we have lived here longer than anywhere else. Thirty years in one place—but not by accident or parents' choice. We came to Austin by our choice, and we stay here by choice.

Remembering Sixty-eight Years in Austin
By Nina Irene White Allen

I'll turn 98 years young on June 8, 2006, if the good Lord's willing. That's a lot of memories of good times, and some not so good times that we survived by helping each other through.

I married Ernest Eugene Allen on April 28, 1928, in Park Rapids, Minnesota. In April, 1929, our first son Harold was born. He had a heart malfunction; they called the condition "blue baby," and there was no medical treatment for it. He passed away after three weeks. Ernie was a carpenter, and he built a tiny new house in Ackley, MN, for our new family, but the house burned while we were at my mother's for the baby's birth. We were not off to a good start.

Ernie's sister, Amy Fleming, lived in Austin. She and her husband Jess came north on vacation to visit and fish. She thought it would be a good idea to move to Austin. She said there was plenty of work available, so we packed our belongings into our old Ford convertible and headed south to Austin. A big gust of wind blew the top off the car during the trip, but at least we didn't get rained on. Back in the old days it wasn't a quick trip like they make now because those old cars didn't go 70 miles an hour, and there weren't any freeways to travel on.

Austin in the distance was quite a sight for me. I had never been there before, and it was a lot bigger than I had imagined. As we drove down Kenwood Avenue, with the beautiful homes lined up on either side and then past a school so big it actually had a street running through the center of it, I knew this was going to be a wonderful place to put down roots. We stayed with Ernie's sister, and he worked with his brother-in-law in his painting and wallpapering business until we could get on our feet and find a place of our own, but then the Great Depression hit full force. Jobs vanished, and times got hard, and we were going to have our second child and desperately needed a home of our own.

The H. J. Holtz dairy farm near Brownsdale needed building repair and farm help. It was a fine example of the bartering system. We got to live on one of the farms in exchange for carpentry work and farm labor and a small wage. Occasionally there was freshly butchered meat to eat. I washed all the milking equipment for all the milk and cream we could use. Ernie Jr. was born in September, 1930, healthy and such a joy.

Making a trip north the next year with the baby to visit relatives, we discovered my mother, Mae White, struggling to care for my 8-year old sister Dolly because my mother's rheumatoid arthritis had advanced. We brought them home, and my mother lived with us until she passed away at the age of 78.

Later Ernie landed a job on the installation of the gas line being brought into Austin (I believe it was a WPA project), and we found an apartment in Austin. The job opportunity offered by the gas line brought my brothers, Delbert, Melvin and Jesse, to town. They call that chain migration now, but then we just called it helping out family members. Ernie also worked as the security guard for the project at night. I landed the job of doing the washing for the out-of-town men working on the pipeline, because my husband offered them my labor. It would have been wonderful had automatic washers, dryers, and permanent press clothing been invented sooner. To supplement the family income I also sold baked goods and horseradish in pint jars. Later on, all three of my brothers got jobs at the Hormel plant, and soon I was cutting hair for the men they worked with, for a quarter a head. During those days people did what they could to survive, and a quarter was a lot of money.

A strong sense of family and community spirit also helped. Neighbors shared, and were as close as kin; everybody watched out for each other, making sure no one would starve. Nothing was wasted; clothing was recycled for the material and used to make whatever was needed, children's clothing or quilts. We moved to a newer house, but it was too cold for our little boy, so we moved to an apartment above Gildner's Clothing Store on south Main Street for a short time. There were two other apartments on the second floor, a dentist office, beauty parlor, and the WPA office pay window, where checks were passed out. Our daughter Darlene was born there in May of 1934. My sister-in-law, Amy, noticed that a neighbor was moving out of her house. We found the owner, Mrs. Howvell, and rented it from her, and we lived there for the next nine years. In November, 1937, our son Bob was born there.

The Great Depression was anything but great, but there were things for people to do for enjoyment. There was a zoo on the north end of Main Street where you could take your children to watch monkeys play. The library had story time during the summer and gave a party for the children with treats and ice cream. The Austin High School was used as a social activity center in the evenings.

The "Clay House" provided clay to make ceramics. There were many molds to choose from to create plaques and figurines for gifts or for home decorations. My brother Jesse had the job of firing clay. After the firing process, people would return to paint their project and enjoy socializing with each other. There was no charge for this activity.

Another community social gathering place was the sing-alongs and band concerts at the band shell. The Old Mill at the Ramsey Dam was another popular place for summer recreation. There was a pasture adjacent to the water, and the man who owned the property let people drive in and spread their blankets on the ground to have picnics, fish and play there. There was a boat that you could ride up the river, but there was a fare for that. Todd Park was also a popular place for family relaxation, and the spring water in the park served as water for the fresh squeezed lemonade (I believe the water became so polluted in the 1970s that it was no longer safe to use it).

People who could afford the privilege could spend an evening at the movie theatre occasionally. But it was common for people to get together and make their own entertainment. Those who could play an instrument did, and everybody else sang along. I played the fiddle and mouth organ, and our friend Tony played also.

Austin had a WPA project called the "sewing room." People, mainly women, worked there making clothing and other necessities that were given out to the folks who needed them. They made sheets, pillowcases, towels, washcloths, dish towels, bloomers (underpants), nightgowns and pajamas, dresses, and shirts. Ernie had bought a truck and was hauling men to their job sites. He also contracted to cook the noon meal for them. I got to wash all the big pots and dishes for the next day while he went to Albert Lea to pick up the material for delivery to the sewing room. During those days it was valuable to be a Jack-of-all-trades because it meant survival. No one could afford a carpenter so you did whatever you could find to do and were extremely happy you had some money to survive on.

The Salvation Army provided prepared meals for people who needed them every day. Government commodities of cheese, butter, canned meat, flour, and cornmeal were distributed to people. If the government had not assisted, people would have starved.

I'm not sure of the year, but when I arrived in Austin there was no East Side Lake. It was created later, and I do believe that was a

WPA project also. The Roosevelt Bridge was another vital project that provided improvement to Austin during the Depression. So even though the times were hard, many good things were being done. People had the opportunity for joy, happiness, and success although their success was measured more by fulfillment of basic needs compared with the fulfillment of wants today.

By the late 1930s, the hard times were over, and we bought our first home and remodeled it. Ernie was working as a carpenter again for Nick Wagner Construction, and the economy was booming. In 1941 National Defense projects were in full swing, and Ernie left for Provost, South Dakota, taking his friend Tony Liposki with him to build government barracks at the south end of the Black Hills. His next stop was the copper mines at Anaconda, Montana. We moved out there with him for the summer and returned so the children could go to school.

Ernie moved on to Hanford, Washington, to work on the Manhattan Project. That was where they eventually processed plutonium for the atomic bomb. One of the structures had walls made of ten feet thick cement, but he wasn't allowed to talk about it. Letter writing was the only form of communication we had because no one had thought up the cell phone yet. When he returned home, he spent the rest of his life being a carpenter in Austin. Ernie passed away in February, 1986 at the age of 81.

During World War II, there was a shortage of goods, and rationing stamps were needed to purchase goods. Every person in the family was given a book of stamps good for specific items such as sugar, cigarettes, tires, and gasoline. The economic situation had come full circle. Money shortages of the Great Depression were gone, and the folks in Austin had plenty of money to buy goods, but there were very few goods to buy.

Our last child, Marlene, was born in May of 1946, becoming one of the first of the baby boomer generation. There was a shortage of lumber, and we had to wait a long time to get enough to build a small new home on the west edge of Austin, a couple of blocks from where the college is located now. Construction is always slow during Minnesota winters so in the late 1940s, Ernie rented a shop over by the fairgrounds and started Allen's Fish Market, which latter moved to 10th Street NW near our home. He trucked fish from Salmon Johnson's in Duluth, besides hauling lumber for Ray Buchner Tomellson's Sawmill south of Austin.

After graduating from high school, Ernie Jr. joined his father in the building business, making him the third generation of carpenters. The building boom that occurred in 1950 continued strong until the 1960s. Our last move was in 1964, when we moved to Burr Wood Addition, south of the Austin airport. I moved to Perham, Minnesota in 1997 to live close to my daughter. They worried about me because they thought I was getting too old to live alone so far out in the country. I have been told that County Road 3 that used to run in front of my house has been closed off for the airport expansion--a sure sign of Austin's continuing growth.

I lived in Austin from 1929 to 1997. I watched the town grow, the suburbs spring up, and the buildings change. I saw the demolition of the old courthouse and the building of the new one, the loss of some of the railroad, and the many expansions of and the building of the new Hormel Packing Plant. Many new schools needed to be built to educate the growing number of children in our community. I remember the addition of the Sterling Shopping Center, the forerunner of the Oak Park Mall.

I watched changes that have occurred on Main Street, like a bank replacing the old hotel that served as a bus stop for many years. Cars and cab service slowly replaced city buses that used to run regular routes for easy transportation. The old library was replaced with a more modern looking building, but the old one had a lot of character too. The Holiday Inn was made into an apartment complex. The Terp Ballroom, where Ernie and I must have danced around the world at least once, has even faded away.

Things have to change to keep up with the times. There will always be something new to replace the old; it's just part of the life cycle. Speaking of cycles, I had my first ride on a Harley in my 96th year, proving that change is just a normal part of growth. Austin was a wonderful place to live life for 68 years, to watch my children grow and become independent, to watch my grandchildren and great grandchildren be born.

Nina lives with her daugher Marlene and son-in-law in Perham, MN. She is in the International Poetry Hall of Fame.

The Paper Lady
By Lynne Andersen

I have been a newspaper carrier for the *Austin Daily Herald* for the past fourteen years. I have walked many of the streets in Austin and have become known as "The Paper Lady." The stories I could tell about my journey! With my daily walks in rain, sleet, wind, snow and ice, I am expected to be out there delivering the news to my customers.

When I became a carrier, most of my customers were carrier collect. That meant I had to collect money from them every month. Now they all pay in the office. I don't like this because when I would go to collect, I felt I got to know my customers on a more personal level. I do like the fact that everyone is paying in the office, because at the end of the month I receive a check instead of having to pay a bill to the *Herald*.

I have been asked for directions to a lot of places too many times to count. I have been asked how much a paper route pays, where to buy a cheap car, and who is hiring.

I have seen dust tornadoes, and I have been bitten by my share of dogs. I have seen car accidents happen. I often watch children playing and fighting. Many times I have been offered help in doing my routes. I have even been sung to. These are just a few of my stories; my list is endless. I have enjoyed delivering the paper all these years. It has kept me in shape, which has contributed to a strong, healthy heart, and I like meeting people.

*Lynne Andersen delivers the **Austin Daily Herald** and the **Albert Lea Tribune** to the Austin Public Library.*

Miracle on Neveln Street
By Lois Anderson

September 1, 1967 dawned bright and sunshiny but turned out to be a dismal day later on. My daughter Cathy, 13 years old, and her little cousin Julie, age 6, rode their bikes to Zip's Store near our house to buy candy. Cathy planned to escort Julie back home about four blocks away.

As they turned the corner near our house, they saw a neighbor's puppy and decided to stop and play with it. Julie left her bike near the front of a parked car on the street, and Cathy's bike was behind the car. As they were getting on their bikes to return to Julie's house, a car driven by an Austin man veered out of control, heading right toward them. He had reached into the back seat to keep his small son from falling. No car seats were required in those days.

Julie was hit, and the parked car, with Cathy behind it, was moved about twenty feet along the boulevard. Neighbors rushed to help, and one lady ran to my house to tell me that Cathy was in an accident down on the corner. I hurried to the scene and saw several men lifting the car off my daughter. Julie was under the runaway car with hot radiator water and battery acid dripping down on her face.

Julie's parents were notified. Someone called the ambulance, and I rode with the girls to St. Olaf Hospital. Cathy had one long, deep gash on her leg and returned home the next day. Julie was in bad shape! She had burns on her face and neck, abrasions and contusions all over her body, and a broken leg. The doctors performed major surgeries and skin grafting, and she was in recovery at the hospital for one month.

It was a miracle that both girls survived and went on to lead successful lives. Cathy graduated from Austin High School and attended cosmetology school at Austin Vo-Tech. She later moved to the Minneapolis area and worked at various positions. She is currently an administrative assistant at Columbia Park Medical Group.

Julie was a pretty young woman. She married and had three children. She was an efficient waitress, enjoyed bowling, and was an avid pool player. She passed away November 27, 2005, at age 44.

Life on Grandpa's Farm
By Lois Anderson

When I was growing up, Austin seemed like a big city. We lived on Grandpa Sukow's farm three miles west of Dexter, a small village about fifteen miles east of Austin. Our parents had three daughters when we moved there. Helen was the oldest, I was next, then Dorothy. Charles was born a year later on Helen's birthday. Just think – four children in four years! What a busy mother! Leo came along later, then Clara and Phyllis.

One day Dad went to the small railroad town of Renova, a mile north of our farm. The store owner, Herman Stern, asked, "Well, Charlie, what are you going to name this one?" Dad answered, "Enough!" Then George and Betty came along. I remember the hired girls who helped Mom. One was our cousin, Evelyn Crane, who will be 91 in April and lives in Sunnyvale, California.

The farm was a great place for nine children. We had to walk the fields in summer to pick out the wild mustard – no weeds in Grandpa's fields! Mom planted a huge garden, and we kids picked potato bugs off the plants. Dad promised to pay us a penny for each bug, but I don't recall that he ever paid us! The boys helped with the barn chores and fieldwork. We girls learned how to do housework, baking, and gardening. We helped Mom can hundreds of quarts of corn, beans, tomatoes, and beef. Grandpa tended his orchard of apple and plum trees, so we canned sauce and jam also.

I was not a typical farm girl. I wasn't fond of animals, and I detested gathering eggs in the hen house because the hens would peck at me. Another chore I hated was washing the cream separator. I liked cleaning house and remember one incident that almost got me in deep trouble. Dad was listening to our battery-operated radio for the noon markets. I was sweeping the living room floor, and Leo kept teasing me and getting in my way. I lifted the broom to hit at him; he ducked, and guess where the broom landed? On Dad's head! Needless to say, I hurriedly ran out of there!

We had few toys so we planned our own fun together, playing house in the grove Grandpa so carefully cleared out every summer. We arranged sticks to designate rooms of our house. We pretended to be

Mom and Dad, with the younger ones as our children. We also played kick the can, tag, hide and seek, ante-I-over and captain may I. We girls made bracelets out of dandelion stems. We also picked wild roses in the ditches and soaked them in water for perfume.

Mom had to be the disciplinarian, and we learned in a hurry! One look from across the room was all it took to make us behave. We four older ones never forgot one incident. Mom told us to take lunch to Dad and Uncle Jake Sukow, who were working in a field a couple miles away. We tarried along the way home, stopping at the neighbors' and taking our time. When we arrived home, a worried Mom was waiting for us. Helen was the first to be escorted in one door of the woodshed and out the other, crying loudly. We knew what that meant – a spanking with Mom's left hand! The rest of us were crying before we even went in the door. What a chorus we made as we came out! Was that our first singing lesson? If so, it was a valuable one.

Dad and a neighbor, Bill Kraft, owned a threshing rig together and were hired by all the farmers in the area. Oh, how I loved those days. We would take lunch to all the farm workers in the morning and afternoon. Dinner served at noon was scrumptious: fried chicken or roast beef, potatoes and gravy, a vegetable, tomatoes, pickles, homemade bread or dinner rolls, pie and coffee. I was often hired to help a neighbor lady serve the meals. I think I earned 25 cents a day.

Grandpa Sukow stayed with us for several years, in the small bedroom downstairs. In the summer, hired men helped with the fieldwork. They slept in the enclosed front porch. I can still hear Dad shout his wake-up call, "Muleskinners, Buckaroos, daylight in the swamp!" The porch was also a play area for us when unoccupied. I recall playing the cylinder records on the old Victrola out there.

We enjoyed music. Grandpa would play a button accordion he brought from Germany, and we kids would dance around the huge kitchen table. We older girls often stayed at Uncle Jake's farm near Elkton with our cousin, Luella.

Uncle Jake was a big influence, teaching us to harmonize the good old songs like "Prisoners Song," "Isle of Capri," and "Put on Your Old Gray Bonnet." We Sukow girls, Helen, Dorothy and I, sang at many functions at our country church.

Uncle Jake played the trombone. I was so proud when my oldest son, Alan, followed in his footsteps and chose to play the trombone. The Sukow relatives compiled family information for a book entitled *A New Song* – again music related.

We kids learned to behave after our spankings and Mom's warning looks across a room. However, I wonder if she ever knew how we teased our grandpa. One day we were playing in the barn while he was outside calling to the horses, "Come, Pete! Come, Bill." We would mock his German brogue – and it was quite a chorus! By the time he came back into the barn to scold us, we were up in the haymow with the ladder pulled up after us. I think he often called us "those Sukow brats!" Later Grandpa moved off the farm and stayed in town with Aunt Lillie, his daughter, and Louis. He passed away in 1945.

We enjoyed free summer movies at Dexter and Elkton, sitting on blankets outside under the stars. Those Westerns were so exciting! Sometimes we would make popcorn to take along, but our favorite treat was an ice cream cone from Lucky Louie's Pool Hall in Dexter. Uncle Louie Budahn owned the place for years.

Our winter entertainment was playing card games. We learned crazy 8 and hearts, and we older ones learned to play 500 from Mom and Dad. They would play with a neighbor couple, Grace and Lyman Richardson. They usually played at our house so we kids could go to bed upstairs. Some of us couldn't resist looking down the hole where the stovepipe ran through our room to watch and listen when we were expected to be asleep.

When we three older girls were teenagers, we rode to Austin with Mom and Grace to see our first movie. *Gone With the Wind* was being shown at the Paramount Theatre. What a special treat!

Grandpa had donated an acre of land from our 160-acre farm for a school. Monitor School was built, and we older ones were students there. Mom was active in Mother's Club for years and years! I loved school, and my favorite teacher was Margaret Fairbanks. I graduated from eighth grade at Trinity Lutheran Church School the year I was confirmed. One day that year Mom let Helen, Dorothy and me skip a day of school and travel to Austin with her to shop. There was a "Man on the Street" program over the radio. The interviewer stopped us to visit and asked us to sing a song. We sang "Ragtime Cowboy Joe." Somehow my pastor/teacher, Rev. Schroeder found out why I was absent that day. I guess singing on the radio wasn't a good excuse!

Helen didn't get to go to high school. She worked at a local farm as a hired girl. The year after eighth grade, I helped neighbor ladies with laundry, canning and babysitting. I wanted to become a teacher, and Mom checked into our attending Elkton High School after Dorothy finished eighth grade. We started ninth grade together the fall of 1939. The bus picked us up, and we rode thirty-two miles each day to get our education. We joined the Glee Club and also sang in the sextet. We graduated in 1943 with a class of thirteen. I attended the Normal Training Department at Austin High School for one year. It was a grueling year of learning to be a rural school "marm." I spent three weeks in March practice teaching at a rural school in the area. My host teacher was Frances Martin, and she is still living in Sargeant, Minnesota.

We moved off Grandpa's farm after Dorothy and I graduated from High School. Dad managed the Hormel Cook Farm north of Mapleview for one year. Then we moved into Austin to a house on West Oakland Avenue. Dad was a truck driver for S. L. Young and Kough's Transfer. Mom worked at Nelson's Supermarket, Austin Candy Company, and the Kozy Nook Café. She and her sister, Elsie Perl, owned the café for one year. Later, Mom and Dad retired and moved to a smaller house within walking distance of their church, St. John's Lutheran on Kenwood. Helen and her husband, Arnold Schlichting, Dorothy, Clara and her husband, Dean Twedt, all worked at the Hormel Plant. Phyllis was a secretary at the Hormel office, and her husband, Bill Myhre, also worked at the plant.

Mom often told us she couldn't cook before she was married, but apparently she learned! She was well known for her cooking and baking. Relatives would drive out from town for a Sunday feast. We all enjoyed her large sugar and molasses cookies, cinnamon rolls, donuts, bread and pies. She never used a recipe, always a little bit of this or that. Her goodies were a hit at Farm to Market days downtown every summer. She would make two bushels of donuts – that's how she measured. All day long she baked bread, dinner rolls and cinnamon rolls, and the entire family helped. We would frost the rolls, then wrap them in plastic bags. Someone would transport them to Main Street, where we had a stand in front of Wallace's. I made two dozen angel food cakes to sell.

One summer our brother George and his family drove from Chicago to help. It was a new experience for them, and they were in their glory enjoying the camaraderie.

Austin has always had a special place in my heart. I raised five children after my husband Harry died suddenly in 1968 of a massive heart attack. All our children attended Neveln grade school, Ellis Middle School and Austin High School. I was a stay-at-home mom until 1969, when I became a teacher's aide at Whittier School and then a secretary at Austin High School library from 1970-1997.

Lois Anderson's family

Lois Anderson is 81 years young. She moved to Austin in 1945. She enjoys reading, traveling, playing 500 and spending time with her children, grandchildren and great-grandchildren.

Swept Away
By Lois Anderson

After a heavy rainstorm the day before, June 26, 1959, was a bright, sunshiny day. My 11-year-old daughter Cheryl and her friends Vicky Strong and Patsy Ferguson, rode their bikes downtown to the swimming pool. On the return home, they stopped at Sutton Park because they heard other kids apparently having fun. They were watching Dobbin Creek, which was swollen from the heavy rains. It was flowing rapidly along, the water a roaring torrent and full of debris.

Cheryl stepped on the rocks to watch the swift water, slipped, and fell in. She was carried away by the current. Her friends jumped in to help her, but she was struggling frantically. The park attendant was just leaving for the day, and he had warned the other kids earlier to stay away from the water. When he heard them screaming and saw them running towards him, this got his attention, and he stopped just before driving away.

He ran down to the creek and waded in but couldn't reach Cheryl. He swam faster, dove in ahead of her, and grabbed her blonde hair. She was pulled to safety, thanks to David Edwards and the powers that be. After receiving CPR, Cheryl was brought home by a policeman. I'll be forever grateful that David Edwards was there to help save my daughter.

City Worker Rescues Girl, 11, From Creek in Sutton Park

The Accident
By Ron Anhorn

Prologue: The following story should have been written forty years ago, but at that time I did not know what I know now. The impetus for this story came two years ago when Phillip Kelly, an aspiring Hollywood screenwriter and Austin High School graduate, contacted me for a series of interviews about an automobile accident in 1959 involving five Austin High School students. His probing questions prompted me to embark on my own research to document what I knew to be the truth. What I discovered in conducting personal interviews and reviewing old court transcripts stunned me. This story is the first written account I have given about that accident and the three court trials that ensued.

In the fall of 1958, I quarterbacked the Austin Packers to an undefeated football season and #1 state championship rating in the *St. Paul Pioneer Press*. I thought that when I graduated the following spring, I would be remembered foremost in my hometown for my achievements on the gridiron. I was wrong.

Whenever I would return to my hometown in the ensuing decade and meet someone new who might recognize my name or my face, invariably the first words out of his or her mouth were always the same: "You were one of the boys in the accident." There was never a need to identify the accident by specifying a time, or a place, or who was involved; everyone instantly knew which accident the person was talking about.

It was the accident that killed three AHS students on February 27, 1959, and paralyzed another. It was the accident that gained statewide notoriety when the earliest Twin Cities radio broadcasts erroneously reported that all five students riding in the 1957 Chevy were instantly killed when their car collided head-on with a semi truck one mile north of Alden on Highway 169. It was the accident that spawned a series of rumors about drunk driving and perjured testimony as to who was driving the Chevy. Few people to this very day know that a third vehicle figured into the equation or which drivers were legally at fault.

The loss for the high school, the community, and the families was immeasurable. Killed in the accident was Bruce Hall, one of the top high school golfers in the state and the starting left guard on our championship football team at the start of the season. A knee injury in the second game sidelined Bruce, but he stood on crutches beside his teammates for every remaining game to cheer them on. Such was Bruce's character. He was a model student, serving as the vice president of our senior class, a member of our student council, and a staff writer for our yearbook. He was a strong Christian who never touched a drop of alcohol or uttered a curse word.

Also killed was Jerry Peterson, a reserve halfback and outstanding baseball player. Jerry and I became close friends in the two months preceding the accident as we began to travel to South St. Paul every other weekend to date two senior girls from Visitation High School. Our plans on that fateful day were to first attend the opening matches of the State Wrestling Tournament at Mankato State College, and then travel to South St. Paul in the evening to rendezvous with our new girlfriends and three of their classmates. We would return to Mankato on Saturday for the final matches of the wrestling tournament.

The third fatality was Steve Nygaard, another of my closest friends. Steve was not an athlete, but his outgoing personality and generosity had endeared him to many. As an only child who had lost his father in an auto accident in 1954, Steve was especially considerate and thoughtful of his mother, Myrtle. She became a second mother to many of us, and her home became a meeting place for Steve's friends.

Left paralyzed from the accident, with no memory of the events of that day, was my closest friend and the spiritual leader of our football team, All State guard and linebacker, Larry Maus. Larry had recently competed against his twin brother Terry to represent AHS in the heavyweight wrestling division. We were on our way to cheer on Terry and four other AHS wrestlers in their quest for another state title.

With the events of that day indelibly etched in my mind, it was left to me to identify who was driving our car, and to challenge the testimony of others who claimed our driver was to blame for the accident. As we left Austin around 11 that morning, a heavy snowfall from the previous night had left patches of snow on the streets and highways yet to be plowed. Larry had offered to drive his parents' cherry red '57 Chevy for our two-day excursion, and it was therefore assumed by many that Larry must have been driving when the accident occurred.

As we drove through Albert Lea on our way to Mankato, we made a spontaneous decision to attempt to purchase booze for the party that evening. At an Albert Lea liquor store, Steve was carded and promptly turned away. He made a second attempt as we passed through

Alden, and we were quite surprised when Steve exited the Alden Liquor Store with a smile on his face and a brown paper bag tucked under his arm. In a moment of exhilaration, Larry gunned the accelerator as we pulled away from the curb, and upon hitting a patch of ice, our car slid sideways down the main street of Alden, with motorists and pedestrians scrambling to get out of the way.

Following a barrage of derogatory remarks about his driving skills, Larry offered to turn the driving over to Jerry. Jerry was known to be a good driver on ice and snow, a reputation he had earned after many joyful days of pulling toboggans behind cars on the country roads of Mower County. They made the switch on the outskirts of Alden, with Larry now riding "shotgun" in the front seat, while I was seated in the middle of the backseat with Bruce on my left, and Steve on my right.

A mile or so down the road, I recall being engaged in a conversation with Steve about the uncertainty of how the Visitation girls would react to the bottle of bourbon, when someone in the car screamed, "Look out!" As I looked up, I saw a black car in our lane in the process of passing an oncoming semi truck.

My first thought was, "Why isn't he getting back over into his own lane? He's way past the semi truck." The answer became obvious as I saw he was fishtailing on the slushy road. When it appeared that a head on collision was about to occur, Jerry steered to his right in an attempt to ride the shoulder.

As I would later testify, it was my belief that our right side tires were riding the right shoulder, and our left tires stayed on the pavement as the black sedan missed our front bumper by inches and narrowly missed swiping our left side as it passed the truck in our lane. The proximity of our two vehicles caused the back sedan to throw a sheet of slush across our windshield, completely blinding our vision. Suddenly Jerry had no way of knowing whether our car was headed in a straight line or veering one direction or the other.

A split second later, I felt our right side tires catch the lip of the pavement, causing our car to jump and slide to our left across the highway. As the wipers cleared our windshield, all I could see was the front grill of the huge semi truck bearing directly down on us. I screamed, "Hit the floor," and threw my body to my left and downwards onto the floor of the car.

The collision knocked me momentarily unconscious. Our car disintegrated upon impact, and the drive shaft came up through the floor and shattered my left leg. As my body was thrust against the back of the front seat, my right lung burst like a popped balloon. Several years would pass before doctors would discover bone chips in both my knees. Yet, I was the lucky one. Jerry and Bruce died instantly, and Steve succumbed to head injuries the following day. Larry Maus broke both legs, his right arm and suffered three factures of the vertebrae. He would never walk again.

There were no seat belts in 1959. Upon impact, bodies were hurled in every direction, causing investigating reporters and stopping motorists to question who was doing the driving. With my memory intact, I gave a deposition within hours of the accident identifying Jerry Peterson as our driver. State Highway Patrolman Phillip Hodap also gave a statement in my presence in which he indicated that the evidence found at the scene suggested that the Peterson boy was doing the driving because his body was "impaled on the steering column."

Understandably, Officer Hodap's statement was never quoted in any newspaper coverage. Instead, newspaper stories cited my deposition to identify Jerry as our driver. As such, a rumor quickly circulated that Larry was actually driving, but since I knew that Jerry had died instantly, I identified Jerry as our driver because I wanted to spare my best friend the anguish of thinking that his driving had killed three of his best friends. This belief still exists in certain circles, despite the existence of a photograph published only in the Albert Lea newspaper, which supports Officer Hodap's conclusion as to which boy was driving our car.

A series of rumors regarding drunk driving also spread throughout southern Minnesota. Three factors undoubtedly spawned the rumors. The first is the fact that the bottle of bourbon was found at the scene of the accident by a stopping motorist and shown to many others before being turned over to Officer Hodap. The second is the fact that Officer Hodap queried me about the illegal purchase in the presence of several doctors and nurses at the Wells Hospital. The third is the fact that numerous newspapers carried articles about the prosecution of the owner of the Alden Liquor Store.

To date, not a single newspaper article has ever cited the irrefutable evidence that we were not drinking. The first proof is the fact that the seal on the bottle was never broken. As the roof of our car was ripped off by the impact of the collision, the bottle was launched through the air amidst flying metal and glass. Miraculously, it landed unbroken in a snow bank in the ditch. Second, blood tests confirmed that not a drop of alcohol was consumed by any one of us. And a third piece of compelling evidence can be found when one reviews the court transcripts. Knowing the results of the blood alcohol tests, not a single attorney in the ensuing three court trials ever raised the question of whether our driver had been drinking at the time of the accident. In the absence of media coverage of any of the aforementioned, many people still believe alcohol was to blame for the accident. The most vicious rumor, and one that remains prevalent in the Alden-Wells area to this very day, is that we were all so drunk that we were deliberately "playing chicken" with the semi truck.

Equally important to the question of blame is the fact that many people to this very day are unaware that the passing black sedan had forced Jerry Peterson to take evasive action. Only one newspaper article ever quoted remarks made by Mr. Harold Drews of Wells at the scene in which he noted that a black sedan had passed both his stock truck and the semi truck seconds before the collision. Newspaper articles covering the court trials only addressed the verdicts, and not the particulars of the testimony during the trials.

Courtroom testimony, however, documented the fact that the driver of the black sedan pulled over to the shoulder momentarily, but then left the scene of the accident as other motorists began to stop to offer assistance. Officer Hodap led a year-long, unsuccessful investigation to find the driver of the black sedan. My review of the court transcripts last year uncovered a startling fact. In the first trial, held in October of 1959, in which Frank Brothers' Feed and Grain sued Bert and Vickie Maus, owners of the '57 Chevy, for damages sustained to the semi truck, partial loss of their cargo, and injuries to their driver, David Roesler. The driver of the black sedan actually appeared as the last witness in the trial.

Though I testified at this trial, I was a teenager somewhat in awe of attorneys, and easily intimidated by them. I allowed myself to be quickly escorted into and out of the courtroom without any opportunity to hear other testimony. Three years passed before I learned the identity of the driver of the black sedan; forty-five years passed before the son of Harold Frank, the owner of Frank Brothers' Feed and Grain, revealed to me in a telephone interview that Henry C. Nelson of Albert Lea appeared at his father's home one week after the accident to identify himself and to discuss the particulars of the accident.

During the first trial, both Henry Nelson and David Roesler testified that our car was out of control "a half mile" before the two cars nearly collided. In fact, both alleged that our car first slid completely across the highway and hit the south shoulder (the shoulder to our left), whereupon it slid across the highway a second time onto the north shoulder before it finally slid across the highway a third time into the path of the semi truck. Mr. Nelson claimed that he had steered his car onto the south shoulder (the shoulder to his right) to avoid a head-on collision with our car. These allegations were in complete contradiction to my testimony and that of Harold Drews, the only disinterested eyewitness to the accident.

Harold Drews testified that he was following the semi truck at a speed of approximately 45 to 50 miles an hour when a black sedan began to pass both his stock truck and the semi truck. Drews testified that he pulled into the left lane directly behind the black car to also pass the semi truck, but quickly pulled back in behind the semi when he saw our red car and realized there was not enough distance to safely pass. In the second trial, he stated explicitly that our car was traveling in our lane, "under control," and seconds after pulling back in behind the semi truck, he saw our car spinning in the air above the semi truck. With the passage of only seconds, a jury could safely infer that there was not enough time for our car to slide across the highway three times before it collided with the semi truck.

Also critical to the jury's verdict in the first trial was Drew's testimony that the brake lights of the semi truck never came on until a split second before the collision occurred. In short, if the jury was to believe Nelson's and Roesler's testimony that we were out of control "a half mile" before the two cars nearly collided, then both were at fault for not hitting their brakes sooner and taking evasive action. Perhaps for this reason, and many others, the jury in the first trial absolved the Maus family and their insurance company of any liability for the accident with a direct implication that Jerry Peterson was not speeding or driving in a negligent manner.

Two and a half years later, the tables turned when the Maus family filed a lawsuit against Frank Brothers' Feed and Grain and Henry C. Nelson for Larry's personal injuries and medical bills. It was during this trial, when I remained in the courtroom after my brief testimony, that I first learned the identity of the driver of the black sedan. I was stunned, but I was the only one in the courtroom surprised by his appearance. It would take considerable research forty-five years later before I fully comprehended why my time on the witness stand was always limited, and why Mr. Nelson's identity had been withheld from Officer Hodap and me.

In 1959, Minnesota statutory law on accidents allowed juries to proportionately award damages based on the degree of culpability of the drivers. Through personal and telephone interviews last year with attorneys and relatives of Mr. Nelson, I learned that he had virtually no automobile insurance at the time of the accident and no personal assets. This meant that if a jury were to find him 90% or 100% liable for the accident, there would not be money to be fairly divided among Frank Brothers' Feed and Grain, David Roesler, the Maus family, the families of the deceased, and me.

From day one, I was always pointing the finger of blame at Mr. Nelson. Yet no one but me wanted to find him primarily liable for the accident. Six lawsuits emanated from the accident, and three went to trial. What occurred during the three years of courtroom fighting was best summed up by an astute defense attorney who made the following remark upon reviewing my findings: "In a personal injury case, morality and the search for truth fly right out the window. You're looking for who has the most insurance and whether you can find them culpable."

The opposing attorneys preferred to fight it out among themselves to find culpability rather than to lay any blame at the feet of Mr. Nelson. In their attempts to look past Nelson, attorneys for the Maus family and the deceased boys unsuccessfully tried to prove that Frank Brothers' Feed and Grain were liable because their company had not performed recent mandatory brake inspections on the semi, the weight of their cargo (sixteen and a half tons of soy beans) exceeded the maximum allowable limits for their truck, and their driver failed to hit his brakes and take evasive action.

Attorneys for Frank Brothers' Feed and Grain and David Roesler tried to prove that Jerry was speeding and therefore lost control long before the two cars nearly collided. It is noteworthy that after losing the first trial, both Roesler and Nelson changed their testimony in the second trial and stated that they "were mistaken" about the distance our car was from their vehicles when it began to slide out of control. And neither claimed, as they had done in the first trial, that our car slid across the highway three times before impacting the semi truck.

The word-count strictures prevent me from expounding further on the conflicting courtroom testimonies and the conflicting verdicts that emanated from three court trials over a four-year period. In the second trial, the jury absolved Frank Brothers and Henry Nelson of any liability and held the Peterson estate liable for the medical bills and injuries suffered by Larry Maus.

Six months after Larry's trial, I filed a lawsuit naming everyone possible as co-defendants. After three years of lawsuits and conflicting testimonies, no one wanted another trial because a new verdict might become the foundation for an appeal of a previous decision. As such, a generous out of court settlement was offered to me, and I was told every named defendant, including Mr. Nelson, contributed to the sum.

Though our careers took us in different directions, a bond of friendship remained between Larry Maus and me. Larry became a partner in the law firm that represented both of us during the trials. After many years of college teaching, I entered the business world and settled in Colorado, where I own a real estate brokerage and a loan company. On rare occasions when we get together, we reminisce about our high school days and the dear friends we lost. To have such promising lives cut short by an accident is tragic. I hope this story will rekindle memories of what they accomplished in their brief lives and finally put to rest rumors that have surrounded the accident for almost five decades.

The accident scene near Alden, February 27, 1959

The Austin of My Childhood Days
By Karin Arsan

I was born in Austin in 1943, and shortly thereafter my father, Stuart Lane, left for World War II, and I don't remember seeing him until I was almost 3. He had grown up here, and his friends and parents were very helpful to my mom, Virginia. My mother worked as a receptionist at the Fox Hotel during those years, and her mother took care of me. My grandparents were Alfred and Lura Lane, and their house was at 306 SW 5th Street. It's still there.

I remember riding my tricycle over to visit them and watching Grandpa shovel coal into the furnace. At Christmas my father's sister Beverly, who was probably still a teenager, played Santa Claus. She rang the sleigh bells upstairs and then came down dressed like Santa with gifts for all of us. This was a wonderful time and probably shortly before my father returned.

After the war we moved to the Twin Cities for a few years, but by sixth grade we were back, and I have so many wonderful memories of those school years here. I had the very good fortune to move in right across from Jan Arney, who has been such a wonderful friend ever since. We went to Banfield together, and then all the seventh graders went to the building where the high school is today. We had a pretty big class of about 400, and I met a lot of kids.

We all had such a good time together, and I really appreciate now how wonderful it was that the Hormel whistle blew at 10:30 p.m. to signal that all the teens had to be home or at least inside for the night. There were no curfew fights with parents. The town set the curfew! It was easy to go home because you knew everyone else had to, and the party was over for the night. I don't remember any drugs, alcohol, or cigarettes; it was just good clean fun.

We could go to The Tower and buy a Coke and dance to the jukebox or go to a movie. The Sterling Theatre was quite new, and I saw many wonderful movies there including *Rebel Without a Cause,* and of course, there was the Paramount. We ice skated on Skinner's Pond and tobogganed down that hill, and for a country adventure we went out past Turtle Creek to that big hill (was it called Nob Hill?) and skied and tobogganed down and walked up. Going down was fast, but coming up was slow and there was no warming house like at Skinner's Pond, so we only went down a few times and then went home to warm up.

That whole area west of Turtle Creek and south of Oakland was rural. There was a farm and then just a dirt road, which I think went to the big hill in winter and was a good lovers' lane in better weather. Turtle Creek was really the city limit, and there was no housing development on the other side.

When we moved to 21st Street SW, we were near the creek and at the far limits of town. I loved being out there where Jan and I could play along the creek, which was ever changing with lovely little violets in spring. And one winter we went down to the creek on the town side and just across from the big hill. Although the creek is deep there, it looked pretty frozen. I tried the ice and went right through! Fortunately Jan pulled me out, and we walked home with me in a very cold, wet snowsuit. I think I was 13 that winter. Fortunately it wasn't my last. And it wasn't the last time Jan pulled me out of the water.

Jan and I had a good friend, Jane Young, who lived out in the country down the road across from the cemetery that goes to the Oak Park Mall now. Her house isn't even there anymore. It was a farm house, and the place was called Plenty Acres. I can remember walking back to town in the fall, and it was all cornstalks along the road.

After we graduated in 1961, I went away to school. I came back to marry in Christ Episcopal Church in 1966 and then left for thirty-five years. In late 2001, I came back to help my parents who still live here, and I've spent a lot of time in Austin in the last few years. But it's almost like a ghost town for me as all my friends are gone, and the houses and many other important buildings, like the Terp Ballroom, now the Vineyard Church, remain. But I wish I could bring all the people back. My, we had a good time.

Teens at the Tower, enjoying Cokes and the company of one another

Main Street Sterling Drug
By Laura Astrup

Main Street Sterling Drug is a family owned business started by my grandpa, Leonard Astrup. This store is great for all ages. People from grandparents to toddlers could identify Main Street as being one of the best places in Austin. I don't think Austin would be the same without it because it's been around for more than fifty years.

This store is an important place not only to me and my family, but to our community. Main Street is very important to me because it's been in my family since I've been alive. I plan to work there when I'm in high school. Main Street helps our community so much. They sponsor a lot of sporting events and teams. Sports are a big part of my life, and I'm super glad that Main Street has helped out with that.

There are many parts inside Main Street. There is a "play place" for kids while their moms or dads are shopping. There's an ice cream and coffee shop to get a snack, a place to wrap your gifts that you buy your friends or family, a dollar store if you can't get the most expensive products, and of course they have what all the Sterling Drug stores are known for, their pharmacies where you can get your medicines.

Main Street Sterling Drug has been a part of Austin's history since before the centennial celebration in 1956. It started way back in 1952 when Leonard Astrup came to Austin from North Dakota to open his first store. There have been eleven stores opened throughout Minnesota, but the one here in Austin is by far the best. In 2002 Main Street celebrated their fiftieth anniversary and that is a reason in itself why Main Street is an important place in our community.

The original Sterling Drugs

A third-generation Austin Astrup, Laura wrote this as an Ellis 8th grader.

Skinner's Hill Stairway
By Donald Barnes

While visiting relatives in Austin during the Christmas holidays of 1933, I was sledding on Skinner's Hill. Ascending the slippery slope was becoming an increasingly tiring task, so I had the idea of a stairway made of concrete blocks to be kept free of snow by a steam pipe running through their holes.

Among the adults at the top of the hill was a friendly man who encouraged me on my slow climb. With all the exuberant confidence of a first grader, I explained to him the advantages of my idea. He seemed adequately impressed.

A few days later the man's identity was revealed as this conversation was recounted in the daily Pot Pourri column written by John H. Skinner, editor of the *Austin Daily Herald*. He lived at 609 South Kenwood Avenue – now 4th Avenue SW.

Winter fun on Skinner's Hill

Donald Barnes moved to Austin when he was 4 years old. He farmed near Lyle and retired in Austin. He enjoys reading and photography.

The Ghost of the Austin Public Library
By Betty Benner

Even new buildings have ghosts. Some buildings are haunted from the time the first shovel of dirt is turned over and the first form is filled.

I believe this brand new building has a ghost. I believe in this ghost, because I almost saw her. And I definitely heard her. Now it may be that Austin's previous libraries were haunted too: the basement of the county courthouse, which housed our first library, and the Carnegie building on 2nd Avenue, built in 1904, and the wraparound 1968 addition. But I've never heard tales of apparitions in any of the former libraries, nor have I seen any signs of such spirits there.

I say it again....this building, these very walls, are not too new for a ghost. This building, at 323 Fourth Avenue NE, is haunted. One afternoon for one split second I saw the hem of her white skirt reflected in the polished granite mosaic of the atrium floor. I looked up quickly, but there was no one there.

In the evening, just before closing, when only a few patrons still browse, I have heard the echo of a child's sweet song, and a tap, tap, tap, like the click of metal on concrete. Don't ask how I unearthed these facts. Only know that this story is true, as true as the small girl child who floats through the stacks and the meeting rooms and hides behind the sofa in the reading places.

Fourth Avenue, which runs by the front of the library, was not always Fourth Avenue. Water Street was its name for many years. And for years there was a house at 321 Water, located in what is now the driveway to the new Austin Public Library. The house was torn down several years ago to make way for the new building. In this home for many years lived a mother and a father and three children, two girls and a boy, who shared their home with an aunt and the uncle.

It was a happy home. There was a playhouse attached to the house out back. And the attic was also a frequent playground, with its three little windows looking out on Water Street. The attic became a haunted house on Halloween, a spooky, neat little place that the little girl loved – the little girl who was the youngest of the three children. She loved that attic especially because it had been rebuilt in 1928, the year before she was born, when the tornado that took off part of Austin

Utilities' smokestack took off the top of the family's home too. After the tornado came through, the family made it their evening's entertainment, when the weather looked threatening, to sit in the living room with a bowl of popcorn and the radio nearby, watching for any approaching storms.

The back yard at 321 East Water went all the way down to the river. It was filled with flowers, tended by the small girl's uncle. A rowboat was tied at the water's edge. The child and her friends would sit, hidden among the flowers, and watch the gypsies who came by. There was always singing and dancing, and the little girl was a little afraid, because of the stories she'd heard of the gypsies who came to Austin. And she had reason for fear, for when they left the town after one of their visits, they took with them her dog Rex. The police followed them as they traveled to the north, but could not find her dog. Then two weeks later he appeared at the back door, with bloody paws and a rope around his neck.

The little girl's grandfather was the very first employee hired by George A. Hormel when he began his small meat-processing operation across the river. Later, her father and uncle used to walk across the railroad bridge to work each day at the packinghouse. That railroad bridge is now a footbridge over the Mill Pond. Where the children played in the flowers, there is now a walking path that continues on around the pond, following a trail between the water and the green lawn of the library.

The child's father was a partner in the Ramsey Ice business, located near the Old Mill, in those days before refrigerators. He cut river ice, which was sold to families for cooling iceboxes. And Young's Ice House was right next door on Water Street. There the ice was pushed down a slide into a truck waiting to deliver it to customers, and sometimes this small girl would get up on top of a block of ice and ride it down the slide to the truck. Just for fun on a hot summer day.

Down the street was Mr. Rainbow's grocery store, where the children could get a sack full of candy for a nickel. Or sometimes the little girl would sing a song and dance a little tap dance, if she didn't have a nickel, and the sack would appear in her hands. Further down the street was Klagge's Ice Cream Parlor, where a cone was just five cents, any flavor.

The neighbor kids came to play a lot at 321 East Water Street, partly because they had the largest sandbox in the neighborhood under the eaves out back, next to the playhouse. And every year the neighbors came for Fourth of July, when back yard fireworks were legal. And on May Day, the little girl was a sprite as she delivered to her friends beautiful May baskets made by her aunt. Then there was the annual doll buggy parade down Main. Aunt and Mother decorated the little girl and the buggy, and several times she came home with first prize.

The house at 321 East Water was located just off the railroad tracks that went through Horace Austin Park. It was natural for the hobos who got off the train at the park to stop by the back door and ask for supper. And they were fed. The word had gotten around. The little girl was not afraid of the hobos. She liked to watch them as they sat by the back door, leaning against the wall and waiting for their food.

The little girl had a sort of deal with the hobos. She would tap dance on the sidewalk for them while they awaited their meal, and when it was served they would share their tales of life on the road. It was a sort of exchange--a dance for a story. They always received a hot meal with a napkin and a flower on the tray, fixed by the child's aunt or mother. The hobos were respectful of the little girl and her tap dancing, and were happy to tell her stories while they ate. They spread the word to their friends: Stop at 321 East Water for food and entertainment. And be ready to tell a story.

When the house was torn down to make way for the library, all that was saved was the front door handle and the lock and key. The little girl who tap-danced for the hobos had grown into adulthood. She now lives in another house in another part of the city. But her daughter, knowing how she felt about the house at 321 East Water, had the handle and lock and key framed as mementos for her mother. Nostalgia pieces they were--relics of a bygone day--symbols of a happy childhood.

The house at 321 East Water

The house is gone, but the view is still the same out over the Mill Pond. The tracks are gone, but the railroad bridge still leads across the river to the Hormel Company. And it isn't too bad a thing to have such a beautiful building arise out of the dust of one's childhood home. But ghosts are ghosts, and a little girl is a little girl. Her spirit remains. She wants the flowers; she wants the fun; she seeks the sight of hobos eating supper on the back porch. She wants the memories to live again and even the fears, the fears of the tornado and the gypsies who sang and danced and carried away her dog.

So.... some evening, when it's almost closing time for the library, and there are only a few last patrons lingering, you may see the quick reflection, gone before you know it, of a child's white skirt in the polished floor. You may hear the echo of a sweet childish song, and the tap, tap, tap of metal toes on concrete. Understand her search. Go back with her, even, to that other day. The ghost of the Austin Public Library will thank you, and will rest easy in the night.

Thanks to Dolores "Pete" Judd, who lived the story, and who continues life here in Austin, and who was most gracious in allowing us to tell the story.

Dolores "Pete" Judd, the little library ghost

Betty Benner worked in the Austin Human Services Adult Community Treatment program. She is a member of the Austin writers' group and edits the Plainview Rural America Writers' Center publication, "The Green Blade."

Cedar River
By Tyler Bentzin

The Cedar River, which is sometimes called the Red Cedar River, has been the site of some of my best memories of Austin. A lot has happened to the river, such as the floods, and a lot has been done to the river. My dad and I like to go canoeing and kayaking in the Cedar River. I was first taught to swim there, and I was also taught how to fish in the Cedar River.

Why is the Cedar River important? The Cedar is important to me because that is where a lot of my memories with my dad and me are set, and because I love to fish there with my family and friends. Another reason it is important is because the wildlife needs it to survive. And without the wildlife, how are we supposed to go fishing? Fishing in the Cedar River is an important memory I will cherish forever.

Austin has had its bad times with floods that come from the Cedar River. One of the most recent floods happened only about two years ago. That was a flood no one in Austin will forget about. I remember that day very well, and I am sure a lot of my classmates will not forget that day either, because it was one of the only days we will get out of school because of too much rain.

It was very sad to see all of the flood victims lose very valuable items and memories such as pictures and yearbooks. And it was sad seeing all the houses that were surrounded by floodwater. When we have floods, the water rises so much that we might miss out on our fun activities and not be able to go fishing and kayaking on the Cedar. And when the Cedar floods, that causes garbage to wash up in the rivers and my dad and I have to go with our canoe and pick up garbage to make the Cedar a better place and also make us feel better because the last thing you want to have happen to your memories is watching them be destroyed. Seeing garbage all over was just disappointing.

It has been very enjoyable to write this for *Austin Remembers*. It made the memories come back to me. After reading this, I hope you know how much the Cedar River means to me, and maybe you will go check it out yourself.

Tyler Bentzin is an Ellis Middle School student who enjoys football.

10-Speed Tales
By Stephan Benzkofer

The stranger leaned against a big, old elm tree. He didn't seem like he wanted to cause trouble, but I was wary. He was about my size, and I felt pretty good that my younger brother Rick had my back. But we were newcomers, and this was his neighborhood, and I didn't know how many friends he had.

I decided to jump in: "Hi. My name is Stephan."

"Hi," he said. "My name is Chris."

"I'm 4," I said, challenging and sharing.

"I'm 4 too!" The amazing coincidence bonded us instantly. I immediately started ignoring my brother. I smiled, delighted at meeting a new playmate so quickly after moving in. I'm sure we both went straight home, Chris to the gray ranch across the street, and me to the yellow story-and-a-half behind me, to tell our mothers of the miracle.

We became friends, a relationship that would outlast that grand, old elm, which was felled by Dutch elm disease a few years later in the mid-1970s. Our friendship would be put to the test by my flunking kindergarten, causing me later to fail to make the move for an additional year from Banfield Elementary School to Ellis Middle School.

The truth is that a 4-year-old's memory is an imperfect recorder of fact. It very well may be that my mother was keeping close tabs on me, not sure how I would react to the new neighborhood. It may be that she had actually been right there meeting Chris Harder's mother, the two women watching their boys interact and sharing in their amazement of the number 4. But that's not how I remember it. I remember being on my own (well, with my brother). I remember danger.

This isn't my first memory of Austin, but it is the most telling. It speaks to freedom and exploration, danger and adventure, and an ever-expanding universe to master. It recalls a time when my backyard was the whole block, which was then the neighborhood from the "highway" (Oakland Avenue) to the fairgrounds, then Austin Acres to the library downtown, and finally the whole city, from the old Bridgeman's Restaurant to East Side Lake. It is a Midwestern boy's natural progression from Big Wheel to banana bike to 10-speed to the family car.

Skip ahead a few years. Our world has expanded beyond the elm tree and our front yard to the Sterling Christian Church's ball field at the end of the block and the Banfield Elementary playground on the far side of the school. It is summer, and for the first time that means no school. Rick and I have tired of trying to dent our impossibly sturdy Tonka trucks by battering them against each other on the driveway. I don my Batman cape, he puts on his Superman 'S' shirt, and we're off to seek adventure. We fly out of the side door of the house, Rick running fast with me close on his heels. We reconnoiter at the corner of the next-door neighbor's giant corner bush.

Our target is Mr. Hill's forbidden yard. It's just one more door down, but we must cross the Brown's broad expanse of front lawn, cross their driveway, navigate a slight berm, and enter Mr. Hill's grove without being detected. Once inside the natural fort, an area created by the outlawed running, climbing, playing and scheming of the neighbor children, we would be on our own for hours. Our piece of the Great North Woods was a couple trees and a few straggly bushes, but it was constantly transformed into much more by the potent combination of our imaginations and the fact it was off limits.

Rick breaks for it, and I follow, but the mission goes badly before it starts. Just as we streak across the lawn, Mr. Hill's car turns onto 2nd Avenue from 19th Street and turns into his driveway. How he knew we were coming, I wasn't sure, but Rick and I veer left, run across the street, and straight into Mr. Thompson's back yard. We pull up behind a bush and try to assess the situation. Did Mom turn us in? She had been threatening to do just that. Or had Mr. Hill been waiting around the corner?

The fact was, it was noon, and in Austin it wasn't unheard of for people to come home for lunch. But despite seeing Dad turn into our driveway seconds later and hearing Mom yell for us to come to lunch, we still failed to realize the coincidence. We were sure we had been busted. We were on our best behavior at lunch—and Mr. Hill's forest redoubt was safe--for a day.

The Sterling Shopping Center was a kid magnet and a gauge of your maturity, or at least the trust Mom and Dad had in you. Around Banfield, past the scary motel and across busy 14th Street, the strip mall was just a hop, skip and a jump from home. But going without an escort was a milestone. Early on, we walked with Mom or slow-walked with Grandma. Later, when we were older, it was a quick dash on banana-seated bikes. It also was our first stop during the annual Crazy Days, that aptly named, citywide sales bonanza. It was a time when Austin Drug's cheap, plastic toys, which we ignored for 364 days of the year, became irresistible when their price went down. (In other words, this was a professional-grade garage sale.)

Sterling was all any kid needed. Sterling State Bank let me stash my paper-route money in their vault. Alger Ace Hardware sold nails, screws, snow shovels—and duct tape. The grocery store stocked gallons of milk, sticks of butter and loaves of bread. And Happy Joe's Pizza Parlor, the mall's eastern bookend for at least a few years, served up ice cream and the arcade games Tron and Joust.

But what drew me and my sister Rachel and brother Rick and the other kids from 2nd Avenue SW was the candy aisle of the Ben Franklin Five and Dime. Any money saved was money spent at Ben Franklin. For a scrawny little kid with an appetite bigger than the two quarters he was rubbing together, the Ben Franklin candy aisle was both Nirvana and Gethsemane. The aisle, at least a mile long and five shelves tall, was packed with a gazillion types of jawbreakers and Sweet Tarts, 38,000 flavors of Bubblicious and Bazooka, every chocolate bar under the sun—even the brand-new Whatchamacallit—and, of course, lemon drops.

A few steps from the Ben Franklin was the Sterling Twin Theatre. The standard procedure was to allow at least an extra ten minutes before the movie was scheduled to start so we would have time to buy candy to smuggle in to the show. I think at the time we had to pay $2.50 for a movie, a quarter for a candy bar, and a dime for lemon drops or a pack of gum. Three bucks sufficed, four dollars was gluttony. Most days, I would buy a chocolate bar, a box of lemon drops and maybe some Life Savers, a nice mix that would last through the opening credits of most movies. One day, though, I didn't live up to my parents' trust. I don't remember if we were going to *Benji, The Life and Times of Grizzly Adams,* or the original *Shaggy D.A.*, but I decided the standard fare wasn't good enough. Maybe I was tempted by the Whatchamacallit. Maybe I dropped a coin on the bike ride over, leaving me short. Maybe I simply miscounted my change. Whatever the reason, when push came to shove, I broke the law. I shoplifted.

After making the rest of my purchase, as the clerk was busy with my brother and sister, I pilfered a box of lemon drops. Mom and Dad should know that I felt guilty immediately—and terrified. I was sure the clerk had seen me. I exited quickly, and I was too ashamed to eat them openly. I was equally sure that Rachel would add up the cost of my haul and find me wanting—financially and morally. I waited until the lights went down in the theatre before I opened the box. The first lemon drop seemed to taste even better than normal. More sweet. More lip-puckering sour. But the fear of being caught gnawed at me, and in short order I was popping six or seven into my mouth at once and just eating them like run-of-the-mill M&Ms. I finished the box in minutes and dropped it quietly on the floor. With a kick, the telltale box was two rows in front of me.

I would like to report that those lemon drops gnawed at my stomach like Edgar Allan Poe's heart, but to tell you the truth, I forgot about the whole affair ten minutes into the movie. It wasn't until later, maybe even a year or so, that the thought of those stolen candies became too much. It was probably Lent, and I had probably just gone to confession and not confessed that actual crime but constructed some believable yet less heinous sins for the priest to hear. So those little white lies, on top of grand theft lemon drops, pushed my conscience into action. I would come clean. The store owner would hear me out but wouldn't think twice. He would slap me on the back and forgive me.

I jumped on my bike and rode straight to the store. I entered without hesitation because I felt sure that my righteous sense of purpose was clear on my young face, clear in the way I set my shoulders and held my head. I walked straight ahead, looked the clerk in the eye, nodded hello—and veered right, into the candy aisle.

Without a seeming care in the world, I bee-lined to the lemon drops, picked up a box, and surreptitiously left behind a dime. The transaction was as smooth as that of a veteran pickpocket. Without a pause, I returned to the checkout, bought my box of lemon drops a second time, thus redeeming my soul, and I walked out the door.

When my brother and sisters and I turned 13, we all received, in turn, a 10-speed bicycle for our birthdays. In August, 1981, my dad took me down to the Schwinn store, which was across from the Dairy Queen on Oakland. I chose a blue model with ram's horn handlebars. It was understood, if not stated, that this would be the last transportation we would get from Dad and Mom. That made it even sweeter, of course, and it seemed to confer a greater level of freedom. No longer must you pedal that one-speed, child's bike all about the neighborhood, the gift seemed to say. Here's a real bike; Austin is your playground.

For reasons that I can't remember, I thought my new transportation would greatly transform the speed and ease of my travels. I would no longer battle winds to and from the old Carnegie building at the corner of 1st Street and 3rd Avenue. I would easily surmount the Turtle Creek hill. Jaunts to Oak Park Mall would be nearly instantaneous. Reality quickly disabused me of these notions. Despite ten gears, a derailleur, aerodynamic handlebars and nifty racing seat, the bike was still powered by my scrawny 13-year-old legs.

En route to Brien Lilja's house in Austin Acres, I still tried to build up (using tenth gear, of course) as much speed plummeting down to the bridge over Turtle Creek as I could. But no matter how fast my legs pumped, and no matter when I down-shifted to third or second or—shame—first gear, I never seemed to climb to the top of the other side with the ease this high-performance racing machine should allow.

I don't know if kids still have the run of Austin; I certainly hope so. The freedom I enjoyed and the confidence I built, were in some ways illusory. The town held me in its grasp; I never traveled that far. But those experiences were important.

I didn't consciously realize it, but by the same measure, I didn't waste it. My friends and siblings and I wrung every second out of those summer evenings. We played football until the forward pass became a tricky option in the dusk. We played kick the can until it was impossible to tell who was who or where the can was anyway. We waited until the last possible minute to hop on our bikes and return home, often arriving after dark, sticky from sweat and bug repellent, and in no way willing to call it a night.

Later, as a high school teen, I would be allowed to venture forth into those intoxicating, warm, summer evenings. I would gather with friends around a campfire at Dreisner Park or play games in the basement of somebody's home or hang out in a friend's car on an empty country road. We would listen to R.E.M., the Replacements, Violent Femmes, Lou Reed and the Gear Daddies. We would drink ill-gotten, cheap beer. In the heart of the vacation season, we would coalesce around whichever home was parentless, on subsequent weekends drifting from the Parlins to the Benzkofers, from the Liljas to the Crumps, from the Jacobsons to the Olsens.

We laughed and flirted; we talked and argued. We belted out lyrics at the top of our lungs and played jokes on each other. We danced like Banshees and put on world-weary airs. And while we complained about how boring Austin was, throughout it all, we were, indeed, having the time of our young lives.

Parked bicycles show evidence of kids shopping inside the Ben Franklin store at the Sterling Shopping Center

*Stephan Benzkofer, born and raised in Austin, is the Page One news editor of the **Chicago Tribune**. He lives in Oak Park, Illinois with his wife and son.*

The Healing Energy of a Prairie Farmhouse
By Judith Bergen

I have visited many homes where a loved one was dying. I am a social worker for a hospice in a rural southern Minnesota community. In hospice we do all we can do to help a person be as comfortable as possible during the last days of his or her life. Most of our patients die in their homes, surrounded by the people and things they love.

It's interesting to see the things with which people surround themselves. We reveal a lot about our inner lives by the objects that fill our homes. A home speaks to the soul, as well as to the eye. I love visiting the old farmhouses, with the front doors nobody uses and the walls and floors that are often a little crooked. Many of these homes in the Midwest are now abandoned because the farms keep getting bigger.

Walter's Farmhouse

There is one farmhouse, however, I can't forget. In fact, I dream about it sometimes in the early morning just before waking completely. The owner, Walter, was an elderly gentleman who was dying of cancer. His home had no carpeting, no upholstered furniture, and no indoor toilet. Time was suspended when I crossed the threshold of Walter's humble farmhouse. It was the most peaceful home I've ever been in.

Walter had a very personal relationship to the things in his home. There wasn't one item placed there purely for the joy of looking at it, yet the home was filled with a serene happiness. It wasn't a typical old farmhouse, though it was one of the oldest in the county. The only entrance to Walter's house was what most farmers refer to as the back porch. It was enclosed but wasn't heated. There was a broom resting in a corner, and a galvanized tub, in which Walter heated water to wash himself, sat along the inside wall. The inside door opened directly to the kitchen.

A square oak table sat in the middle of the kitchen, and the floor was covered with gray linoleum with faded red flowers in the design. The linoleum was worn but immaculate. On one wall, there was an antique hutch where Walter kept his dishes. I winced the first time I saw the wooden towel bar that was nailed to one side of the wonderful old hutch, but I got used to it. Everything in Walter's home served a purpose.

There were two worn wooden chairs by the table and an aluminum lawn chair in one corner, where Walter sat to watch TV. Yes, Walter did have electricity, even though he had no hot water and no flush toilet. He believed in cleanliness, in frugality, and in using modern conveniences to simplify his life when he was sure that's what they really did.

A hand pump brought water from the well to the kitchen sink, and there was an outhouse in the backyard. As Walter got weaker and could no longer make the trip to the outhouse, we brought a commode for him to use. The second room on the main floor, the bedroom, was quite small. There was a bed, a simple chest of drawers, and a door leading to a tiny room that he used as a closet. A large armoire pretty much filled up the tiny room. The smell of mothballs permeated it. In contrast, the kitchen had a very clean, piney smell.

I know this sounds strange, but these opposite smells both belonged in the house. They smelled so right, each in its own place. I never saw the second floor, but a neighbor who checked in on Walter regularly said it had a narrow wooden spiral stairway that led to three, small, low-ceilinged rooms. Very little was stored there, according to the neighbor, because Walter sold what he couldn't use.

When I entered the home for the first time, I immediately felt the sense of peace and contentment that filled the rooms. Walter had all he needed and, most importantly, all that he wanted. He was a happy man who lived life on his own terms. The neighbor told me that Walter had a wonderful, clear mind—and that he usually got his way.

Although there was tranquility in the sparse furnishings, I know that if I had lived in Walter's house, I would have had to bring my rugs, candles, books and plants. I need to have softness in my surroundings. Walter stared life right in the face. He also did so with death. He was not afraid. He had lived his life the best that he could and was ready for whatever the next chapter would bring. He didn't belong to a church, but there was a well-worn Bible on the table next to his bed.

To me, his home was a holy place. It was so pure and simple. When entering it, I pulled out of the fast lane that I'm in so much of the time. Even now, when I think of Walter and his home, I again pull out of the fast lane. I slow down and get in touch with what matters most to me. Walter was a shy, private bachelor. Yet he was always friendly to the hospice staff and volunteers who came to help. He said many times that he appreciated all that we did. I was always amazed how everything was so clean in his home and how he always had on fresh bib overalls and a crisp, blue cotton shirt. With no indoor plumbing, it must have been a challenge to keep everything so clean. His exterior space matched the interior to the greatest extent that I have ever seen. His life had order, joy and purpose. He loved being a farmer, and he loved the land.

On a gray November day, a year after Walter died, I drove out to the gravel road he used to live on. I hadn't been down that road since he died, and I wanted to see his place. I knew that a neighbor had bought the farm and had sold the land the house was on to a couple who wanted to live in the country. In the fog I recognized Walter's driveway, but the house standing where his home had been looked so different. I couldn't see clearly because it was so misty, but it looked like it was much bigger, with blue siding on it and new combination windows.

I tried to reconstruct Walter's home in my mind. I removed the siding and the windows, made it smaller and put the porch back on. It didn't work. Walter's house was gone. The healing energy was gone. I heard later that the couple who bought Walter's house had it burned to the ground. The local fire department used it for a practice session. In its place, the couple put a farmhouse they bought for one dollar and completely rebuilt it. It was an old farmhouse with a new face. It was larger than Walter's home, but it didn't look as solid.

Sometimes I dream of being old and of sitting on the steps by the door of Walter's farmhouse. I imagine hollyhocks growing in the front yard and the rows of corn in this rich, black soil whispering to each other throughout the hot summer nights. It is good to live on what used to be called the tall grass prairie, where the four seasons are always filled with so many beginnings and endings.

Judith Bergen was the social worker for the Austin Medical Center Hospice. She now serves as a consultant for the hospice program.

Summertime in the 1950s and '60s
By Linda Vietor Blom

I grew up in the Decker Acre area, and I'm the fourth child in my family. There were my dad and mom and my siblings Nancy, David, Joan and the three little boys, Bruce, Bill and Tim. We lived in a house that our parents built, located on 4th Avenue NE.

One of my fond memories of growing up in Austin begins with a long walk. My sister Joan, our friend and neighbor Vikki Swanson and I would take off after lunch. We were so brave that we would even walk over the old railroad bridge, wearing our 39-cent thongs, now called flip-flops, to help keep our feet from burning on the hot pavement. We'd go to free time swimming at the old Austin Municipal Pool. Did I mention that it was unheated? The lady who would hand out the baskets to hold our clothes was rather cranky, and we were somewhat afraid of her. After changing, we'd return the basket and pin the number on our swimming suits. Next, we'd run fast through the hallway that led to the pool because it sprayed COLD water, which was either to rinse us off or prepare us for the blast of cold when we jumped in. Burr...at first we'd scream until we got used to it, no going in slow, as that would be rather wimpy or pure torture.

How we loved to gaze at the cute lifeguards. Their noses were covered in a white cream to protect that part of their tan bodies. We also enjoyed watching the swinging of the whistle back and forth. That is when they weren't blowing on it and pointing their finger at the rotten kids making trouble in the pool. After a long afternoon of playing tea party and jumping off the little board, not "the tower" (it was just too scary), Joan, Vikki, and I would load up on nickel candy from the refreshment stand. My favorite was the big taffy.

Sometimes we'd stop at the little Park and Rec Building. Each one of us would sculpt a clay figurine. You could pick it up and pay for it when it had dried the next time you were there. We never paid, however, so we didn't get to bring home our masterpieces to share with our mothers.

If we were really tired, we'd take the shortcut and walk the old back road that is now the Mill Pond walking path. The new library wasn't there then, just old houses and storage buildings. We carried our heavy wet towels around our necks and headed out. Our sister Nancy was a carhop at Klagge's Ice Cream Shop. Joan and I would often raid her tip jar to be able to afford our daily snack attacks. We'd stop there for a 25 cent frosted malted cone. It was big and delicious and gave us the strength to make the long journey back home.

This is just one of my many memories. We kids always kept busy making blanket tents on the clothesline, building a tree house, taking long bike rides for a fun adventure and even playing school when we really got bored. I can't believe that I'm saying this, but we knew how to keep out of our mothers' hair. We played and laughed, and sometimes stayed up late to watch our black and white television sets. We even got to see the test pattern that came on at midnight, after the National Anthem played.

Can you imagine parents sending youngsters off for a day at the pool the way our parents did in the '50s and '60s? Well, it just wouldn't be done that way now. They'd be dropped off at the door. After the swim, Mom or Dad would get a call on the kid's cell phone to come and pick them up. Oh yes, and don't forget the ten bucks for the drive through at Mac & Don's.

The Austin swimming pool

Austin native Linda Blom and her husband Joe have three children and four grandchildren, who all live in Austin.

Twenty-one Years and Counting on Meeting More Personalities
By Lee Bonorden

When I bike the streets of Austin and see new immigrants, I wonder what they think of us. I always have since I moved here in 1985. For some reason, Asian immigrants, particularly women and children, caught my attention first, particularly when Minnesota's winter grabbed us in its cold clutches. I would see them on the streets and ask myself, "What possessed them to leave warm climates and come here?"

My idea of immigration reform at the time was based on winter weather. I had my own doubts that moving to Austin was the right choice in the spring of 1985. A divorced, single parent with two children, I had more than a little fear and trepidation that I was making the right decision for my family. When a labor dispute erupted on the scene, the doubts grew.

The *Austin Daily Herald* quickly became my extended family and an oasis of semi-calm amidst the chaos of the mid-1980s in Austin. Ed Smith, the feisty Irishman was retiring as publisher, and another Irishman, Mike Mahoney, replaced him. Walk into the newsroom and there was the inimitable Patsy Sargeant with hoop earrings, rouged cheeks and glasses slipping down her nose. Roger Larson in tennis shoes, dress pants, dress shirt and tie was always moving, always in a hurry, always on the phone.

Judy McDermott chain-smoking--this was before common sense in the work place prevailed--was an alluring sight for a single man. Bruce Lindquist, the managing editor, had whiskers, a sense of humor and a strong will. Unique personalities were everywhere.

On the other side of the second floor of the old Marigold Dairy building was the advertising department. More personalities: John Uecker, Julie Guckeen, Rita Kester, Gayle Peterson and Cindy Samuel. The latter had a great laugh she used frequently. Downstairs the composing room was noisy and crowded. Everybody carried a pica pole -- don't ask -- a tool of the trade at the time. Dick Pacholl, then and now an Austin City Council Member, held court on what city officials had done and why. Jerry Laskewitz actually looked fierce to me in Marine-style crewcut and dark beard. Bob McGinnis smoked cigars and sang hymns at work. Len Parlin talked politics and wore his DFL heart on his sleeve. In the midst of all the males was a lone female, Arlene Hueman.

In the pressroom there was Don Enzenauer, sitting on a stool looking over that day's pages. The days when Don brought wild game he cooked and shared with co-workers were treasured. The mail room had its share of personalities, too. Genial Fred Krofta is still around today, as a matter of fact. Evelyn Culbert came to work with bowling stories. She was a good one. A very good one.

Marcella Schabacker brought her home-baked pastries for the weekly potlucks in the mail room organized by the McGonigle sisters. In the front office were Linda Wehner and Lisa Dunlop-Judd at the front desk; the wise-crackin'-est pair you'd ever want to meet. Dee Quam was there, solving circulation problems, and still is today. In the rear was Vi Christensen, the bookkeeper and payroll clerk, whom we all came to admire at least twice a month.

When I hit the streets of Austin, the first people I met outside the assigned news beat were attorney Bob Leighton and businessman Lee Robbins, both classy guys and missed today. My first impression of life in Austin was being shaped with each new face I saw: Don Hoffman, police chief and Dan Miller, fire chief. Tom Kough, mayor, Darrel Stacy, city administrator, and Kermit Hoversten, city attorney.

Mower County Courthouse looked different too. Don LaValley, Eileen Tapager, Dick Anderson and Fred Wellmann before the judgeship. Wayne Goodnature, sheriff, and "the four oldest commissioners," Bob Shaw, Butch Finbraaten, Dewey Hanson and Dick Cummings, the latter still serving on the county board. Personalities to remember wherever I went.

Art Dubke approved a loan to buy a used car. Otto Volkert and Ron Whalen changed the oil in my car. I filled up with gas at Nicol's with the original Nick Nicol behind the counter, bought groceries at Elden's IGA, went to Dr. Mansur Taufic or the Lommen Brothers when the kids got sick and filled prescriptions at Wold Drug. I spent an inordinate amount of time at Nemitz's on North Main Street and still miss that place. Talk about your personalities.

And then I discovered--a good word choice--the rest of Mower County. That was an epiphany for me, starting with Harlan Boe and going on to Glen Davis and finally Tom Mullenbach and "Them Adams Folks," with hundreds more personalities in between. Truth be told, I saw the light on a summer's day in 1988, three whole years after we moved to Austin.

I was on my way out of Austin and headed someplace, probably Adams, when it struck me. "This place feels comfortable," I said to myself as I drove Highway 56. "The kids are going to good schools and making good friends. Got a good landlord, Dale Peters. Pastor Henry Mayer and Grace Lutheran Church are welcoming. Bud Johnson makes the best root beer and hard-served ice cream anywhere. The Mower County Fair is a blast. Got a good library in town (I could see better then). Going for walks over the walking bridges over the Cedar River is fun. There's nothing better than watching the son play an Austin youth baseball game after supper. Got a job I like a lot. Maybe, I should ask Judy McDermott out for a date? All this, and everyday I'm meeting new and interesting people wherever I go and getting paid for it." My heart was speaking to me, of course, when I heard it say, "This feels as good as a pair of blue jeans, flannel shirt and tennis shoes. I think I'm going to stay here." And I did.

The Austin Herald Staff several years before Lee arrived.

Austin Herald *reporter Lee Bonorden raised a son and daughter in Austin. His two grandchildren live here too.*

A Trip to Trowbridge's (Circa 1963)
By Ramona Borchardt

When you lived in the country, going to town meant going to the big town of Austin. My favorite memory was going for groceries, because that meant we were going to Trowbridge's. Trowbridge's was a huge supermarket in the Sterling Shopping Center, and it seemed like a whole different planet to us kids.

With five or six girls in tow, Mom would drive twenty minutes to get to town. A small lecture on town behavior usually laced the drive, and before we knew it, we were there. We always found a convenient spot in which to ease the massive Olds. The parking spots were angled in front of the store's windows, and as we disembarked, we always stopped for a few seconds to gawk at the window advertisements. Mom shuffled her list and coupons at this point, reconciling her needs with the specials to maximize her budget.

The adventure began right off the bat, as we stepped on the automatic doormat. We younger kids would hang back, repeating the open/close sequence as many times as we could without looking like hopeless country bumpkins. Time would not be wasted on this frivolity, however, because through that automatic door was probably the best part of Trowbridge's. Today I call that entryway "The Supermarket Narthex." It was where kids paid homage to the Gumball Gods.

That entrance could hold about six machines, typically arranged three abreast and two tiered. There was the basic penny multicolored gumball sphere, always a favorite, unless it dispensed the dreaded white gumball. There was the nickel M & M dispenser, another favorite, but considered a gyp for the amount of candy dispensed. Then there were the "prize machines." These babies took a whopping 25 cents, but had the potential to yield rings, glow in the dark skeletons, plastic spiders or even handcuffs! I don't ever remember anyone ever actually using those machines, but we all liked to look at them and manipulate the knobs, on the outside chance that someone would have previously put in a quarter and then forgot to turn the knob. So much for youthful hope!

The "Narthex" behind us now, Mom collected herself and was ready to roll. The wire cage-like carts were predictably queued to the left of the entryway. A firm tug would usually release the cart, but sometimes they seemed welded together, as if engaged in some kind of grocery cart mating ritual. We were farm kids and knew enough to leave things be.

A different row would yield a cart, and we would soon turn it into a hot rod of horror. We all wanted to push. Mom would protest, then back down and let one of us give it a try. The carts were huge, and the wheels all had a mind of their own, which made navigation difficult. We would be quickly demoted as driver once we ran up Mom's heels. We would lose interest in the cart once someone got wounded, and Mom would take her rightful place as skipper.

This place! This massive place! It smelled and looked like nothing I knew. The aisles were long and tunnel-like. The lighting was harsh and intense. A dim roar of voices was all around. There was no climbing under or peeking over the aisle, and no one had any idea what would be around the next bend. Every face was a stranger to us. We followed Mom like ducklings. It occurred to me that someone (like maybe this little kid) could get lost in a place like this. We weren't in Kansas anymore.

A predictable shopper, Mom would stock up on canned goods, especially those on special. The baking goods aisle held hope for us kids. Maybe a bag of flour would be torn and we could "accidentally" walk through the mess and leave white footprints. We were ever alert for overhead announcements appealing for, "Clean up on aisle 5, clean up on aisle 5!"

Each aisle was a new experience. We would marvel at the variety packs of cereal, although we seldom ate cold cereal at home. There were familiar faces along the way, like the ruddy face of the Quaker Oats Quaker, the Snap, Crackle and Pop elves, and Tony the Tiger. Marketing was lost on us.

The meat counter was only briefly visited, since we frequently had home butchered meat in our freezer. That didn't stop us from seeking out liver, tongue, kidneys, and brains to gross out over. The butchers tended to the meat like fussy mothers, arranging the packages just so. They were always large men wearing white aprons spattered with blood. The sight of these awful aprons intimidated me on some level. I never gave the butchers a smile and wouldn't even make eye contact. These men worked intimately in a world of guts and sharp knives. Any kid who valued their digits would know better than to mess with them.

I never liked the cleaning products aisle. I wasn't old enough to realize that the bald genie from the Mr. Clean bottle wasn't real. I guess I figured he lived at Trowbridge's when he wasn't on TV.

The frozen food aisle was next, and now we were back in exploration mode. In those days, the aisles were lined with open chests lined with frost. They were just the right height to peek into, scrape off some frost, and suck it behind Mom's back. It tasted vile, but the intrigue was in the taking, not in the eating. Mom targeted vanilla ice cream and Popsicles, and we were on our way.

The bakery department was an olfactory experience. Yeasty, sugary aromas wrote seductive messages in the air. Our eyes would glaze over as we pressed our faces to the glass display cases. Mom would embarrass us by loudly condemning the "outrageous prices" for what she considered to be inferior baked goods. We knew she was right...our cookie jar was never devoid of her excellent treats. We would lateral our pleas to the bread, hoping it would stand up to Mom's standards. We never got Wonder Bread, and believe me, we tried everything. Mom didn't even crumble when we pointed out that Wonder Bread built strong bodies twelve ways. If it was strong bodies we wanted, Mom replied, she had some chores in mind that were waiting back home. Bread was bread, and Mom liked Trowbridge's store brand.

The checkout marked the last leg in the Trowbridge adventure. We kids were oblivious to the anxiety I now know my mom must have felt as the clerk tallied our total. There was something about that black rubber conveyor belt that intrigued me. Sometimes I would snatch an item from the front of the belt and move it back, just so I could replay the journey. The conveyor belt ranked close to my one experience with an escalator with its potential to suck in a body part, so it felt wonderfully risky to place a hand on it.

In those days there were grocery carryouts. I remember them as clean-cut, cute, young men who were obviously mutes... not that they could have interjected a word into the clerk's nonstop chatter. Extremely efficient, the carryouts were able to maximize the space inside the serrated edged brown bag. They scored big points with Mom for double bagging heavy loads, keeping the eggs whole, and the bread from getting squashed.

I liked those carryouts, but I dearly loved the checkout clerks. Most wore bright makeup, painted fingernails, and a smock with their name stitched on it. They were lightning fast on the keys, friendly, and I was sure they were making a lot of money. I was confident that if I lived right, said my prayers, and studied hard, I too could aspire to the glamorous life of a Trowbridge checkout clerk.

If all went well, and the total wasn't too shocking, there was a chance of a ride upon the "Supermarket Steed." Five cents gave one a pitiful lurching ride on this stationary mechanical horse. Never mind that we had real horses at home. We preferred this public equine. What a memory…two or three of us crammed on top, holding on for dear life!

The adventure was over as we stepped out the back door. (Yes, we *did* open and close this automatic door a few times as we left). The carryouts accompanied us the few feet to the car and helped us load it for a ride home. No one sat comfortably with all the groceries perched between them and around them. The bigger kids had to hold the bags on their laps. God forbid it might be the one with the cold stuff in it, or there would be griping all the way home.

There was rather a Neanderthal feeling to unloading the groceries from the car. It was as if we had gone on a hunt and were bringing home the kill. We were at the end of our trip to the big city of Austin. Trowbridge's would be there when we returned. The party was over, as they say, so we would scatter once we hit the door, and Mom was on her own to put it all away.

Ramona Borchardt, a registered nurse, lives in Woodbury, Minnesota with her husband Marty and dog Tanner.

A Walk With Charlie
By Roger Boughton

My dog Charlie and I often find ourselves walking each day through the Austin neighborhoods. He was rescued from the dog pound in Eau Claire, Wisconsin several years ago. I do some of my best thinking on these cold winter walks while Charlie and his nose do the exploring.

On one of our most recent walks, I got to thinking about my first visit to Austin some twenty-nine years ago. Our family was living in Kalamazoo, Michigan at the time. I was invited to Austin to interview for a position at Austin Community College. Arlan Burmeister, who was the president at the time, had just been promoted and was looking for a replacement for the Dean of Students. My wife Cheryl, daughter Wendy, sons Nathan, Matthew and I had lived in Kalamazoo for the past eight years, and we were looking for new challenges.

Several students from the college met me at the airport. My first impression of the community twenty-nine years ago was how attractive and neat the neighborhoods looked. The new Ellis Middle School was remarkable, and the downtown busy and energized. There did not seem to be any poverty, and plant workers lived next door to executives. It was a community without class distinction, or so it seemed. In addition, the college campus was small, neat and tidy with an excellent faculty and reputation. The support staff at the college looked me over, and I passed muster. However, the experience did not pass without incident. During lunch at the Country Club, I spilled ketchup down the front of my white slacks. A quick trip to the bathroom and a sponge bath did not cure the problem. This was not a very good beginning for a guy applying for a job.

Nevertheless, an offer was made and after several conversations with my family back in Kalamazoo, we accepted and found ourselves together in Austin on October 10, 1976. The community welcomed us by providing a winter snowstorm. Students, along with Alan Burmeister from the college, helped unload the U-Haul trailer, and we were in business in a new community and a new home.

Our intent was to stay just five years and then move on. That five-year plan translated into twenty-nine years. Our out-of-state friends inquired as to why we stayed. We had lived in seven different states prior to Minnesota. The question was not difficult to answer. Our three children loved the schools, the college provided a wonderful opportunity for area residents, and the community of Austin was welcoming to newcomers. It became our home in a matter of months and wore like an old shoe. The Twin Cities was our city, and Rochester was close enough to remind us of what a larger community afforded in the way of entertainment.

However, I must remind myself that one of the reasons we originally chose Minnesota was that it was the "land of ten thousand lakes," or at least we thought so. I had as a hobby taught sailing at a college in Michigan and thought a move to Austin, Minnesota might just be the cat's meow. Was I surprised! My sailboat that I trailered from Michigan remained docked and anchored in my driveway until I sold it three years later to a family who put the boat in Lake Superior. East Side Lake was just not the same.

I am retired now. My children are adults in their own right and have moved on. We are still in Austin and our out-of-state friends ask, "Isn't it time you moved on?"

Not for the world would we pick up and move to another community or state. Our friendships have expanded, and our roots have grown deep. Our friends nourish those roots and provide support when needed. The different languages heard at the grocery store or the various cultures found in the church pews on a Sunday morning remind me how rich our lives have become. The community college has become a powerhouse of opportunity.

Austin remains a community where neighbors know one another, a place where one stops at the corner stop sign and waves at a friend. It is a community where I can walk to my daughter's home or visit a grandson's football game or granddaughter's dance recital. Yes, Austin is just where I want to be. Home is just around the corner as I walk with my best friend Charlie. Our walk has ended for the day. What will we recall tomorrow, and where will we walk?

Two Hometowns
By Roger Boughton

I am fortunate to have two hometowns. One is in Minnesota and the other is in Ohio, some 750 miles away. One hometown is where I grew up, and the other where I have chosen to live. On a recent walk through the southwest part of Austin with my best friend and dog Charlie, it was snowing and a blizzard was about to occur. The clouds were closing in, and the wind was out of the northeast. Driveways were slowly being snowed over, and children were headed home. Tracks were disappearing, and it was quiet. The weatherman predicted that we would have sufficient snow to close schools and suggested we stock up on milk and bread.

I also heard that a possible worldwide flu pandemic could arrive at any time, and it is only prudent to be careful. This is a "new" reality and quite different from anything that we have experienced in the past. Hearing about it reminded me of another hometown at another time when I grew up.

The year was 1959. Vermillion is a small fishing village located in Ohio adjacent to Lake Erie. It was a village at the time I was in high school, about the size of Blooming Prairie. Eighteen hundred residents called Vermillion home. Main Street was two blocks long with the north end of town being in Lake Erie and the Vermillion River dissecting the town from north to south. Downtown included several fisheries, a lumberyard, hardware store, barbershop, shoe store and several restaurants. Its small downtown was struggling with being competitive with "new" shopping centers in towns close by. The local meat market, dairy and grocery store were struggling and soon would disappear.

The family farm was changing as well. Weather was unpredictable, and when winter storms came out of the northeast, we referred to them as nor'easters. When the storms occurred, schools were closed, and we stocked up on milk, candles, bread and other essentials. We knew it would be only a day or two before we were back to normal. The lake was wild from time to time with large ice mountains pushed tight against the shore or breakwater. A friend and I often would grab a snow shovel and head to Main Street to shovel out stores. Ford Motor Company was bringing in a new, large assembly plant a short fourteen miles down the road. Numerous new homes were being built, and retail stores were busy on Friday evenings. The populations were quickly becoming diverse. Everything was about to change.

It is now 2006 and the weather looks threatening in Austin. A winter storm alert has been broadcast with the weatherman suggesting no travel unless necessary. As Charlie and I head north, we pass the fairgrounds. All is quiet, and you can barely see the sidewalk with the snow falling in large flakes. I am reminded that I checked my computer prior to leaving and found Hormel stock doing quite well. The community is prosperous by having a Fortune 500 Company headquartered in town. Employment is strong, a new Wal-Mart is about to begin construction, and a local businessperson will close his doors at the end of the month after a number of successful years. Illness and competition with big stores have had their effect. Austin has become a tourist destination with its new SPAM Museum and has picked up the name SPAM Town. The world is changing.

Back in Vermillion, Ford Motor Company has just closed its doors after forty-seven years as the largest employer in the county. How could that happen? Schools are not sure how they will fund their students, and laid off workers are wondering where they will work next. Retail stores on Main Street are closing, but tourism is booming. Property tax continues to rise, and the sale of real estate is strong. Vermillion has grown to over 11,000 citizens. The world is changing.

While walking along Oakland Avenue, I gaze at our refurbished Wescott Athletic Field. How attractive the athletic complex is, and it illustrates how much pride the community has in its schools. Attractive churches suggest that the community has invested in its soul along with issues of the wallet. Banfield School on our left is busy, and the community has adopted an all-day kindergarten. One wonders why it took so long to do. Charlie and I have walked nearly two miles, and we are tired. There is much to be proud of in Austin. The future looks bright, but one must remember that the world is changing.

Vermillion and Austin are similar but quite different. Each has its own beauty but has struggled in a world where companies are changing and skills once celebrated are discarded or replaced by machines. Vermillion is called Harbor Town, and Austin is referred to as SPAM Town. Downtowns are changing as populations change and new needs evolve. Thomas Friedman reminds me in his book, *The World is Flat,* that what each community needs are people who dream, who wake up each morning and imagine that the world can be better. Communities also need individuals who are flexible and committed to change. This thought brings me to the end of my walk with my dog Charlie. I know that tomorrow will be better than today, and I will help make it so!

Launching a New Life
By Astrid Brown

The stately gray granite Union Station in Denver loomed ahead, and we looked for the gate marked "Burlington Zephyr," where we boarded a train that was to transport us to our new life in Austin, Minnesota. Frank and I were married early in 1948, and he graduated from Colorado State University and accepted a job in the Engineering Department of the George A. Hormel Co. Frank had been in the Navy in World War II and served in the Pacific. I had only traveled as far as Wyoming. We bid a sad farewell to our families who had come to see us off. It would be nearly two years before we could return for a visit.

After we boarded the sleek, silver Zephyr, we were on our way to Omaha, where we spent the night at the Blackstone Hotel, an imposing building whose dining room reflected old world elegance. The next morning we switched trains to board the Great Northern Railway. Most of the day we rolled through Iowa past huge, red barns and large farmhouses and miles and miles of fields ripe with standing corn.

Ever since we had left Denver with the Rocky Mountains as a backdrop, the landscape had been flat. As the train pulled into the Milwaukee Station in Austin, the town seemed bleak and sparse to me. It was hot and humid that September day, and I remember noticing several bars along 4th Street, the East Side Furniture Store and a bakery.

We got into a cab with our few belongings in a couple of suitcases and we told the driver we would like to go to a hotel. We were dropped off on the corner of Main Street and 4th Avenue at a three-story, red brick building built around the turn of the century. Today this is the site of Wells Fargo. Frank and I walked up the numerous steps to the lobby of the Fox Hotel to register with the desk clerk. He told us we could stay for three nights. After that, the hotel was booked for the Barrow Show. "Whatever is that?" we thought.

The next day Frank walked the mile to the Hormel Company, and I began a search for an apartment. Just west of the Fox Hotel was a Red Owl grocery store. Then turning left on St. Paul Street (now 1st Street NW), I saw a row of churches. First to my left going south was the Episcopal Church. On the other side of the street were the Congregational and Presbyterian churches, both of which burned down in the '50s. In the next block was St. Olaf Lutheran Church, where it stands today.

I continued on past the Carnegie Library next to the First Methodist Church. Crossing Oakland Avenue and walking west, I came to Greenwich Street (now 2nd Street SW). There I saw a sign that said, "Room for Rent" on a large, frame house, now the Ramseth Beauty Shop. After I assured the landlord we were not there for the Barrow Show, he said he had an apartment for rent over the double garage in back. It had a living room, dinette next to the kitchen, a small bedroom and a bathroom. There we began our life in Austin.

That same September of 1948, the campaign for the election of president of the United States was in full swing. The Republican candidate, Thomas Dewey, came by train to Austin. We were excited to see this man whom newspapers claimed would be the next president. Frank met me at the yards of the Milwaukee Depot. We waited for the train to arrive in Austin. There were others from the Hormel office dressed in suits and ties along with farmers, plant workers and housewives pushing strollers. There was a crowd of perhaps 300 people, not a great showing for a city of over 20,000.

It seemed like quite a wait before we heard the whistle that announced the arrival of the train. It took even longer before Dewey appeared on the banner-bedecked caboose and waved to the crowd. The crowd listened respectfully and clapped sporadically to his message. It seemed there was a lack of enthusiasm for the dapper New Yorker. Would he win the presidency? Some weeks later Harry Truman made a similar appearance and drew a more enthusiastic response. Could this be a precursor of the final outcome?

On the regular date of a national election, the first Tuesday after the first Monday in November, Frank and I, both 22, voted in our first presidential election. That night we tuned our radio to the returns as they slowly made their way through the polls from the East Coast to the West Coast. Before midnight, the Chicago Tribune declared Thomas Dewey the winner. We stayed glued to the sounds from the radio as votes from the country were changing the predictions. Our personal prediction, based on attendance at the two campaign trains, was confirmed.

Cheaper by the Dozen—Plus Two
By Merle W. Burton

The Frank and Sarah Burton family won the "Cheaper By The Dozen" contest, held in conjunction with the opening of the movie by that title in 1950. The *Austin Daily Herald* photographer came out to take a picture of our family, and we won a meal and theatre tickets so our whole family could see the movie at the Paramount Theatre. I don't know how many families entered the contest, but we won because we had fourteen children. My mother entered our family in the contest. I had just come home from the Navy, where I had served in the Pacific for about three and a half years. My oldest brother Harry was out of the Marine Corps at that time, and he had five children of his own.

We had eight boys and six girls in our family. Mother had a flag with six stars on it during the Second World War and the Korean War, and six of us boys served our country for a total of about 23 years. There were two boys in the Korean War; Darrel was in the Navy and Jerry served in the Air Force. Frank and Doug were in the Army in Germany when they were flying into Berlin. The other boys were Clint and Micky. There were six girls in our family: Donna, Betty, Phyllis, Rosie, Dixie and Paula. Paula was born when I was in the service, and she was a surprise when I got home. Only eight of us are still alive.

When the picture was taken, we lived on 900 Harmon Avenue NE. There were three bedrooms upstairs and one down. Many years separated us kids, but at one time thirteen of us lived there. We had outdoor plumbing, lights and power. Dad bought the house in 1933, along with two blocks of lots. He sold the lots for about fifty bucks each. It was nice growing up in a big Austin family, and we all got along.

Fourteen kids and two parents posed together for the Herald photo.

I Remember Pearl Harbor
By Margetta G. Byers

We didn't have TV then, only radio when I heard that a little country like Japan went up against the USA by bombing Pearl Harbor. My Mapleton cousin, who was on leave while serving in Pearl Harbor, was with me when we heard. How lucky he was to be home on leave.

My husband Leonard enlisted in the Navy, and he was in Nemitz's Fleet, which went from island to island fighting right on to Japan. He never talked much about that time and all the fighting. Most men under the age of 40 enlisted, whether or not they had wives and kids.

I lived in Austin, and I didn't drive. In those days there were city buses that would take you anywhere you needed to go, and I had a lot of good neighbors who would take me grocery shopping and to movies.

There were many young wives like me in Austin who were waiting for their husbands to come home. Some of the war wives from our church would go down to Sutton Park and have picnics. We would talk about the letters we received from our husbands and have a good time keeping each other company.

The letters we received would have parts blacked out, and we weren't supposed to know where the men were, but we had a kind of code. "How's Jimmy?" meant Iwo Jima, and "Phillip" was a code name for the Philippines. My dad had a big map, and we would try to figure out where everybody was.

The day he went off to war, I found out I was pregnant with my third child. Leonard came home once after boot camp, but otherwise I didn't see him for about two years. I don't think anybody realizes how hard it is for a mother, especially one who doesn't drive, to get along when her husband goes off to war.

I sent word by mental telepathy that the baby was born and that he was a boy. My husband knew before he received the mail, and his friends razzed him and said he couldn't possibly know. But when the mail arrived two weeks later, the news was confirmed.

When Leonard came home in 1945, my three children and I were glad to have him home again. We had to go to Albert Lea to pick him up. Since I didn't drive, I had to get my folks to drive me over there to meet the train. The excitement was electric as all the wives waited for their husbands. Another Austin guy hitched a ride back to town with us, and although giving him a lift was the sensible and right thing to do, I just hated having him in the car because I had waited so long for this reunion, and I didn't want to share it with an outsider.

Leonard worked as a butcher for Hormel until he retired. We enjoyed our years in Austin, and I still get back once in awhile. We had five children in all, and at the age of 81, I have fifty descendants. I think of life as an adventure, and enjoy every day.

The streets of Austin in the 1940s.

La Historia de un Rio, A River Tale
By Ruby Campos

My adventure started before I was born. My parents were traveling in their old car hoping for the best since they were going to cross the border to the United States for a better life for my brothers and me. My brothers are three and four years older, and my mother was pregnant with me at that time. She was due in a couple of weeks when she decided to travel with my dad and my brothers.

While traveling, my mother was starting to feel some pain but there were no hospitals around. All of this happened in Chihuahua, Mexico, something that no one expected to happen! Believe it or not, I was born in that old car that my father was driving to get us to the border. My mother told me that we had to stay in Chihuahua for a couple of months until I was a few months older because it was very risky for a newborn baby.

A year went by when my parents decided to finish their adventure. In those times the easiest way to come to the United States was by crossing, or you can say by swimming, since you needed to be a good swimmer to cross the Rio Bravo. Of course, my parents would need more help. When I saw the movie *My Family (Mi Familia)* where Jennifer Lopez is holding her baby and crossing the river to come to the United States for a better life, I remember my mother doing the same thing.

A couple of years after we arrived, the government offered amnesty. That's how my parents, my brothers and I became U.S. residents and then citizens. I came to the United States in 1981 when I was only 1 year old, and in that same year my sister was born. She was lucky she didn't go through all that we went through.

I grew up in California, went to school there and graduated from high school and went to school two more years; next year I plan to go back to college! Wish me luck. I got married very young. I have two kids, a girl and a boy. My son is 13 years old, and my daughter is 10.

In 2002 I started another adventure. My husband decided to try his luck in another state, since the minimum wage in California wasn't enough, and everything was very expensive. So he decided to go first. It was going to be only for one year, that's what he told me, but deep in me I knew it was going to be more than that, and I knew he knew that too.

Once he started working in Minnesota he started to notice that he wasn't going to be away for one year. He started to convince me to move where he was. Deep in me I wanted to but at the same time, I didn't; I didn't want to leave behind my parents. Yet, I had two kids who were growing and needed a better and safer place to live.

California wasn't the place where I really wanted my kids to grow up and go to school. He knew it was going to be difficult to convince me to leave, since he knew I didn't like quiet areas. I call them ghost towns. When I was 10 years old my parents separated. My father went to live in San Bernardino, CA. It was the quietest community I had ever been to, and I hated that place with all my heart. I don't know why my dad still lives there.

My husband knew it was going to be difficult to convince me to move here. He started with his lies. He told me that there were a lot of shopping stores, big buildings, food markets and a lot of job openings. So I went with my two kids and bought three airline tickets to Austin. It was a long trip, with delays and change of airlines. There was a point when I was starting to regret it.

Finally I arrived around 1 a.m. and I noticed when I was leaving the airport that yes, everything my husband told me was true. There were tall buildings and a huge mall--the biggest Mall of America. It was a big city, but what he didn't tell me was that we were in Bloomington, right next to St. Paul and Minneapolis, and not in Austin. We were almost two hours away from home still.

It was a long trip. I thought it was going to be just a couple of blocks. When finally we were a few blocks away from where my husband lived, suddenly something came into my mind. I remember that as my husband was driving into this small town, it reminded me where my dad lives.

The next day I woke up late. Aaaaaaaaaaaa! A bunch of people were eating at the table. I thought it was party time and that they came just to welcome me home, but no! He never told me that we were going to share the apartment with his brother, sister-in-law, two more kids, a cousin, and our family! Ayyayaya. I asked myself what I had gotten myself into. They started telling me the rules. The women would cook for everybody, so I would be taking turns with my sister-in-law, and we would be doing all the cooking.

I was so mad that I decided to go for a walk. I noticed the more I walked the fewer things I saw. Well, I said to myself, this is only one side of the town; downtown is on the other side of the town, and that must be where all the people are.

The weekend arrived, and my husband's niece and her husband came to visit us. She proposed that we go for a walk to the mall so that the kids wouldn't be bored and just to get a tour around the big city.

Here comes the good part. We went to the mall. Oh my God! It was the smallest mall I have ever been in. In half an hour I walked to all the stores, and I think we were the only people inside the mall. My husband could sense that I didn't want him right next to me. He could see that I was so disappointed.

Then we went downtown. I remember that my husband didn't want to go. He proposed we go home and eat something when not so long ago we had eaten. Well, I wasn't going to waste the opportunity to go and see the tall buildings and many shopping stores. What was my surprise! Haaaaaa… a one and a half block downtown with a couple of buildings that didn't reach to a second floor.

I was so disappointed and mad for many weeks because I couldn't find a job. I missed California. I had everything there. I was working, and they were paying me well, but the problem is that everything was upside down now; I wasn't working and he was, and they were paying him a good wage.

Several months passed, and I had decided to go back to California. Thank God finally I found a job that I never thought of doing. I started working for the WIC office as an interpreter for non-English-speaking clients. Soon I started working for the Austin Public Library. I don't know if my husband prayed to all the saints because now I was working in two part-time jobs. I started to like the town. Yes, it was quiet, but I don't know, it had a different feeling from where my dad lives. I started to like it a lot. It was the perfect place to raise my children, give them a good education and a safe place to live.

What surprised me most were the schools, compared to the schools in California. The people in Austin are very trusting. They trust each other, and they are very polite. With these people you can smell peace. You can trust that your kids are going to be safe if they go outside and play.

Sometimes I still remember when my husband told me he just wanted to see me happy. "Do you want to see some shopping stores? This weekend I'll take you to the stores." He took me to the Mall of America. It is spectacular and the biggest mall in the U.S. If I need to go there sometimes, I can.

Coming to Austin was a new change for us; it changed the way we live and the way we look at people. Now I can say that I don't miss California. Neither do my children. The only thing I miss is my family. Austin is a great place to live. I have everything I need, well almost everything. The good thing is that I'm working, and the most important thing is that my co-workers are very nice people, especially the people at the library. All of them help out whenever someone needs it. It's like working with family. They are so extremely nice that when they take their vacation, I miss them. And I think it is rare when you feel that good about a place where you work. Actually I get excited when we plan something fun to do with them.

Not so long ago, Kathy Helle, who works with me at the library, proposed to me that once her kitchen was done being remodeled, that I come to her house and show all the staff of the library a Mexican cooking lesson. We did that, and had a good time.

Well, what more could I say. There's no better and peaceful place to live than Austin. I don't regret coming to live in this beautiful, small town that is full of nice things. Well, this is how the river ended. Maybe in the future it will continue running, but for right now the river is happy where it is.

Library staff Maureen Steenblock, Gayle Heimer, Jeanne Steinbrink, Ann Hokanson, Little Ruby, and Ruby Campos

An Austin Boy's Fun in the 1940s
By Kenneth Carlson

One of the memories I'll always cherish is going fishing with my grandpa on the Red Cedar River. Our first step was to take a spade and go out back to our garden and dig for worms. Grandpa always took a coffee can, punched two holes in it and made a handle out of wire; I always thought that was so neat.

We'd take our can of worms, cane poles with a cork and small hook, and walk to the Cedar River between Water Street and the railroad bridge. Our favorite spots were on the east side of the river. There were several spots where we could get down to the bank to fish. Sometimes we'd go out on the railroad bridge and fish from there, but that was really scary, always thinking that a train would come any minute, but it never did. The best part of all was when our cork went down and we'd pull up a nice blue gill or sunfish. We didn't always catch anything, but I can remember having an occasional meal of fish from the Red Cedar River. It was one of the highlights of my youth in Austin.

Winter fun time in Austin always involved going ice-skating with my dad. We'd either go to the big rink on North Main Street on the Red Cedar River or what we called "the lagoon" below Skinner's Hill, where kids still enjoy sliding in the winter. Each place had a nice warming house with wood ramps down to the ice, although the one on North Main was especially long. One year the city flooded a spot on Driesner Park north of the highway (now Oakland Avenue). We lived there before the city extended Oak Street through to the highway and took out the houses. That year we could just put on our skates at home and make our way over to the rink. My dad was a great figure skater. He did the grapevine, which was a beautiful thing to watch, as he seemed to float around the rink. He could also do the figure eight, always keeping one skate in front of the other. I never could quite get that one right.

He worked at Hormel as a foreman when Jay Hormel was still active in the plant. He knew Dad was a great ice skater and told him to come out to the estate and skate on their rink anytime he wanted. I'll never forget going out there with Dad at night, stopping at the guard house, waiting while the guard turned on the lights, and going into the warming house to put on our skates. I also remember the three pairs of small ice skates hanging on nails on the wall, each belonging to one of the three Hormel boys. Skating with my dad all alone on that rink at night is something special that I will never forget.

Being a Part of the Austin Bands in the 1940s
By Kenneth Carlson

As a kid in Austin High School, I always enjoyed playing clarinet in the band. C. Vittorio Sperati was the director of all the bands at school. I started out in Beginners Band, of course. Then came Junior Band, where we even got uniforms. We provided white pants and white shirt, and the school provided a bright red and white cape. We thought it was pretty neat.

Then came the Austin High School Band with our nice new uniforms. Mr. Sperati, as we all called him, was a great band director, and we all liked him. I always thought he was a great musician. He wanted our concerts to be perfect. I enjoyed going to other schools for our band festivals, in which we competed with other bands in the area. We'd take a school bus, and I remember that when we got there and as we left the bus, Mr. Sperati stood at the door and gave everyone a dollar bill for lunch. Yes, a dollar really did buy lunch in those days.

One thing he insisted on was that we were absolutely not to tap our feet to the music. To emphasize his point, he used to say, "If I catch any of you tapping your feet, I'm going to nail your shoes to the floor!" I can't remember anyone tapping his or her feet after that. There was a good reason for it. It looked terrible to the audience to see everyone tapping their feet. In addition, it made it harder for the director to change the tempo. There was one high school band (that shall remain nameless) in our district that was notorious for foot tapping.

Mr. Sperati wanted us to keep one eye on the director. He would have us look at the music at rehearsal, then he would do something with his hand, and we would have to tell him what he had done. As a kid I didn't think too much of that, but years later in my music experience, I decided it was extremely good advice.

After graduation from high school, I played in the Austin Municipal Band during summer vacation from college. Mr. Sperati also directed. I was never a great clarinet player, but it was so special to play with some of the great older, experienced musicians, of which there were plenty. We rehearsed in the Shaw Gym and played our concerts in the Austin Band Shell when it was still just like new.

There was a light engineer who controlled the beautiful colored lights. When we played soft parts of an overture, the lights would dim, and then they grew brighter as the band would crescendo. The frosting on the cake was when we ended every concert with the Star Spangled Banner. The lights were red, white, and blue. It was really very moving.

My wife Signe and I moved away from Austin for twenty-three years before returning, and I have often thought how thankful I was to grow up in Austin!

The Austin High School Band

Austin Remembers The Flood of 2004
Katrina Carolan

On September 15, 2004 in Austin, a big storm hit with heavy rains and started what we call a flood. Some parts of Austin were under water. During this time our community was affected in many ways. People's houses became deteriorated, many people couldn't get from place to place, and some of the grocery stores and gas stations were under water, causing them damage and loss of business. Septic tanks backed up in many homes, and there was a lot of residue on the streets, sidewalks, and everywhere else you looked.

During this time my neighborhood, in the northwest part of town right by the Cedar River, became flooded. Even though my house wasn't under water, the flood still affected me. I couldn't take a shower because the septic tank in our house was backing up, and we had to use our water wisely. The house belonging to my good neighbors and friends was flooded.

While I was off school, I spent time working at my neighbor's house by helping them sandbag and move their furniture to a higher level. I watched their children so they wouldn't get in the way or so they wouldn't get in a dangerous area. I also helped by cooking meals for families who were going through this hard time and for the people helping the families who were directly hit by the flood.

Even though I was only 12 years old at the time, I will always remember this experience because it was very hard on my neighbors. They had recently finished their basement, and then the flood came, and they had to do it all over again because it got ruined.

Although the flood happened two years ago, the effects are still in place today. Many people are still waiting for their houses to be remodeled or sold. Some people still worry every time it rains because they live in the part of town where their house may become flooded again. Although the flood of 2004 was a hard time for Austin, it was also good for us as a community because we became closer as we helped people in need, and we got to know our neighbors and friends through this experience.

1956
By Colette Frisk Chaffee

I was 9 years old in the summer of 1956 when Austin celebrated it's centennial. There seemed to be a lot of excitement in town and like today, lots of old photographs in the newspapers.

The first thought to come to mind about this great event was the men growing beards. I can still see them, some with very long beards and big mustaches. My Dad grew a beard. Dad had always had a mustache, and I was used to that, so much so that once when he shaved it off I thought he looked awful without it, and I couldn't wait for it to grow back. The beard I did not like on Dad, and I recall that I could not wait for the events of that summer to end, so he would shave it off.

I remember taking baton lessons along with my sister Marcia, and we marched in the parade. We marched north down Main Street and past the courthouse. I had been in parades before, usually as a Brownie or Girl Scout, but twirling the baton was more exciting. I cannot recall who we took baton lessons from, but do remember going to a building downtown. We started in 1955, and I don't think we continued after the summer of 1956.

Another big event was the birth of my brother Tom at the end of July. My Mother took a photo on a Sunday, as Dad and I returned from church. We were dressed up, so she probably thought this was a good time to photograph Marcia, me and my brother Michael. My father, Merrill Frisk, is in the beard he grew for the centennial and wearing his centennial button. Another sister Mary missed out. My mom always had duplicates made to send to our grandparents.

Marcia, Merrill, Colette & Mike Frisk, 1956

The Marble Sink and Other Memories
By Colette Frisk Chaffee

For the most part, I grew up in Austin, living briefly in Rochester, as a youngster. We would return occasionally to Austin by bus to visit friends or to watch parades. Austin had the best parades in this part of Minnesota, according to my mother. At the end of the day, we would head back to the Fox Hotel and catch the bus back to Rochester.

We returned to Austin for good in November of 1951. I had started first grade in Rochester and transferred to Columbus, the Catholic grade school in Austin. I vividly recall my first day. A Sister stood on either side of me, each holding a hand, while I cried, screamed and tried to break away to run after my mother, who was swiftly walking down the dimly lit hall of the old building. I can still see her walking toward the light coming in through the south door window at the end of the hall. Things did improve after that day.

Christmas vacation from school meant sledding on Sunset Hill on South Kenwood Avenue (4th Street SW) or pulling our wooden sleds north a half a block from Sunset to Skinnner's Hill, which was actually private land behind a house owned by Mr. and Mrs. Skinner, early publishers of the *Austin Daily Herald*. The elderly couple would at times be visible, looking out a window at us, but we did not know who they were. I'm certain it didn't dawn on us that they owned the hill! No one ever stopped us from sledding there in the 1950s, and early '60s, but that probably wouldn't be the case today. The house and hill are still there. We skated at the lagoon, next to Sunset or at Galloway Park, for hours at a time, showing off our skating ability and watching others.

Summer meant swimming at the municipal pool several days a week. We usually swam during free time, when most of our friends were there. We weren't allowed to bring towels into the pool, so they went into a wire basket, and we pinned a numbered metal tag to our suit to retrieve the towel and/or clothes after swimming. We sometimes brought a nickel to use at the snack bar, clinching it in our hands or diving for our nickel in 3-4 feet of water, until ready to spend it on a candy bar.

On the way home, clad only in our suits with our towels over our shoulders, we ran across the hot tar streets as fast as we could go, to get to the cooler sidewalks beneath the store awnings. We usually stayed on the west side of Main Street, which was shaded. Sometimes we walked on the east side. I recall the day when we curiously peered into the open door of the Colonial Bar. It was smoky and dark, except for the advertising signs, and the men were rather loud. We were promptly chased away by the patrons.

We liked to window shop, and we often ended up in Woolworth's looking at parakeets, little lizards and fish in the lower level. We'd go back to the main floor and smell the little bottles of Blue Waltz perfume, admire the lipsticks that we were too young to wear, and try on rings. I will never forget the gold colored ring with the December stone. A little gold heart hung off one side of the stone, and a little cross hung from the other side. I put the ring on and was unable to get it off. I remember a feeling of panic. I recall quickly picking my towel up from the floor and running out of the store and to the huge red brick courthouse about a block away. I ran down the stairs to the basement restroom. Along the north wall was a large, gray marble sink. I began frantically soaping my finger, and the ring flew off and nearly went down the drain. I wiped it off and ran back to Woolworth's as fast I could and put it back in its slot on a very large tray of rings.

I remember that event as being rather traumatic. I had never heard of shoplifting and had never stolen anything and didn't know anyone who had. I apparently didn't see anything wrong with leaving the store to get the ring off. I do know I learned quite a lesson that day. I eventually bought the ring, one that fit, of course.

In 1970, my husband and I bought our first home. The tour of the home ended up in the basement bathroom. Standing in front of a large, gray marble sink, obviously very old, the homeowner proudly announced, "This marble sink came out of the old courthouse." Yes, I instantly recognized it and many memories surfaced, especially of the birthstone ring. This year the sink will be replaced. I managed to keep it when we did the first remodel, but this time my husband says it is going to go. I'm just trying to figure out where it will go, as I have a soft spot in my heart for it, partly because of the ring, but mainly because it is a part of Austin's history.

Childhood Memories
By OryAnn Champlin

This I remember, one memory at a time, then and now. I am writing an overview of memories from my life and families. I am 84 years old, and I will try to express some of the many changes through the early years of my life. I have been told it was a cold wintry day the 30th of December, 1921, to be my forever birth date. I was the youngest of five children. Harold was nine years older, Caroline, was seven years older, Adeline was five years older, and Ruth was two years older. Only my sister Adeline Henricks is still alive. She is 89 years old.

We lived on an 80-acre farm twelve miles northwest of Austin. Dad was a farmer and carpenter who built our home a few years before I was born. The memory of our home is still very vivid in my mind. The house was square and had two stories. There was a large kitchen with two cupboards between the kitchen and dining room. The kitchen was the room with the most activity. There was a square oak table with fancy legs and several leaves to enlarge it, and it was used for eating and baking. Mom made a cream cake, donuts and several loaves of bread during the week on this table. If the sale of eggs brought in extra money, Mother would get extravagant and buy a new oilcloth for the table. Mom usually crocheted rag rugs from old print dresses and men's shirts. There was a fold down treadle sewing machine and a wall telephone. There was a half window higher up on a shelf where my father kept his pipe and Prince Albert tobacco. This also held his shaving mug with brush and soap, barber scissors, and clipper. Dad gave us all haircuts. He also had a wall mirror for shaving.

We had a washstand with drawers below and a washbowl with soap on top. Mom made long linen towels to put on the rollers. The wash machine stood in one corner. On wash days there was a big copper boiler on the stove, and we boiled the white clothes and added Mrs. Stewarts's Bluing for whitening clothes. Later the wash machine had the wringer attached and was run by a gas engine. It was some improvement!

In the summer we hung clothes outside on lines strung between two large cottonwood trees, and in the winter we hung them on drying racks and on a round spinning rack with extended arms. I still have the rack in the basement. We put it over the floor furnace so the heat would dry them faster. We did ironing with a flat iron that had handles, and we put it on the stove to heat. Many items were starched with Argo starch and boiling water. In later years we acquired a gas iron.

There was a large rain barrel by the back door to catch "soft water" that came down from the downspouts. This was the best water to wash our hair and take baths. We had to get our drinking water from a well that was located quite a way from the house. There was a gas engine to start the pump. We would carry pails of water to the house for fresh drinking water. Every day Dad or one of us kids would get a cream can full and push it back to the house on a two-wheeled cart, and we would also push each other around on the cart. The well water was pumped into a large, round, wooden tank for the cattle and horses to drink from.

The water was heated on the stove in a large copper boiler. We always had our drinking water in an enamel pail on the table with a long handled dipper and blue enamel cups to drink from. There was a large cook stove or range, as it was called then, with four burners or plates that lifted off to put the wood in and two warming closets above to keep the food warm. We had a reservoir on one side to keep water hot for dishes and the separator. There was always a gray coffee pot and an aluminum teakettle. Beside the stove was a wood box for the chopped wood, and sometimes we started the fire with corncobs.

There was a large dining room, and in this room was a large round floor furnace with flat grates to fit. We adjusted the heat with chains. Sometimes it got pretty cozy, but the heat register was above to let the heat rise upstairs. This was really needed in the winter months. I cannot guess how many marbles and pennies went down through those grates.

For the special days when we had company and for holidays we usually used the big round oak table in the dining room. We had a buffet and a radio console that was battery operated. We got our first radio, a console Motorola, when I was about 12. We listened to the news, politics, which did not interest me, comedians Lum and Abner, George and Gracie Allen and music. I think we had WLS from Chicago and other stations.

Mom had long black hair, and she wore it braided and put in a pug or crossed it to the front and used metal pins and side combs to hold it up. As she relaxed I brushed it, and she would sit as long as I had the patience to brush it and braid it. She sometimes dozed off as she sat there.

In the basement there was a large fruit cupboard. The blue fruit jars were filled with peaches, pears, applesauce, and homemade strawberry jam, apple butter and vegetables, all raised in our garden. Of course there were lots of meatballs and canned meat. We did not have refrigeration so when they butchered beef or pork, Mom canned a lot of our meats. She often made a combination of beef and pork as meatballs to be baked in the oven in a double layer in big black pans. They were super-delicious!

When I was very young we had a big open porch to the west of the kitchen. We would often sit out there in the evenings after dark, and we had to contend with mosquitoes! It was cool and peaceful on the porch. Mom and Dad told us stories about the old days, and we got to learn about the Big Dipper, the Seven Sisters and the North Star. Mom was one of seven sisters in her family so that was a fascination for all of us. We watched for the full moon, quarter moon and half moon. They often spoke of certain days being best for planting and things that needed to be done for the week.

We did not have a barn, but we had a long stable for our horses, Barney, Nancy, Nig and June. There were about eight to ten cows, milked by hand both morning and night. The pails filled with milk were brought to a De Lavel cream separator turned by hand. The milk and cream separated were hauled to the Moscow Creamery about five miles away. From the sale of milk, cream and eggs in wooden crates we made some money. These items were usually taken to Blooming Prairie and sold at Martin Nelson's Variety Store for groceries and sometimes yard goods, shoes, overalls, etc. By the stable there was a tall silo in which they put up corn stalks after the corn had been hand picked. There was silage to feed the cattle and horses. There was also an outside haystack. The big straw pile was used for bedding. The hogs were in a smaller building close by. They sure were noisy and stinky, but very cute when they were born. The cats also found their place in the stable.

The Great Depression in the late 1920s and early '30s started when I was about 8 years old. I remember Mama and Papa speaking in low voices and sometimes Norwegian about the Depression. They were afraid of losing the farm. I guess Papa made arrangements with the banker Sam Rask at Blooming Prairie so we could keep our home and the farm. Many people went bankrupt and lived on the county and had to rent homes and farms. We felt fortunate to survive this time.

A couple of things I remember Mom saying were, "If you live through the winter, spring is worth waiting for." And, "If something is worth taking, it is worth saying thank you for." We learned some words in Norwegian as Mom spoke Norwegian with Dad. He sometimes answered her in English.

When one of the five of us would leave the farm, we would say, "See you, Dad, or goodbye." Dad would always answer, "Hope so, God willing." He had a good sense of humor, and at family reunions he liked to discuss politics and the farm crops with his brothers and brothers in-law. Dad would often say how fortunate and thankful he was that all the children and grandchildren were born healthy. Many illnesses at that time were incurable and difficult to recover from.

Dad and my brother Harold farmed with "horsepower" with plows, corn planters, disc, and a manure spreader. There were wagons, and the neighbors also did threshing with a threshing machine. The grain was seeded, cut and bundled and then threshed in the late summer with a machine that the farmers owned together. We did not have a tractor until the 1940s.

Dad liked trees, and we had abundance around the yard. He planted evergreens on each side of the driveway. We had willow trees, and to one side there was a big stone pile and a pond farther to the southwest. This pond is where we went wading and caught polliwogs and frogs in the summer and skated on the ice in the winter.

Our playmates were primarily our cousins as they lived across the road. When we could have time together, we would go up the hill and yell, "Yoo-hoo," and we would play on one farm or the other. There were six cousins across the road and five of us, so we each had someone our age to do things with. Harold, Caroline and Addie, being older, had friends from school come to our home or vice versa. My grandma (Dad's Mom) had my Aunt Thea living with her because she was a young widow with two children, my cousins, Hazel and Gordon. These cousins were older so they spent time with my brother and sisters.

My first movie was when Harold, Ruth and I went to the Paramount Theatre, which was built in 1929. I was watching the screen with real intent, getting into the excitement of the movie, and all at once I saw a train coming down the track in the movie. I really believed it was going to run over me so I ducked under the seat. Ruth and Harold never let me forget it.

We often played school by setting up chairs, getting books out, colors and tablets. We colored, drew pictures and read. We made flash cards for addition, subtraction, multiplication and division. One of the older kids would play teacher. We also had books from the school library. Our sister Addie spent more time reading than the rest of us. She loved to read. Checkers and dominoes were the games available. We had a newspaper from Austin and Blooming Prairie and a Sunday paper, the *Saint Paul Pioneer Press*. I looked forward to receiving the paper as it had paper dolls and clothes to cut out. "Boots and her Buddies" and "Freckles" were my favorite comedy strips. Mom would often get a handed down Norwegian newspaper from her parents called the *Dakota Posten*.

Dad made whistles from green willow branches and slingshots with a rubber band and tree crook. We used stones for target shooting. We were warned to be careful! He also made stilts, a pair of poles with a footrest, and it took some practice to stay up on them. None of us had bicycles.

In the summer we set up benches by putting boards on bricks and then got dirt and water, and we made mud pies. We would get metal play dishes, can covers and whatever and make pretend food. We made bird nests and put mud eggs in them and hid them around so the next person could go and find them.

We also played "Annie-I-over" the garage, as that was a lower building. We divided up and had kids on each side of the garage. We would yell "Annie-I-over" and throw a ball over the garage. Someone on the other side would catch the ball and they would come a running around the building and catch us. We had lots of places to play hide-and-seek. We played cricket with sticks and stones. After a rain we would love to go barefoot and wade in puddles and in our pond. We trapped gophers in the early summer and sold each tail for a nickel. We had a slough located on the southern part of our farm, and duck hunters in the fall needed to ask permission to hunt there.

May 1st was May Day and quite a special event. We would make May Day baskets from boxes and cover them with colored paper and crepe paper and fill them with peanuts, popcorn and candies. We prettied them up with spring flowers such as violets, mayflowers and cowslips. We would deliver them around to kids, mostly our cousins.

Dad had bought a Nash open touring car. I am not sure what year it was. It had side curtains made from what they called "isinglass" so they could be snapped on if it was too cold or raining. We sure enjoyed the breeze if it was warm. Later my dad bought a Model A, and it sure ran nice and quiet. I never drove a car as a teenager.

Sunday school and church were not always regular. Mom was strict on memorizing the catechism lessons for confirmation. It seemed that Pastor H. J. Rasmussen was at our church for as long as I can remember. He sometimes spoke Norwegian sermons, and I did not understand the language. We met once a week for classes, and I was confirmed at age 14 at Oak Grove Lutheran Church.

In late summer we kids enjoyed threshing, but it was a long, hard day for Mother. The threshing machine was owned by more than one farmer and used cooperatively. There were several hungry men to feed at noon. Before we sisters were old enough to help out making food, our neighbors helped each other out with the menu. Mom usually just put in a big roast and a couple of chickens, lots of mashed potatoes, garden vegetables and always cakes, cookies, doughnuts and pies. We also made lots of lemonade and pots of coffee. Lunch was usually sandwiches, donuts and cookies. The wheat was put in the granary in bins and the straw was a big stack outside tied down with ropes to the ground.

These are just a few of my treasured memories of growing up in Austin. Some of the things that are good about me are from my mother and dad. It meant a lot to us as a family to have devoted and caring parents. All through the cold winters, pleasant springs, hot summers, and colorful fall seasons we went about the serious business of work and the happy joys of playing. The farm was never far from our hearts. How could anything ever have been dull and monotonous among these very alive, original and hardworking Norwegian people?

Our life on earth does not depend upon our talents or IQ, our social standing, influences or bank accounts. The great achievements we spend our days striving for fade into insignificance in the little dash between birth and death. Let us in our ordinary lives be an example of how in faith, we can make a difference by reflecting the extraordinary love of God.

OryAnn and Donald Champlin married in 1942. They had five children, seven grandchildren and eight great-grandchildren.

The Gopher Magnate
By David J. Chrz

For kids growing up in the 1950s, money didn't grow on trees. I don't suppose it did for their parents either, but parents were reluctant to share any resources they may have had with their 12-year-olds on a cash basis. This left few avenues of capital generation for an enterprising youth such as myself.

Oh, there was allowance all right, but parents expected you to actually do some kind of chores to earn that. Besides the ubiquitous pop bottle redemptions, there were always sidewalks to shovel in winter, and lawns to mow in summer. If you had particularly long-suffering neighbors, you might even get to mow and shovel for the same people, but that never seemed to happen too often. Mowing had its drawbacks too. The mowing itself wasn't so bad, but weed-eaters in those days looked suspiciously like scissors, and required you crawling on your hands and knees around house, garage, flower beds and trees, furiously snipping away.

I really kind of enjoyed shoveling snow, though, except that some of my best customers lived on a stretch where the sidewalk was made of bricks, instead of concrete. The corners of those bricks were extremely hard on a shovel, as well as the shoveler's temper. What I needed was a way up and out of both poverty and work. It's not that I was particularly avaricious, mind you, but I required some semblance of the good life. There were always bicycle accessories and repairs to buy, root beers at the A&W, and fishing lures (the gaudier the better), plus everybody needs some money to just waste.

Then one spring I hit on a plan: trapping gophers. The Minnesota state mascot is a little chipmunk-looking varmint called a gopher. He is basically harmless, and except for the old "catch a gopher on your rod-and-reel" trick, we never bothered them much. There may be a handful of readers out there who have never heard of that trick, so I'll explain. You ride your bike about six miles out of town to the golf course, carrying your fishing rod across the handlebars. Once there, you find a gopher hole. You make a slip knot in your fishing line, put a loop around the gopher hole, then let out enough line to get to a hiding place. Gophers are fairly curious, and often respond to a particular whistle, so you watch the hole, and whistle that call; if a gopher sticks his head out to look, you set the rod, thereby simultaneously snaring the gopher around his neck and snatching him out of the hole. As you reel him in, things often get sporty, and you should expect to draw a crowd of golfing onlookers.

The most exciting part is the release. For most beginners I recommend cutting the line and running. That's about it; nothing could be simpler. These were called striped gophers, and as I've said, we didn't bother them much.

The gophers worth money were called pocket gophers. They are much larger than striped gophers and live entirely underground. They look like really big moles, and make serious pests of themselves, as they harvest the roots of plants for food, killing large sections of lawns and crops, so much so that individuals often paid to have them removed. Not only individuals, but also townships in those days offered a bounty on pocket gophers, and that's where I came in. Pocket gophers can be fairly difficult to trap, as they rarely come above ground, but I eventually hit upon a successful method. It would have been easier, of course, to poison them, but most folks didn't want to spread poison around under their lawns or fields, and rightfully so, plus you had to recover the deceased gopher to collect the bounty.

I spent two memorable summers in pursuit of the wily pocket gopher, sometimes even living for days at a time with the farm family for whom I was trapping. It boggles the imagination to calculate those folks' cost per gopher, when you factor in room, and especially board. When I was ready to leave they would pay me, usually twenty-five cents per head. My next step would be to collect the bounty from the township in which I had caught the gophers, and I usually preferred to wait for that until just before back-to-school, drawing one huge lump sum.

A note about township bounties: they of course required proof of performance. It was my great good fortune that Lansing Township required the front feet, while nearby Oakland Township paid on the tails, soooo........ In a good summer I might catch as many as two hundred gophers, and with the monies paid by individuals, as well as the twenty-five cent and forty-cent Township bounties--well, you can do the math; it was Easy Street. Among other things, I went with my dad and proudly bought my first wristwatch with gopher money.

Even now, I'll occasionally hear someone use the phrase, "salting something away," and I can't help but smile, thinking of those days, when my entire net worth was out in the garage, packed in mayonnaise jars full of salt, awaiting that final bicycle ride that would turn a summer's enjoyment into spending money.

1965 Pacelli graduate David Chrz lives in Abilene, Texas.

Entertainment
By David J. Chrz

I am and have always been a true devotee of play, and just generally having fun. Although I'm not sure my grandkids would recognize it as such, we had a ton o' fun growing up in Austin in the 1950s and early '60s. The following paragraphs are not written to inform or educate, but I intend to have a really good time remembering this stuff.

My earliest memories of play involve the neighborhood kids; we probably bore a startling resemblance to The Little Rascals. There were various dogs, mostly mutts, and in the few photos I have, the dogs look better than the kids.

There were forts to be dug and dirt clods to be thrown, the clods replaced by snowballs in the winter. The Red Cedar River comprised the rear property lines of the houses right across the street, so we had a really handy twofer when it came to getting in Dutch. Not only was I forbidden to go down to the river, but I was also forbidden to cross the street to get there. This convenient arrangement saved a lot of time, trouble, and suspense, as both parents and kids pretty well knew in advance when and why the next spanking was due.

By the time we were 6 or 7, Davy Crockett and Lone Ranger paraphernalia had supplanted freestyle play. Cap pistols (occasionally even loaded with real caps), rifles, and coonskin caps were the uniform of the day, every day. In a rare total lapse of good judgement, my parents bought me a Lone Ranger tent. If I don't make it into heaven, it will be at least partly their fault for making that purchase.

By the time I was about 8, my folks had decided to build a new house, so we moved into a rented house while the construction was underway. All the kids had bikes by that age, and were extremely proficient in their use. This changed everything. Wheeled transportation brought all the coolest entertainment into range, and first on any 8-year-old's list of cool entertainment is the city dump.

In what could only be described as a pack, we would feverishly peddle to the dump, in hopes of beating the "ragpickers" to the best junk. The ingenuity used to haul home on a bike some of the more unwieldy treasures we found defies description. Not only did this Monroe Street house boast easy (if you had a bike) access to the landfill, but it also had a park with a hockey rink, and a railroad track at the end of the block.

This perfect setup allowed us to pick up broken hockey sticks at the rink, sharpen the ends to a wicked point, and then in the summer we would walk the tracks, trying to spear the occasional rabbit or pheasant flushed along the right-of-way. A scarcity of rabbits or pheasants usually led to civil unrest, and I'm still not sure how none of us was ever speared through and through.

Sugar beets were hauled down those tracks in gently rocking open cars, so there was never a shortage of them to gnaw on as we crept along, on the alert for game and each other. Fall was great on that block too, as a neighbor across the street had a small field in which he raised popcorn. I don't know about all varieties of popcorn, but his variety produced an ear of perfect throwing size and weight, and hard as any rock. Formal contests required a Snow Coaster (this was a round aluminum sledding dish with canvas handles on either side); you put your arm through one handle, and grasped the other, making a dandy shield which gave off a really satisfying BONG! when you deflected a shot. Your head gave off a somewhat meatier BONG! when you failed to deflect a shot. Informal contests only required concealment sufficient for ambush. I believe the slang term "pop-knot" was derived from these Monroe Street skirmishes.

Construction over, a new house meant a new neighborhood and new friends. This house was on Water Street, and located, appropriately, near East Side Lake. The hours spent fishing in those mostly sterile waters, both summer and winter, would total an embarrassingly large number.

We also were getting pretty heavily into roller-skating at about this time (these were the old-timey clamp on your shoes skates), so we built a plywood jump. I'm certain our mothers shuddered as we worked, but what can you do? Once the jump was finished, a tow rope was tied on behind a bicycle seat, the rider pedaled furiously, and at the last second the skater swerved out toward the jump in approved water-ski fashion. I clearly remember one broken arm and a broken tailbone, but I'm sure there were others I've forgotten (mercifully).

This was all happening in the late 1950s, and if you can recall the cars of that era, you'll understand. My next door neighbor and I would ride over to the highway, and sit on the front steps of the Lutheran church there. For hours, as cars approached, we would compete to see which of us could correctly identify the make and model of a distant vehicle just by looking at its front end. Try that now!

Another favorite pastime was looking for agates. As the north shore of Lake Superior was a little distant for a bicyclist, we had to use the resource at hand, and that was the Ready-Mix plant. There was one aggregate bin there that contained the occasional agate. If you could climb around on that pile long enough before the yard boss saw you and ran you off, there were treasures to be found. I still have my agate collection from those days. The easiest way to identify an agate is to moisten it and hold it up toward the sun to see if it is translucent and has stripes.

"Where are you kids going?"
"To the Ready-Mix to lick rocks."
"Be back in plenty of time for supper."

Starting at about this time, and continuing for several years, was a truly favorite pastime, swimming. Family outings were usually to the river at Lansing or the gravel pit at Owatonna, and occasionally to Lake Pepin or Roberds Lake. However, the swimming I remember best was at the Austin Municipal Pool. A mob of us would ride bikes clear across town to the pool. Once there we would swim for two hours with no admission charge, in what was known as "free period." The pool was then cleared, admission charged (15 cents), and we had two hours of "pay period." We weren't often flush enough to afford to pay, but when we could, it was great, because we didn't have to contend with the free period riffraff, who were our friends at all other times.

There was a snack bar at the pool, and my favorite treats when I could afford them were Sugar Babies, or a Slo-Poke caramel sucker, and a cream soda. In retrospect, a cheaper, quicker alternative snack would have been to snort a cup of sugar, but we hadn't thought of that yet.

I do not want to fail to mention winter activities here; there were the usual sledding at Skinner's and Whittier hills, ice fishing, cottontail hunting, etc., and of course, skating. Usually we skated on a neighborhood rink provided by some spectacularly patient parents. Not only did they have to build and maintain the rink, but also had to put up with a herd of occasionally unruly, always loud and exuberant kids.

One of those generous parents I still remember. He was completely bald, and honestly fancied himself a serious speed skater. Every kid in the neighborhood called him "Bullet" year 'round, and I never decided if it was because of his skating or his hairdo. Once I hit about the fifth grade, my favorite skating was at the municipal rinks, especially at one called "the lagoon." There were the usual warming house with kerosene heater, music piped out over the ice, and lights at night. However, the main attractions were girls. Skating at night under the lights, to music, with your arm around a girl's waist and holding her other hand was, I thought, too hot for words. To this day, I still feel romantic when I smell a kerosene heater. Summer evenings often found us playing the usual group games: kick the can, and Annie-I-Over among them. Who in the world dreamed up, "Annie-I-Over....... Pigtail!," and what does it mean?

The closest thing to vandalism we ever were parties to consisted of standing around a city streetlight for hours and throwing a rubber ball at the light. The ball wouldn't break the glass cover, but if you hit it just right, it would unlatch and hang down from the hinge side. Nothing was better than getting to watch the guy in the city cherry-picker have to latch the cover back in a day or so. He would give us dirty looks while we pretended to be nonchalant and completely innocent.

Along about this time, I got really interested in tennis. This proved to be an excellent activity for me, as I later got to play on both high school and college teams. There were not a lot of courts in Austin, and the ones I used almost exclusively were at the sports complex known simply as the Athletic Field. For the actual hundreds of hours spent at those courts, some of my fondest memories are not of tennis.

Next door to the Athletic Field someone put in a trampoline center when that craze got underway. Music played constantly, and I KNOW I heard "Muleskinner Blues" by the Fenderman a thousand times...... "Bring the buck-buck-bucket round." Besides the ubiquitous Fendermen, the drum and bugle corps known as the Lancers used the Athletic Field for marching and musical practice, and over the years I learned every note of every song they played, and frequently marched in time to pick up stray tennis balls.

In Austin, the last momentous event before a boy got his driving learner's permit was getting a Shaw Gym card. The facility had been donated years earlier, and was then operated by the Parks Department. It consisted of several basketball and volleyball courts, ping-pong tables, handball courts, and a boxing/wrestling ring. The main draw, however, was about a dozen beautiful old Brunswick pool tables. If I remember correctly, once you reached the seventh grade you were eligible for your Shaw Gym card. If you were caught swearing, or skipped a ball off a pool table, the supervisor punched your card. Five punches and you were out for two weeks, the seventh grade equivalent of banishment to Siberia.

There were always more prospective pool players than tables or cues, even though four players to a table was requisite, so every forty-five minutes a supervisor would blow a whistle, and there would ensue a mad scramble to stab cues into a fiber barrel at the corner of the supervisory area and get back in line to get another cue. Most of the aspiring pool sharks at Austin's real pool halls got their start at the Shaw Gym. One of the most distressing sights in modern-day Austin is the empty spot where that most revered old building stood.

The last thing I want to remember here is that famous institution of my generation, the Tower. Some involved parents decided that kids needed a place to let off steam under adult supervision, so they purchased and renovated a second-story series of rooms above George's Pizza Parlor. The main room had a wonderful hardwood floor, and because it was on the second story, it had just enough spring to make a perfect dance floor. With a snack bar and tables, occasional live music, and the excellent jukebox music of the era, the Tower was an institution for teenagers of the entire area, not just Austin. A particular style of dancing evolved there, and no matter if you were in Owatonna, Albert Lea, Rochester, or anywhere else in southern Minnesota, you could immediately recognize someone from Austin, or at least the Tower, by the way he or she danced. The stairway from the ground floor up to the second story was wide and open, and had a landing half way up. I will never forget the rush of anticipation I felt as the music cascaded and echoed down that stairway, meeting us on our way in.

It strikes me that my friends and I truly had a good place to grow up (as much as some of us have grown up, anyway). It may seem that we lacked parental supervision, but that is part of the point. We neither wanted nor needed much, and never suffered for lack of it. My parents, as well as those of my friends, invariably pointedly asked where we were going, with whom, and when we would be back. Satisfied on those points, they basically cut us loose to go and have a good time. The "soccer mom" concept was unheard of, and I believe we were better off for it.

I don't understand why things have changed so drastically, but they have. Too few parents allow or encourage minimally supervised play, depriving their children of circumstances in which they can develop imagination, social skills, and perseverance. On the other hand, who can blame parents, when every day brings to light some new horror? I suppose things as they are don't require my understanding or approval. One thing of which I am certain: I am both fortunate and grateful for the time and place in which I spent my childhood.

I Love Austin
By Daniel Clayton

On July 12, 1955, as a young man of 18, I traveled from Ada for a weekend visit with friends and relatives in and around Austin. On July 12, 2006, that weekend will have lasted fifty-one years. Over this period of time, I have of course, joined a church of my faith, and many other organizations, one of which was the Fraternal Order Eagles. I have raised six children, the youngest of whom is 36 years old.

Several years ago, with a select choice of delegates and city officials, we traveled to Willmar, host to the 1989 State Eagles Convention and presented our reasons for choosing Austin as their convention city in 1991. After the presentation we spent not less than an entire evening visiting the many delegations pleading for their consideration.

We happily shared the reasons they should choose Austin over other host cities. We told of our huge arena capable of seating more than 5,000, our large armory, ready and available for the meetings and banquets, our many fine housing facilities, the many choices of entertainment, supper clubs, parks and shopping. We convinced the people who would soon choose that Austin was very qualified to provide the hospitality and atmosphere necessary for a state Eagles convention. The following morning, Austin was selected by a two-to-one margin.

After the Minnesota State Eagles Convention was completed, I offered my gratitude to the American Legion Post 91, both the United States and Canada, for sharing their beautiful display of original colony flags, and to the merchants for their financial support, as well as their willingness to share our community with our guests. The Austin Chamber of Commerce, our city officials and the entire staff of the Holiday Inn and the Austin Police Department did a terrific job. Our convention was one of the finest ever. During that week I saw grown men cry as they were recognized for many years of dedication. I saw grown men saddened that they had not been able to do better. They raised many thousands of dollars that year, which was then given to a variety of charities, including the Minnesota Sheriffs' Youth Ranch ($23,000), cancer research ($280,000), Our Lady of Good Council ($44,000), to name just a few. I saw tears when it was over and time to say goodbye.

To our community, I am proud to say that all our guests noticed and appreciated your hospitality. That is why, fifteen years later, I am still very proud to say, "I am an Eagle from Austin, and I love Austin."

Cora Conklin
By Timothy Conklin

Cora Conklin, my grandmother, was a woman of the 20th Century; her life spanned it entirely. When she was born, William McKinley was president of the United States, and Queen Victoria sat on the British throne. She was 4 years old when Orville and Wilbur Wright launched their *Flyer* above the dunes of Kitty Hawk, North Carolina. She told me once that she screamed for her sister Virgie and ran to the house when the first plane she ever saw flew over their farm sometime before World War I.

Cora was the second of eleven children born to Edward and Molly Hubbard. She was born near Hubbard, Iowa and lived near Indianola and Austin before her family settled on a place near Wells. For Cora, Wells meant home, and she referred to her family, the farm, and all those family reunions as taking place, "over home."

In 1918 Cora attended Simpson College in Indionola, Iowa for a term. Inside her textbook, *Domestic Science, Principles and Application*, she wrote her name, and throughout the book she wrote sparse notes. One note reads, "War ended. November 11, 1918. Peace treaty signed at 2:00. Algebra class Thursday."

She was just 20 years old in 1919 when she married Melvin Conklin from Indianola, and the couple moved to a farm of their own near Lansing, Minnesota. In 1925 she gave birth to Muriel, and three years later their son Dale was born. When Cora was 30, she was working on a farm with her husband and taking care of two little ones when the stocks crashed and the U.S. entered the Great Depression.

Cora was a farm wife and a farm mother, and she made sure there was always food on the table for those kids of hers. She was resourceful, and she knew it was up to her to help provide for her family. One year she raised turkeys. She slaughtered and butchered them and packed them into barrels to ship to Chicago. Cora made $400 on those turkeys, and with that money, she went out and bought a Ford Model A--black, of course.

In the early 1940s, Cora's family moved off the farm and into a house in Austin. They took in a 7-year-old girl named Alice Dahl, who made her home with them. Cora always worked hard. She took in boarders, she took in ironing, and she baby-sat for the neighbors.

She cooked and washed dishes for the Elks, the Eagles and the Country Club. She clerked at Averbrooks and Wallace's on Main Street in their yard goods department, and sometimes her grandchildren would visit her there after school.

Cora loved to cook, and I remember her tarts that she made with leftover pie dough and her own homemade apple jelly. She said that the secret to her flaky crust was Fluffo brand shortening. I don't know about the shortening, but I do know that as a little boy I would be surrounded by grandmotherly love whenever I went to her house. Whether it was her greeting to me, "Hey, Barney Google," or her homemade apple jelly tarts, I felt loved.

When I was 5 or so, Grandma was watching me at her home while my parents were at work and my sisters and brother were at school. On those long quiet afternoons, Grandma would sit with me on her front step there at her home at 510 2nd Street SE, and together we would watch the trains load up boxcars on the tracks behind the neighbor's house across the street. And she would say to me, "You know, Barney Google? Someday you and me, we're gonna climb aboard one of those trains and we're gonna go."

Of course, my 5-year-old brain was fired with thoughts of adventure, but beneath that, was almost a sense of wonder that my 68-year-old grandmother would even say such a thing as, "we're gonna climb aboard and we're gonna go." And I think that more than just stirring her grandkid's imagination, she was confiding something to me about her own desire to take a journey and leave her mundane world filled with its responsibilities and travel, footloose and fancy free--just for a bit. Just enough to get away for awhile and then come home. It was revolutionary talk coming from my grandmother, and I always remembered.

In her last years, she lived with Alzheimer's disease that gradually took her out of our world. But she always seemed comfortable, cheerful and content with the care she received from the wonderful staff of St. Mark's Nursing Home. She lived in three centuries and died in 2002. When she was born, mankind hadn't yet learned to fly. When she died, we had flown through space and put people on the moon. But when I think of travel I think of those trains, Grandma, and I think you have finally climbed aboard.

Tim Conklin teaches writing at the University of British Columbia.

Victorian Era Teacher
By Bertha Case Cooke-Written in the Late 1950s

My father and mother's people, the Cases and Coffins, had come to Minnesota from Vermont and Ohio in 1854 and taken homesteads near Chatfield. My father's brother, Uncle Gehial, had moved his family to Mower County and bought a farm seven miles east of Austin. When he was elected Treasurer of Mower County, he had to move into the city, so he asked my father to come take over the farm, a whole section, and work it for him. This we did after the close of my second year in high school. I wanted very much to graduate from the Chatfield school, so arrangements were made for me to spend the school year with Grandpa and Grandma Coffin until I graduated.

On May 18, 1883, I graduated from Chatfield high School and went with my parents to the farm in Mower County, seven miles directly east of the city of Austin, the county seat. The farm consisted of 640 acres, a mile each side. There was some pasture land, and we had a number of cows. Most of the land was planted with wheat, oats, rye, flax and corn. Brother George was too young to do a man's work, so Father had to have two or more hired men to help with plowing, sowing, harvesting and milking. The next year a quarter section was sold, leaving only 480 acres to care for.

The first year, the grain was cut with a reaper. The grain had to be bound by hand, shocked, stacked and later in the fall, threshed. The next year a harvester and binder succeeded the reaper, which made the work much easier. Nowadays a machine goes into a grain field, cuts, threshes and sacks the grain in the field and eliminates the need for most of the men.

With the extra help in the fields that summer, there was plenty to do helping Mother in the house. After the threshing in the fall, which required a crew of about twenty men for five or six days, I knew I would have time to do something else. I wanted very much to go on to college, but I knew my father couldn't afford to send me, and there was not much girls could do to earn money.

There were about twenty of us young people, and we would have our parties. My sister Nora and I made up our minds when we first went to the farm that there were some things we would not do. For one thing, we would not play cards nor dance nor play kissing games. When the young folks found out we wouldn't do those things, they never suggested them when we were present. But we had good times. We sometimes held socials at the homes during the winter months, and all the folks, old and young, would attend. Sometimes we would have a program of singing, recitations, reading and games and all seemed to enjoy themselves.

Sometimes we would pile into a wagon with a hayrack to sit on and go maybe ten or fifteen miles for a picnic. In the winter we would go several miles to find a small pond of ice to skate on or go to Austin, where there was an ice skating rink. We didn't have enough practice to become good skaters. My time was usually spent in falling and getting up. That was fun too…then!

The first summer on the farm I read *Paradise Lost* with Miss Emma Ware, who was teaching at our school and boarding with us. I believe it was the hardest thing I ever tried to read. I intended to read it again sometime but I never have.

Instead of taking the country children by bus to a large central school as is done today, each township had a little red or white school building located near the center of where the children lived. There would be two terms of school; one in the summer after the plowing and seeding was done, and the other beginning in the fall after harvest was over. And maybe there would be four months of school during the winter. The older children who could help with farm work could in this way get to attend school.

I decided that if I could pass the teacher's examination and get a school, I could teach. At that time one didn't have to have a normal education nor a college degree. Age didn't count either, so I tried the examinations and to my great delight I passed with a second grade marking. However, I had to have one term experience teaching before they could give me a second grade certificate. So I started out to find a school. At the first place I applied they had already engaged a teacher and I was quite discouraged.

Father took me to another school, and there they had no teacher engaged so they said they would try me for three months at $25 a month. I found a place to board with Mr. and Mrs. Rugg, who had two daughters, Mary and Hattie, and two sons, Jay and Willie, not yet of school age. Hattie was the teacher who got the first school I had applied for.

This school was about three miles from our home, and Father would take me over on Monday morning and come for me on Friday after school. I believe I paid $3 a week for my board, and it was good board too, with honey and hot cakes for breakfast during the cold weather! Just think! What could you get for $3 a week now?

I had, as I remember, thirty pupils all the way from one beginner to three taking junior high school work. One boy was older than I. I had passed my sixteenth birthday that summer. I had about forgotten some things I had once known so I had to do a lot of reviewing so as to keep up with, or a stay little ahead of my numerous classes.

The County Superintendent of Schools, Mr. Belden, came to visit my school, and he seemed to approve, so he recommended me to the school board, and they asked me to stay for the fourth month. When I received my pay with board taken out, I was paid with a $50 gold piece. That's the first and only time I was ever paid in gold, at least of that denomination. I had really earned some money!

Uncle Gehial had given a corner lot on his section for a school building, which was about three quarters of a mile from the house. Miss Ware, who taught the winter term, was not coming back, so they offered me the school for $23 a month. You see, I could board at home, so I could teach for a little less than I had earned in the winter.

Enrollment was small. My sister and brother were two of my pupils, and I never had as many as twenty. I taught them three years, and the last term had only six children part of the time. It wasn't the teacher's fault either. Some were transferred to another district; some were sick and taken out of school. One family had a sickness that left two of the children deaf. One of them came to school for a time but finally was sent to the school for the deaf at Faribault, where she received a good education, became a teacher, and held good positions.

I decided a change would be better for me so I applied for what was called the Centennial School, two miles south and two miles west of home. The families in the neighborhood were mostly Danes or Norwegians, good farming people, and the school had a good reputation. So they took me for the summer term, and I had a very pleasant term. I boarded with Mr. and Mrs. Jensen. They had two teenage sons who were in school unless they had to stay out to help on the farm. They had fine new barns and farm buildings, but they lived in a small log house. I slept in a small room just off from their bedroom. The cot-bed reached the whole length of the room, and when lying on the cot I could stretch out my arms and touch the other wall. There was one window so it was really comfortable. Mrs. Jensen was a fine housekeeper and a good cook, so I was well cared for.

We usually got paid for our teaching at the end of the term, and then we paid our board bill. When I asked the Jensens how much my board bill was they said, "Three dollars for the term." Now where can one board for a dollar a month? And it was good board too!

I began to wonder at this time if perhaps I couldn't get a position in a city school. To teach in a city school, I would have to hold a first grade teacher's certificate and would have to take an examination in plane geometry, physical geography, civil government, and physiology. So I spent the summer studying up and reviewing these subjects and took the exam. Mr. Belden considered my marks in the common studies good enough for first grade, so I took the exam and passed my teacher's first grade. And thanks to Mr. Belden, that was the last test I ever had to take. When I went to other city schools, some college graduates and others who had taught had to take the whole list of examinations, but Mr. Belden sent my marks, and they were accepted. He was certainly a good friend.

I started out to find a city school that would have me. My sister Nora was ready now for high school, having already done some of the regular work, so if I could teach where she could be with me, we could be together, and she could attend high school. I applied in Austin, and they selected me to teach second grade. I think I was to get $30 a month.

We went to Austin and secured two rooms just a block from the high school and were ready for school. The teacher who had been engaged for the seventh grade had failed to come, and the grade I was to teach had not been organized. The principal came to me and asked me if I would be willing to take the seventh grade instead until they could make some other arrangements. I very foolishly said I would. I had a fine class of pupils, and during the six weeks I was there I had a fine time. My cousin Frank, a son of Uncle Del, was one of my pupils. Years later at the Chicago World's Fair, I met the mayor of Austin and his wife. She said she had been one of my pupils in the seventh grade.

Miss Gertrude Ellis, the eighth grade teacher, came to me one morning before school. She was considerably older and had been teaching for some years. She was quite elated. She said, "On my way to school this morning I was called into the office of the county school director and they asked me if I would run for County Superintendent, and I told them I would. Now you are the first one I have told this to. Will you vote for me?" Women 21 or over had been given the privilege then to vote for County Superintendent. I said, "No," much to her surprise. When she asked why I answered, "I am only 19, and they wouldn't allow me to vote." Even if I had been old enough my vote would have gone to Mr. Belden, who had been such a good friend. Mr. Belden was elected, but some time later Miss Ellis did become superintendent and held the office for many years.

The grade six teacher thought she could manage older children better so she asked to change with me. I did not want to do it but felt that I was just substituting where I was. So one morning I walked into her room, and she took my place, much to the dismay of the seventh graders. She could do no better with them, so soon had to resign.

So long as I could keep everyone busy, all went well, but as soon as a lull came, pandemonium broke out. This was my first year in city schools, and I was at my wit's end. When my boss asked me if I would prefer to have the second grade for which I was hired, I said, "I certainly would!" So his wife took over the sixth grade, and after thrashing some of the youngsters (it was allowed in those days), she finally brought order out of chaos.

I had about thirty pupils, and how I did enjoy them. This grade was in a small building just across the corner from the high school, and only the first and second grades were there. Miss Gertrude Sherwood taught first grade. She was a good teacher, and we were friends for many years. On the other corner of the block was a Catholic school for small children. Sometimes pupils would come to us and we would get called "Sister" instead of "Teacher."

I had a rule about spelling that I insisted on. Every word missed in spelling was to be written ten times correctly before they went home. One little boy missed twenty words one day, and he decided that would take too long, and he wouldn't do it. I said, " I can stay here as long as you can." So we sat there. It took a long time, but he finally wrote his words, and we got home at suppertime.

Before the end of the second year, I was switched to a third grade, and I decided I'd like some time off. I had some interesting experiences and made some good friends in Austin.

The Bronco
By Michael Cotter

When I was a young boy on that Minnesota farm, we had many large draft horses, and they were an important part of our lives. They provided the power for most of the fieldwork, and occasionally we rode them. Their backs were broad, they had large hooves, and most of them stood very tall. Sitting on the back of one of those large draft horses, my feet would stick straight out, and I only had that thick, heavy mane to hang on to. These horses were for work, and I dreamed of a horse just to ride. I didn't know enough to ask for any particular breed, an Appaloosa or a quarter horse. I just wanted a riding horse, and I knew exactly what he would look like and what his name would be.

In our newspaper, in the funnies, there was a comic strip named "Red Rider." I don't know why they called it a funny paper, cause it was never funny at all. Red Rider was a lean, red-haired cowboy trying to do a little good in his part of the world. His companion was an Indian boy named Little Beaver. I didn't think that Red Rider was the most important part of that comic strip. It was his horse that I loved. The horse was a tall, graceful, black horse with three white stockings and a long black mane. His long black tail always seemed to be blowing majestically in the wind while he stood gracefully, figuring out how to help Red Rider out of his last problem.

I thought that horse was perfectly beautiful. And to cap the beauty, he had a white star on his forehead. I knew that someday I'd have a horse that would look like him, and I would name him Thunder, just like Red Rider's horse. I did what kids do, and I begged and begged. And finally my father, in an uncharacteristic move, agreed to get me a horse; but I would have to wait for the right one. The right one meant it would be a good horse, but it would be cheap.

After a seemingly endless period of time, one day he said, "Let's go look at your horse." There had been a notice in the paper that carloads of broncos would be arriving in Austin, so on a Sunday afternoon we went to the rail yard.

Now if you drive by Austin on Interstate 90 where the new Hormel plant is, back in the early '40s that area was just a pasture. East of that, where the industrial park is now, there was a rail yard. All sorts of animals, cattle, sheep, and goats, were brought in from the western states in livestock cars and then were unloaded in those large pens. It was a common sight to see them grazing in that pasture in front of the Hormel plant where they waited for their time to be slaughtered.

On this Sunday in those railroad pens with the high boards and the railroad tie posts, my dad and I went looking for my horse. I was not prepared for the sight that greeted me. At one end of the pen, the local people who were interested in the horses were standing. In the center of the pen were two cowboys, tall and lean, with dusty clothes and faces the color of the fence itself.

What caught my attention most were the horses they were sitting on. I had only seen our big draft horses, sleek and grain fed, muscular and healthy. These horses were like skeletons, tiny and thin, their manes and tails missing, and there was only a scab where the mane had been. I learned that the other horses had eaten the mane away. Their tails were just stumps with no hair. All the long hair was gone.

The cowboys looked a lot like their horses. They weren't the real cowboys like we know today, like the late John Wayne and President Reagan. These were the dusty old-fashioned kind. There was a cowboy with a home rolled cigarette hanging from his mouth. The cigarette was fat in the center and twisted on the ends. His horse's head hung down, and his neck without a mane didn't arch beautifully. It kind of had a bow in it, and the horse's ears didn't stand up straight. They sort of tipped out. That horse looked like he was just too tired or too old to stand straight.

At the bar end of the pen was a whole bunch of little broncos, thin and pitiful and wild. They too had no manes or tails. and as they tried to crawl over each other, they got tighter and tighter into the corner. Their eyes had a wild look with a white ring around the edge as they struggled to get into the farthest corner. They reminded me of a pile of maggots moving up and down and going over.

If you wanted to buy a horse, you gave the cowboy $25. Then he reached into the gunnysack hanging from the saddle horn and pulled out a new white lariat rope, unfurled the rope, and touched his spurs to his horse. His horse had those wild eyes too. You pointed to the horse in the pile you wanted, and a loop sailed out. Out of that pile of struggling horseflesh came a little bronco, spinning and twisting in the air, squealing and rolling on the ground. Then the cowboy handed you the rope, and you got the rope and the horse for $25.

My dad was an old-timer, and when he saw the situation, these horses wild and untrained with the rope, he had a change of heart. Whenever he wanted to intimidate someone he called him Shorty, no matter how tall he was. He went up to this cowboy who looked so tall, and he said, "Shorty, what'll you take for that horse you are riding?"

Seventy-five dollars later, the cowboy stripped the saddle from his own horse, and I got up on its back. That horse's back was sharp as an arrow board, and there was no mane to hang on to. A friend of my dad had opened its mouth, and after checking his teeth, he announced, "He's just comin' three." He was a young bronco.

As I rode him out of that pen that evening, we passed several of those other young broncos, lying in the dirt. They just would not give in to that rope, and they had broken their necks. My horse was broke, and you knew he was broke, because he had spur marks on his side, just scabbing over. He'd had one rough encounter with a cowboy, and like the other horses, when he looked at you he had those wild eyes. It was a long trip home.

This horse was a long ways from my dream. When I let him walk, his head hung down and he sort of plodded, but if my heels touched the spur marks, he went up in the air like a wild animal. When I got near our farm, my brother came out to meet me. I think he was jealous that I was getting a horse, but when he saw us, he just laughed. And that made me mad.

At first my horse would not eat the hay and the grain that our big draft horses ate. He didn't seem to know what they were. He would just eat the weeds along the fence and the old bedding in the horse stall. Very soon he began to eat that grain, and he was crazy for it. The energy that hit that young bronco was unbelievable. About a week later, my brother rode him out one morning, and the horse came home without him. When I saw Dick walking, I didn't even feel bad.

It was then I noticed how my horse was changing. His head had come up, and his neck was arched. This young bronco was coming of age. In a few weeks he grew a long black mane and a long black tail, and he became the deepest chestnut I'd ever seen. He stood majestically, and for the first time I realized he had three white stockings and a white star on his forehead. And I named him Thunder, and he ran like the very wind itself. And I never had another.

I loved him like a 12-year-old would love a horse, but it was a one-sided love affair. I think his beginnings had been too harsh, or the cowboys had been too rough. He wasn't mean, but if I ever let go of the reins, or if he was able to jerk them out of my hands, he ran away, except for one time, and that's my story.

It takes place a few years later when I was about 16. We had a herd of stock cows on our farm. My dad called them western cows. They were mostly Hereford breed, and they spent their summers on a distant pasture where they had their young. In the winter, they were fed among the sheds on the farm.

One of them was going to have her calf out of season, and one of the characteristics of a stock cow is to go off by herself to have her young. On a bitterly cold January Sunday, this cow got away from the herd, and we knew she had gone to have her calf. To search for her I rode my bronco through the snowdrifts to the far corners of the farm.

I found her where Interstate 90 now runs. Then it was a marshy area with tall grass and brush growing. The calf had already been born. She had cleaned him off, and he was lying in that tall grass with the snow drifting around him. His ears were already frozen in the bitter cold. She had done everything she could, and she was standing over him as I rode up.

It looked like some famous painting, the cow standing there quietly, both of them waiting for the inevitable. I got down off my horse into that deep-crusted snow, and tried to pick up the calf, and even though he was half frozen, he was slippery and heavy and awkward. And my horse was nervous and jerking on the reins.

I turned to that horse and I said, "You've gotta stand," and I let go of the reins, and I picked up the calf. When I turned around I expected he would be gone. I don't know if it was the wind, or the desperation in my voice, or just the way things are; but I will never forget the scene as that wild-eyed horse danced around me. His neck was arched, and his ears were pointed. His nostrils were flared wide as he snorted sounding almost like train's whistle in the distance.

He danced around me, but he didn't run. And eventually he let me lay that newborn calf across his back. He stood long enough so I could get up behind the calf, and we started for home with the cow following.

Later, in the warm barn his frozen ears dropped off, but the calf lived. And I never let go of the horse's reins again but what he ran.

****

Many years later I was asked to do a program in a nursing home in Rochester, Minnesota. It was St. Patrick's Day, and I was excited, being quite new as a storyteller. People were being wheeled into this big recreation room, and some were coming in and sitting in chairs, and I was talking to the people in charge, and there was a lot of excitement in the air. Some of the residents were hard of hearing and talked out loud to each other during the program. Sometimes right in the middle of my story they would say, "I can't hear him. Can you?"

For the most part, things seemed to be going quite well, except for one little man who was sitting almost directly in front of me. I didn't know why they had brought him; he looked so pitiful. He sat in a wheelchair, and his frail little body was supported entirely by straps. His head would have been right down on his knees had not that strap held him back. His arms hung down by the side of the wheelchair, and he seemed totally out of it.

I told my stories, and I tried not to look at him because there was no response from him. The program ended, and it seemed to have gone quite well. As the aides were coming to wheel the people away, I wanted to talk to one of the directors. On my way past this man, I almost missed seeing his hand down near the wheel of his wheelchair. That hand was fluttering. It was the first movement I'd seen from him. Because his head was near his lap, I had to get down on my knees in front of him to see his face.

It was the first time I'd seen his eyes. They were not out of it as I had imagined. They were very bright and rolled way back as he was trying to see me. When he spoke, his voice was only a raspy whisper, but I'll never forget it. He said, "One time, my dad, brought two carloads of broncos, and I helped him." Then his body relaxed, he sagged back into his straps, and his head dropped down closer to his lap.

I tried to respond, saying, "Two carloads of broncos-- they are wild!" But he had finished, and the nurse came and wheeled him away. As I drove home that day, I thought of that man, helpless and pitiful; but he knew if he could tell me that he had handled broncos, that I would know he had once been powerful. He needed to tell me his story, and I had almost missed it.

Grandpa and Grandma McShane
By Michael Cotter

I think grandparents are important. I only really remember one grandma and grandpa, because my dad's father died before I was born, and though my Grandma Cotter lived till I was almost 3, I barely remember her.

When I think of grandparents, I immediately think of Mary and Michael McShane, and I think of them in that order. I remember the big white house on Kenwood Avenue and the large front porch with the green porch swing. When I was a little boy and my grandmother would get mad at Grandpa, she would always say something that would make me feel bad. She would say, "If there is a wrong way to do something, that man could find it." I didn't think he deserved that criticism, and as I got older I was even more puzzled, because they had thirteen children. But maybe that's where her anger came from.

Mary was a large woman, not fat, but large, and I think her personality made her seem even larger, because I always felt that her opinion was very important. Michael was a smaller man, with sandy hair and twinkling eyes, and just the right kind of a mustache. Even in the face of criticism like that, he would wink and bob his head and pretend that Mary was about he cutest thing that he'd ever seen.

Grandpa Michael McShane was my very special friend. He told stories about the wee people of Ireland, the fairies, and the leprechauns, and it was easy to see that he believed them. When we would say, "Is that true, Grandpa?" he would just laugh and shake his head and not answer.

He had some rituals that we loved. One was he was always so happy to see us. Another was when you'd get a new pair of shoes, he would pick up your foot, put it on his lap, and tap a forefinger on the toe of the shoe. This is the little jingle he would always say. "Well to wear, soon to tear, plenty of money for another pair." The other ritual that he did was on Easter when they always came to our farm for dinner. Grandma would be in a most festive mood because she liked dinners out. Plus, she was going to use our outhouse and save wear and tear on their plumbing, which she considered a thrifty thing to do.

After the dinner, Grandpa would take my brother and me out into the woods back of our house. There, we would set our caps, filled with soft paper Easter grass, under some new little evergreen trees. Then all three of us would try to drive those hiding Easter bunnies towards the caps to lay one more time. Grandpa gave detailed instructions how to tap on the trees lightly, so we didn't scare the bunnies too badly, and how to herd them toward those caps.

It was quite a process, and when we reached a certain point and our excitement was high, Grandpa would say we had to wait while he crept ahead and checked to see if the bunnies had been there yet. We'd feel wonderful when we saw him waving to us, signaling that it was time to come. Sure enough, in each of the caps would be three or four Easter eggs. When there was a very small amount in each cap, Grandpa would have us go back through the hunt, all the while thinking about how we might have frightened the bunnies, so they didn't have enough time to lay their eggs.

After Grandpa and Grandma McShane would go home, my older brother Dick, who had watched very carefully, often decided that we should make one more round up of those rabbits. We did everything just like we'd done with Grandpa, but when Dick left me at the edge of the woods, so he could go and check on the caps like Grandpa had done, instead of that wonderful signal that I could come now, there was just disappointment and disgust in his manner, for there were no eggs in our caps. We knew that Grandpa had some secret with those Easter bunnies that we could not understand.

On stormy winter nights, when my dad would have a hard time getting to town to get us from parochial school, we would have to go to Grandma's and wait. She would be sitting on that cast iron, hot water heater in front of that big window, watching the street. She would be looking longingly for our car, or if the weather was too bad, a team of horses and a bobsled to come up that snowy street. Grandma was a frugal woman. She did not want extra mouths to feed. She was putting off fixing the evening meal as long as possible.

"Better get your homework done," she'd say in a stern voice, "so you'll be some help to your mother when you get home." I was probably in first grade then, and of course, all I could think of was how long it had been since I'd eaten and how hungry I was. With having left home at 7 in the morning, and carrying a cold lunch for noon, and now with darkness beginning to fall, I was just starved. With Grandma looking longingly out into the street for my dad to appear, I knew there was not much hope for any lunch there.

Then it happened. I saw Grandpa in the kitchen doorway, with his eyes twinkling and his fingers to his lips signaling to be quiet. He was signaling me to come. Grandma never seemed to notice as I slipped into the kitchen, and Grandpa carefully opened the door of the pantry. The cold air and the smell of all the wonderful baked goods rushed out. He'd take out a loaf of Grandma's homemade bread, and then with a bread knife, he'd cut off a huge piece. Humming a little tune, he buttered that bread with large sweeping strokes of that wide old butter knife. I could hardly wait.

There were other reasons for my impatience besides hunger. Grandpa smoked a pipe, and a long drip often hung from the bowl of that pipe just above that bread. I hoped against hope that he'd finish buttering before that drip fell. No such luck. I'd try to mark with my eyes the place on the bread where the drip fell, so I could eat around it. But it was so good, and I was so hungry, and besides I couldn't remember the exact spot. So I would just eat it all. It was wonderful.

Grandpa McShane had been a railroad man, and one time he took me on the train. I'd watch him flip open that gold pocket watch with the Roman numerals. He had a railroad man's pride, knowing the trains were running on time.

Grandpa died when I was 11, and I knew that I had lost a special friend. Grandma lived on for many years. She seemed to prefer living alone in that large, white house, and as I grew into my late teens and early 20s, my mother would ask me to stop and see her some nights to make sure she was all right.

When you'd come up to that darkened house, you would think it was empty. But those of us familiar with her habits knew she was in there watching. With all her knitting and other daily chores finished, Grandma's night work consisted of praying and listening to the radio. She'd be all bundled up in a heavy shawl or sweater to conserve heat, and she'd have a good flashlight to get around the house and a full view of the street for entertainment.

Grandma was fine. She loved her life. There were only two things that she needed to do, and on those she wouldn't compromise. She liked to go to church most every morning, and on Tuesday nights she had to go to Bingo, which was also at the church. By now she was in her 80s, and most of the time she could get a ride, but on stormy nights, when the snow was blowing, she needed help. She would call early in the afternoon and say to my mother, "It doesn't look too bad. I think I'll start on over." This would send my mother into orbit, and she would lay a guilt trip on me.

My dad, who liked to have his black Mercury in the shed on nights like this, would also get involved. He'd say something like, "You'd think that damned woman could find a way to entertain herself on a stormy night without having to get out on the road."

My mother wouldn't tolerate this kind of talk, and we all knew, no matter what we thought, Grandma's will would prevail. So with the chains on the Mercury and a shovel in the trunk, I would soon be plowing through snow trying to get into town to get Grandma to Bingo. When I would pull up in front of her darkened house, I had to jump right out of that car and run for the porch, because Grandma had been sitting in front of that window with her coat and her overshoes, and she was ready.

She was right out that door, across that icy porch, and down the steps that had no handrail. She expected me to be there helping her. Grandma would not wait. She would lean heavily on my arm, and there was always a strong scent of perfume in the air, because, as she said, "Old ladies should be stylish." As we moved down the sidewalk, Grandma got heavier on my arm, and her breath became wheezes as I helped her into the car.

When we got to the parking lot and saw the other Bingo goers hurrying through the snow, Grandma's leaning and wheezing became worse. Middle-aged women called to her in surprise, "Grandma, you're out on such a night? Grandma, you are so brave." By now I was almost carrying her as she was leaning so heavily on me and breathing so hard. The other women would rush to help her as we went down the stairs to the church basement. She outlived most of those women.

Grandma would rush in, shedding her coat and sweaters, heading right for the women's bathroom with the little step in front of it. Those women around her looked at me sort of embarrassed, thinking that Grandma maybe had a bladder problem, but I knew she had been sitting in that darkened house and had probably timed those flushes that afternoon, wanting to save water, because she knew the church had plenty. So, there was a real urgency in getting to that bathroom.

The coming out was worse. She remembered that step on the way in, but in exiting, she was thinking only of Bingo, and she always forgot the step. She would just sort of catapult out toward the Bingo tables. I had to be there and kinda catch her, and it was always embarrassing to me. Then Grandma would sit down, play either five or six Bingo cards, and also watch the one that I was playing. She played to win, and if a card didn't seem to be doing well, she would call to the volunteers for a new card. She didn't just turn in her card, she wrote on it. She would write, "no good" or "it stinks," or something appropriate on her card, and you'd see the red face on the volunteer, as he would try to erase her inscription before he handed the card to another patron.

Grandma won fairly often, and when she would win, she would lean back, adjust her glasses and say, "I think I will have a Coca-Cola." Then she would look at me sort of wondering why I wasn't more caught up in the festivities of the evening. When the Bingo ended, Grandma made one more trip to the bathroom, and this time had no problem remembering the step. She said good-bye to the women who were helping, and then as we walked across the parking lot, told me in front of all of them that I was a good grandson. The heavy leaning and wheezing had disappeared.

During the trip home in the car and across the icy porch, Grandma's was breathing like a thoroughbred. She went into her darkened house, put one light on, told me again that I was a good grandson, and then left me to figure out as best as I could how I could get home.

Years later, when Grandma held my first child, I was proud when she pronounced it a good baby, because you always knew Grandma McShane's opinion mattered. Grandma was well into her 90s when she died. As I remember Grandpa and Grandma McShane, he was a dreamer and she was a hard cold realist. They raised thirteen children on a meager income, and many of those children were college educated. I believe that's the combination it takes to make it in life-the dreamer and the realist. I'm glad that I have blood from both of them running in my veins.

Michael Cotter is a well-known radio personality, storyteller and writer whose many books are available wherever good books are sold.

The Pink House on the Corner
By Alverne Diekman

I grew up in a little pink house kitty-corner from the Terp Ballroom. My bedroom was an upstairs loft, and on weekends and holidays, I could sit by my window overlooking the front door of the ballroom. I would watch the couples, all dressed up, holding hands and laughing, as they walked past the house on their way to the Terp. Music from bands like Tommy Dorsey, Glen Miller and Lawrence Welk would float out the doors in the warm summer nights and serenade our neighborhood.

My parents very seldom had the money or energy to go out dancing. It cost $1.10 to get into the Terp then. But on New Year's Eve it was a tradition. My parents, my mother's sisters and their husbands always went out for an evening of dancing that night. The sound of the joy and laughter of the women getting dressed and putting on their makeup still stands out in my mind. I dreamt of someday going dancing there in a fancy gown with my Prince Charming.

The neighborhood was also home for the Marigold Dairy, a laundromat, a greenhouse, a lumberyard and the old brick house. I delighted in hearing the train whistle at the crossing by the lumberyard and waving a greeting to the engineer as the train rumbled through town. The engineer always waved back at the crowd that gathered to watch. The old brick house, which was just around the corner from my childhood home, is now a coffee shop, but when I was a child I loved going there with my doll buggy and dolls to play house in the shade of the trees. Our neighbors, Tiny Bassett and his wife, enjoyed watching my parenting skills with my dolls from inside their brick home.

When my sister and I arrived home from school, my mother would be in the living room ironing our clothes, sheets and pillowcases. Mother had baked chocolate chip cookies, and she was anxious to hear about our day at school. For a special reward, my mother would treat me to ice cream at Klagge's. Ice cream cones were a nickel a scoop. The flavors were peppermint, spumoni, licorice and rainbow, to name a few. I also enjoyed going to the Paramount Theatre to see Laurel and Hardy, the Stooges, or Shirley Temple movies. It cost 25 cents for a child's admission. I never bought candy during the show, as I wanted to save my nickel for ice cream after the show. In the evening my mother would read me books like *Old Yeller, Black Beauty*, or *Tom Sawyer* while my father rested from a hard working day at Hormel.

My sister Jan was seven years older than me so her tastes differed from mine. Her favorite spots in town were the Tendermaid, the Tower and Woolworth's. Jan would meet her friends downtown and shop for the latest trend-setting shoes, penny loafers, and poodle skirts. She would spend hours listening to the jukebox tunes and sipping on malted milks. In the evening there was always dragging Main Street and going to the dances on the weekends at the Tower.

My parents selected a charming town to watch their two daughters growing up and forming their childhood memories and family values. There was warmth throughout the neighborhood, and we were rich in the relationships we formed there. The pink house is just a memory for me as it was torn down to make way for the Senior Center. My mom, dad and sister have left this earth, and I remain here without them. I did find my Prince Charming. My prince and I do go out dancing, and on the dance floor I think of my bedroom loft and the security of love and family.

Terp Ballroom

Dien's Story
By Dien Doan

When I was just a little girl about 12 years old, I lived in my village, Bac Binh, with my family. I had my grandpa. He spoke a little French. My country was at war. I lived in South Vietnam. America helped South Vietnam, and they sent many soldiers to help South Vietnam.

One day the Army came to my village and came to my house. Some Army men spoke French with my grandfather. At that time nobody spoke English in my family. I don't know what they said to my Grandpa.

The soldiers loved children. I know because they wanted to play with the children and speak with the children, but the children didn't speak English. They gave my family SPAM, a can of what the Army ate. We liked the SPAM because at that time people were very poor in my village. We ate it and felt very good.

The Army men stayed about two or three days. They stayed in the back yard, not in my home. Later, I think the Army came back to my village every two or three days. For four or five years they just walked by. Every family in my village made a hole in the ground. We stayed underground just sometimes when they were fighting.

My dad went to South Vietnam, serving in the South Vietnamese Army from 1972 until 1975. He was wounded in the stomach but came home to Bac Binh to teach school. My grandfather was killed in 1972 in a B52 bombing raid on the city of Quang Tri, Vietnam. I was there, but not hurt. Too many people died; my uncle, cousin, soldiers from North Vietnam, along with their animals, chickens and cows. Sometimes I saw whole families in the ground die.

The war ended. My husband came home from prison in 1980. He was a policeman in South Vietnam and was put in prison by the Communists for four years. The program between America and Vietnam said that if a Vietnamese person was a political prisoner more than three years, he could apply to come to America. In 1991 he filled out the paper and sent it to the government. When I went to the interview in Vietnam after I filled out the papers, one Vietnamese and one lady from America talked to me. I think she lived in Minnesota but I don't know where. She asked my family, "Why would you like to go to Minnesota?"

My husband said, "My uncle lives over there in Austin. My uncle served in the South Vietnam army." He had been in prison and he went to America first before my family had the chance.

I came to Austin. I asked my friend who came here before me and she said, "Over here the weather is very cold, but the school is good for my children." So we came to Minnesota. I lived with my uncle and aunt. My cousin drove me to school every day. They cared for my family and me. I came with my husband and the children. Vu was 13 and Uyen was 8 when we came in April, 1996. Nobody in my family spoke English at that time. After two or three days I went to school for English as a second language.

When I first came, Roberto Romo and Sue Grove helped me find a house, food, clothes and a doctor. My husband made an application to work at Quality Pork Processors, and I stayed home for two years to take care of my kids and go to school. Many teachers and friends helped me.

Now I am a United States citizen. My husband will be a U.S. citizen on the fifteenth of February. My children, Vu and Uyen, are citizens. Vu finished five years of college this summer and will be a computer engineer. This summer he will graduate. Uyen just finished her first year of college at the University.

I think the way things turned out is very interesting. I thought when the U.S. army came back I would never have a good life again, but right now I work at QPP, and I eat SPAM, and I live in SPAMTown, USA.

The New Dress
By Janice Duncan

When I was about 4 years old in 1946, my family lived on Mill Street, a short half block away from the railroad tracks. Our house was right across the street from the Marigold Dairy, now occupied by the *Austin Daily Herald*. If you followed the tracks south to 3rd Avenue SE, there was a long loading dock.

The loading dock was endlessly fascinating. It was made of huge timbers and was full of marvelous things. Where else, except in a Tarzan movie, could I find large branches full of green bananas and boxes of coconuts? I would edge closer and closer, so tempted to touch these tropical delights, but I knew that in among the pretty green fronds were deadly snakes and giant spiders. So I would admire them from a safe distance. The sights and smells were pure delight and fueled my imagination for many fanciful adventures.

The loading dock was great, but my favorite memories are of the days my mom would buy her flour. I remember her holding my hand as I skipped along, talking a mile a minute, as Mom would say. Mom bought her flour in large, hundred-pound bags. These cloth bags were made of printed cotton that had pretty flowered prints and so many choices, and I had to see them all. The chosen bag would make a dress for me, not a hand-me-down from my sister or cousin. I would dance from one bag to another, agonizing over all the patterns and bright colors. Finally I would make the wrenching choice. A dockworker would set the bag behind the counter and put our name on the paper tag. Later, when Dad got done with work, he'd stop by and get the chosen bag.

Oh, the excitement when he came through the door with the flour on his shoulder! Soon the bag was carefully opened and the contents transferred to a metal barrel and a flour dispenser in the old green cabinet. Three times a week Mom would bake the best bread for our large family. We all loved baking day. The day after the bag was carefully emptied, Mom would wash, dry and iron my flowered material. Out would come the pattern, and she would shoo me away so she could sew in peace. I loved the rhythmic sound of the treadle on the Singer sewing machine. She might put white lace on a collar, puffed sleeves, and a pocket for my hanky on the gathered skirt. Mom would work her magic, and soon I would be twirling and preening in my brand new dress. I knew I was a very lucky little girl to have such a pretty dress made just for me.

Monumental Memory
By Shirley Snyder Earl

"Huge Crowd to See Statue Unveiled Here: Impressive Program at Dedication of Weber Gift Planned" read the headline atop the *Austin Daily Herald* article reporting the dedication and unveiling of George Washington's statue.

Judge Henry Weber greatly admired George Washington and the principles for which he stood, so he commissioned a bronze statue to be cast and placed on the courthouse lawn, dedicated to the children of Mower County.

Henry and his wife Hannah had no children so he requested that his cousin, Emma Loomis, ask one of her grandchildren to do the unveiling. I was Grandmother Loomis' youngest grandchild, and when she broached the subject to me I was honored, but I grew apprehensive as the day neared. Mother sewed my pink taffeta dress and curled my hair for the occasion.

On September 18, 1937, Main Street was partially blocked off, church bells rang, roses were dropped from a plane overhead, and the Austin High School Band, directed by C. V. Sperati, played patriotic selections. Speeches were made, and also on the platform were state and local dignitaries, school and clergy representatives, Hannah Weber and the sculptor. The *Herald* story covering the day's events read, in part, "Little Miss Shirley Snyder, daughter of Mr. and Mrs. Fay Snyder, and a grand niece of the late Henry Weber (actually a third cousin) was introduced as the one to unveil the monument."

Henry Weber did not live to see that September day, but his gift, given to the city of Austin and dedicated to the children of the county, still stands after nearly seventy years on the courthouse lawn.

The Boys of Summer
By Larry Engelmann

On any given summer day in the early 1950s in the little town of Austin, if you stepped outside in the early morning you would inevitably witness what appeared to be an unusual and felicitous mass migration. The movement down sidewalks and streets of the sleepy town was not one of birds or of other familiar migratory animals, but rather a migration of boys. All appeared to be happy and expectant as if heading for a carnival or picnic. They were generally dressed the same-white short-sleeved tee shirts were universal. The trousers varied: some wore wide-wale corduroy, some denim, some nondescript cotton or gabardine of several hues. Most boys were blond and blue eyed, betraying the Scandinavian origins of the early settlers of the region, but there was a scattering of dark-haired, brown-eyed boys. Almost all of them were lean. Someone said later that they all looked underfed, but they were not. They were well fed and thrived on the pure air and water of that time and the incredible abundance of vegetables and fruits produced by the fertile loamy soil of southeastern Minnesota.

A few carried baseball bats slung over one shoulder. Some strung baseball gloves on the bat. All wore black high-top sneakers. One in a dozen brought black spiked baseball shoes, tied together by the strings and slung over a shoulder. Half rode bicycles, and half of those carried another boy on the crossbar, handlebars or back wheel brace. The brands were Schwinn (the 24" Phantom was the Cadillac of bicycles at that time), Shelby, Huffy, Radio, Monarch Gene Autry, Rollfast Hopalong Cassidy, Raleigh, J.C. Higgins and Columbia. Several local bicycle stores sold and serviced these, and they could also be purchased at the local Sears office (not a store, just a catalog ordering facility) or at one of the town's sporting goods stores. Some parents purchased bicycles with Green Stamps that were given out by retailers. Some bicycles had battery-powered horns between the crossbars. Some had streamers snapping from the special handlebar grips. A rubber band around the right ankle of many riders held trousers fast and prevented them from getting caught in the chain. One or two of the boys used a clothespin to attach a small piece of cardboard to the back wheel frame. The cardboard flapped against the turning spokes and made a sound vaguely like a two-cylinder engine as they pedaled down asphalt, tree-lined streets.

Lush branches of large oak and maple trees canopied Maple Street where I lived and the streets just north of it. The boys rode and walked as if through a gorgeous, quiet forest. All were going in the same direction toward the same place, moving with determination and resolve, like iron filings toward a magnet, to a huge grassy swatch of land four blocks long and two blocks wide, known throughout the town as merely the Athletic Field.

Around the green grass that blanketed the Athletic Field, ringing it and making it impossible for an automobile to drive onto the grass, were hundreds of evenly spaced thick posts, sunk deep in the earth and virtually immovable. They were painted white up to about ten inches from the top, where they were bright red, and they looked like a nearly endless row of matches embedded in the ground. They rose four feet tall and were spaced about six feet apart.

At the northeast corner of the field, adjacent to Highway 16, were six tennis courts, usually vacant on weekday mornings. Their nets were thick wire, permanent fixtures just like the fencing enclosing the courts. And on the west side of the field, right smack in the middle of the north south access, lay the football field, ringed by a quarter-mile cinder track. Along the field were white concrete bleachers. Beneath the east bleachers were storage facilities with huge, padlocked wooden doors. Inside were also dressing rooms for the Austin Packers and for visiting teams from the Big 9 conference.

On Friday nights in the fall the stadium came alive and was packed with local fans. And in spring the high school track team used the track for practice and meets. One small sand pit for the high jump and another for the pole vault were at the south end of the football field close to the large electric scoreboard. Except during fall and spring, nothing much happened in the stadium. Sometimes in summer afternoons and evenings, a half dozen boys climbed over the tall, barbed-wire topped fence to play touch football on the pampered, cushioned grassy field and to dream of someday playing in real games on that grass in front of a large and enthusiastic home crowd, running up and down the field while the gray-clad band blasted out the Austin fight song and everyone cheered. But on summer mornings the field was silent as a cemetery. A few birds perched on the top of the stadium or searched through the grass on the field undisturbed. Once a week a motorized lawn mower made its way up and down the field keeping the grass neatly trimmed.

The migrating boys passed between the white and red posts. A few dismounted from their bikes, wheeled them between the posts and crossed the grass to gather along the outside east wall of the stadium.

Many sat down and shielded their eyes from the rising apricot sun just starting to peek above the treetops. A trickle of boys soon became a sizeable flood of more than 100. Bikes were parked and leaned along the fence. There were no locks on the bikes. A stolen bike was not a concern or a worry or even a passing thought. The homes in Austin, people said with pride, were never locked, and people parked their cars on Main Street usually leaving their keys in the ignition.

At the southeast corner of the Athletic Field and directly across the street was a small storefront soda fountain, The Rush Inn. It was owned and operated by the Rush family, and Barry Rush was one of the ball players. The place had only half a dozen red-topped stools along a short counter. The specialty was root beer. The Rush Inn gained its fame among the boys of summer because whenever any one of them hit a home run, he was given a hand-written note to take to the Rush Inn. There he was rewarded with a tall, icy mug of root beer. These were the days before fast food. There was no McDonalds or KFC. There was no pizza at the time, and when that treat finally arrived, it could only be bought in a box of mixings at the grocery store where it was known as "pizza pie." For a good hamburger one had to go to the Tendermaid on Water Street and then a bit farther to Klagge's for an incomparable Frosted Malted. Those who hit homeruns got a seat of honor in the Rush Inn, and those who hit singles, doubles and triples either waited outside or gathered around their fortunate friend and watched him sip down his sweet reward.

The new arrivals abandoned their bicycles and sat or stood around talking or pacing. A few played catch. Others wrestled or pawed at each other in a pastime known as "horseplay." They watched a car pass on the street bordering the east side of the Athletic Field. Now and then to the south a car or truck would be seen heading west toward Sterling Addition, Turtle Creek and Albert Lea. But these were of no interest to the boys. They knew exactly what they were watching for. Any car brought an apprehensive moment of silence. But when the first one spied the big, four-door, two-tone tan Oldsmobile roll slowly around a corner, a shout went up to heaven. One or two voices at first and then, inevitably, a loud and enthusiastic chorus. "Ove! Ove!" they chanted. A few broke from the others and ran toward the car as it slowed just on the other side of the white and red matchstick border.

The car slowly rolled to a stop. The driver's door opened, and out stepped a very tall, slim man, Ove Berven, supervisor of the summer baseball program and basketball coach of Austin High School. He was a big man, somewhere around 6'5", although these boys might have described him as about 10 feet tall. He walked ramrod straight toward the field house in a familiar slow and graceful gait. The boys ran to meet and greet him and whirled around him like a human tornado as he walked. Some leaped into the air in enthusiasm, shouting again and again their one word hymn of praise. The others, waiting by the field house, stood and watched as if a major religious figure was approaching. We expected – and I am not exaggerating here – that if any small body of water separated us from Ove, he would without hesitation walk across it to get to us. He would never fail or hesitate. He was as solid and as certain and as good as that rising sun.

Another individual, coming seemingly out of nowhere, joined Ove. This man, affectionately known by Ove and the boys as Jerry, was also tall, but he walked with a deep stoop so that his face was only a few inches above that of the boys. His eyes were always open wide and alert, his mouth agape. His arms swung loosely at his sides, palms back. His walk was more of a lope, recognizable from a distance whenever he moved through the town.

I don't know where Jerry lived. I knew nothing and I knew no one who knew anything about his past. I never learned what had happened to him after I outgrew Peewee league baseball. In the early 1950s Jerry was probably in his mid-20s, but his mind was forever that of a 9 or 10-year-old child. He was a friendly guy with a laugh that was louder and shriller than ours. He wore trousers high on his waist, held up by a belt drawn two or three notches too tight. His trousers were too short, coming only to the tops of his ankles. Every day he wore a long sleeved checkered shirt buttoned all the way to the top. Ove treated him with the same deference and respect as we treated Ove. Some of the boys began to shout, "Jerry! Jerry!" When Ove and Jerry arrived at the field house in the midst of the tangled swirl of boys, Ove handed Jerry the keys to the big double-doored storage facility.

Jerry turned the key and pulled the doors wide open. Inside were bats and bags of baseballs along with several sets of equipment for catchers. We could see where the tackling dummies were stored along with several dozen red and white football helmets piled in a corner. The boys huddled outside, and Ove and Jerry went in and handed out the equipment and distributed clipboards with official scoring sheets attached. A stubby yellow pencil went with each board. Players were handed small plastic "clickers" that showed strikes, balls and outs. These were to be held by the umpire as a reminder of the count. As they scooped up their equipment, many broke and began running for one of the eight diamonds that had been laid out from one end of the Athletic Field to the other. Ove and Jerry threw out bases – large padded sacks – and boys snatched them up and raced off to their respective diamonds.

At the start of the Peewee season these boys had been divided up into teams – picked partially by Ove and partially by each other. The teams were supposed to be balanced by talent. Each was given the name of a major league team, but there were no uniforms. Not even caps. And midway through the season all the teams were dissolved and reorganized. There was no real season championship and no season-long triumph by one small group. These games were to be played day after day with one goal – the love of the game itself. In this organization it did not matter if you won or lost but only that you played the game and had fun doing it. I cannot remember how many games my own teams won or lost. What overwhelms me most after all these years is the sense of unfettered and unbounded joy of those mornings. Being with other boys, waiting for Ove, running for our selected diamond. Playing the game. What happiness! What freedom! What singular joy it brought.

Not all the boys brought gloves. Many could not afford them in those less affluent times. This presented no problem. Possessiveness or selfishness was not yet a vice of these youngsters. Sharing was the rule. Whenever one team left the field and another ran out, those in the field just dropped their gloves near where they were standing for someone else to use. A center fielder or first basemen might use his own glove or use the one he found nearby, whichever felt best. The important thing was that everyone be given the chance to play his best, and a fielder with a bad glove could skew things the wrong way. Every opportunity was given every player. Every opportunity. And every player.

Umpires were chosen from the side at bat. One of your own teammates stood behind the pitcher – nobody stood behind the catcher or the backstop--and called strikes and balls. Every effort was made to do it fairly, and if someone proved to be bad at making calls, he was simply booed down, and he came to the sidelines while someone else took his place. There were no threats. There was only the shame, temporarily, of trying to make the game unfair. There was no pride in winning a fixed game. As with the gloves, nobody wanted to win or lose from bad calls, so every effort was made to make calls as accurately as possible. Often strikes and balls were protested and settled by an argument. Decisions were changed. Howls of protest rang out. The same was true of stolen bases. There were no threats, just groans and boos and cheers. Boys in their adolescent melodramatic stage fell to the ground clutching their heads in despair when an awful and unfair call was made. When Ove heard a difference of opinion expressed, he either hurried over or sent Jerry as his emissary. After listening for a few moments and trying to let the boys themselves decide the issue, he'd make a decision or Jerry would decide, and the game continued. Sometimes a pitch was "re-thrown" or a player was sent back to his former base if there was a question. Jerry went from diamond to diamond to watch and listen, and if he didn't think the umpire was doing a good job, he'd take the position for a few innings before tossing his clicker to someone else and moving on to another game.

Honesty was pure and unquestioned. That is what made the game fun and more. And Ove had another firm rule. Everyone had to play. No matter how many players on each team showed up, everyone had to play and everyone had to bat in proper rotation. There was no pinch-hitting, pinch running or pinch fielding. If a team had eight players, they played with eight. Tough luck. But if a team had fifteen players, they played with all fifteen. To accommodate them, Ove created new positions. Nobody disagreed with his wisdom on this matter.

Since most boys batted right-handed, right field was the least desirable position, and those who were lazy or who could not catch a fly or who needed more experience were usually consigned to far right field, where they fended off boredom for a few hours. Most of their excitement came from throws to first base that went too high or wide. Seldom were they called upon to field a ball actually hit to right field.

The umpiring was anything but consistent. Batters learned to accommodate the often loony inconsistencies of the umpiring. The strike zone on any particular morning might be as large or as small as players might reasonably agree upon. It also was dependent upon the stature, record and needs of the batter--and upon the score. As one team fell further and further behind, the strike zone grew smaller. Sometimes if a team was far ahead, it was as big as a garage door. A pitch that went twelve inches over the head of a batter or that hit the plate in front of him might unashamedly be called a strike. And nobody argued. A team too far ahead should be going for every pitch, after all. The explanation was that, "You shoulda hit it. Easily." Protests sometimes got the call reversed, or in rare cases the umpire might plead that he wasn't watching closely, and the pitch would be done again. As a consequence of this unpredictability, scores tended not to become embarrassingly one-sided by the end of a game

My dear friend Ron Anhorn told me recently that he remembered once retiring twenty-one batters in a row. At the end of the day, Ove gave him the scorecard, and he still has it tucked away in a closet in his Colorado home. I cannot remember that accomplishment. I do, however, remember one particular morning when a team using a series of pitchers walked twenty-four batters in a row and ran up a 0-21 deficit in the first inning. I think every member of that team pitched that morning.

Jerry and Ove, hearing shouts and howls of protest, came to stand behind the backstop and watch the melodrama unfold. Several umpires were called and then dismissed. Even Jerry went out to stand behind the pitcher. The poor team seemed incapable of getting the ball anywhere near the plate until bases were loaded, and the score was 21 to nothing. Ove seemed less concerned about the score than about the length of the game. Finally he allowed pitchers on the opposing team to stand two or three feet closer to the batter. They aimed their pitches like darts thrown at a board and got them in the vicinity of the strike zone, and the batters started to swing wildly and miss.

I do not recall who the first batter was to strike out after his team scored 21 runs in a row. It may well have been me. I really don't know for sure. The fact that I cannot remember means that there was not much of a stigma attached. Everything was fun, absolute, total and unrestrained fun. I recall, as one batter after another advanced to first base, falling down laughing along the third base line with tears of happiness and silliness streaming down my face.

Getting on base was not merely a function of calling strikes and balls. Pitchers in the Peewee league were notoriously wild in flinging balls toward home plate. Each player could look forward each day to being beaned several times. In fact, when the game was in the late innings and a batter did not have a formidable record that morning, he could certainly look forward to his teammates crying from behind the backstop, "Come on, get in there and get hit. Crowd the plate. Lean over it. Shut your eyes."

I cannot remember how many times a pitch hit me. I can only say with complete confidence that it was many, many times. At least once a game. At least. The batter stepped up to the plate several times each morning. Everyone tended to use the same bat, even though a few boys brought Louisville Sluggers from home with necks carefully taped. The pitcher looked over each new hitter and took his windup. Despite the choreography of more experienced and accomplished players, everyone seemed to realize that the pitcher was concentrating on getting the ball roughly across the plate and into an area that the umpire might call a strike. I was hit in my knees, arms, hands, feet, chest, gut, and many times in the head.

The pitcher's windup was as much a warning to the batter as a threat. Teammates begged me not to step out of the batter's box to avoid getting hit. "Come on Engelmann, get in there and get hit," was a common bit of cheap advice given to a batter in a critical part of a game. Dodging a pitch or stepping out of the way was usually met by a chorus of groans; the batter had just avoided a sure journey to first base.

I recall a couple of times in those pre-helmet days, being struck in the temple, the neck, the cheek and the forehead. These left swellings the size of half a golf ball that disappeared in a day or two. Twice I turned away and was hit in the back of the head, the ball bouncing over the backstop with the catcher madly scrambling after it. I have no idea what the rule is for a ball that bounces off a batter's head and is caught in flight by the catcher. I remember a pitcher grimacing as I turned back to him after being struck and then limped to first base.

I am still amazed and impressed by the absence of tempers. Nobody lost his temper. Hitting was accidental, always, and everyone knew it. The pitcher would far rather strike out a batter than strike him. Some players refused to take first base after being struck. They denied that they had been hit, even when everyone saw them get beaned in the head. But they just refused and demanded another pitch. The umpire argued with them and the pitcher, demanding that they go to first base. Finally, inevitably, they slowly went to the base, disappointed that they'd missed another chance for a root beer.

Because everyone had to play and bat, Ove created many new positions not heard of before or since. I personally played some of those positions. If a team had fifteen players show up, Ove usually began placing players at shortstop position. A team might have two or three or four shortstops. These were labeled by their nearness to a base. Consequently there was third short short, third short, short, second short, second short short. There were times when the infield was crowded with players, all eager to snatch the ball. Ove then moved to the outfield. Between left and right field there might be three or four players – left left, left, left center, left center center, center and then moving right.

In at least a half dozen instances I clearly recall two pitchers on the mound taking turns. The umpire was behind the mound, and sometimes Jerry was there with him, so the mound was crowded. Crowds on the field meant a lot of fun for everyone and a virtual stampede between innings as players left or took the field.

Decades after baseball was done with me I was not done with baseball. I watched major league games in person. On television I witnessed a genuine rarity when Jose Canseco was standing in right field for the A's and a fly ball hit him on the head and bounced into the stands for a home run. This was shown again and again on television, much to the consternation of Canseco, who may have been thinking about his salary, his sports car, or his steroids at that time.

But I witnessed such scenes in Peewee league a hundred times. Any time a ball was launched by a batter into the outfield, any number of things could happen, and the least likely was that someone would catch it for an out. I remember stunned silence on the field, indeed, even on nearby diamonds, when that familiar crack of hickory hitting horsehide cut quickly through the air. It was rare, and everyone stopped and turned to watch. The ball rose into the blue sky as players on the sidelines stood and shielded their eyes to follow it. Cars passing up and down Highway 16 might slow to see what happened next. There were a dozen shouts of, "I've got it, I've got it" as players ran every which way in the infield and outfield. If someone snagged it before it hit the ground, there were loud groans and cries, shouts of utter astonishment, yells of praise. Ove or Jerry rushed over to congratulate the boy who caught the ball and to praise him lavishly.

But catching the ball was a rare event. Players ran into each other like the Three Stooges times three. They tripped each other up, fell down, got up, pointed, yelled, used their glove to block out the sun and try to find the elusive white ball. Players running in opposite directions collided and fell. Desperate players flung their gloves high into the air to try to stop the ball. I have no idea what the rule is on a glove without a player catching a ball twenty feet in the air. I think I saw it happen one time. The boy threw up his glove, the ball went into the webbing and fell back down, but he dropped the glove. It was a hit.

I've seen the ball bounce off the shoulders or head of an outfielder and continue on its way. In one game the ball, as if it were inside a pinball machine, struck three different heads and bounced up after each one, only in the end to be caught by a fielder, amidst the cries and laughter of the other team. The surprised fielder–dumbfounded really – found the ball suddenly in his hands and threw it twenty feet over the head of the third baseman into an open field. Runners tagged up and bases emptied.

How glorious our games were. How full of praise and admiration Ove and Jerry were for us all. How full of admiration and love we all were for each other. How much fun we had at the end of the morning, pulling up our bikes and heading home, perfumed with sweat and the rich clean scent of grass. Our shirts and trousers were stained with grass and dirt. How exhausted we were, and how utterly full to the brim with happiness. We knew we were the luckiest boys on the face of the Earth. We knew it for a fact. We could not imagine a more felicitous condition than the one we lived in. We waited eagerly for the next game. We really were in a pastoral paradise that most boys around the world seldom dare dream about.

Amidst the scent of new mown grass and sight of huge cumulus clouds passing overhead like gigantic icebergs drifting slowly across the sky all the way from Antarctica, the boys laughing and screaming and running around were having what surely was the time of their lives. But they were not yet quite fully aware of it. For a few this was as good as life would ever be. The next years – and each was given a limited number of them – would be a slow descent from the highs of those summer days.

I cannot remember a serious injury in Peewee baseball. I cannot even recall a bruised ego. Everyone was good; everyone was bad on any given day. We realized the teams would be dissolved and reorganized mid-season, and we'd start all over again so who cared if you were on a winless team half the summer or an undefeated one. We tasted equally victory and defeat, and the lesson was sweet.

The one thing that stands out from those days is not the lack of uniforms or spikes or gloves or balls or bats. It was the absence of parents or older boys. There were never any family members along the sidelines, no family or even peer pressure. Ove and Jerry were the only adults. We were alone in our own world with each other and with the gods and with Ove and Jerry.

Whenever I pass an athletic field where boys' or girls' baseball is being played and I see the sidelines and bleachers crowded with parents, some with ice chests or elaborate folding chairs, cheering their children on, the children all in uniform, a uniformed umpire, uniformed coaches pacing up and down the baselines, I feel only sad for the players. What pressures they face. And the poor extra players who must sit on the bench. What happened to the rule that everyone must play and everyone must bat? They will never know, I am sure, the joy, the unpressured joy, that my friends and compatriots and my childhood sharers felt as children playing a game for the fun of it all. What bliss. What pure bliss.

When the ball game was over and a lucky few ran to the Rush Inn for their root beer, we returned home. My favorite lunch was peanut butter on homemade bread and a glass of whole milk poured from a real glass bottle. About 1 p.m. I usually got on my bicycle and pedaled to the public swimming pool beside the Red Cedar River.

Free time at the pool was 1:30 to 3:15. Once an hour there was a ten-minute rest. Children pulled themselves out and lay on the hot concrete while lifeguards circled the pool looking for foreign objects. There was a roped off area with two diving boards. The rest of the huge pool was marked off in lanes or areas for merely splashing around.

At 3:15 we had to exit the pool, and fifteen minutes later "pay time" began. There was a dinner break for the lifeguards, and the pool opened at night for paying customers. But money was scarce in those days, and I don't remember ever going to the pool during pay time.

In the summer evenings of the early 1950s, there was a man with a large telescope on a tripod who set up his own concession on the corner of Main Street just outside the Austin State Bank. We called him Elmer the Moon Man. Elmer called out as the light was fading, "See the mountains and the craters on the moo-hoon." I think he charged two or three cents for a look through his telescope.

I remember the time my dad paid Elmer, and I looked in the eyepiece. I was stunned. I straightened up to make sure he wasn't putting a photograph over the end. The moon was brilliant and beautiful and was as close as the other end of Main Street. I'd seen many science fiction thrillers at the Austin or State or Paramount Theatres, had seen the stage mockups of the moon and stars, but had never seen anything like this. What a thrill! What dreams Elmer inspired.

He was gone by October of 1957, when the Soviets put Sputnik into orbit and the demystification of space began. Before that time we could believe whatever we wanted about outer space. After that, the immediacy of the Cold War came home to us, even in Austin, and space became synonymous with race rather than with enchantment. One of the myths perpetuated in those Cold War days was that in case a war broke out with the Soviets, bombers from Siberia would cross the Arctic and Canada and descend on America to bomb it. One of their targets, I recall being told in school, was Austin. I could not figure out why our little settlement should be a primary Soviet target. But we were told that Austin was the primary producer of SPAM, and that an army traveled on its stomach, and that during World War II, SPAM fueled the American fighting man. My uncles, all war veterans, heard this story and told me that in case of war, Austin would be *our* first target, to prevent SPAM from being fed to U.S. troops again. I was obviously confused by the conflicting accounts.

Our activities were limited in the early 1950s because of the polio epidemic. Nobody knew what caused it, but everyone knew it was contagious and often fatal. Between 1952 and 1954, when Peewee baseball was in its prime, well over 100,000 cases were reported each year. This was a children's disease usually, that struck down countless youngsters. As a result we avoided movie theatres, where the air was not as fresh as it was outdoors. In August we were restricted in our use of the swimming pool. The long period of fear came to an end in 1955 when Dr. Jonas Salk announced the discovery of his vaccine. The world, for my generation, was divided between 1955 and after, the years of fear and the years free of fear from that awful affliction.

In August we went to Saturday matinees to see Superman, Roy Rogers, Gene Autry, Lash LaRue, and Whip Wilson. We inevitably went up north fishing with the family. My cousin, Bobby Doty, who lived next door, spent much time sitting on the curb of Oakland Avenue, counting and naming out of state license plates as they passed through town.

Downtown, if one waited long enough, one might see Leslie Caron, who had married Geordie Hormel and lived part of each year at the Hormel estate just outside town. She married Hormel in 1951 and divorced him in 1954, the year after she was nominated for an Oscar for her role in *Lili*. Hormel went on to compose music for television shows and to sing back up for Frank Zappa. I always thought Ove Berven might have given that blessed boy and his rich siblings some much needed guidance in life. But he never really had the chance that we all had.

Bill "Moose" Skowron played first base for the Austin Packers at Marcusen Memorial Field before he was called up to the Yankees to become a legendary player, hitting 211 home runs in 14 major league seasons and playing in seven World Series.

The years raced by. Too soon my time in Peewee league came to an end. I never went on to play in other leagues. I swam more, and watched the younger boys playing as I rode my bicycle past the Athletic Field. One generation followed another. I watched Ove Berven's basketball teams repeatedly win Big 9 titles and go to the state tournament. All the boys went their separate ways. Elmer the Moon Man suddenly stopped showing up in the late 1950s. I don't know what happened to Jerry. He just wasn't there anymore.

I can truly say I have never had as much carefree and guiltless fun as I did during those summers playing baseball with the other boys of summer in Austin. We watched each other get older, went on to live our lives, experienced just about all the good and bad that life has to offer. I think only with the passage of time did we come to recognize what a time we'd had, how special those summers were. Never again would we be so carefree.

I have seen many things since that time and been many places I'd never dreamed about as a boy in Austin. I've seen things I should not have seen and done things I should not have done, and I am wiser and better for it now. I slowly gained my bearings in life, and I gradually got a grip on the importance of my time growing up in Austin. And by then, it was all gone – a lost world, completely erased. Many of the boys I watched playing in those green fields are now gone too, and the echoes of their laughter and their protests remain only in my memories, fixed there for as long as I live.

Ron Anhorn spoke the truth for all of the boys of my generation when he summed up Ove and those beautiful baseball summers. I told him I was going to write this piece. He told me during our conversation, "You know, I really loved that man." I was not surprised by his words. We all loved him. And I like to think that he knew that every morning as he pulled up on the eastern edge of the Athletic Field and heard the boys of summer begin their divine chant, "Ove! Ove! Ove!"

I have come to realize over many decades how very innocent all of the boys of summer were. We were happy and we knew it. We were innocent and artless, and we did not know it yet.

Innocence means living in a world without mirrors. Everything is as it seems, exactly. There is no lonely or solitary self. There is only the group. There are no perceived contradictions, no puzzling complications and no problems that cannot be solved. When we were laughing boys running through the rich green grass of the Athletic Field, watched from a distance by Ove and Jerry, we truly were at play in the pastures of heaven. Today I can close my eyes and see four or five boys lost in right field, where no baseball ever landed, eyes to the ground chasing a bumblebee or butterfly. In left field I can see and hear a crowd of boisterous boys running after a rolling baseball in the way that a litter of puppies might chase a ball. The whole world is right there for the boys. Bathed in summer sunshine, rooted in dewy grass, they live entirely in that perfect morning.

But none of us was immune to the passage of time. We grew up. If we'd had our way, of course we would have stayed the way we were forever, and the innings of every game would have been endless and eternal. Days and nights might pass, and we'd play in the sunshine and starlight, the rain and the snow.

Ove Berven and his family

Now those days are gone, and most of the boys are also gone. Yet, whenever I hear laughter that seems sincere and unbridled and deep and genuine, I can see them all again in their felicitous gathering, their morning migration, the sun rising over the town, the tinkle of bicycle bells and the clap-clap of cardboard on wheel spokes, the hum of the approaching Oldsmobile just beyond the red and white posts. At those moments I know that some things, even after they pass, must exist somewhere forever. I see the boys of summer.

*Larry Engelmann is the author of several books, including **Tears Before the Rain** and **Feather in the Storm**. He lives in San Jose, California.*

The Big Fire
By Gloria B. Falconer

On a Sunday night in October of 1953, my husband George and I were in the basement of Central Presbyterian Church. We were in charge of the young people, and there was a service upstairs. Later in the evening it started to thunder and lightning and rain cats and dogs. All of a sudden, there was a loud bang, and I said to George, "Oh boy, that was close. It must have hit something!"

After the service was over and people came to pick up their children, I asked, "Does anybody else but me smell smoke?" Several of us looked over the entire church and found nothing. About 2 a.m. the police called Rev. Schendel, and told him, "You better get down to your church right away. It is on fire. See if you can save anything."

He managed to save the cross and chalice. I think he also saved some records out of his office. Word just spread, and there were so many people down there watching and crying as we watched our church completely destroyed. One of the greatest losses was the beautiful, irreplaceable stained glass windows.

It was determined that the lightning we had heard was the cause of the fire. My circle went through the rubble looking for anything to salvage. We found the old stove, and it was cleaned up and later taken to the new church. That stove served us well for at least forty-five years! The burners worked, but finally it was the oven that didn't work. You couldn't buy parts so we bought a new stove about five years ago. The Conservation Club took the old stove, and it is there today!

Someone came up with the idea of cleaning the bricks and selling them for doorstops. So for many days we cleaned bricks and decided we would paint some of them gold and charge $2 instead of $1.

The picture of us cleaning bricks includes my son Richard, who came along because the other boys were in school. I don't remember everyone who was there, but the picture shows Delores and Daryl Franklin and me. We sold some bricks, and Bob Guy later transported those remaining to the new location for the building of the new church.

Central Presbyterian Church was on the corner where the downtown Sterling Drug store is now. The Episcopal Church was across the street.

The Congregational Church was in the next block south along with the Lutheran and Methodist Churches. This street was often referred to as Church Street. The Congregational Church offered the use of their facilities to us during the building of our new church. We met at 7:30, and they had their service at 9.

Due to the very close relationship Dr. Griese had with the Jenks family who owned property on Kenwood Avenue that extended through to what is now Sixth Street SW, we were able to purchase the back half of the Jenks' property. However, there were stipulations that we could not cut down any trees as long as any member of the family was living. Upon their deaths we were able to purchase the lot on which their home stood, which is the present location of Westminster Presbyterian Church. A new era had begun. It was very hard to see our church burn, but we all knew that it would not be the end, but a new beginning.

After the Presbyterian Church fire workers cleaned and salvaged bricks.

The Mower County Fair
By Paige Fisher

When I was younger, I was terrified of the double Ferris wheel. That fear continued until my older sister and cousin reassured me that those who ride the double Ferris wheel could grab cotton candy from the clouds when they were up in the air. My other sister and I, being too little to know any better, wanted to feast on some of that cotton candy in the sky. At that point, my sister and I weren't afraid of the heights we had to climb in order to reach it. So, we climbed onto the seat, and waited for the ride to begin.

As the ride started to lift off, my stomach began to feel a little queasy. As we climbed higher in the air, we realized that we didn't care about the cotton candy anymore. We clutched onto the bar until our knuckles turned white. We screamed as the ride went on, and couldn't wait to be let down.

When we got off the ride, we marched over to my other sister, demanding that she provide the sticky treat that we were deprived of. Lucky for her, we were distracted by the aroma of Tom Thumb Donuts wafting through the air. The savory smell of sizzling steak kabobs and creamy fruit smoothies further whetted our appetites. After our nerve-wracking adventure, we were absolutely starving. So we gobbled down what we could in order to be on time for the grandstand events.

After we ate, we headed over to the grandstand to watch people perform and to see the rodeo take place. We always had a fun time when we got to the grandstand. We then walked over to the historical buildings that are right inside the main gate. We visited the one-room schoolhouse and the horse and buggy building.

Our day ended by looking at all the animals in the barns. The Mower County Fair is a place where anyone can have a good time. It is usually at the beginning of August, and runs about a week. All ages are able to participate in the many activities that go on, so it's a place for everyone. There is always something a person can remember about the Mower County Fair.

Tunney
By Janet Anhorn Gaughran

It was 1926 when my father, Art Anhorn, brought home a new puppy, a three-quarter bulldog/terrier, whom he promptly named Tunney after the world's heavyweight champion boxer of 1926, Gene Tunney. Tunney would turn out to be no ordinary bulldog. By 1928 he had become the protector of Art and Mildred's oldest son, Donnie. Still in rompers, Donnie had only to stray a little outside of their large backyard on Maple Street, and Tunney would grab Donnie from behind by his diapers and gently pull him back to the safety of the yard.

When he got a little older, Tunney became known to all the townsfolk as the Pure Oil Dog who rode on the running board of Art's company pickup truck. If Art went around the corner too fast, Tunney often tumbled off, but he always came up running to jump back on the running board again.

Art Anhorn, along with his cousins from Owatonna, Andrew and John Anhorn, had founded the Mower County Oil Company in Austin in 1922, selling Pure Oil products. The company opened on Brownsdale Avenue, which became their bulk plant near the railroad tracks. In 1925 the company expanded and opened the uptown station at Main and Oakland. A third station opened on Water Street, along with eight other outlets.

Tunney liked to make the rounds each day of all the Pure Oil Stations in Austin. Because doing that would involve a lot of walking, Tunney made friends with all the bus drivers in the city. Tunney had merely to go to a bus stop and wait until the bus came along. The driver would then open the door for him, and Tunney would ride to the next station where the driver would let him out. As the townspeople came to know Tunney, they would often stop for him as well when they spotted him waiting at the curb.

Using his personality and intelligence, Tunney soon made friends with the pilots as well at the Austin Airport. They were also generous with their rides, and Tunney came to love flying. At the stations, Tunney again showed his protective qualities. He placed himself at the stations' entrances and, if a man was ragged or smelly, Tunney would not let him enter the station door.

At 11 years of age, Tunney was proposed for membership in the Old Timer's Club by a group of dealers from the Mower County Oil Company. Tunney also became their official mascot, and was in evidence at all of their dealer meetings.

Tunney lived a long and useful life. He will always be remembered as the Pure Oil Dog who was named after the famous boxer of his time. Like Gene Tunney, he was a champion as well. Well known to the townspeople of Austin, he captured many of their hearts. Tunney was much more than a dog; Tunney was a person

Tunney and Donnie Anhorn

Janet Anhorn Gaughran lives in Jordan, Minnesota.

Two Colorful Local Characters
By RoseMary Anderson Gerlach

There have been many colorful Austin characters throughout the years, but two I remember are Charlie Pitcher and the iceman. Charlie Pitcher, the junkman, lived in his junkyard with his swaybacked horse. The junkyard was located at the corner of Oakland Avenue and old Kenwood, where the Bamboo Hut stands today.

He had affixed a tall post on each corner of his cart, with a pair of posts midway. He had nailed beams to them, six in all. On these beams he hung pots, pans, ice tongs, other household items, and some clothing. You could hear him coming from a distance-- "clank, clank." He not only sold, he bought things. That was before rummage sales.

One time my mother needed a special knob for her kettle cover. He looked through everything, but he didn't have the right size knob. He told her he'd have one the next day, and he did. I suppose he rummaged around at the junkyard until he found it.

Charlie the junkman covered all of Austin, so everybody knew him, and everybody liked him--except little kids, because he never smiled and was kind of scary looking. I have a warm memory of Charlie the junkman because one day he gave me a penny, and in those days that was quite a bit. I wish I had kept it!

Although I don't remember his name, I remember the iceman. The iceman came once a week. We had a big icebox in the kitchen, and the water from the melted ice drained into a pan we'd have to empty. We'd order many pounds of ice, and he'd grab them with a big claw and lug them in on his shoulder. Ice blocks were cut from the Cedar River in winter and stored in sawdust in the big icehouse down near old Ash Street near the new hockey arena.

When the iceman came down our street (South Kenwood), all the kids would run out with a washrag, because if he was in a good mood, he would take out an ice pick and give us each a sliver of ice that we'd wrap up and suck on, not minding the sawdust bits that clung to it. In the summer we loved the iceman! It was just as good as going to the Dairy Queen nowadays.

The Tap Dance Kid Bites the Dust
By Joan Claire Graham

With the firm understanding that I would not under any circumstances be allowed to participate in the June recital, I was admitted to Mary Lou Regner's tap dancing class right after Easter in 1952. A Spartan room in the back of the first floor of Albert Lea's Hotel Albert contained the requisite dancing school barre and mirror, and from the moment I walked through the door, I loved the place, the teacher, the taps, the classmates, the music, and the idea of being a tap dancer.

The tune was "Chicago, Chicago, That Toddling Town," and I caught on immediately to the tap steps. By the end of that first lesson I could do the entire dance the class had been working on for several months, with the exception of a tricky "shuffle step-hop shuffle step" that I later mastered at home. Much to my delight, Mary Lou expressed surprise at my aptitude and said she thought I should dance in both her upcoming recitals in Albert Lea and Austin. Although I've dabbled in many artistic and academic areas, this was my first and only experience with instantaneous gratification and meteoric success.

After my successful and intoxicating stage debut, the following year I paired off with Pam Schuhmacher, and we became the darlings of local tap dancing. Our big number was "Me and My Shadow," and we performed at several area talent shows, mother-daughter banquets and service clubs. Our big show business opportunity came when we received an invitation to appear on the "Hemmenway Talent Parade" on KMMT television in Austin late in 1954. Undoubtedly the inspiration for "American Idol," the "Hemmenway Talent Parade" was a 15-minute early-evening show that featured three local acts, and audience members sent postcard votes to determine which individual or group would win an encore performance on next week's show. I don't think there was any other prize, but just having a chance to appear on television in Austin was incredibly exciting. Pam had an autographed photo of Johnny Western, and we hoped we might bump into the handsome young KMMT singing cowboy while we were in Austin.

When we arrived at the studio we learned that Johnny Western had quit his Austin show and headed out to Hollywood. Although disappointing, Johnny's departure was the least problematic situation we had to deal with. When we handed the sound guy our 45-RPM record, he told us that their record player only played 78s—or maybe it was the other way around. The key point is that they didn't have the right speed turntable to play the record to which our routine had been choreographed. We didn't have time to spare before the start of the live show, but the folks at KMMT pitched right in to help us because, as everyone knows, the show must go on. They had a piano so they called in a pianist. She miraculously sprinted in on short notice, but she didn't have sheet music for "Me and My Shadow," and she didn't know how to play it. Could we possibly do our dance to any other tune--one she knew by heart--possibly "The Syncopated Clock?"

"The Syncopated Clock" was a nice song, but it certainly didn't make sense with our "Me and My Shadow" choreography in which Pam did a step and I copied it, with one of us being the person and the other being the shadow until we teamed up for the big finale. On the positive side, "The Syncopated Clock" was written in 4/4 time, and the pianist knew how to play it with two minutes until airtime.

Troupers that we were, we smiled our show biz smiles and tapped our toes and did our best to look confident while we danced our clever shadow dance to a song about a clock that went "tock tick tock" instead of "tick tock tick." We probably looked pretty silly to legions of viewers who tuned in to the "Hemmenway Talent Parade" instead of watching the test pattern that was playing on channel 10, but all was not lost. Our hopes to win the competition were bolstered by the fact that the third act booked to perform that evening failed to show up.

Despite our optimism, adaptability and talent, the majority of voters cast their ballots for a pair of Austin girls who actually did show up with the right kind of record and lip-synched a song. We didn't say "lip-synch" in those days; we called it "pantomiming." We received a nice letter of condolence from someone at the television station, who said that the vote totals had been very close. That letter was no consolation, however. To be defeated, even by a narrow margin, in a two-act contest by a pair of girls *pretending* to sing shook my confidence and raised self-doubts about my talent as a *real* tap dancer.

After the "Hemmenway Talent Parade" debacle, my tap dancing career quickly unraveled. Mary Lou closed her Albert Lea studio and invited us to attend lessons in Austin. Mom didn't drive, and my dad wouldn't have considered driving me twenty miles for life-saving medical treatment, let alone for tap dancing lessons. Pam's mom didn't want to drive that far either, so the tap dance kid bit the dust.

*Joan Claire Graham is the author of the **Minnesota Memories** book series.*

The Perfect Dress
By Rosalie "Rose" Grebin

This picture was taken of my Aunt Shirley and her boyfriend, Harold Gomer, in 1942. As you can see, he was in the Navy. They had known each other since their early teens, and they started dating in high school. He went to work at Hormel's after high school, and then like many at that time, he went into the Navy. When my aunt got the news he was coming home on furlough, she wanted something special to greet him in. Meeting your fellow who was coming home on leave was a big deal. She went to Buttrey's Dress Shop (now where Curves is located) and found the perfect dress. It was a Navy style dress.

After awhile the war drove them apart. My aunt went to California to work, and Harold was shipped out to sea. When the war was over, my aunt came back to Austin as did Harold. Once back on their own turf, they started dating again. They were married in a small wedding at Queen of Angels Church on April 27, 1946.

Uncle Harold went back to work at Hormel, and he retired after forty years there. When the kids went back to school, Shirley worked at Woolworth's, where the Main Street Coffee House is located now. They had four children, who all grew up and graduated from Austin schools and moved to other towns. Shirley and Harold have grandchildren.

We helped them celebrate their sixtieth wedding anniversary this year. Since they had already celebrated their golden anniversary, they didn't have a big party. We all went out to eat, and we celebrated. We talked about old times and remembered that perfect dress she bought at Buttrey's so many years ago.

Shirley and Harold, 1942

Childhood Memories
By Rosalie Grebin

During my teenage years my address was 317 E. Water Street. I went from collecting movie star pictures to being a married woman while living in that two-family home. My mother, my four sisters and I moved in sometime in 1944, during World War II. Food and savings bond stamps became a part of our life. Friday was the day savings stamps were sold at school. We hoped Mom could spare a dime so we could at least buy one stamp to put in our savings book.

Also in those early years we hoped for the fare so we could take in a Sunday movie. I can't remember the exact amount needed, but movie and treats were under 25 cents. The Paramount was only two blocks away, and we always got our money's worth because we sat through two shows. The shows gave us a zest for living. We left the theatre with visions of being an actress and living in a beautiful movie star home.

The part of the house we lived in had three rooms and a bath downstairs and three bedrooms up. No hot water came out of our taps, only cold, which meant bath time was a real chore with heating big pans of water on the kitchen stove and hauling them to the bathroom. Washing your head was even more of a challenge. I don't know how my mom managed the laundry, but during the winter months, I do remember she laid clothes over our heat radiators to dry. There was a basement with a dirt floor, cobwebs and probably rats. We never ventured down there.

The house was located east of what used to be the CIO Union Hall. Also located in that brick building was Joe Bear's Grocery Store, and on the second floor of the building were several apartments. Down behind us, next to the river, was the old icehouse. During the winter months ice was harvested from the river. We were customers because we did not have a refrigerator; therefore, we put a big sign in our window that said "Ice," so we would get a delivery that day. Of course, we always had to remember to empty the pan that sat under the icebox that caught the water as the ice melted.

We were so poor during those years, but we also felt lucky. Not many kids had a tennis court and swimming pool in their back yard, the Paramount Theatre two blocks away, and the Tendermaid just one block down the street. A rare treat for us was a Tendermaid, which cost a mere

15 cents. In our mid teens we spent many hours skating at Sarg's Roller Rink, which was only about four blocks away.

The house is long gone. It, along with many other buildings, was torn down to make room for the beautiful public library. At age 75, I look back and wonder how we managed to be happy. We had no hot water, no refrigerator, and no car, but I wouldn't change my teenage years with any teenager in this day and age.

Lafayette Park swinging bridge

The Candy Lady of the East Side
By Dorothea Guiney

I had my first bottle of Dr. Pepper at Auntie's store. I was 4 years old, and other than a sip of 7-Up when I was sick, it was my first real taste of soda pop. My mother would not have been pleased. She had just groomed me for a birthday picture. Auntie was watching me while my mother ran an urgent errand before taking me for my picture. Being left under Auntie's guidance was no different than being left to my own devices in a candy store – Auntie's candy store. My great aunt was "The Candy Lady of the East Side."

Elizabeth Smith McCormick ran a little candy store near the railroad station on the east side of Austin, next to the old overhead pedestrian bridge. It was actually a neighborhood convenience store that carried a range of household staples. However, I doubt the majority of young visitors to the store saw beyond the large glass candy case that engulfed the store.

This magnificent case housed every imaginable type of penny and nickel candy. There were licorice wheels and whips, root beer barrels, Sixlets, Smarties, Pixie Stix, chalky cigarettes, sweet and sour balls, tiny wax juice bottles, chocolate coins, jelly coins, cinnamon bears, taffy, chocolate bars and kisses, jawbreakers and unlimited varieties of bubble gum. Children from near and far brought their pennies to the store, pressed their foreheads against the glass case and began dictating their orders to Auntie. As they rattled off their choices, Auntie filled miniature brown paper bags with the order while calculating the transaction in her head. Many children stayed to talk and laugh. She loved children and they loved my Great Aunt Elizabeth. She loved hearing their jokes and stories, but she especially loved telling them her own riddles and rhymes. The walls behind the candy counter were plastered with decades of children's school pictures. The store was close to Webster, Lincoln and Queen of Angels and was a stopping off point for children on their way home from school. It was unusual to drive by the store and not see a bicycle or sled parked outside. The store was also a spot for neighbors and friends to share gossip.

Running a candy store was probably not Elizabeth McCormick's life ambition, but in her later years it became a joy. Because her face was worn with the kind of wrinkles one gets from smiles and laughter, you would not suspect her life had not been easy. She was born Elizabeth Smith in Janesville, Wisconsin in 1888. Her father died when she was a young girl. Elizabeth and her three sisters helped support the family by working in strawberry and tobacco fields near Janesville.

To help ease the financial burden of the family, her eldest sister, Sarah Ella, was sent to Austin to live with relatives. After graduating from high school, Elizabeth came to Austin to be near her sister. She moved in with her aunt Sarah, who was married to James T. McCormick, a railroad conductor. She attended the Southern Minnesota Normal College, studying business. Following graduation Elizabeth worked at the First National Bank until her marriage to J.T. McCormick.

J.T. "Dooly" McCormick's family operated a coal, ice and kindling business on Railway Street (now 10th Street NE). J.T. worked in the family's business and was well known as an actor in local theatre productions. The Depression of the 1930s hit the McCormick's business hard. Customers had difficulties keeping up their payments for coal and ice. Like many businesses it became a casualty of the Depression and closed. Elizabeth and J.T. McCormick opened a gas station at the site. At that time gas cost five gallons for one dollar. Next door to the gas station they opened the little store. J.T. McCormick died in 1939, leaving Elizabeth to manage the property on her own.

Today the candy store would not hold up to contemporary standards of decor defined by popular franchises. To the discerning eye, the store was homey, poorly lit with peeling plaster and ceilings damaged by years of leaking rain. The walls were layered with yellowed signs and calendars from soft drink and snack cake companies. An old refrigerator held soft drinks, and a chest freezer with a glass lid contained ice cream and frozen treats. A couple of painted wooden chairs were placed around the store for people to sit on. But for those who entered the store, whether seeking something sweet or a joke to giggle at, Elizabeth McCormick made the store bright and cheerful. The candy store operated on the east side from 1937 until it was closed in 1972, when Elizabeth was no longer able to manage it on her own. She died in 1980. To this day, a sip of Dr. Pepper still brings me back to that magical candy store, and I am reminded of my great auntie, Elizabeth McCormick.

Dorothea is a fourth-generation Austin Guiney. She is a museum contractor who does exhibit development. Her first museum job was at the Mower County Historical society when she was a teenager.

A Homestead in Austin
By Francis Guiney, Circa 1931

Pardon me for being personal. I will take my grandfather, the late Daniel Guiney, as an example —his case being typical of all pioneers. He and his wife Hannah and two small children left Illinois in a covered wagon drawn by oxen in early spring, 1856. They brought two cows along, which furnished milk on the way for the babies. They also had chickens, household goods, and provisions with them. At Prairie du Chien they met Mr. Andrew Mack, who was on his way to Minnesota to prove up on his claim. He told them of a claim nearby. So all came on to Austin, arriving June 1, 1856. Here my grandfather purchased 160 acres of land from J.S. Decker for $5. Mr. Decker had been holding this land for another party who failed to show up.

The early settlers always settled near a woods and a stream, if possible, so as to have fuel and water. My grandparents built a four-room log house – two rooms on the first floor, two on the second floor, and a log barn for cattle and chickens.

The nearest trading post was at Winona. The men went to Winona in groups with their wheat to exchange for flour, lumber, dress goods, sugar and other necessities. These trips with oxen took about three weeks. One of the stopping-off places was High Forest, where men and beasts rested. The men exchanged the news of the day over a mug of liquid--coffee for some, and something stronger for others. They traveled the old territorial road from Winona to High Forest through Brownsdale, through the north part of the John Guiney farm, through Ed Wehner's farm and came in north of Austin. Part of it may be seen yet.

There were many friendly Indians hunting along the Cedar River who often went miles east and west of Austin. One day my uncle was fishing, and an Indian crept up behind him and slapped him on the shoulder. Needless to say, Uncle jumped a foot. The Indian laughed and laughed. But in 1862 the Indians were not so friendly, due to the Indian massacre in New Ulm. In October the settlers were warned that the Indians were coming this way. A number of the men in the area had gone to help General Sibley quell the uprising. This left the man shortage acute. Many of the settlers went to Fort Snelling, and others went to Austin with their personal belongings, living in dread and praying that the scare would soon end. After that they all returned to their homes.

The early settlers were as one family and helped each other in trials, sickness and death. Many died during the black smallpox and diphtheria epidemic, and relatives had to bury their dead. Many were buried on their own homesteads. There were no special roads or bridges on which to travel through woods and streams. They had good times visiting each other, and if company came the mother served whatever she had. They held singing schools and dancing parties at their homes. To hear them tell of their amusements we wonder why it takes so much for our generation to have a good time. If we of this generation had a part of the courage and patience to carry on in difficult times as our forefathers, we would think of our trials as passing incidents.

This essay is from a high school history project written by Francis Guiney in the 1930s. It is the true story of his Irish grandparents who homesteaded in 1856 in what is now Red Rock Township of Mower County. Daniel and Hannah Guiney raised twelve children on the farm homestead. They were active in the establishment of St. Augustine's Church, where a stained glass window with their names can be seen to this day. Today eighty acres of this original pioneer homestead remains in the Guiney family. Francis Guiney, who is the third generation to farm a part of the homestead land, owns it.

Francis Guiney, around the time he wrote this story.

The Enterprise Threshing Company
By Shirley Guy

The Enterprise Community has roots south of Austin, centered around the Enterprise School or Hall, as it is called today. The early settlers in the area always searched for ways to improve themselves. Their untiring efforts gave rise to such organizations as the Home Study Club, the Enterprise Cemetery Association, the Happy Thought Club and the Enterprise 4-H Club.

The Enterprise Threshing Company, which was organized in 1903 and played such a vital part in this community for fifty years, is equally interesting. It is amazing that in 1903 a group of ten young farmers were investigating various makes of threshing machines. The machines were not displayed in local stores so the men had to travel to the cities to see them.

Finally, after thorough investigation and conversation, a special meeting was called on July 9,1904 for the purpose of deciding on the purchase of a company machine. A report by Lew Lewis and H. R. Mills was carefully studied. Mills had observed a Geiser machine in action, he thought it was well built and durable, and he wondered whether it could provide the service they wanted. After further study, ten eager farmers agreed to buy this machine. The signers included H. R. Mills, C. H. Lott, C. O. Brownell, John Schottler, C. B. Sayles, P. N. Weinert, Thomas Fulton, Charles Mills, Lew Lewis and E. V. Hart

Before the meeting had adjourned, it was learned that the signers were expected to pay freight from Minneapolis to Austin. A general uproar followed. There was intensive discussion. Finally the president was authorized to write an order and deliver it to the company agent. The order was to include an insertion asking for three things: The men wanted 10-inch wheels on the separator, also a perfection sacker, and the company selling the machine was to pay freight charges to Austin. The total amount the farmers agreed to pay was $2400.

The men went home and waited. Would the order be accepted? By July 30, only twenty days later, the Enterprise Threshing Company knew they were in business. A tank wagon was ordered. Coal was to be burned in the steam engine. One stockholder was delegated to buy coal where he could get it at the lowest price, and they agreed that a building had to be constructed to shelter the new machine.

This was built at the H.R. Mills farm, which is the present home of Raymond Sayles. Various notations in the minutes tell us they discussed the size of the shed, the posts, cement, stock boards, roofing nails and other things needed for the shed. A busy summer followed, and the threshing was done in due time.

December 15 was the payment date. All ten members gathered at the First National Bank at Austin to pay for their purchase. While they were assembled at the bank, they agreed that the first Tuesday after the first Monday in January was to be their annual meeting day. At the annual meeting, bills were to be paid, necessary purchases discussed, and if there was extra money, dividends would be declared.

The dividend checks were never very large. Oats and barley were threshed at 2 cents a bushel, succotash at 3 cents, wheat at 4 cents, flax at 8 cents and timothy 10 cents a bushel. No stockholder would receive dividends if his threshing bill were not paid. This was real democracy in action.

In 1910, a coalhouse was built on the C.B.Sayles farm so that they could take advantage of special buys on coal. Frequently a carload of coal was hauled from the train at Varco Station to this shed. One item in the minutes tells us the company bought seventy tons of lower vein Brazilian black coal in 1909.

For fifty years an annual meeting was held at the home of one of the stockholders. With the passage of time some changes occurred in the names of the stockholders. The sale or transfer of shares was a personal matter, and we find very few notations in the minutes. We know that Joseph Mueller bought Lew Lewis' share in 1908. Claude Sayles bought a share from Elmer Loucks in 1917. In studying the minutes, one finds that Orin Varco's name appears as a shareholder after the year 1933.

Whenever everything was running in order and no large replacements were needed, and the balance in the treasury was sufficient to pay the outstanding expenses, then very few members showed up at the meeting. Sometimes no more than four members were in attendance. The only one who regretted this small attendance was the secretary-treasurer, as he was retained in office for 22 years, C. O. Brownell.

But not every meeting was so harmonious. When it became necessary to replace a separator or engine, the interest at the meeting was high. Sometimes, the active stockholders who wanted to use the outfit to thresh grain had to assess themselves to pay for whatever was needed. Some who had gone into other occupations and were no longer threshing could not be expected to pay an assessment. In order to continue the threshing company in 1925, a new separator was needed, and seven stockholders each added $200 to the treasury. In previous years, they had paid smaller amounts.

The first separator was made entirely of wood. A sacker was attached to the machine, and the grain was collected in bags as it came from the separator. The men placed the bags on their shoulders and carried them to the granary. In 1919, an elevator was purchased. A gasoline engine provided the power to run it, and the grain was elevated into the granary. This was a great improvement.

The number of stockholders varied from time to time. So did the value of the shares. It was never intended that large fortunes should be made. The only purpose for which they united was accomplished. Each member had a reasonable assurance that his grain would be threshed within a short period of time. Each man had to learn to give as well as take. Without combined effort from all of them, the machine would not be any good to anyone. Community spirit prevailed. The shareholders were considerate of each other and when new people moved into the neighborhood, their threshing was done also.

Through more than fifty years a large number of people had their grain threshed, or were helpers or stockholders or operators. One cannot begin to name all of them, but one individual, George Hall from Rose Creek, stands out as being unique to this neighborhood. He served as the engineer for many years and was totally dedicated to his job and tried to make the Enterprise Threshing Company the best there ever was. George stayed overnight at each home where threshing was to be done the following day. He would rise before dawn, build his fire and have steam ready to run the threshing machine when the farmers forked grain into the separator. Very rarely was the power in short supply if George was on duty.

In the early years, stack threshing was done, and ten teams of horses brought wagonloads of bundles from the fields. The gigantic loads were a sight to behold. The men had acquired a skill for loading bit by bit with the heads of the bundles turned to the center of the wagon and the butts shaped up the outside. Building a load required skill, and no bundles fell to the ground if the load was built correctly.

It was hard work. This crew was determined to build the tallest most perfect loads in the entire farming area in the county and perhaps the state. In the 1940s, Austin residents followed along County Road 4 and parked their cars beside the road to watch the men load and observe grain going through the threshing process.

In about 1920, a big change was made. The steam engine was replaced with a tractor. A Hart Parr tractor was purchased. Gasoline cost 10 cents a gallon. Interest in threshing machines decreased when the pull type combines came into prominence. In 1951, there were only five farmers interested in threshing this way. When Carleton Sayles decided to buy a combine, the four remaining farmers decided it was wise to discontinue threshing, and Julius Schottler, Ed Schottler, David Sayles and Adolph Mueller each invested in a combine of their own.

People celebrate fifty years of life. But the Enterprise Threshing machine was too worn out to celebrate. The organization was dissolved in 1957. Notices of dissolution were sent to all who were shareholders at this time. The shareholders included Claude Sayles, Carleton Sayles, David Sayles, Raymond Sayles, Julius Schottler, Adolph Mueller, Edward Schottler, Mrs. Charles Ulland, Irene Hart, Viola Voight and J. S. Schottler, the only charter member living at this time.

Threshing

Both sets of Shirley's grandparents lived in Mower County. Shirley attended Enterprise School, graduated from AHS, and worked at the library for 23 years.

The Playground in My Mind
By Iris M. Hansen

In the early 1970s, when I was raising three small boys, there was a popular song, "Playground in My Mind." My children loved that song because it had a simple melody and words that were easy for them to understand and sing. I loved that song too, as it brought back wonderful memories of when I was a little girl growing up in Austin. I recently purchased a CD with that song, and once again those memories came flooding back.

My playground was Dreisner Park. Every summer the Park and Recreation Department sponsored a structured program for all of the kids in Austin. We would go to our neighborhood parks, where life-long lessons awaited us. We discovered that the park wasn't just a place to play, but it was also a land of learning.

Our teacher was the park leader, a high school girl who was grateful to have a summer job. She arrived every morning carrying a folder containing projects, a set of keys to the box of park equipment, and a chain around her neck made out of a material called gimp, with a whistle on it. Even though she was a young girl herself, she was a kind adult to me. In short, I idolized her, and my goal was to be an assistant park leader and wear that whistle.

Our typical day at the park consisted of making crafts, singing songs, playing games, running races, telling stories and cleaning up the park. There were also special events, one of which was our talent show. All of us chose exactly what we thought would wow our parents when they came to our big performance, Talent Night. After our show we all voted for the three best performers. The winners went on to audition for the citywide competition for the talent show held at Marcusen Park after the Hobo Gypsy Parade.

I will never forget how proud I was of my older sister when she won in the talent show. She performed a duet with her best friend. Her costume consisted of a pair of striped flannel pajamas with a man's straw hat on her head and a cane in her hand. She sang "Yes Sir, That's My Baby." Her best friend was dressed up in an old flapper dress and sang "Five Foot Two, Eyes of Blue." I was not surprised when she and her friend were chosen to perform in the talent show at Marcusen Park.

The Hobo Gypsy Parade was also a special event. All the kids from their neighborhood parks dressed up like hobos and gypsies. We would then march in the parade behind the banner identifying our park. A committee from the city picked the best hobo costume and the best gypsy costume. The lucky winners won brand new bikes.

As an adult, I understand that our park leader and the Park and Recreation Department may not have realized that the projects they helped us with were life lessons. The Park and Recreation Department trained a young girl to entertain and keep children in the park busy.

I hope all of those women who were park leaders and the administration of the Park and Recreation Department realize the impact they had on our young minds and what a gift they were to all of us. The life lessons they taught us were: 1. You can be whatever you want to be – an artist, an athlete, a dancer or a singer. 2. Be fair and be happy for your friends when they win, even when they are competing against you. 3. Respect each other and always clean up your mess. And the most important life lesson for me was: 4. You too can make a difference in your community and in the lives of the most impressionable by living these life lessons that were given to you.

Todd Park robot slide

The Oldest Fraternal Organization in Austin
By Larry Hanson

The histories of Austin and Fidelity Lodge begin but a few years apart. The history of Austin begins in 1853 when Austin Nichols, on a hunting expedition along the Cedar River, reached the present site of the city of Austin. In his reminiscences he does not state where he spent the winter, but it is known that he drove his first claim stake in the vicinity June 8, 1854. One year later the settlement was laid out, and in 1856 it was regularly platted.

The history of Fidelity Lodge began in 1861 with a meeting in the office of the *Minnesota Courier,* the second newspaper published in Mower County. The first issue came off the press in December, 1860, when the present city was but a settlement of four hundred people and seven years before it was incorporated as a village. B.F. Jones, founder and editor, was a Mason.

The following announcement appeared March 20, 1861: "The Free and Accepted Masons residing in this county are requested to meet in the *Courier* office, Austin, on Saturday, the 6th day of April next, at 7 o'clock p.m., to take under consideration the propriety of establishing a lodge in this place. A general attendance of the Fraternity is solicited."

After the meeting, the *Courier* carried the following item: "The Brothers of the Mystic Tie will not forget the meeting of the Fraternity on Saturday evening."

On May 1, 1861, he reported: "At the meeting of the Fraternity on Saturday afternoon, the election of officers took place, and the preliminary steps taken to establish a lodge. On the 8th the officers will go to Albert Lea to get recommendation for a dispensation. The next meeting will be held in the *Courier* office on Thursday evening next at 7 o'clock. They have leased the hall now occupied by H.B. Kimball as a paint shop and will commence fixing it up the present week."

Dispensation to form a lodge did not arrive until late in November, 1861, and the first regular communication under dispensation was held December 5, 1861. In dim candlelight, eight men gathered around Austin's first Masonic altar. It consisted of a dry goods box, a borrowed Bible, a carpenter's compass, and a square made of tin. Not much of an altar, but it was fully as sacred to those eight men as our more elaborate altars are to us today. In the progress of the meeting, B.F. Jones was chosen Master. Others elected to positions were E.W. Ford, Abraham L. Lott, Oliver Somers, Charles H. Huntington, and E. Parliman. After some discussion it was decided that they should meet at six and one half o'clock p.m. on the first and third Thursdays of each month, and that the fees of the Lodge should be $20.

The lodge hall was above the paint shop of H.B. Kimball in a frame building located where the Armory now stands. The second floor was not finished. There were rough floorboards, no paper or plaster on the walls, and no curtains. Such was the Spartan atmosphere in which the first meetings were held. The brethren used newspapers for curtains while they held their meetings by flickering candlelight. They paid 25 cents a pound for candles, and the cost of illumination was not lowered until later when they began using lamps.

In the *Courier* January 12, 1862, we read of the business activities of the little city and of twelve business houses, which were in the course of construction. And, more important, that, "One large business house is being erected south of the Public Square to be used for law offices of Allen & Short, the upper of which will be occupied by the Free Masons as a Masonic Hall. The building is 28 by 30 feet."

At the second meeting held in January 1862, the first petitions for the three degrees were received from V.P. Lewis and R.O. Hunt. Lewis was a merchant on Main Street, and Hunt was a blacksmith with a shop just back of the present post office at 1st Avenue SE.

1865 was one of the really big years in the history of Masonry in Austin. In answer to their request, Minnesota Grand Master G.W. Prescott granted members of Fidelity Lodge a special election which February 1, 1865. The results were as follows: Oliver Somers, worshipful master, V.P. Lewis, senior warden, C.W. Sawyer, junior warden, E.D. Fenton, treasurer. and J.C. Smith, secretary. The Master Elect appointed C. C. Hunt, senior deacon, Allan Malison, junior deacon, Thomas Varco. Tyler; H.C. Huntington and A.S. Lott, stewards; and Smith R. Gunn, the first man to hold the office of chaplain in Fidelity Lodge. Since the Master Elect did not have the Past Master degree and as a result could not install officers, it was voted that he should proceed to St. Paul and receive the degree, and on February 15, 1865, officers were installed.

The first person to be elected to membership in 1888 was George Hirsch, one of the city's most prominent and well-known citizens. His first store was on the northwest corner of Maple and Main Streets, the present location of the People's Bakery. As the opportunity presented itself, he moved up the street until finally he erected his own building on the northeast corner of Main and Water Streets, formerly the site of the Davidson House. He was alderman from 1916 to 1918, and mayor for the term of 1918 to 1920 and again from 1922 to 1924.

The following were initiated December 27, 1888: H. Eugene Kearney, a locomotive engineer; J. Charles Scullen, a farmer at Oakland; George A. Hormel when he petitioned called himself a butcher and packer, and there can be no one in Austin who will not agree that he has proved himself to be a butcher and packer par excellence; William F. Kearns, a farmer near Moscow; John A. Harrison, a locomotive fireman, August Olson, an engine dispatcher; James R. Martin, a locomotive fireman; Joseph E. Gilbert, a locomotive fireman; Newton S. Gordon, a printer, art owner and owner of the *Mower County Transcript*, one of the city's early newspapers; Theadon C. Harris, a farmer, George W. Bliss, a clerk in the law office of French and Wright; and William M. Crane, a clerk.

On March 8, 1902, the following article appeared in the *Austin Daily Herald*.

An event unparalleled in the history of Masonry draws attendance of nearly 500 Masons from all over the Northwest to Austin. Gov. Van Sant and Grand officers in attendance. Event closes with a fine banquet by the Eastern Star.

An event unequaled in this country, and probably the world, occurred in this city Friday night when six brothers, sons of the late David Aultfather, were made Masons by Fidelity Lodge Number 39, A.F. and A.M.

Such an event drew Masons from all over the country. Every train arriving in the city carried a load of Masons. Among the prominent Masons present was Gov. Van Sant when he is in the Lodge, for he was where all men meet upon the level. Excellent music was provided by a quartet composed of: J. J. Mitchell, Wm Crane, M. S. Detwiler, and J. S. Wood.

It was an imposing and impressive scene when the candidates were brought into the lodge to be raised to the degree of a Master Mason. Only those upon the square can realize the impression that was made on the great throng when six stalwart brothers were made Masons.

After the ceremony that lasted until 11 p.m., Brother Todd announced that the Eastern Star had prepared a repast to which the lodge and its guests were invited. A half hour later, a procession was formed, and the Masons marched to the armory, where one of the finest banquets ever served in this city awaited them. The tables were loaded down with lots of good things, and fifty ladies of the Eastern Star stood waiting for the signal to wait on their quests. As soon as the chairs were full, grace was said by Rev. Sommerville. After the 442 guests were through eating, cigars were lit and many speeches given. It was 1:45 a.m. when Governor Van Sant proposed three cheers for the ladies, which was given in a manner that shook the building.

The banquet was a spread that involved a lot of hard work, and the ladies are to be heartily congratulated. After the party broke up at the Armory, many returned to the Masonic Hall, where they enjoyed a social session. It was 7 in the morning when the last Mason left.

The 1902 armory was a hall located where the Brick Furniture Store now stands. Fidelity Lodge #39 has met since April 6, 1861 to the present with 145 years of continuous meetings.

Fidelity Lodge #39
Austin, Minnesota

March 7, 1902
7:30 p.m.

Larry Hanson is a retired building and heating contractor. Members of Fidelity Lodge #39 helped him compose this article.

Ellis Middle School
By Sydney Hataye

I love to learn, and what better place is there to learn that at Ellis. When you think of Ellis, you probably think it's just another school, but Ellis has been nearly destroyed by a fire, it was rebuilt, and it has been here in Austin for a long time. It's a great place for kids to learn and have fun, yet it has its rules like every school.

Ellis Middle School is important to me because when I was a student there, I had the chance to learn, to be with my friends, and have fun all at the same time. At times school can be a drag, but when you think and remember that it's helping you for the rest of your life, it makes it a little better. Ellis was my school, and I'm proud of it. We had great classes, teachers and more, and I'm just glad that I actually got to be a student at Ellis Middle School.

Our town has great educators, and if we didn't have Ellis Middle School, everyone would be crammed into Pacelli or Austin High School, and there would be quite a few more people without jobs. Austin gets pretty good Minnesota Comprehensive Assessment scores, and many students work hard to get those good scores and grades.

July 3, 1986 Ellis School Fire

In 1834, in Potsdam, New York, Allen V. Ellis was born. He was a schoolteacher, farmer, road miner, soldier, and adventurer. In 1857 he came to Austin, Minnesota. He bought about 800 acres of land over time and sold some to the Austin School District in 1948. In 1957, Ellis Middle School was built and named after him. A.V. Ellis' daughter, Gertrude Ellis Skinner, and her husband donated a sculpture called *The Burning Bush,* by John Rood, to the school.

On July 3, 1986, a fire started in the school. No one was sure what caused it, but they guessed it might have been a copier with a faulty light. The only parts of the building that were saved were the gyms, swimming pool, and the music area. It took about three years to rebuild the school, during which time the students and staff moved to the high school. Then in 1989 the middle school students and staff returned to the new and improved Ellis.

I believe that Ellis is a pretty amazing place with some very amazing people, staff, and students that work very hard day and night to get work done. It's an important place that I don't think the people of Austin could do well without. I'm proud to live here in Austin, I'm proud to have graduated from this school, and I know that it's important to many other people as well.

Sidney Hataye, who enjoys figure skating, will enter AHS in 2006.

Children gathered on bicycles to watch firemen battle the blaze.

Cow Eyes
By Kathryn Helle

I remember well the summer I met Dr. John Patten. I was a preteen in a predicament. School had just ended for the year, and summer fun was just beginning!

I lived on a farm south of Austin, on the infamous "River Road." Five sisters, a neighbor friend, the Cedar River, the curvy road, bikes and animals made my summers full of fun and discovery. It was Trixie that caused me to meet Dr. Patten, however.

Trixie was our large, red, family horse, and as gentle as a horse can be. Since she only liked to walk, and had to be coaxed into a faster gait, we were allowed to ride her without too much supervision. On this particular day, for a little variety, my two younger sisters and I decided that we should all three ride Trixie together.

Because we rode her with no saddle, there was plenty of room for all of us on her broad back. We figured that if the first person held on to her mane and reins, the second person held on to the first person and the reins or mane if they could reach them, and the third person just held on to the second person, we would be good to go! So youngest sister Carmie was put in the first position, Monie was boosted into the second, and I climbed into third. With a little click of our tongues and nudge of our feet, we began our ride.

It was a short ride. Something went awry. We all began to slide and soon toppled off. Trixie stopped, side-stepped around us, and stood waiting while we gathered ourselves up off the ground. Carmie and Monie popped right up, ready to give it a go again, but I laid there experiencing a vicious pain in my left arm. Mom and Dad were summoned.

It was a long ride, the ride to St. Olaf Hospital in Austin. On this ride, I did not welcome the charming twists and turns of the River Road, as my arm rebelled at each movement. Finally we were at the large, old, looming, mysterious hospital. My injury was diagnosed as a broken, dislocated shoulder.

Dr. John Patten was the artist who repaired my shoulder in surgery. When I awakened, I was surprised by my surroundings. I discovered a cast that wrapped around the upper part of my body, connected to my shoulder, and extended the length of my arm, which was pointed out to my side and held out by a sort of bar. I was in a bed, surrounded by a metal frame, from which a small trapeze hung. The bed was one of four in the room. It was the children's ward in the old hospital, which was like a house with a sun porch room with windows and a door facing west. The nurses wore white hats and uniforms, and visitors had to be 16 years old. After a few days' stay, thanks to Dr. Patten, my shoulder was proven to be on the mend, and I was released. My innovative mom designed a couple of unique, split-sided blouses for me to wear, and I resumed my summer activities with a little extra baggage.

One afternoon Mom and I were shopping on Main Street when a young boy stopped, stared and pointed at me in the cast contraption, and told his mom to "Look at her!" I wasn't bothered by his comment, however. I was much enamored with Dr. John Patten, the doctor who just weeks earlier said I had beautiful eyes—eyes like a Jersey cow!

Main Street Downtown Austin

Kathryn "Cow Eyes" Helle lives the rural life with her husband Jeff. They own the family farm on the River Road along 105.

Oh Boy... Lefse!
By Mable Hjelmen

It's that time again – the winter holidays. Thanksgiving is more than just another holiday. It, along with Christmas, is a time of many traditions to add to our thankfulness. The pilgrims, who started our Thanksgiving and brought Christmas with them too, did it in spite of the number of loved ones they lost during that first hard winter. The Norwegians who came and settled in this area brought with them the traditions of their old country. I married into a full-blooded Norwegian family. When Thanksgiving is close, there is always anticipation of lutefisk, and the menfolk don't think we could have one without the lefse.

Many people in this area are of Norwegian descent, and the holidays would not be the holidays without lefse. My mother-in-law remembers learning to make lefse with her older aunts, and I remember my sister-in-law and me learning to make it for our husbands and families. Now it falls to us to pass these traditions on to our children. My daughters are ready to learn, and my time has come to teach them. It happened in Auntie Goldie and Uncle Gordon's kitchen last week on the farm outside Blooming Prairie.

Lefse, for those few who might not know, is a traditional Norwegian delicacy for the holiday table. The men in the family insist upon having their lefse. When the lefse comes out, the kids will say, "Oh boy, lefse!" (at least mine do) and we will smile. They are almost as excited as they are with their gifts at Christmas. It helps if you have eaten lefse at Grandma's or one of the great aunt's houses. Is hubby pressing you to learn how to make it? Your turn will come. Count it a special privilege if you have been invited to join the aunts and grandmas in the kitchen at lefse-making time. My three daughters were excited, and so were the grown-ups.

Put your anxieties to rest. Learning this process is not so difficult. With special lefse griddles hot and special lefse rolling pins poised, the old-timers are ready to take you under their wings. The daughters and I and a boyfriend gathered for the occasion. We rotated around the table with various jobs to share the work. Rolling is done on a floured board with a covered rolling pin. The rolled pieces then are lifted onto the griddle with a flat stick.

The potatoes are boiled and put through the ricer and cooled the day before. There can be no lumps in these potatoes. Cooling ensures that they won't take on too much flour when they are rolled out. Forming the potatoes into golf-ball sized rounds is also done the night before. This gives uniform size when you are rolling your lefse. If there are any that don't come out right, of course they will be eaten by the workers, and they need to be tested anyway, we think.

If all goes well, the results are fantastic. The lefse must be thin, and jokes will be made about being able to read through it. It must be round and just the right size (a large dinner plate is a good measuring tool). It must also be very delicately browned. The addition of a token amount of white sugar will see to it that the lefse is lightly browned. This will be credited to each woman's recipe, also handed down from some other grandma or auntie. My recipe came from Great Aunt Hazel. These recipes are as cherished as the homemade turning sticks, made by the great-grandfather or some uncle. The turning stick my daughter uses was made for me by Uncle Gordon. This and the russet potatoes from his garden are his contribution to the family meal.

When the job is finished, we are all covered with flour, and the kitchen is full of the good smell of lefse. When cooled, it is divided into small stacks to be put away and kept under guard until Thanksgiving or Christmas comes, when it is brought to the table to be devoured by almost all.

Everything about lefse is traditional. Even the way it is eaten. One family may sprinkle brown sugar generously on it and eat it that way. Another may put cranberries on it, and yet another may put lutefisk on it, roll it up and eat it that way, with the butter dripping out. Now children will say once again, "Oh boy, lefse!" when the plate is brought to the table. Someday they will learn to make it and their children will say, "Oh boy, lefse!"

Mable Hjelman was born and raised in Austin. She has three daughters, nine grandchildren, and one great-grandchild. She is an on-call LPN at a nursing home. She enjoys spinning, weaving and writing.

A Famous Austin Building
By Mable Hjelmen

One of the most famous places in Austin, on one of the main streets in the city, is the Hormel Historic Home. Fifty years ago on June 2, I had my wedding reception there. It was a beautiful Saturday. There were already two wedding receptions in my church, so I had to find another place, and what a perfectly lovely place it was too, for an afternoon wedding reception. We took pictures in front of the living room fireplace. I have attended many functions there since that day, including spring luncheons, an open house honoring my friend who returned from a mission trip, and a Strawberry Lane fundraiser.

George Hormel purchased this building in 1901 and modernized it in 1902. The pillars were brought from Italy. It was originally a red brick building, purchased from Austin mayor and state senator John Cook, who built it in 1871. The Hormels had one son Jay, who was 11 when they moved into the home. Mrs. Hormel was interested in civic things. She was a schoolteacher, and the family went to church right next door at the Presbyterian Church, which burned down when I was in high school.

Between the time the Hormels lived there and the present, the Hormel Historic Home was the YWCA. The YWCA had its early meeting upstairs over a store, and when the Hormels moved to California in 1927, they donated their home. The YWCA moved out eventually, and the place became the Hormel Historic Home, and it is on the state registry of historic places.

I have been a member of the Hormel Historic Home and have attended a lot of functions there. It has been social headquarters for many women's groups, including Art and Travel, Floral Club, Austin Garden Club, Zonta, Degree of Honor, Milwaukee Women, Business Women Networking, League of Women Voters, Y Matrons, Women's Aglow Fellowship, Social Concerns, and various 500 and bridge groups. Once a month I meet in the Carriage House with our quilters group. From time to time we have lockins; we are there from six till midnight, if we can stay awake that long. We order pizza and act giddy as kids.

Girl Scouting has always been an important part of the Hormel Home, meeting in the remodeled Carriage House. During my high school years I attended a Girl Scout hayride. Later, when I was 20 years old, I helped Opal Smith lead a Girl Scout group, which also met there.

Changes are always happening in and about this famous old building. Two years ago I attended a shower honoring George and Lillian Hormel. George and Lillian would have loved the shower to replenish their kitchen. Attendees brought crock-pots, a toaster oven, microwave, dishtowels and many other items. Lunch is always a big thing with women and showers, and this was no exception. This shower is a fond memory. I look forward to many more years with the Hormel Historic Home.

The Hormel Historic Home

A Child Again, Just for Tonight
By Richard D. Hogan

Elizabeth Akers Allen wrote, "Backward, turn backward, O time in your flight. Make me a child again, just for tonight!" When I remember my childhood in Austin, so many warm and pleasant experiences come to mind. My hometown was a wonderful place to grow up. God has given us the gift of memory to relive those happy days so many decades ago.

Soon after class was over at the old Shaw School, I would make my way to the newspaper office of Ray Swain, perched on a hill behind Peck's Grocery and overlooking the viaduct. It was time to deliver the *Minneapolis Star*. My route began at Kenwood Avenue and continued down Park Avenue. I didn't enjoy the weekly collection time on Saturday, except at Christmas, when sometimes a customer would give us paperboys as much as a dollar tip.

Christmas time! Our house was within a block of the end of Park Avenue, which in those days hadn't yet expanded with the post-World War II additions to the west. As Christmas time neared and I came to the last few houses in Sterling addition, the sun had set and the typical Minnesota winter evenings were cold and snow-packed. The Streveling Farms had huge speakers that sounded out Christmas carols across the open fields. It was wonderful, and I would sing along with Carl Kehret's annual Advent gift to the community, and to a young paperboy. I doubt that those who broadcast the carols knew the joy they brought to one faithful listener, or that the memories would be so fondly remembered more than fifty years later.

Skinner's Hill, the lagoon and the band shell, taken from the east

Granny Visits Her Daughter and Austin
By Mary Hokanson

I step off the curb on Main Street. Traffic this time of the morning is light, so I quickly cross the street and step up to the sidewalk. Carefully watching my feet, as I have learned to do so as not to sprain an ankle, I brush my head into something swishy. Above my head is a startling display of fuchsia and purple flowers. Lush, full and healthy, the hanging plants dangle in the morning breeze.

Flowers are my first impression of Austin, where my daughter, Ann Hokanson, is director of the Austin Public Library. As I look down the street toward the library, I see baskets and baskets of flowers, each a turgid mass of color and vitality. I identify petunias, but those little tendrils, growing by inches right before my eyes, what are they? They are beautiful! They make the whole street seem cheerful and make me happier than I was seconds before.

The same potted flowers surround the library itself. I recognize a building that looks very similar to the Frank Lloyd Wright structures I have studied. Coming from a town a handful of miles from Taliesin in Spring Green, Wisconsin, I am very familiar with the Wright concepts. This building looks like the designer has been influenced by one of my favorite architects.

Inside, I immediately get a feeling of welcome. Though I am anxious to find my daughter, who is working today, I forget the reason for walking downtown to see her. I must check out the floor plan, wander through the spacious aisles and glance at book titles. I have to see how the flow continues to pull me into the comfortable surroundings.

My fingers touch the wood patina and the copper accents. My feet slide over a smooth—marble? Am I walking on a marble floor, and what kind of a design is that in the middle over there? Mentally I start a list of questions to ask Ann.

With my love of children and books, I gravitate to the children's section, and as usual, find the old-time books so much a part of my childhood. The edges of some are spread with usage and the cover illustrations blurred with age. Not far away are the new additions to my collection of favorites: the *Redwall* series, good old *Harry Potter,* and the striking, high-quality magazine, *Zoobooks*.

In the corner of the library is a fireplace. With the serene view of the pond, a thought of a glowing fire, and the knowledge of sure peaceful quiet, how on earth does the staff ever get people to leave at the day's closing! As for me, I must leave after setting a date with Ann for an afternoon adventure along with her son Ben and husband Peter.

Fishing in Cedar River is the project. At our house on 4th Street, we collect our gear for the fish hunt. More importantly for Ben, who does not really understand the idea of catching a real fish, we pack goodies for humans. Into a sack go a plastic carton of Cheerios and goldfish-shaped crackers. Another carton contains red grapes, apple slices, raisins and another jar with peanut butter.

Armed with bottles of water, mosquito spray, fishing poles, tackle box, jackets and sunglasses, we grab the dog leash and Simon, the big, black dog. Off we go. I walk with Simon; Pete and Ann act as llamas for the expedition, and Ben rides his new three-wheeler with all the skill of a first-time biker. The two-hour segment of time we scheduled may be enough for us to actually get to the river's edge. It should be a five-minute walk, but there is way too much to see, and part of the adventure is certainly just getting there.

River current brings floating debris just itching for a young boy to snare. Ben confiscates a big water-soaked stick and uses it as an exercise toy for Simon, who is busy sniffing every square inch of river walk. We settle down at our first spot we think most likely for successful fishing. Peter readies the fish pole while Ben devours half the goldfish crackers, some of the Cheerios, and eyes the water bottle. Ann baits the hook and tosses in the line. She picks out a mound of soft grass and arranges Ben on her lap. I pop a few grapes into my mouth and watch the bobber.

Not two minutes later, down goes the bobber! While Ben chases the last cracker around the bottom of the carton, the rest of us jump up yelling, "A fish! It's a fish!" All three adults are clueless as to how to land the fish. Since none of us thought we would actually hook or catch one, of course we have no net.

The pole bends as if we have a huge rubber tire or a submerged log. Pete and Ann encourage each other to "keep the tip up" as they take turns holding the pole until Ben can unravel his legs from the picnic supplies. He holds the pole and tries to see where the line enters the water. We do not know if he now gets the idea of "fishing" or not. All three of us help Ben land the fish.

It is a huge fish, the ugliest fish I have ever seen. The idea of eating such a terrible fish makes me nauseous. Ben is fascinated and enthralled with the size and the enormity of standing so close to an actual, alive fish. While I get my camera set up, Pete holds the fish up. Ben moves his head within inches of the gaping mouth. Picnic food long forgotten, Ben enters the world of true fisherman fantasy.

After the last ripple of the freed fish disappears, Ben reluctantly leaves his fishing hot spot, and we all head for home. Next on the agenda is something Grandpa and Granny dread. Ann tells us, "You must visit the SPAM Museum; you just must." Jim and I look at each other. I whisper, "How can we get out of this?" He says, "Let's just go and get it over with. She'll keep insisting until we see the darn thing."

With that positive attitude, we hit the museum with sneers plastered on our faces. Oh, well. It will be over in fifteen minutes, we can go have coffee in that cute place downtown and then lie about how long we were in the Hormel tourist trap that will probably cost a fortune to see. Two and a half hours later we leave the building. We grin, laugh, smile and wear our bright yellow SPAM hats.

The somewhat longer version of our tour: From within a darkened tent, a soldier appears. He tells us about life near the war front. Jim and I stand before him and feel like we are there with him. We move a little bit and read a letter from Eisenhower. He congratulates Hormel for the SPAM, but because they eat it so often, he wonders if anyone will ever eat it when they return stateside.

Jim and I remember our SPAM experiences. I begin to grin with the memory of the cold jell, the suck as the hunk of stuff frees itself from the oval can. I am 5 years old, not 67. Mother cuts it in thin slices. Dad eats it with relish. I cannot get by the gel goop. What? I miss what Jim just says. "We should buy a can. How long has it been since you tasted SPAM?" I wonder if I ever did and can't remember.

That night we don our SPAM hats and set up the video camera. Pete grills SPAM and puts crunchy, juicy slices on French bread. With the camera running, we bite into our SPAM sandwiches. I say, "This is good; this is really good! Wow, this is good! Why didn't Mother heat it up? There's no jell-goop here at all...this is good...is there any more?" It's all on tape, and that's the truth!

The Children Who Sit on the Boulders Reading
By Denyse Hompe

The new Austin Public Library had been built in 1996, and we were just getting things in place when we received an unexpected windfall in 1999 of nearly a million dollars from the estate of a bachelor farmer named Walter Wienke. The library board, under the guidance of head librarian Melissa Brechon, felt that there should be a tangible memorial dedicated to Mr. Wienke, and a piece of sculpture was suggested.

The project was turned over to the art committee that consisted of library board members Judi Bergen and myself, library secretary Jeanne Steinbrink, and Jim Wegner, art teacher at Riverland College. Then the search began. Carmen Tribbett, wife of board member Ken Tribbett, suggested sculptor Dennis Smith of Utah, who had created the bronze sculpture, *Once Upon a Time*. The art committee was satisfied that this figurative bronze sculpture of a girl reading to her brother was the best choice to help commemorate the Wienke gift and to serve as a lasting tribute to him. The library board commissioned the work in the fall for spring delivery.

The art committee felt a boulder native to the area would be a good choice for the base of the sculpture. Jeanne's maiden name was Gerber, and she grew up on a farm just outside Adams. A stream ran through acres of oak pasture at the back of the farm where she played as a child. The pasture had lots of very large boulders that had been harvested from the farm fields, and we thought some might be ideal bases for the statues of the children. As a group, the art committee went out to the farm in the fall to look and found two boulders that we felt might work. Since the statues had been ordered but would not get here until the next spring, Jeanne's brother Mark, who now owned the family farm, said he would move the boulders up to the edge of the cornfield until they were needed.

Spring came, and so did the bronze children—life size. One beautiful spring morning in May, the committee set out again for Adams to match them to their boulder bases. Since the bronze statutes were too heavy to maneuver into a regular car door or trunk, Jeanne put the top down on her red convertible, latched them in with seat belts and off to the farm we went. It took awhile to find the chosen boulders in the tall spring grass. Once they were located, the sculptures were placed on the boulders, and the young girl fit perfectly on her base. On the longer, lower rock the young boy was placed, and he too would be perfect with minor adjustments. We hired Jeff Anderson, award winning cemetery marker designer, to tow the boulders from the Adams farm to the Austin Public Library. The boulders were "glacial erratica" and quite heavy. When they were hoisted onto the truck, the flatbed strained under their weight.

The art committee chose the cove between the front of the new library and the arbor along the brick walkway as the permanent site of the bronze statues. Jeff hired a "master-of-his-craft" crane operator who carefully lifted each of the boulders over the wooden arbor and gently set them in place. With approval of the board, Jeff then drilled anchor holes into the boulders and attached the children firmly in place. It should have been filmed; it was such an example of skill. Spotlights were added to shine on them at night and wild grasses and flowers were added to create a prairie look, in keeping with the design of the building.

Once Upon a Time, by sculptor Dennis Smith

Denyse Hompe was born in New Hampshire and studied art in Boston. She and her husband moved to Austin from Saginaw, Michigan and raised five children.

Whittier School in the 1940s
By Polly Jelinek

There it was, Whittier School, the "big" school, just across the street from the apartment house I lived in. I had been waiting to go there for years...almost six of them, because my birthday was in January.

There it stood, the brick building, waiting as it had for years, for classes to start. It was originally three stories high, with four classrooms. A double door entrance on the ground level of the east side opened up to a huge double wide wooden stairwell that led to the large first floor landing, where there was a classroom to each side of the stairwell. The stairs split at the landing, and the stairwell curved around to single sets of stairs leading up to a mezzanine area. The mezzanine had a large window on the east, and cupboards on that wall. A wide double stairway then continued up to the two classrooms on the top floor.

Each classroom had cloak halls on the west, one for boys and one for girls. On the top floor, there was a small stairway that led up to a principal's room, which had windows all across the front and a window looking east. As you came in the wide front doors on the east side, there were doors on both sides, where you could turn and go down a short flight of stairs to girls' lavatories. On the north side you could go down a flight of stairs to a boys' lavatory and the school basement.

Later four classrooms were added to the west side. These classrooms had metal lockers at the back, and there was a stock room on the first floor and a nurse's room on the second floor. They also added a new gymnasium to the north, which was reached by going down a set of wide wooden steps similar to those at the east entrance. It also had a separate entrance on the east. There were water fountains in strategic places, especially outside the gym doors. They added a small kitchen area, between the gym and the school proper, and there was a stairwell to the restroom areas. Years later a kindergarten room was added to the east side of the gymnasium.

I was on needles and pins just getting to go up the back stairs of the school, turn right, walk past the stock room into the kindergarten room. What fun, my friends were there, and it would be so much fun learning. My biggest hurdle was to keep quiet. I was a constant talker so I spent much time behind the piano in the corner, learning to be quiet.

The teacher finally put me in the stockroom with all the school supplies to see if I could learn to be quiet. It was quite interesting in there with all the colored paper, glue, paste, scissors, pencils, and all that good stuff. Consequently, I grew bored all by myself, and being a very creative child, I took a pair of scissors and cut the edges of the colored paper as far as I could reach, and it was so much fun to open a big jar of paste, stand on a stool, and paste paper together, as far as I could reach. Stapling other things together was fun too.

The year progressed, and I must have learned some control, as I don't remember other opportunities to express myself so creatively. Visiting Miss Daily in the principal's office a couple of times helped me learn about being a good listener. Everything was just going along dandy when Easter came around, and we were to color baskets with eggs, grass, and other goodies in them. I finished mine, and was waiting for the rest of the class to finish when I started to think about my grandma's neighborhood grocery store, just across the street, and the baskets she had on display there. Each was wrapped in some cellophane wrap and tied with a big bow, so I proceeded to draw the yellow wrap around my basket, and a great big bow on the top. When the teacher saw what I had done to my color sheet, she immediately grabbed it, crumpled it, and threw it in the wastebasket. Again my creativity was thwarted.

I must have managed to complete the rest of the year okay, as I was promoted to first grade. Maybe she just couldn't handle having me around for another year. First grade was just great. Miss Quigg believed in children being creative. We had a play area, and she had us take the furniture outside on the sidewalk and paint it. We drew illustrations to put on the bulletin boards instead of coloring dittoed sheets. We wrote and presented a shadow play for other students and our parents and lots of other fun stuff. My only embarrassing moment was when we made visits to each child's home. When it was my day, I completely forgot that I left my nightgown hanging on the doorknob. It was still there when the class came to visit.

Another funny thing that happened was that one of the boys in my class, Fred Requa, came down with chicken pox. His mother felt so bad that many of us caught it from him that she brought each of us a bottle of calamine lotion.

We learned to read, write, and do math, along with fun things in social studies and science. I really liked reading, and have had my nose in a book ever since. My mother always said the house could have burned down around me, and I wouldn't have noticed until the pages of the book I was reading caught fire.

Miss Quigg must really have liked me, or nobody else wanted me, as I was in her room the following year as a second grader. I was allowed to go up to the hallowed ground of Miss Rupner after school to join a class learning to knit afghans to send to the Army hospitals for soldiers who were injured while fighting in World War II. Miss Rupner stitched a piece of cloth on each afghan telling where it had come from, and when I was in junior high school, they read thank-you letters from some of the GIs who received them. She also made each of the knitters a cute little knitted mitten cuff, knitted with tooth picks, that had a small safety pin attached to the back, so we could wear them identifying us as part of the after school knitting club.

Second grade must have gone very well. Reading again was my favorite pastime. At the end of the year, Miss Quigg put books on the ledge around the chalkboard, and we each got to pick a book to have for our very own. I have mine in the bookcase yet.

Third grade with Miss Baxter went great. She encouraged independence and creativity. We learned to do cursive handwriting, and were encouraged to show it off in all the creative writing we did.

In fourth grade, I got sent to the principal's room, and boy, did I have to practice being good. Every time I tried anything I seemed to get noticed. When I bit that kid on the hand, I just said he put his hand in my mouth, and he didn't disagree. Maybe he had a crush on me? But the next time, I tore the shirt off his back, and he ran home and changed it before he came back to class. Miss Daily was a teaching principal, and used her office for a variety of things. We went there for special reading classes, play practice, and other activities that involved small group work. The principal practiced loving discipline here.

We read from the *Allison Wesely Readers* great adventure stories, with sketches of tools the pioneers or sailors used, as well as folklore and stories from around the world. We could draw items for our own stories that went with the topic we were reading about. They were really great. Even now when I am volunteering in the old schoolhouse on the fairgrounds during fair week, people will ask about those books, and we get them off the shelves and share memories. Reading was still my favorite thing to do, and my friends and I would get together on Saturday afternoons and have reading parties. I believe these years introduced me to the joys of history, and wanting to know more about family beginnings, as well as local history.

Oh, the years of student council work! On Fridays, we could bring money to buy defense stamps, and student council representatives would sit at a table on the mezzanine and sell them to students. It was fun to buy a few stamps each week, and then paste them in your stamp book until you had enough to take to the post office or bank to get a defense bond. Just $18.95 worth of defense stamps would earn $25 in ten years, and that was a bundle to us in those days.

We had great big scrap drives and paper drives to raise money for defense. There would be a huge snow fence stretched into a circle on the south side of the school, and everybody dragged in all the old scrap metal they could find, and it would be sold for the defense effort. I remember bringing the cans of grease that were saved from cooking for the defense effort too. We filled Red Cross boxes each year to send to children overseas in war-torn countries. Pencils, toothbrushes, toothpaste, combs, hankies, erasers, small tablets, bars of soap, and washrags were many of the items sent. Pen pals across the nation and overseas were established, and their letters were shared with the whole class, and the different stamps admired.

Whittier was located in a diversified and integrated area. We had a melting pot of students and were instilled with values that made us one big family. During the war many military families came back home to live, and there were families from other parts of the nation whose families came to our city for employment. One boy came with this family of migrant workers from out West. He came the first day, barefoot and in bib overalls. Miss Daily knew all about him, and she knew he had a very good singing voice. On that first day, she had each student tell one thing they thought was special about themselves. When it was his turn, she had him sing for the class, and we were all amazed at his beautiful voice. We had him sing for us again and again over the year.

We were very privileged to have Miss Harriet Nordholm for our music teacher, and Mr. Stan Whittmore for our art classes. Exposure to the arts whetted our appetites for the arts, and the experiences we shared became lifelong enjoyments.

During the war, down by Lafayette Park, where the ballpark is now, we planted Victory gardens. Each spring the ground would be plowed up and made into plots, and we would walk down there and plant vegetable gardens. Every week we would weed them, and make sure they were growing fine. Then in the summer we were on our own to take care of them, and our families could enjoy the vegetables we grew.

Parents had monthly PTA meetings in the afternoons, and some were in the evening, but they always had a program, and each month different grades put it on. The favorite was the Christmas one, where the whole school participated. We sang songs, did poems and skits, and the grand finale was the telling of the Christmas story. When they acted out the story, all the characters and singers came down the stairs on the way to the stage in the gym, singing all the way. There was this big stage at one end, and chairs were set up with a middle aisle all the way to the stage. The students all paraded in for their parts of the program and then sat on the floor right in front of the stage to watch the rest of the pageant. Santa handed out treats at the end.

Another fun thing the parents did was have a candy and bake sale. They put up tables all around the gym, and the students came down by the classroom to look and buy, our hands full of pennies on the way in and bags of goodies on the way out. For Mother's Day the parents sponsored a special program for their meeting. Students sang, recited, and did skits, but the most fun was that the dads, wearing fancy aprons, prepared and served a pancake supper to everyone.

We started many days by all going out to the front of the school and standing in the semicircular driveway to say the pledge, followed by a patriotic song. We would file back into the school ready to start the day's work. As this was during the war, Mr. Bloom, the custodian, always made a big ceremony of raising the flag when we all got out there, and at the end of the day we saw him do the ceremony of lowering the flag and folding it up.

On the last days of school, we brought lunches and walked down to Lafayette Park for a picnic. The whole school shared the park with games, races, and all kinds of fun. At the end of the day a tired bunch walked back to school. One of the most exciting parts of going to the park was that we got to go over the swinging bridge on old Franklin Street twice. We had to stop and wait for it to settle down before another group could cross over. It was enjoyable to see the parents watching us from the doors of their houses as we walked by.

For fifth grade, I had Miss Rupner, said to be the strictest teacher ever. With the Whittier crew, she probably earned her salary many times over, and those gray hairs. She started out very strict, but as the year went on, she mellowed, or we shaped up. What a great year! In the winter we watched the birds on the feeders outside the window and wrote reports on them. If a bird would hit the window, Miss Rupner would go and get it, and bring it into the classroom and show and tell us about it. We studied about pioneers in the United States, made reports, and did pioneer projects like making candles, carding wool, knitting, and other crafts. We learned to square dance and do other pioneer activities. At the end of our study, we walked over to Shaw School and shared all our learning with the fifth graders there, and Miss Beck's class came over to Whittier and shared some of their projects with us.

My favorite sharing was a science unit. We all brought old electrical appliances to school, and proceeded to take them apart. We drew all the parts and wrote down how they worked. We made different posters to go with them. We walked over to Shaw one day carrying all this stuff with us, and then shared it with those students. The school system sponsored a play for all the elementary schools to attend at the high school auditorium. There was always this big giraffe's head that came out in between the curtains to entertain us before, during breaks and after the play. Its name was Jo-Jo the Giraffe. This was a great time for us to see all the kids from the Austin schools having fun together.

Apparently I didn't lose all my creativity by fifth grade, because I asked Miss Rupner why girls couldn't be school patrol guards. She told me if I could get three other girls to share the four corners it would be possible. So, the next morning when school started, I asked for volunteers. Joanne Cummings and June Miller raised their hands, but no one else volunteered. I waited for awhile, and it looked like we wouldn't have enough, but just then Elvina Cafourek came in late, and I told her to quickly raise her hand. I counted out loud "1-2-3-4," and told Miss Rupner we had enough, and we were in. That spring at the patrol banquet at St. Olaf Lutheran Church there were four girls. Now you see girls on patrol at all the elementary schools.

I think I met my match in Miss Rupner. For some reason the parent group decided they would sponsor a picnic, but it would take place in the school gym with all the activities on the playground. I just decided I was not going to participate, but would go home for lunch that day. Miss Rupner found out, called my grandmother and had her prepare a lunch for me and send it over to school. Imagine my surprise when the teacher told us to line up for lunch with our lunches. When I got in line with my silly smirk, she just handed me that brown sack lunch, like it was no big deal. She was my favorite teacher, and I always tried to follow her example for dealing with children, and also her teaching style. It was my privilege to be able to student teach under her, and also be able to substitute for her in her classroom.

I began teaching in one-room country schools in Mower County, and then went into Elkton to teach during the great consolidation years, so when I finally came to Austin, it was a great thrill to begin my career here at Whittier School. Although I did not get Miss Rupner's old room, I did start in my old fourth grade classroom. It was a wonderful way to continue the art of teaching in the school where I received my fantastic background for learning, positive discipline, and facilitating others to learn. While there, we did many of the projects and ideas that I had learned, including knitting. I also had a knitting class after school, and one of the boys wanted to learn how to knit mittens so I had to learn to do it on four needles and show him how. Rose Daniels, who ran a little neighborhood store around the corner, would put some of the students' knitted projects on display, and she sold some of the items.

My mom and her siblings went to Whittier School. My grandmother was the first PTA president, and my brother and cousins and I also went there. After the school closed, it was used as the Austin Senior Citizens' Center, and after the center moved to Woodson School, Whittier was torn down, and the present Whittier Apartments were built on old South River Street, now 4th Street SE, near the Roosevelt Bridge.

Whittier School

Polly Jelinek retired after 50 years of teaching. Her family roots in Austin go back to 1858.

Fifth Generation Stories
By Polly Jelinek

Stories told over the years remain in the memory. Grandma Lillie told of when they moved south of Austin, where the Boys' Ranch is now, and she finished eighth grade in the country school nearby, the first Woodson School. The next winter, the snow was deep, and her older brother Daniel made a path through the snow all the way to the Franklin School, which was located where the Austin High School is today. Her family later moved next door to her uncle's residence, on the north side of the river by the Old South Bridge, where there were several businesses on their property.

There was the story about when her mother worked in a diner just off Main Street, between Alex Hirsch's men's store and where the Paramount Theatre is now. When it was noon, her uncle's dog would come over to the diner from the gun repair/roller rink store that he owned (where Thirsty's is now), get her uncle's lunch from my great grandmother, and carry it back to the gun shop to her uncle in a brown paper bag. It was a great big dog, and he is sitting in front of my great-great grandmother in her rocking chair in a photo I have in my living room. Beneath the photo sits the rocking chair.

Both my great-great grandfather Wait and my great grandfather Wiseman died in 1888, so my family became very matriarchal. My great-great grandmother came to live with her boys (the uncles), and my great grandmother purchased the land where the Boys' Ranch is today and lived there for several years. She sold the land to her son Daniel, and she moved near her brothers until her mother passed away. She had worked in various places such as the diner, and did home nursing; and then she came to the area near the old South Bridge and ran the grocery store there until her death. It became known as "Aunt Polly's," and she even had some merchandise marked with her name on it. When she died, my grandparents moved the store to the front porch of their home, which they had built right next door to the apartment complex of the uncles. My grandparents, especially my grandmother, operated it until 1953.

When she was 17, my grandmother, Lillie Wiseman, began teaching in the county schools. She taught at the Gregg School by Lyle, Woodson School near her old home (her great-great granddaughter will be attending kindergarten at the present day Woodson School). She taught at Sunnyside School east of Austin, where she and the students planted the pine trees that grew so tall on three sides of the school, and she also taught near Lansing, Sargeant, and Waltham. She was the temporary county superintendent while the regular one was on leave for a short time.

One time while she was teaching out by Lansing in the spring, the river was starting to flood, and as they crossed over a bridge, her suitcase almost floated away as she was being driven out to her boarding place. At Sargeant, her school was near the railroad, and the fellow she was going with worked for the railroad, and the train he was working on passed near the school during the afternoon. She always managed to have recess at about that time, so she could wave to him. He gave her a small locket with a pearl and two small stones in it that went on his watch fob. It is still in my jewelry case.

She kept a journal, and when I was about 16, I found it and read that she paid $8 for a hat, and she mentioned some other clothing she had purchased, a skirt, and a top. When I innocently mentioned how expensive clothes must have been then, she informed my mother that the journal must be returned immediately so I never did finish reading it.

She also mentioned that while teaching, she wore a small black apron over her skirt, and that they had celluloid cuffs to go over the sleeves of their blouses at their cuffs, so that they would not get all chalky or dirty, as they could not wash their clothes as often as we do. She also mentioned that at one school a little girl began to have a really bad body odor, so my grandmother had a lesson on personal hygiene, and mentioned that children should bathe and change underclothes every week. Well, this little girl came to my grandmother later, and said she couldn't do that, as her dad had sewed her into her long underwear in the fall, and she had to wear them until Christmas vacation when he would wash them. Since the girl's mother had passed away, my grandmother had a talk with him about personal hygiene, and the little girl did not have that problem anymore.

My grandmother was very open-minded about her students, and at one school she was teaching at, one of the school board members came at the beginning of the year, and started to tell her about the students, which were the good ones and which were the problem children. My grandmother told him she was able to determine that herself, and that she probably would not look at the previous behavior reports on the children for at least the first month. She never had any problems with students, and she even had immigrant boys who came when they were 18 and 19 to learn English. When I started teaching, I used this same technique of not looking at previous behaviors of students in years past, and this process proved very helpful to me too, in all of my years of teaching.

As my grandparents had built their home right next to the uncles' home, which later became the apartment house I grew up in, the family was very extended. As the years passed, the old chicken coop had living quarters added to it, and then other structures were added on to and combined to make a seven apartment building...but there were interesting additions as the buildings grew.

Over the years the building in front housed a tavern, called the Bloody Bucket, a dance hall with stabling for horses, a barbershop, a buggy repair and umbrella repair shop, a grocery store, and a place where a person could get documents handwritten in Spencerian script. There had been an old rug factory just behind the front house, which was converted into an apartment, and when the uncles closed the boat livery, it was attached to this rug factory building to make two more apartments.

When Aunt Polly, died, her daughter Lillie and her husband Lafayette Crandall converted the front porch area of their home into a storefront, and moved the grocery store over there, and it was open until 1953, about the time supermarkets started popping up in the town. Until that time there were about eight small neighborhood grocery stores within a ten block area, my grandparents having the most centrally located one just across the street from Whittier school.

In the early years, the Kolb Bakery operated out of a building next to Whittier School, and there was a shoe repair shop nearby. The building where the Boys' Ranch Store is now used to be a Singer Sewing Machine store with apartments over it, then it became all apartments, then Hi-Way Sales Furniture store and finally the Ranch Store. Beyond the back or east boundary line of the estate, was a bottling works or plant where Mr. Cummings made glass bottles. Later houses were built in this area and it was Peck Street.

About the time of the Depression in the 1930s, the WPA constructed the Roosevelt Bridge. My mom told of pulling bloodsuckers off my legs, as we would sit out in the yard and watch the bridge being built. Sometimes she said they lit a match and put it near the critter to get it to loosen up before they could pry it loose and toss it back in the river. Some the other projects done at this time were Todd Park, Wescott Field, East Side Lake, and the band shell.

Uncle Sim ran a boat livery on the shores of the Cedar River just north of the old South Bridge, which crossed the river on River Street. It was part of the old Red Ball trail leading to early Austin. The name Red Ball came from the way they marked the old trail posts with a red ball on the top to help early settlers keep to the trail.

Many early residents of Austin used to come down to the boat works to go for a boat ride on the river. Some fished, others took boats down to Lafayette Park to enjoy a picnic, or to attend the chautauqua, tent shows in the summer. There were tales of how during Prohibition the bootleggers would rent boats later in the evening and go out along the river to specified spots, and drop bottles of their merchandise in the river with a cork tied to a string. Early the next morning their customers would rent a boat and go pick up their merchandise.

Decoration Day was a very important day. Everyone went to the cemetery to decorate graves, and then attended the big parade that went down Main Street, with a family picnic afterwards. Looking at old family albums and talking about the family always followed our picnics. One story was about one of the uncles who was crippled. He always worried that no one would be around to put flowers on his grave. As the years went by, a wild bleeding heart plant was found growing on his grave.

Later in the summer we would have a family picnic. The oldest member, or the matriarch of the group, Aunt Rhodie, came to the park and sat in a special chair that was brought for her. She was a grand old lady with a full head of snowy white hair wearing a straw hat and sitting very stately in the chair. I remember an old folksong about an old lady named Aunt Rhodie and her goose...I always thought that song was written about her. After she died the picnics never seemed so well attended, and now the relatives are scattered to the winds.

When the Fourth of July came around, Uncle Clint had someone up at the crack of dawn to get the flag flying from its holder on the front porch, and at the first sign of the setting sun it was taken down and put away with ceremony. There were tales of the battles, especially those of the Civil War, when four of the uncles, as well as my great-grandfather and others, went with the First Minnesota Regiment. They told about the moonshine business in town, people pushing baby buggies with bottles of stuff besides milk tucked in with the babies, or the long hauls to La Crosse, which ended with some of the fellows going to Georgia as guests of the government on chain gangs. They told about kitchen sinks that had to have the traps changed after Prohibition was over.

During the tough days of the Depression, everyone you knew had popcorn and milk for Sunday supper, and they just added another handful of spaghetti or a cup of water to make the soup go farther if company stopped in at mealtime. Then came the big war, World War II, the draft, listening to the news reports, having the huge world map on the wall, and being able to locate all the places we heard about in the news. Every week the kids took their quarters or dimes to school to buy defense stamps to paste in the stamp books until they had filled the books up with enough stamps to go to the bank and buy a defense bond

Helping Grandma in the store was fun too…sacking up the eggs in paper bags and being careful not to break any of the twelve when you twisted the top of the bag shut. It wasn't much fun to have to dust the shelves and change the prices or the number of food stamps people needed to buy groceries. When the fellow from Fox Candy would deliver the candy and cigarettes to the store, Grandma would close up for an hour so that she could put a pack of cigarettes away for each of her regular customers, or those who had charge accounts before re-opening. When all the people who followed the Fox delivery truck came in and demanded to purchase some of the cigarettes they had seen delivered, she could run out of them very quickly.

There were so many students in our school during those years that students had to go to the high school for sixth grade. What an experience! There were grades K-12, plus the junior college, and the teacher training class all in one building. It really seemed huge. Junior and senior high seemed to fly by, with all the usual hubbub. Exciting events seemed just a part of growing up, and then those days culminated with graduation ceremonies. We were off to college and a new life style. I went to normal training, and what a misnomer that word was for me, a city girl going out to teach in a one-room rural school. But that is another story.

Aunt Polly's store

Woolworth's on Main
By Polly Jelinek

Oh, what a great day it was when the F. W. Woolworth store came to Austin. It was a glorified general store of pioneer days, with the grocery line. It was the place to go if you couldn't find an item. If it wasn't there, it wasn't anywhere.

The store, located in the 300 block of North Main Street, employed many of the young women of Austin. There were many opportunities for employment here. Clerks, office personnel, floorwalkers, stockroom help, managers and assistant managers were some of the options available. The brother of Gustav Borglam, who carved the four-faces national monument in South Dakota, was one of the managers of the Austin Store. As the years went on, some of the local stock boys became assistant managers, and then managers of stores of their own. Some of the clerks advanced to department heads, and there were opportunities for the office help to advance too.

Memories of the early store next to the Ford-Hopkins Drug Store are many. Seasonal promotions were a child's delight. The colored baby chicks to buy for Easter were always surrounded by "oohs and ahs" from spectators, and customers always noticed frosting decorations going on at another end of the counter, with names being inscribed on those delicious, large chocolate eggs. Other Easter fare included jelly beans, solid chocolate novelties, and those candy coated white center eggs.

Christmas brought all the candy canes, peppermints, stockings, stocking stuffers and toys on display around the four sides of the toy counter, enhanced by the lovely window displays. And of course, Santa was there to hear all the wishes of the children. I remember being able to buy alphabet stickers in little boxes to write names on your packages, as well as huge assortments of stickers, tags and cards, all on display on the huge counters.

Valentines could be bought individually from huge displays on the counter. I remember one of a huge carrot in overalls carrying a heart, which said, "I wouldn't carrot all if you would be my Valentine." Of course, there were all kinds there with the heart doilies, and heart stickers, and again the chocolate hearts that you could have someone's name written on, as well as all the other heart candy.

The regular candy counter at the store was a marvel in itself, a long counter with candy delights of all kinds, and you could buy them by the pound or the ounce--whatever your choice. They had chocolate-covered sea-foam, cherries, or crèmes-- the list goes on and on-- always weighed and sold in little white bags.

The cosmetic counter held delightful beauty products such as Tangee lipstick, Evening in Paris cologne, some of the rose waters, bay rum for the men, all kinds of powders, and rouges, nail polishes, emery boards, and that white stuff you put under the tips of the nails, because you left a half-moon at the cuticle and didn't paint to the outer edge of the nail, but put that white stuff under the nail.

Later years brought the machines that enabled you to stamp your name on billfolds, wallets and other merchandise. I even had a pair of shoes with a strap, and they engraved my name on the strap. Then, there was that big ice cream freezer that stood by the front entrance and held that three-colored ice cream sandwiched between those ice cream cone squares that sold for nine cents--my mouth just waters at the thought.

One of the most romantic things I remember about Woolworth's was waiting for my mom to get done with work on Friday nights. Near the double doors at the front of the store, at about ten minutes before 9, congregated a row of young gentlemen spreading across this area, all waiting for their dates to get done with work so they could go down to the Terp Ballroom for an evening of dancing and entertainment.

When the drugstore on the corner went out of business, Woolworth's expanded into that area with more good stuff. I can remember that along one wall was a counter just filled with books of all kinds that you could peruse and choose. Then came the move. The whole corner was demolished and a NEW store was built, involving the whole corner and the old store too. There was a lunch counter and booths along the windows to the east. The other departments were spaced around the store in a customer friendly pattern. There was a very neat record section, which carried all the top tunes, especially the 45s, and you could listen to them while waiting to purchase some.

There was a hobby section where customers could choose patterns for knitting, crocheting, and embroidery work, and often meet other crafters there to share patterns and chatter. Paint-by-Number kits were a favorite of this area, as were other crafts. A downstairs store was added with clothing and household goods, including lamps and some furniture, and a huge toy department. A pet shop that had chameleons, hamsters, birds, and fish with all the paraphernalia was located in the basement store. Sometimes a bird would escape from the cages, and pandemonium took over the entire store.

There was a checkout area at the base of the stairway. This stairway divided into two small stairways at the bottom and created a space for checkout there. On the main floor was a really neat back door. The Woolworth store just teemed with all kinds of items to entice even the most wary shopper. Housewares had all the equipment to supply cooking, baking, dining, and all the other needs. They even had a china pattern that could be found there. Clothing needs for all the family could be found in the basement store, and the cosmetic counter was a center for all ages. Jewelry abounded here too, and all the fashion choices were here, at five-and-ten-cent-store prices. Everything from shoe polish to toothpaste was available.

Ah, yes, they had a lunch counter where all kinds of yummy foods were offered. Those delicious hoagies, I never have found ones that could replace the taste of those, not to mention that delicious cheesecake they made. This was the place to eat lunch, have a coffee time with friends, and enjoy those delicious Friday night supper specials.

The first Crazy Days that they had in Austin were fun. Main Street was closed off, and all the stores put marked down and special sale items out on the street. The neatest thing about these early Crazy Days was that all the clerks came to work dressed in the craziest outfits they could find. The Woolworth crew were among the craziest attired clerks on the street.

The F. W. Woolworth Company was a good employer; good wages, stock opportunities, and retirement benefits were available to the workers. When the company closed, these stocks were transferred to the new organization, and are still paying profits to these workers.

The Woolworth Store was the center of town for many shoppers. This continued for many years while the store served the city and surrounding area. Now, the Woolworth store is gone but not forgotten, because the present Chamber of Commerce, and other community interest groups are located right in the old Woolworth building on Main Street, and you can walk in and remember the good times shared there, with the food counter in the same place, and you can still walk down the old staircase to the basement level. The sale of merchandise for the enhancement of life in Austin is not available, but the concept of a better life for the citizens of Austin is still the aim of the people in the building.

Cheesecake Served at F. W. Woolworth

One 3-ounce package of lemon flavored gelatin
One cup boiling water
One 8-ounce or three-3-ounce packages cream cheese (Philadelphia)
½ cup sugar
1 teaspoon. vanilla
1 large can whipped condensed milk (milk must be cold)
3 cups graham cracker crumbs
½ cup butter or margarine (melted)
Dissolve gelatin in boiling water. Chill until thickened. Cream together cheese, sugar, and vanilla. Add gelatin and blend well. Fold in stiffly whipped condensed milk (this can be done with electric mixer).
Crust:
Mix graham cracker crumbs and melted butter together.
Put 2/3 mixture in 9" x 13" x 2" pan.
Add filling and sprinkle with remaining crumbs.
Chill several hours or overnight.
For more lemon flavor add 3 tablespoons lemon juice

Ushered to a Better View
By Richard W. Johnson

It was the moviegoers who crowded the Austin Paramount Theatre in 1949 that compelled me to find them the best seats in the house. Sometimes lines would extend on Water Street east to the Tendermaid and west to Hirsch's Clothing on Main.

I was hired as an usher with the responsibility of making popcorn, selling candy, polishing brass rails and seating hundreds of patrons. Karl Lindstaedt, the manager, was a kindhearted man who was a pleasure to work for. I was 16 years old, and he employed me at 40 cents an hour. I dressed for the part, wearing slacks, a white shirt with bow tie, and a plaid sportcoat. I would carry a flashlight and usher moviegoers to their seats and watch for others to come. I was also responsible for making certain that nobody sneaked in the back exits.

My job came with a couple of perks, the first being that I could have free popcorn if I supplied my own small brown paper sack. The second benefit was that I had free access to other movie theatre shows that I could view on my own time. I was also given a couple of gifts that were priceless. It was here that I met my loving wife of over fifty years, Connie Reisinger. We say here at the Johnson home, "It all started at the Paramount!"

I also gained a bit of wisdom concerning the ability to stay focused on the task at hand. It was imperative that I face the doors and keep an eye out for those entering so I could usher them to their seats. Although this was in my job description, I was easily distracted and would often feel the draw of that big silver screen.

One night Mr. Lindstaedt caught me gawking at the feature film, and I felt his tap on my shoulder and a signal to follow him to the office, where he gave me a warning. "Richard, I didn't hire you to watch the movie, but to keep a watchful eye on the crowd." That admonition kept me in line for a couple of weeks, but it was not long before I was sliding back into my old ways. Along came Mr. Lindstaedt's guidance. Once again he tapped me on the shoulder, but this time he said that he needed my assistance in the entrance foyer. I followed immediately for I was more than willing to somehow make up for my negligence.

Mr. Lindstaedt asked me to help him move one of the oversized, red, throne-type chairs from the foyer. I followed his lead and was amazed that we were headed back into the theatre while the movie was not even half way finished. We set the chair up in the back, behind the last row of stationary seats. Mr. Lindstaedt then leaned over and whispered softly, "Take a seat here, and enjoy the rest of the movie." I felt my face glowing, along with what seemed to be the stare of many eyes now returning the glare of my earlier guiding flashlight. I sank and faded into the red throne, humbled and embarrassed.

I learned a lesson that night that has stuck with me through many decisions. The best seat in the house doesn't come without a price. I am thankful that I was ushered to that seat so I could see from another point of view.

The inside of the Paramount

Richard Johnson owned and operated R.W. Johnson Construction Company in Austin. Retired since 1995, he enjoys fishing.

The Square Deal Grocery
By Peggy McLaughlin Keener

Wallace Lee McLaughlin had an idea. Not just any little piddling idea, mind you, but a significant new way of doing business idea. What would it be like, he mused, if each time customers came into his grocery, they paid cash for their purchases right then, on the spot, instead of waiting to pay an entire thirty days' tally at the end of each month? The end-of-the-month-business was a slow, cumbersome way of conducting commerce.

Furthermore, what if customers carried their own groceries home instead of having him deliver them? Revolving around in his enterprising brain was the one promising answer to those two questions – "cash and carry."

With funds on hand every time of the month, Wallace conjectured he would be able to make more frequent and significantly larger purchases. Buying bigger lots of food at one time meant the producers' prices would go down. With Wallace paying less, this savings could be passed on to his customers. Glory hallelujah! Who wouldn't applaud such a concept? Certainly not the practical, money-wise folks of Austin.

If truth were told, Wallace already had established such a grocery business in Perry, Iowa. The store flourished under his cash and carry plan. Indeed, it was the first of its kind in the entire Midwest. The next step was to start a second such enterprise in Austin, one he would call The Square Deal.

Wallace McLaughlin liked the ring of that name, the honesty it imbued. Moreover, he sincerely had every intention of living up to its ethical promise, as well as bringing to his new community fair and affordable food prices. But first he had to explain his unconventional plan to the Austin public.

He introduced himself, along with his concept, in the *Austin Daily Herald*. He explained that his store was arranged in aisles where costumers could browse and select their own purchases, and he tried to sell them on the unseemly and socially suspicious idea of carrying home these purchases, another surefire way to save them and him money. As strange it seems now, customers used to call in their orders, and the grocer would fill and deliver them himself. Customers were not able to select exactly what they wanted. Now all that was about to change.

Austin Daily Herald, January 18, 1921

To the people of Austin and vicinity, we introduce ourselves to you as The Square Deal Self-Serve Grocery Co. A few words at this time may not be out of place. We came from Perry, Iowa, where our reputation for truth and accuracy is "good" and our financial standing is "just and fair." We are locating in Austin without friends and, bless you, without enemies.

We bought a small tract of land here in 1918, and from the first time we put our feet in Austin, we liked the town and the few people we met. We believe there is room here for a Self-Serve grocery store. We did not come in order to drive anyone out of business or to cut and slash prices below a legitimate profit. We believe that what is best for Austin is best for us.

The price of our groceries is based on a small margin of profit while relying on a large volume of business to make us money. Frankly speaking, we will figure on a profit of 10% on gross sales. The great volume of business we expect to do will enable us to sell groceries at amazingly low prices.

For example, in Perry, Iowa, a town of 5,000 people, our first month's business was only $4,000. Our sixteenth month's business showed that we sold over $16,000. Naturally, you ask how we did this. Our power in selling for on-the-spot-cash, no delivery, and no bad debts eliminates overhead expenses.

Volume is the whole story in our store as you wait on yourselves buying just what you want and no more. You carry your groceries to the cashier, pay for them, and carry them home. We do not have $1,000 tied up in a delivery automobile, nor do we have a $1200 a year man to drive it. Also, we do not have extra high priced clerks to sell you something you do not want. Our store must not carry an overhead of over 5%; sometimes 4%. Thus, you can figure on a saving of 10% with our system, which means annual business for us of $150,000, and a savings of $15,000, of which you will get the benefit.

Now a word about quality. We sell only advertised groceries. Whenever possible, you will find groceries of standard quality, and we will give you satisfaction. Don't worry, people. If you are not too proud to carry your groceries home, you will trade with us!

The article concluded with a note from someone at the newspaper: *Just a word about management. Mr. McLaughlin, the manager, you will find to be an honest and Christian gentleman. I cannot speak too highly of him, as in his previous home, where he was a resident for over thirty years; people agree he is a gentleman in every sense of the word. Truly! By Donaker of the Herald.*

The rest is history. The Square Deal Grocery opened in 1921 in the old Hormel Provisions Market at 404 North Main Street. Several years later, it moved across the street to 417 North Main Street, their location for the next thirty-some years. In approximately 1935, ownership was handed down to Gene McLaughlin, Wallace's son.

Grand Opening Advertisement – January 20, 1921

NO SUCH THING AS FREE DELIVERY

Every thinking person knows that each delivery costs the merchant a certain definite sum. To cover that cost, he must put a high price on his goods. People are fast breaking away from the idea that a lady or gentleman never carries a package. Market baskets will become numerous on the streets of Austin as housewives decide our type of marketing is more economical.

The Following Day's Advertisement:

Our cash registers at the close of our first day's business showed that 683 people of Austin and vicinity bought groceries at The Square Deal Grocery Store. The smallest purchase was 10 cents, the largest $12. This showing was very gratifying to us, and proves to the management one thing – the people from Austin and Minnesota are just like Iowa people. They ask – and demand – a Square Deal.

Our opening prices were our everyday prices, and we believe you will find our prices are always right and will give you a savings of at least 20%. It's certain you may look other places in Austin for lower prices on groceries, but we ask you now in fairness, why are the prices in Austin cheaper now than a week ago? Because we opened.

The words of encouragement we received yesterday from the people of Austin will ever be remembered. And, we thank you very, very kindly.

This photo reveals a store packed with inventory stoically stacked upon itself in long, impeccable rows. High above the canned goods are two shelves running the length of the store. Atop them is a variety of intricately woven, colorful shopping baskets. These, of course, were meant to entice shoppers into carrying their purchases home, thus saving them big money. If, that is, they could overcome the social stigma of hauling home the food themselves! You can see the shoppers were free to gather up their groceries rather than calling in their order on Wallace's two digit telephone number or handing a list over to be filled by a clerk. Wallace McLaughlin is standing on the far left.

Stock, which other merchants purchased in small amounts, Wallace now began ordering in bulk. The result was well received lower shelf prices for customers, as well as the anticipated profits for Wallace. With more cash on hand on a regular basis instead of all coming in at the end of the month, Wallace began buying whole railroad boxcars of food and household supplies, an unheard of procedure in 1921.

Time was to prove Wallace McLaughlin's theory right. In 1926, the advertisement in the _Austin Daily Herald_ for the fifth anniversary of Square Deal showed that prices had indeed gone down. Sugar (10 lbs) .60, Flour (49 lbs.) $2.45, Prunes (2 lbs.) .20, Raisins (1 lb.).10.

In 1931, ten years after the doors first opened, the following advertisement ran in The _Herald_. Even though an entire decade had passed along with the value of the dollar. The Square Deal prices continued to go down. Wallace was living up to his promise to the people of Austin. (By now his telephone had four digits.)

Sugar (10 lbs)	.50
Flour (49 lbs.)	1.45
Prunes (2 lbs.)	.15
Raisins (1 lb.)	.07

Additionally, there were fantastic bargains in the meat department:

Pigs feet (1 lb.)	.05
Pork hearts (1 lb.)	.05
Pork sausage (1 lb.)	.09
Spare ribs (1 lb.)	.11
Chicken (1 lb.)	.20
Pork Roast (1 lb)	.14
Fresh Oysters (1 qt.)	.55
Fancy young ducks	.20

Gosh, it makes you wonder what kind of deal you could have made on an unfancy, old duck. Notably, there is the historic part. The Square Deal played in the evolution of SPAM. You see, Jay Hormel was perplexed over the sagging sales of his spiced ham. What could be the problem with his product? It was indisputably superior to the spiced ham his competitors were producing. After much reflection, Mr. Hormel realized his product, at six pounds, was simply too large. If he wanted his spiced ham to sell, he determined, it would have to be a small, one-meal sized loaf. Twelve ounces sounded like the ideal weight, enough to feed a family of five with possibly leftovers for the next day.

The problem with his plan was that there was no twelve-ounce can. Furthermore, this can had to be distinctive, unlike anything already on the market. With that in mind, one of the Hormel technicians was sent on a can finding mission. He was directed to go to The Square Deal, where he walked the aisles diligently studying the merits of every can. Suddenly he spotted a Mazola oil display. Bingo! He liked the rounded corners, and even though the can was too tall, he could re-fashion it to accommodate the smaller chunk of meat, with the help of his tin snips.

That is exactly what he did. The rest is history. And, believe it or not, the SPAM Museum claims to have the actual first "Square Deal" SPAM can tucked away in its archives. While you're looking for it, you might also notice the impressive golden cash register that is displayed near the front door of the museum. That is the very cash register Wallace and Gene used from the day their store opened in 1921 until the day it closed in 1953. Whether it came with the Hormel Provisions Market building (which Wallace took over) or whether Wallace purchased it new for his Square Deal is another of life's mysteries.

During the Great Depression, the McLaughlins were keenly aware of the toll the ordeal was taking on its customers. They took seriously the plight of their shoppers, knowing no matter how hard the times, people had no choice about eating. And their customers were earnest in every sense of the word. Contrastingly entwined with the easily recognized pathos were also moments of unheralded patriotism when the folks of Austin mustered up their best heroic displays of allegiance to America and their president.

Just such a person approached Gene's counter one day with a fully loaded shopping basket yanking heavily on her arm. Her appearance was one of abject misery. A chalky, gray pallor stretched across the swollen puffiness of what had been recognizable cheekbones. Little was now left of the former contours. In their place slouched a striking resemblance to an aging Pillsbury dough girl.

Along with her groceries, the woman's bloated arms and hands proceeded to shift seven cakes of baker's yeast from her basket onto the counter. Alarmed at her physical state, Gene (always a master of diplomacy) inquired caringly as to her health. Then gazing at him through bleary, puffed eyes, the stricken woman proceeded to tell her tale.

On the radio, the dough girl had heard President Franklin Delano Roosevelt express concerns over the poor nutrition many Americans were getting as a result of difficult times. He elucidated on each person's need for healthy, balanced eating, and then went on to suggest numerous ways in which this could be accomplished. One piece of advice Roosevelt gave that day was that if everyone would eat a cake of yeast daily, their Vitamin B needs would be met.

Taking her president's concern and nutritional know-how to heart, this loyal citizen had followed FDR's instructions to the letter. Each day since hearing the broadcast, she had consumed the obligatory cake of yeast. And, with the setting of each sun, she had felt progressively worse.

Woefully she confided in Gene her strong doubts as to how much longer she could carry on this patriotic practice. Being a curious, yet compassionate young man, Gene probed further into the details of her most unfortunate plight. He suggested that together the two of them could scrutinize FDR's health plan. Possibly there was a flaw in it, or in her understanding of it.

Thereupon the woman recounted her president's words. Everything seemed to make sense. All, that is, until the work "cake" was further examined. It was then that Gene grasped what had gone amiss. The distressingly distended damsel had daily been consuming not the one-ounce cake of yeast that FDR had been talking about, but rather the one-pound cake!

For other customers, there was the problem of salmon. You see, back then the salmon was looked upon as a down-and-out sort of food, somewhere on the lower gastronomical level of its indigent cousin, the bean. Some of The Square Deal regulars had serious bouts of self-image consternation when it became necessary for them to painfully reveal the penury that these items revealed when laid upon the check-out counter for all to see. To make matters worse, the wooden counters had, before the Depression, been updated to a more glamorous Italian marble, such distinction only highlighting the salmon's lack of it.

Habitually these salmon phobic shoppers slipped their tall cans of fish, as inconspicuously as possible, onto the satiny marble surfaces, hoping beyond hope that no on was watching, in particular no one they knew.

One such patron was an incorrigibly haughty woman whose pride was way out of line with the current trying times as well as the state of her coin purse. Her bored, droopy little boy accompanied her. The woman guardedly looked at Gene as he rang up her three cans of the disreputable fish, then declared in a loud but tremulous voice making sure all those around her could hear, "And, of course, these are for the cat." This was just another day in the long but happy life of The Square Deal Grocery.

Kehret Family Farm
By Jerry Kehret

My memories of Austin center mostly around my father, Carl Kehret, his land, Crestwood Farm, his dairy farm, and his Streverling Guernsey Dairy. The dairy's original location was on a small hill, about 100 feet to the northeast of Banfield Elementary School. The house, barns, and dairy building site had a half-circle drive to and from Highway 16 West.

During a trip to Florida in the 1940s, Dad experienced the playing of Christmas carols over loudspeakers at a city square. He brought the idea back to Austin. After borrowing an amplifier and speaker from auctioneer Paul Hull, he set them up along with his manger scene along side the half-circle driveway. My mother counted cars, and averaging the number of people in the cars, estimated that several thousand people saw the manger scene display with carols in the first night, alone.

Where Sterling Shopping Center and Banfield School now stand was our cornfield. Barbed wire around the border of the Athletic Field kept my dad's purebred Guernsey dairy cattle off the field. Straight north across Highway 16 West, the pasture became the site of the First Baptist Church.

Mr. Banfield, a banker, owned the land from there to the west up to and past Turtle Creek, including Crestwood Farm. Mr. Banfield sold the Streverling Guernsey Dairy land (Dad was renting this portion) for the construction of the school that now bears his name. Dad built a new dairy plant a mile to the west of the original in about 1952, which still stands.

Before the houses between Banfield and Turtle Creek were built, Dad's Guernseys grazed there, fording Turtle Creek heading west up the hill to Dad's huge 70-foot high dairy barn to be milked. I don't remember how many hay bales Dad said the barn held, but the cupola held sixteen, meaning the barn was totally full, the rest being stacked outside and fed first. The land the dairy sits on and the land between it and Turtle Creek to the east of the dairy was all once part of a country club in the 1920s. Gypsies used to camp along the highway, and arrowheads and spear points have been found there, along with a lot of broken golf clubs!

A Fair to Remember
By Peg Kehret

From the time I was 8 years old until I got married, I lived on what was then South 6th Street, just a few blocks from the Mower County Fairgrounds. I tingled with excitement all during fair week as cars parked on my street, disgorging passengers who headed quickly toward the fairground's entrance. As a child, I sat on the curb in front of my house each night during the fair to watch the colorful bursts of fireworks that marked the end of the grandstand show.

Every year I went to the fair as often as I could. I enjoyed the animal exhibits, the home arts exhibits and the displays of fresh fruits and vegetables. Like every kid, I went on as many rides as I could afford. I especially liked the dizzying Tilt-a-Whirl, but it took all my courage to climb into the Ferris Wheel basket. I rode with my eyes squeezed shut, relieved when I stepped back on the ground. I tried my luck at the carnival games, too. Once I won a baby duck, which I carried home and set to swimming in the biggest container I could find, my mother's electric roaster. She was not pleased when she got home and found a live duck in her roaster.

Even more than the exhibits, rides, and games, I liked the food at the fair. The smells of sizzling burgers and onions competed for my attention with sweet taffy and fudge, making me ravenous before I got through the gate. For me, the fair was synonymous with eating, especially junk food that I didn't get any other time. I loved letting tufts of pink cotton candy melt on my tongue, and I always bought a bag or two of small donuts, which came warm and covered in powdered sugar. Fair food tastes better than other food; it even tastes better than the same food eaten anywhere else. My motto was, "One can never have too many pronto pups."

In the summer of 1950, the Austin Methodist Church had a booth at the Mower County Fair where the church members sold barbecued hamburgers, known as lushburgers. The Methodist Youth Fellowship was asked to help staff the lushburgers' booth, so I signed up to work one shift. When I got there I met the rest of the crew, one of whom was a tall, handsome boy who was about to start his senior year at Austin High School. His name was Carl Kehret.

When we finished our shift that night, Carl and I strolled around the fairgrounds, ostensibly to pick up discarded glass bottles to be turned in so our church group could collect the deposit. We did gather some bottles, but the real reason for our walk was to spend time alone together and start getting to know each other. That process would last for more than half a century. Surrounded by twinkling midway lights and excited shrieks from people on the rides, he took my hand as we walked. It was a good fit in his.

He led me to the cattle barn to show me the Guernsey cows that his family had brought for the competition. I knew nothing about cows, but was impressed that he got to sleep at the fairgrounds.

I went home that night with my head full of starshine, knowing I had met someone special. In the next few years, we had many dates-- movies at the Paramount Theatre, dances at the Terp Ballroom, bowling, Austin High School football and basketball games, concerts and plays. But our favorite times were the warm summer evenings when we returned to the Mower County Fair.

As soon as Carl graduated from the University of Minnesota, we got married, and two years later we moved to California. For the rest of his life Carl and I went to the fair together every summer, no matter where we lived. Hand in hand, we strolled fairgrounds in California and later Washington. While traveling, we attended fairs in Nebraska, Iowa, and Oregon. One year we went to the Oklahoma State Fair. Through the years, we ate a lot of fair food in many different states. As we munched "elephant ears" and admired intricate quilts and viewed gigantic pumpkins, we felt like teenagers again, back at the Mower County Fair, holding hands and anticipating a joyous future. We knew how lucky we were to have sold lushburgers together in Austin. We knew.

Carl died in 2004, but I still go to the fair every summer. I take one or more of my grandchildren and let them eat as much fair food as they want. We view the exhibits, always including the cattle barn. While they ride the roller coaster and throw darts at balloons, I smile, eat a scone, and let my thoughts float back to a long-ago fair in Austin, where memories of a good man and a good place live on.

Peg Kehret is an award-winning author of many books for young readers and adults, including **Small Steps, My Brother Made Me Do It,** *and* **Nightmare Mountain.**

The Old County Courthouse
By Betty Keller

The year was 1940. I had graduated from high school in 1939, and in the fall I went back to take a post grad course. In April I heard there was going to be an opening in the county treasurer's office; I applied and was hired. In those days they didn't call it "making a difference," but I realize now that is what I hoped to do. I felt honored to meet Mr. C. C. Terry, county treasurer, and I was pleased and proud to be hired as a clerk in his office. I remained at the treasurer's office for seven and a half years and retired as deputy treasurer. Mr. Terry remained at his post for many more years.

Austin residents, or those who remember, now call it the old courthouse. It was built in 1869, and it was the most beautiful, stately building in town. It had three floors, plus the basement. The very top of the building was crowned with an awesome dome, so beautiful it seemed to watch over the city. There was open work around the center and the birds, particularly the pigeons, called it home. At special times of the year, music poured from the dome, making it a magical place.

The east and west entrances were reached by climbing twenty stone steps. Inside there were marble floors, stately halls, and county offices opened all around it. The treasurer's office, where I worked with Mr. Terry, was on the main floor near the county assessor, county auditor, register of deeds and others.

I learned quickly that tax work and tax money were the backbone of the economy in Austin and Mower County. The assessor's office was given the task of assessing property owners of their responsibility, and the auditor's office informed the treasurer of the correct amount to collect from the property owners.

It was an awesome responsibility and one that everyone took very seriously. May and October were the busiest work months, of course, and we worked early and late, and I made many trips to the bank. The other ten months were very busy as well. The bookkeeping was all done by hand; there were no computers. We had huge ledgers that we worked in and a large vault to keep them in when the day was done. Some of the other officers of the court at that time were Mr. Sherman, clerk of court, Mr. George Jennings, register of deeds, Mr. C.M. Hubbard, county auditor, Mr. Carl Baudler, district judge and Mr. Ira Syck was the county sheriff.

The courtroom and auditor's office were on the second floor. There was a freestanding stairway between the first and second floor. The sheriff and his family lived in a large white house that stood where the Twin Towers building is now. The jail was located in the same building, directly behind his home, and his wife cooked for the inmates. At that time there were fewer problems and fewer prisoners, not more than six or seven at a time. The basement of the old courthouse housed the welfare department, and offices for the county commissioners, county health department, roads and bridges, and the agriculture extension.

I had a great teacher in Mr. Terry. A highly respected man, he set an example for everyone. I learned responsibility when handling taxpayers' money. I believed the monies collected, through tax assessment, helped to make our city and county a great place to live, just as it is today. A growing community cannot function without a strong tax base, and it was interesting to see how it all came together. I learned that every night before the books were put away, they had to balance to the penny, and what a great feeling to know they always did. All of us who were employed in the courthouse seemed to have the same sense of pride. We enjoyed each other, and I made many friends among my co-workers. A special friend to me at that time was Florence Vogel, a deputy treasurer; she is still my good friend to this day.

In the 1970s, the old county courthouse was torn down to make way for the present complex. It needed to be much larger to better serve the county. There were more departments to house and more employees to man departments, so change was needed. In the nearly sixty years since I worked there, government has expanded its role, but more than that, the population has increased greatly in the county. With the advent of computers and the technical age, the work is far different than when I worked in the treasurer's office. One thing that hasn't changed, though, is the responsibility of handling taxpayers' money with the utmost care and honesty.

In 1947, I married Howard Keller and became a wife and later on a mom. We have two children and like all moms and dads, we believe they are the very best. When the children were in high school, I went back into the work force as a teller at Northwest Bank, later changed to Norwest and now known as Wells Fargo Bank. I worked there for eighteen years, and it was a delight to meet customers who knew me from the old courthouse days.

I served on the Historical Committee Board for two years and for a time was on a committee called "Save the Dome." It was an attempt to preserve a bit of history, a memory of days gone by, when life was simpler. The old courthouse dome had been saved when the building was torn down in the 1970s. The plan was to showcase the dome in a special place, so generations to come would know the grandeur of one of Austin's most historic buildings that had once graced the city. Because a location could not be found, the project failed. The old county courthouse will remain a memory.

A postcard picturing the old courthouse

Betty Keller retired in 1980 from Norwest. She lives at the Oaks with her husband.

A Tribute to Some Wonderful Coaches
By Charlotte "Chuck" Keller

I have many wonderful memories of life in Austin. My husband Cliff and I came here to live in 1947. We were expecting our first child in 1948, and we felt confident that Austin would be the best place to work and raise a family. The beautiful parks, playgrounds with so many trees, beautiful churches, a thriving downtown with many stores and incredible schools awed us. Keith was born in 1948, Tim and Tom in 1949, Kevin in 1952 and Colin in 1956.

As our sons grew, we knew we had made the right choice, as there was a sense of belonging and camaraderie in the community for us, and the boys made excellent friends. We had already begun to make memories because we knew raising a family is a combined effort that involves home, school, friends, rules of conduct to live by, respect for each other and lots of laughter. The early years in Austin were full of opportunities for the boys. The five of them, early on, were inclined towards athletics, and they associated with kids who liked the same activities. Their home away from home, in the spring, summer and fall, was the Athletic Field. Summer sports were the best. There was always a baseball game and a team to hook up with, also there were dedicated volunteer coaches who organized and saw to it that every kid had a chance to play. What a gift to parents and one we took for granted. Fair play was the rule, and we, as parents, were always watchful that our boys would be good team players.

The specific memories I wish to tell about cover a span of fifteen years, 1960 to 1975. One by one our sons began a journey that took them through elementary, Ellis Junior High and Austin High School, and along the way they became athletes participating in football, baseball, track and basketball. My story is about the good men who coached them, taught them, and became their friends and ours. It is also about our sons and how they responded to the opportunities offered on the field, track, and in the gymnasium, all as part of Austin schools. It is a long overdue thank you for all the great leadership provided for Austin's youth. Some will say it was their job, but we say they went far beyond. It was a matter of loyalty, fun and responsible action, and all kids benefited.

The coaches I wish to recognize from Ellis Jr. High are Marv Kallenberger, John Steffen, Dick Lees, Chuck Prunty, and Bill Lloyd. At AHS there were Dick Seltz, Howie Strey, Art Hass, Al Lehrke, Oscar Haddorf, Larry Gilbertson, Hal Cuff, Don Fox and Ray Wescott. Ray was not a coach but served as principal, an incredibly gifted man. For fourteen non-stop years one or another of our sons came under the training and guidance of these men.

Life was good at the Keller home. School was important, and they loved learning. I commend the teachers in all of Austin's schools. You were the best, and when our sons graduated they were well prepared to attend any college they chose. It wasn't all athletics that helped them get their degrees in college; it was study habits and knowledge.

We learned the importance of parental support, whether it was at conferences in the classroom or sitting in the bleachers at every event, we were there. I remember a high school teacher telling me one time, "Of all the things parents can do for their kids, nothing is more important than being with them every step of the way." For us it was easy. We loved every minute of their school life, and we took great pride in their accomplishments.

In the span of years I have mentioned, the football stadium would always be filled to capacity, as public support was tremendous. Football was exciting, and the coaches during those years had winning teams with a lot of talent on the field. All five of our sons played the game, and four of them played for Art Hass, head coach. Art retired to become Athletic Director after a great many years at the helm, and Don Fox became head coach so Colin played for him. After Colin graduated and we no longer had anyone playing, we gave up our season tickets that we had held for fourteen years. We did so with regret. Austin sports had been such a major part of our life, but we concentrated more fully on the college games.

In Austin and in the Big Nine Conference, Dick Seltz and baseball went hand in hand. Year after year Austin Packer baseball teams excelled, and they won team and individual honors every season, much like the football teams. Keith, Tim and Tom were baseball players. Keith was a senior when Tom and Tim were juniors, which was exciting for us to watch. The games were played at Marcusen Park, and on a beautiful spring day there was nothing better.

Every coach wanted to win a state title as well as the Big Nine Conference title. Every year football, baseball and track teams consistently won their share, as well as many individual honors for the players. Colin followed Kevin in track participation. Both of them had their special events, and we were able to switch spring sports from baseball to track quite easily. It was exciting to see that kind of competition, and of course the track team was well coached by Larry Gilbertson and his staff. There is nothing like a warm spring afternoon watching your kids and their team run dashes, relays, jump high or low hurdles, pole vault, long jump and the list goes on. They worked as a team and yet individually each team member made his own mark and set his own records.

Rivalry between Big Nine schools was a healthy, fun part of sports. The student body, in their endeavor to make each contest a win, would come up with signs and slogans. Assemblies were held between games, and pep fests made an exciting atmosphere on game days. Cheerleaders and pep bands enhanced school spirit. Coaches and their staff were encouraging because they knew how important it was for the student body to be a part of the team. During our fifteen years, there was a bonfire on Thursday night before homecoming and a parade on the day of the game, as well as a homecoming queen and her court. The memories of those days are unforgettable, and we are forever thankful to the men and women of Austin schools who made it possible.

Athletics is not an easy vocation; it requires dedication, courage, endurance and loyalty. It requires training mentally and physically and a commitment to team play. The athlete has to learn how to lose graciously and then get up and try again. We are grateful that the men who coached our boys did an outstanding job of instilling in them the ability to congratulate the winner when they lost.

The parents of athletes are a special brand of people with a lot in common, not always worry free, but we wouldn't trade our role for anything. We worried about injuries, but we knew the coaches had the best interest of their athletes in mind and would try hard to keep them from harm. The best way to do that was to keep them in shape, and there was a strict regimen the kids followed. There were trainers watching over them, and in contact sports, a doctor would be on the sidelines.

Another concern parents had to deal with was the mental attitude of the player because so often there were missed goals, leg cramps, strikeouts and disappointments. The men who coached helped with that concern as well. Traveling to other schools was a highlight in competitive sports. Again we relied on our coaches to safeguard their travel, getting them to other cities safely. Since Austin was in the Big Nine Conference, cities were the same size and a fair distance away.

I want to share one special sports memory about each of my sons. When Keith was a senior, he received the Nat Goudy Award, named for an Austin coach. Tim ran the only touchdown in the Mankato game, thus helping the Packers earn #1 ranking in the state. Tom played solid baseball and hit doubles and singles in nearly every game he played. Kevin played halfback in one of the best high school games ever played in 1969 and helped the Packers defeat Albert Lea. When he was a senior, Colin received the Terry Larson Award for his outstanding football and track accomplishments. The award honored the memory of a young athlete who died of cancer during his junior year.

I believe Cliff and I are the luckiest parents, to have raised our sons in this city and at that time in the history of Austin. We were so fortunate to have had these experiences, to know the wonderful people we were surrounded by, and to have sons who, though far from perfect, were great kids. We are proud to have contributed to our community and very proud our sons contributed to sports and schools that gave them so much. The memories we are left with are the very best and we are forever grateful to all the good people who helped make them so.

We know that alone, one is limited as to what he can accomplish, but on a team that is well coached by men who care for the boys for whom they are responsible, boys with natural ability and a strong desire, the game well played is worth all the effort that goes into it.

Colin, Tom, Keith, Tim and Kevin Keller join their mom and dad to thank not only their Ellis and AHS athletic coaches, but all the coaches who made it happen for thousands of Austin boys and girls in their programs.

Fetching Rufus
By Kevin Kestner

When my brother Kraig and I were little boys about 4 and 5 years old, our parents moved us from our house out by the little town of Oakland to an old farmhouse near to the town of Austin. It was located on South Main Street, about a half mile south of the Sheriff's Boys' Ranch.

This house was situated near two gravel pits and three woods, and our pasture was adjacent to the Cedar River. The Sheriff's Boys' Ranch, at that time, was a place where thirty or forty boys ages 11 to 16 were kept. It was sort of a last chance stop before they went to a reformatory, a fancy word for teenager's prison. Many were the times when our parents told us to behave or we would end up at the Boys' Ranch! Right across the fence on the north side of our property were our nearest neighbors, the Getchell family.

The Getchells had three sons and a daughter that I knew of. Jim was the oldest, and he had about a hundred pigeons and about fifty horribly ugly ducks, called Muskogee ducks. Those ducks drove me batty. They used to waddle over to our lawn and poop all over our grass. In the summer I never wore shoes, so each time I went outside I would end up stepping in at least one or two piles of duck poop. Yuck! Few things are more disgusting than stepping in duck poop with bare feet.

One day I had stepped in one duck dropping too many, and it was like the straw that broke the camel's back. I went into the house and grabbed my trusty Daisy one-pump BB gun, and I then went duck hunting. I walked to the duck's favorite hideout, which happened to be our big pole shed. I went up to the nearest duck, pumped my BB gun and shot it in the back. The duck barely flinched due to all the feathers on its back. So I began shooting the duck in the head…the first ten or fifteen BBs didn't do much, but by the time I nailed it in the head for the twentieth time the duck finally keeled over.

With the murder of one of Jim Getchell's beloved ducks haunting me, I immediately did the next thing that occurred to me…I hid the evidence! I picked up my victim and carefully hid it from the view of the house as I walked south across the field toward the gravel pit. I crawled under the fence and went down to the bottom of the pit, where I dug a shallow grave and buried the poor duck. Then, as I was crawling under the barbed-wire fence to go back home, I was feeling rather guilty, and because I was preoccupied with my feelings of guilt, I didn't realize I wasn't all the way under the fence when I stood up. It ripped my shirt and put about a one-inch gash in my back. I eventually did tell Jim I killed his duck…about three years ago.

The other Getchell boy was Lee. One time Lee bet me a quarter I wouldn't chew up a horse turd. He didn't realize how much I valued a quarter at that time in my life. After I chewed it up he welched on the bet and refused to pay! Fortunately for me, his girlfriend gave me a quarter. I used that quarter for a purpose that exemplifies the meaning of the phrase "worth every sacrifice," when I rode my pony over to Petey's Drive-In and bought a 25-cent ice-cream cone.

Actually, they didn't have a 25-cent cone back in those days. The largest cone they sold was a 20-cent cone. When I asked the nice young girl to sell me a 25-cent cone, she said, "We don't make them that big anymore because they fall off." I told her to make me a 25-cent cone and that I'd be real careful. Little did she know what I had to do to get that quarter!

Right after I ordered my cone, my brother Kraig also ordered a 25-cent cone. He, however, had not heard the nice young girl's cautionary remark, and as he took his first lick, the whole top of the cone tumbled off onto the gravel drive out in front of Petey's! It had barely hit the ground when a big yellow dog stepped up and gobbled it right up. The nice young girl had mercy on Kraig and made him another cone.

The youngest Getchell boy was Donnie, and he had a cat named Rufus. I was the one who always got stuck cleaning up after Rufus. That cat was cute, but it had some kind of stomach disorder that made it vomit about three times a day. Each day when I went over to their house, Donnie would meet me at the door and ask if I would please clean up the pile of puke that Rufus had recently produced. I asked him why he didn't clean it up, and he said he had a weak stomach, and he was afraid he'd throw up. Do you know what the word "gullible" means? That's all right; neither did I, so I went ahead and cleaned up Rufus puke every day until they finally brought him to the vet. This brings me to my next story, "Fetching Rufus."

Patty Getchell was about three years older than I. She was the youngest of the Getchell children and the nicest. She had a fat Shetland pony like Kraig and I had, and we played together five days a week all summer long. One day Patty told us that we had to go fetch Rufus. I was wondering where he had been, as nearly a week had passed since the last time I cleaned up one of his messes. She said he had been at the vet, and we were going to fetch him on our ponies that day. What an adventure!

We took off heading north down the half mile of gravel Main Street until the road hit a tee at 23rd Ave SE. Then we took a left on 23rd and went west about another two hundred yards in the ditch on the trail. We were sailing along at a gallop when all of a sudden Coppy came to a screeching halt. We never rode horses with saddles in those days, and since I wasn't ready for her "unannounced" stop, I promptly flew in a perfect arc over her head (still clutching the reins in my hands) and landed on my butt in the middle of the trail.

I wasn't hurt, just sort of stunned. I wondered what had caused such an abrupt halt, so I turned around and looked to see Coppy with her head to the trail, happily munching on a pile of horse poop! And nobody had even bet her a quarter! Later I learned that sometimes horses will eat manure if they have worms; that's probably why she did it. That same scene happened two more times that summer until I caught on to her obsession with eating road apples.

Anyway, after Kraig and Patty stopped laughing, we started again on our journey to fetch Rufus. We crossed the road and entered a big woods, which I believe was the property of the Boys' Ranch. There were no roads in there, only horse trails. We knew the woods by heart because we spent about seven or eight hours every day playing in them. The trails were narrow with moist, black dirt.

On either side of the trail were tall grass and weeds…but mostly weeds. Some of them had long, stiff stalks that you could pull out as you rode by on your pony. The dirt would stick to the roots at the bottom, which added a little weight to the normally light weed, and then you could throw it like a spear about twenty or thirty feet. You had to be careful though; some of the weeds were itch weed! If you even let them brush against your leg as you rode by, your leg would itch for two days!

After traveling about a half mile through the woods we came to the Cedar River. It was mid-summer, and the river was at its normal shallow depth of about "knee-deep to a 7-year-old." The river was about forty yards wide where we crossed, but only a foot deep. After the river we rode through another half mile of woods until we finally emerged at Calvary Cemetery.

Patty's family was deeply superstitious so we never went into the cemetery with our ponies. I went to an abandoned cemetery in Whitewater State Park one time with my pony, and her hind legs collapsed the grave over a hundred-year-old coffin! No doubt the wood had all rotted away, and when we walked over it, both her back legs sank down about 18 inches as the ground caved in. Boy, did we get out of there fast!

Anyway, we never rode our ponies in that particular cemetery. After another mile of curvy streets in a newer growing subdivision called Austin Acres, we came to the vet clinic. Kraig and I stayed outside while Patty went inside to fetch Rufus. Rufus was orange and white and about halfway between kitten and cat. When Patty came out, she gave Rufus to me. I asked why I had to carry him. She said it was because it wasn't her cat; it was Donnie's cat. Once again I refer you to that word, "gullible."

So we left the vet clinic and started for home. Now before I go any further, I should explain that there are two things in this world that cats absolutely despise, and riding on top of Shetland ponies is one of them. In order to maintain control, I had to smush Rufus down on top of Coppy's back to keep him from exiting. With my other hand I had to hold the reins to steer Coppy in the way I wanted her to go.

Patty was in the lead with Kraig right behind her, and Rufus and I were in the rear. All went well until we got past the cemetery and reentered the woods. Patty decided it would be a great day for a race. We did that quite often, but she was forgetting (I think) that I was transporting aboard my horse a rather discontented kitten.

My pony was kind of a marvel. She hated to run…unless there was a race. Then she couldn't be held back until the race was over. Patty took off at a dead gallop, and so did Kraig. Even though I tried to hold her back with my one free hand, which wasn't enough, Coppy broke into a wild gallop. All may have gone well if they had slowed down for the river…but they didn't. Patty and Kraig crossed at full gallop, and Coppy was not about to be left behind.

This brings us to the other thing in this world that cats despise… water! When Coppy hit the edge of the river at a full gallop, you can imagine how high the water was splashing. Well, Rufus went bonkers! He immediately started looking for "higher ground." Due to my position at the moment, I was the "higher ground" he chose. With strength and determination of a thousand cats, Rufus clawed his way up my t-shirt, past my ear and up on top of my head, where he proceeded to dig all twenty of his claws into my scalp!

I wish I had video footage of that river crossing. It would win the grand prize on one of those funniest video shows. I crossed that river at full gallop with one hand on the reins, and the other hand trying in vain to pluck a crazed cat from the top of my head, all the while screaming at the top of my lungs from the sheer pain of Rufus' claws, which had gone through my scalp and were sunk into the bedrock of my skull. I don't remember very much about that adventure once we reached the opposite side of the river. I think I managed to peel Rufus off about the time we exited the woods. I never had to clean up any more Rufus puke after that day either. That was just as well because Rufus and I never got along very well after that trip.

The moral of the story, if there is one, is this: I started out holding on to Rufus. I had him. But in the end, he was holding on to me; he had me! If you let Rufus represent our material possessions, the moral will make sense. It's okay to have things; just don't let your things have you.

Kevin Kestner on Coppy (front), his brother Kraig and dad.

Kevin and his wife Mary Jane have seven children. He is an evangelical minister and the author of the SPAM Joke Book.

New Substitute in Town
By Joyce Kinney

We moved to Austin in 1964, when my husband Fred was hired to teach at Austin High School. I was a teacher also, but at that time the school district would hire only one teacher in a family. That meant I had to give up any aspirations of securing a teaching position in the Austin schools. So what was I to do?

The alternative was to be a substitute teacher. I would still be able to teach kids, which I loved to do. Thus began a twenty-five-year career as a "sub," which involved being called at 6 a.m. to fill in for teachers who were sick, at meetings, or taking a personal leave day.

It was quite a stressful challenge to be new in the community and be a substitute. First of all, I had to figure out where the schools were. In 1964 there were ten elementary schools in the Austin area: Lincoln, Neveln, Shaw, Woodson, Southgate, Banfield, Whittier, Sumner, Lansing, and Oakland. The buildings were located all over Austin, in the middle of neighborhoods or in the next little town. I had to memorize the city map and surrounding areas.

On a typical morning of substituting I had many challenges. Once I got to the building the next challenge was to find the principal's office, get directions to the room, and then find a custodian to unlock the classroom door. There were many things to know and prepare before children came into the room. Where were the teacher's manuals? What were other assignments and preparations for the day? Where were the bathrooms, the lunchroom, and the gym? How do I take lunch count, and attendance? Fortunately the principals and other teachers were very helpful. And so began each day.

The children came into the building, and as they hung up their coats, the news spread rather rapidly. "It's a sub; it's a sub!" They would come into the room, look me over, and try to help me figure out what they thought I was "supposed" to. Some teachers would indicate with their lesson plans which children were dependable and could be my helpers. That was wonderful.

I tried to adjust each teacher's rules and methods, and for the most part things would go quite well. But, there were always those comments, "You're suppose to do it this way," or "the gym is the other way!" Oh, it was fun!

There were those gratifying moments, however, when, at the end of the day, a little third grader would come up to me and say, "You're the best substitute we've ever had," or a first grader would hand me a note on a small scrap of paper that said, "I love you!" That made all the difference in the world, and I would go home with a smile on my face.

In time I learned where the buildings were located, the attendance and lunch routines at the various schools, and the reading programs for the various grades. How to cram the reading, math, social studies, science, language, and spelling plans into my head before twenty-five bubbly children entered the room remained a challenge for twenty-five years.

For the most part I have fond memories of those days and the many wonderful children I met and taught. The teachers and principals were always helpful to those of us who chose to enter the halls of their schools as "subs."

Sumner School

A former schoolteacher, Joyce was director of family education at Our Savior's Lutheran Church for fifty years.

Former *Herald* Carrier Boosts City With Illustrated Lectures
By Mel (Chaunce) Kirkpatrick

I recently found a clip from the *Austin Daily Herald* back in 1945. I sent the editors a letter from Antwerp, Belgium, where my ship, the U.S.S. Augusta, had taken Harry Truman to the Potsdam Conference in Germany. We picked up the president in Plymouth, England, and took him back home again a few weeks later. On the last leg of the trip, the president dramatically announced that the atomic bomb had been dropped on Hiroshima.

M.E. (Chaunce) Kirkpatrick, former Herald carrier, now serving on the *USS Augusta,* which took President Truman to Europe, writes that he is doing a public relations job for his hometown of Austin.

Letter to the Editor:

For a long time I've been telling the guys on this ship about my hometown. The Chamber of Commerce would be proud of my work. But last week that photo book from the *Herald* came through, so I now offer illustrated lectures.

Now some of these Brooklynites, Boston Beans and Quakers can see as well as hear about the SPAM City. There are a few who do not appreciate SPAM, but I show them the city's other strong points. So, thanks for the book. I'm making good use of it.

Another note of interest: The *USS Augusta* found itself in Antwerp, Belgium the other day. Granted liberty, a couple of New Yorkers and myself skipped over to the beach to see the sights. We'd been ashore only a few minutes when we entered a café. The first voice to greet us was Cedric Adams, Minneapolis newspaper columnist, speaking over the Armed Services Radio Network.

And as I stepped in he was saying something about "the patriotic Staneks of Austin who have (I think) eight members of their family in the service and one recently honorably discharged. All I did was turn to the New Yorkers and snap, with a sneer, "See?" The town's fame is going around the world. That's the dope from this end. Thanks again for the book. Chaunce Kirkpatrick

P.S. I didn't get a chance to talk with President Truman about holding the next Big Three meeting in Austin--maybe later.

The Day Hollywood Came to Austin
By Kaye McMasters Klukow

Movies were one of my favorite entertainments when I was growing up. I started going to Western movies on Saturday afternoons when I was in elementary school. Being a bit of a tomboy, I loved all Westerns, and because I went so often, I had memorized the characters and the actors who played them on the big screen. The Lone Ranger, Hopalong Cassidy, Gene Autrey, Roy Rogers and Dale Evans, Lash LaRue, Tom Mix, Red Ryder, Pat Buttram, Gabby Hayes, Andy Devine, Tonto, the Sons of the Pioneers—all of them entertained me for a couple hours on most Saturday afternoons. The movies started at 1:30 or 2 p.m., depending on the season of the year, and my parents would give me a ride to the Austin Theatre, sometimes with a friend and sometimes alone.

As I got old enough to ride the city bus on my own, I would complete the trip and get off the bus back at home about 4:30. We lived in Decker Acres so when I rode the bus I had to catch it at the corner, only two houses away. I would sit near the front and watch the scenery going by as the bus took its usual route through "Dutchtown," past the east side business district making a loop past Hormel's, then up Water Street to the Fox Hotel. Getting off at that point, I would walk down Main Street almost four blocks to the Austin Theatre. Having spent a nickel on the bus trip and saving a nickel for the ride home, I only had enough to buy the movie ticket, if I had a quarter. Admission was a dime, but there was "excise tax" of 2 cents. I always had to carry a couple pennies in my pocket if I wanted a treat, which I *always* wanted!

The best seat in the house, as far as I was concerned, was halfway to the front of the theatre in the middle of the screen. It was not always the same row but in proximity, depending on my place in the line waiting to buy tickets outside the theatre. I would sit mesmerized for an hour or two and then stumble out the door into the bright sunlight to start my trek back to the bus stop.

To catch the bus for the trip home, I had to walk to the same intersection, but the pickup point was on the north side of Holtz Drug Store. To get there I had to walk past the county courthouse, Buttrey's, Elam's, Cleveland Hardware, Wallace's, Gildner's, Lane's Drug Store and several other Main Street businesses. Sometimes I would cross the street to look in Kresge's or Woolworth's, and because I rarely had money with me, I knew I wasn't supposed to be in the stores without my parents. Occasionally the urge to check out the canaries and goldfish overcame me for a brief moment. Usually the trip from the Austin Theatre to the bus stop was straight and brief with only a few minutes of waiting for the next bus heading in the direction of my home.

One day on my trip to the bus stop after a movie I noticed a small crowd on the sidewalk in front of Lane's Drug so naturally I stopped to see what was going on. The people were eyeing a large, dark car with California license plates. Almost as soon as I stopped to look, a white haired man walked out of the doorway of the drug store, and it was Hopalong Cassidy! I was frozen on that spot, and I couldn't stop staring at him. He smiled and talked to the people around him as he walked to his car. He was not driving, but he got into the passenger's side, and I was still immobile and mute! He signed a couple autographs, and as the car finally pulled away from the curb, William Boyd reached out the car window to smile and wave. I could not even manage a wave or a smile back.

I was alone that day so I could only think about all that I had seen while I traveled home. I burst into our house with the news on my lips. And my parents didn't believe me! They said it was probably just someone who looked like Hopalong. I was crushed because I *knew* what I had seen. I tried a couple of times to tell them something more about what I had seen, but I could tell by the looks they gave me that there was no convincing them that a movie star had been in Lane's Drug Store.

I was eventually vindicated when during supper that evening we were listening to the news on KAUS radio. The announcer clearly told the same story I had told my skeptical parents only a few hours earlier. They believed him!!?!

Postscript: Evidently William Boyd had been to Mayo Clinic and was on his way back to California. At that time, U. S. Highway 16 was a main road westward, and it went through the heart of Austin.

Hopalong and Topper

Paperboy
By Kaye McMasters Klukow

Our family moved from a rental house south of Austin to a new development on the east side of town when I was entering second grade. Our house was on Oakland Avenue, on the northern edge of several blocks of story-and-a-half bungalows and single story ranch style homes built right after World War II for returning veterans.

In September of 1947 I started school in Miss Francis Baxter's second grade class at Webster School. It was a six or seven block walk from home, and I had to cross US Highway 16 as it wound its way around East Side Lake and through downtown Austin on its way west. I often crossed the highway at the site of the dam on the lake rather than walk the extra block to the corner on Division Street.

After attending Webster for second, third, and fourth grades, I had to walk farther to the northwest to attend fifth grade at Lincoln School. Webster was bursting at the seams with "war babies," as they were called then. Although Austin had a new elementary school in the works for Decker Acres that I would attend for sixth grade, I had to spend a year in one of the three fifth grade classes at Lincoln. I met many new classmates as we "Websterites" mingled with the kids from the east side and Crane addition, on the other side of the railroad.

To get to Lincoln School I walked the old, regular route to Webster, cut across the school yard, and walked the overpass to get to the east side business district, then on three blocks toward the packinghouse to the school. The overpass was a block-long wooden pedestrian structure built over the Milwaukee Road switchyard that connected the east side to Dutchtown, the area between the switchyard and East Side Lake. The railroad tracks, switchyard, and roundhouse were a manmade barrier. To cross the tracks safely, a pedestrian would have had to walk to Oakland Avenue on the south or Brownsdale Avenue on the north, if the overpass had not been built. Since the two streets were about eight blocks apart, the overpass served as a shortcut for shoppers, workers, and school children.

Instead of steps, the structure had an incline ramp at both ends, with wooden cleats to keep walkers from slipping on the wet or snowy surface. Curved iron railing, built higher that a fifth grader's head, ran the entire length of the bridge. On the west end, the ramp ended at a wooden barricade to keep the walkers from continuing forward into the traffic on Railway Street. At the bottom of the western ramp, one was in the heart of the east side business district. The Milwaukee Depot, the Harrington Hotel, a drug store, a couple grocery stores, the Roxy Theatre, a furniture store, and several bars were all situated in a two-block area. The only business I got acquainted with was a small grocery store just north of the ramp. On the rare occasion when a friend or I had a penny or two to spend, we would stop there and contemplate McCormick's candy counter.

The overpass was an exciting place to be. From the top I could see the roundhouse and watch the maneuvering of the steam engines for repairs. I could look north and south to the point where the tracks ended in a dot. To the far west I could see the steeple and cross of St. Augustine's church. Water Street extended from the base of the overpass, through the downtown area, past the Paramount Theatre and Fox Hotel to the front door of the large Catholic church.

It was always breezy, in desert heat or arctic blast. The scariest part was the trains traveling under the overpass. It was especially thrilling to stand directly over the passing engines and look down the roaring smoke stacks. My friends and I had to force ourselves to stand there because it was like looking into the hell's inferno. We would hold the rail to make sure we didn't fall into hell passing beneath our feet. It was thrilling and terrifying all at the same time.

One day on the overpass the paperboy from our neighborhood was riding by on his bicycle while we were preparing for a coming steam engine. We were occupied with our position and our grip on the railing and didn't notice the cowardly paperboy and what dastardly deed he was about to perpetrate. Just as the smokestack went under our feet, the paperboy grabbed me from behind and made a feeble attempt to push me over the side. Little did he know what fear could inspire me to do! I whirled on him and attacked with a ferocity few have ever seen. I was not going over the edge without a fight. The paperboy quickly got on his bicycle and took off for home.

My friend Susan and I were proud of the defense we had shown and talked about how the events had unfolded as we continued our walk home from school. We had talked it over completely by the time I got home, so I never thought to mention it to my parents. Before supper that evening my mother called me from the kitchen. When I got there she was standing at the door talking through the screen to the paperboy.

"Keith said you beat him up on the way home from school today. Is that true?" my mother asked. Embarrassed, I backed up and shook my head no.

"Uh huh," the paperboy insisted.

Mother seemed incredulous. "Kaye, is that true?" Again I shook my head no. Keith was pretty insistent and said I had socked him in the eye. "Kaye, I am disappointed in you." Mother looked at me waiting for an admission. Finally I had enough.

I shouted, "He tried to push me into the train on the overpass. He grabbed me and tried to throw me over!" I was nearly hysterical.

"Oh?" my mother said as she looked at the paperboy.

"Just tell your daughter to quit beating me up," he flung over his shoulder as he turned tail and escaped. That incident was great fodder for my parents for several years' teasing me about the time I beat up the paperboy!

A line-up of Herald paperboys. Who was the guilty one?

A 1958 AHS graduate, Kaye lives with her husband near Conger. Both are retired. Kaye is a published poet.

Traveling to Austin
By Helen A Knutson

Our family of four lived in LeRoy. I believe we were the poorest family in town. But we were the proud owners of a Model T Ford with an oval back window. It was the oldest car in town.

My sister Marion and I would get so excited when Dad said we'd go to Austin on Saturday. Why, that was thirty-four miles one way! As we rode along we would watch for meadowlarks on the fence posts and red wing blackbirds in the swampy ditches. When we were tired of that, Mom would suggest we count the crows eating animals that had been killed on the road. We were so anxious to see our cousins. Mom would say, "Now watch for the Hormel smoke stack." Dad would skirt around the city. When we were near St. Augustine Church, we'd look at the tall steeple. Going west on Grove Street we'd soon be at our relatives' place. Where the Congregational Church stands today was a pasture of dairy cows. Across the road was my Uncle Elmer's new house.

Now the fun began. Our uncle worked at Hormel's. He'd take us three cousins to town in his brand new Ford. Each of us was given a dime to spend. We'd hurry to the bakery, where I believe Hasting's Shoe Store is today. That bakery had a whole glassed counter of penny candies. Behind the counter stood a patient clerk dressed in a white uniform. It took a long time to spend a dime in those days. Next, we'd go to the north end of Main Street to visit the monkeys. They lived in a cage surrounded by large rocks pressed into cement. Nearby was a large swamp.

If the weather was nice we'd go to the railroad bridge near the Milwaukee Depot. Oh, what fun it was to go where we could look over the city and down the many railroad tracks. My mother told us her experience involving the railroad bridge. She worked at the first class Fox Hotel as a cook. This area is now the home of the Wells Fargo Bank.

Mom would walk over the bridge to visit an aunt who lived in Dutchtown. The bridge was icy when she returned on that dark, wintry night. Mom said how foolish she was, with her twenty-dollar muff on her wrist as she held on to the railing. She dropped the muff. When she got to the foot of the bridge on the west side, she walked under the bridge. She found her muff in the dark. That was scary.

We'd stay over night. Dad didn't like to drive at night as headlights weren't bright. The tail light of the Model T was a lantern with red glass, which you lit with a match. Next morning we'd wake early, and Aunt Clara had a good breakfast for us. We'd put on our Sunday clothes and drive those thirty-four miles to LeRoy in time for Sunday school.

In 1954 I moved to Austin to teach school. I taught many children during my thirty-two years at Sumner School. I enjoy those who are still in Austin or come to visit. I don't drive a Model T with an oval window now. I drive a 1982 Oldsmobile Omega. It's as outdated for today as that Model T was back when I was a kid. When I have visitors from other places, I take them to unique attractions in Austin. I think we have a beautiful and interesting city.

The Fox Hotel, where Mom worked as a cook

Helen Knutson was a teacher at Sumner School for thirty-one years. She now teaches Bible studies at two Austin nursing homes.

The Paramount Theatre
By Rachael Landherr

Most people my age don't really have special memories of the Paramount Theatre, other than watching school plays there, or being dragged along with their parents, but the Paramount Theatre is more than that to many natives. Since 1929 the Paramount Theatre has been an important part of Austin.

Throughout the years the Paramount Theatre has been used for a movie theatre, dance clubs, a teen hangout, and also a historic center. Around 1988 the Paramount Theatre closed, and it was one of the Midwest's last striking movie theatres still standing. After years of deciding what to do with the empty building, Austin Area Commission for the Arts raised enough money to reopen the Paramount. Within ten years of the purchase, it was finally reopened.

Although many things were changed and updated, a lot of things remain the same. One of the changes to the theatre was to restore its original 1929 marquee. With the help of local painter John Durfey, the ceiling is back to its original state. The theatre would not be where it is today without the generous donations of citizens and local funds.

Even though it might seem like the Paramount is just the way it used to be, there were things the renovators needed to change for today's use like heating, air-conditioning, handicapped accessible bathrooms, and expanding the back of the theatre to make dressing rooms for the actors.

With the help of donations and non-profit organizations, Austin hopes to have the theatre open for everyone for years to come. Although a lot of citizens who remember the Paramount Theatre from the days when it first opened are not living, there are a lot of memories that people from Austin can trace back to the Paramount: fun times with friends, first time watching a movie, or first loves. The Paramount Theatre has special memories for many Austin people, and if you look closely you can see those memories appear every time an elderly or middle-aged person steps in there. All the memories seem to come back to him or her, and you see the smile on their face. That is why the Paramount Theatre will always be remembered in downtown Austin.

The daughter of Mike and Sarah Landherr, Rachael will enter ninth grade at AHS in 2006.

Why Hormel Inspired Me
By Stuart (Tate) Lane

I spent my early years as a salesman for Hormel in New York City, a dream town for someone who originated in the small locale of Austin! During my initial years as a Hormel salesperson introducing SPAM to grocery stores, I was privileged to live in many New England states. During that time World War II was brewing in Europe, as Hitler was conquering all his neighbors and spreading terror with his Gestapo troops and concentration camps.

It soon became evident that America had to become involved to help our allies stop the Hitler regime. Our own American economy was strained for many reasons, and rationing was becoming an enforced attempt to restrict consumption of food, resources and energy. I received a phone call from Hormel expressing their concern for me. By then I was married to my college sweetheart who, after graduation from Perk College, had come out East to marry me.

Our first years of marriage were full of wonderful experiences. We had become owners of our first dog, an Irish setter, who we felt would help us prepare for the time when we would also have children. It was an idyllic time in my life in many ways – and all thanks to Hormel.

But as the World War II clouds were brewing, the American corporations and civilians were feeling threatened. While my wife and I were located in the mountains of Pennsylvania, I received the reassuring call from Hormel that they wanted to bring me "back home" at their expense.

They knew I was certainly going to be drafted, and they wanted to be sure my wife was located in Austin. So back we went, into the good hands of thoughtful Hormel execs who created a "war time" job for me, dealing with Washington edicts and regulations. And all too soon the fateful call came from Uncle Sam to join the Air Force.

I was a part of the early invasion at Omaha Beach, and then went to Paris as the Germans slowly retreated. I was among those fortunate enough to live dangerously but be spared death. All through the World War II days, I was aware of Hormel support for the war, and boxes called "care packages," arrived from home.

The happy ending for this story is that when the war ended, I was allowed to attend Shrivenham University in London to start law courses. I never did want to become a lawyer, but it was always helpful to get an understanding of the legal system. That was something that made it easier in corporate life to understand the role of lawyers in functioning legitimately…even in marketing decisions.

Well, now you know why Hormel has always inspired me. I did go on to a multi-faceted career, working for every Hormel president starting with Jay Hormel and ending with Jim Holton. Mr. Holton happened to be my age, and it was easy to explain to him that "when you retire, I also want to retire." Isn't it great that today we are still both alive and still enjoying our many friends here?

Landmarks and Street Names
By Virginia Larsen

When I moved to Austin in 1970 to teach at the junior college, all streets, avenues, places and drives had numbers, not names - with the exception of Oakland Avenue and Main Street. However, many older Austinites still used names like Old Kenwood, Water Street, and Bridge Street when they talked about the past. I liked that. I considered "Old Kenwood" a more stately designation than "Fourth Street." Numbers make a city more navigable to strangers and pizza-delivery people, but names have more character.

I noticed something strange when I moved here. I heard several people use Petey's Drive-In as a point of reference when giving directions to addresses located around 16th Avenue SW. For example, someone would say, "Go south past Sterling to Petey's Drive-In, and then turn west," or, "Southgate Baptist is located just south of Petey's Drive-in." The odd thing was that Petey's Drive-In no longer existed. But it must have been very popular, as it continued to be an invisible landmark for many years.

In fact, I myself have used Petey's Drive-in several times when giving directions. It's probably time I get into the habit of saying Casey's General Store, but for some reason I feel an odd fondness for Petey's, even though it's been gone for at least thirty-six years. I have no idea who Petey was or what his drive-in looked like. Do you?

Virginia Larsen taught German and French at Riverland Community College.

Skinner's Hill and The Lagoon, Our Year-round Playground
By Darrell Larson

I was born and raised in the city of Austin, and most of my childhood was spent in the southwest area, which is now called 10th Avenue SW, but then it was Gleason. I lived on the east end of that street about a half block from what was then the chicken hatchery on Kenwood Avenue. North, across the road from the hatchery, were Skinner's Hill and the lagoon. Both are still there, but have changed considerably from what I remember as a child.

In those years, the south end of the hill had a much steeper grade than it has today. The north end is much like it was in those years – maybe a little steeper with bushes and trees dotting the hill. It had the added hazard of sending sledders onto the lagoon if one was able to build up enough speed. If you were lucky, the ice was thick enough to support a kid and his sled.

In the summertime, seven or eight of us neighborhood kids played baseball at "the hill." In those days there was a nice backstop and very crude base paths. Home plate, first, second and third base were simply large dirt spots dug out of the surrounding grass. Usually we just played amongst ourselves, but occasionally kids from some other neighborhood would challenge us to a game. To us it was like playing in the World Series. In fact, it was just a bunch of kids sharing bats and gloves and baseballs and having the time of our lives. A baseball hit into the lagoon was an automatic home run. A run would score, but we often lost the ball in the process.

During winter months, we spent our time skating on the lagoon. The warming house sat next to the lagoon on the south side. I can still feel the warmth from that small building – and I can still smell that very special aroma produced inside. The bitter cold didn't seem to bother us in those days, and our parents were unable to understand why we would venture out to skate for several hours at a time. It was especially fun during the nighttime hours. Lights were strung high across the length of the ice allowing for activity well into the evening hours. And, of course, there was always the comfort of the good old warming house when it was needed.

A Salute to George Hirsch
By Elliot Larson

I had been in the armed forces for 39½ months when I returned home in April of 1946. This was in the days when, if you wore a suit, you wore a white shirt. Like most Army men, I was looking forward to getting out of my olive drab uniform, so the first thing I wanted to do Monday morning was go clothes shopping.

I went to Leuthold Peterson, but they had no white shirts available. I went to Gildner's, and they also had no white shirts available. The demand for white shirts had been so great the factories had not been able to keep up.

I happened to meet an old classmate on the street, and he told me to go to Hirsch's Clothing. I walked in the door, and Mr. Hirsch said, "I'll bet you need a white shirt." He took out his tape, measured me, looked around under the counter and said, "Here, this one will fit you." I've been ever grateful for this and heard that if a non-serviceman walked in, he was sold out. Mr. Hirsch kept all his white shirts for ex-servicemen like me.

After I bought the white shirt and a suit from Mr. Hirsch on Saturday, my wife and I decided to attend Sunday services at the Methodist Church. I stepped into the sanctuary and saw room for two in the back pew. I asked three elderly ladies to let us in. It was a nice spring day, and the church doors were left open.

I was still a little jumpy and uptight after just returning from the war. A car backfired, and I dug the elderly ladies' legs out of the way as I ducked under the pew to take cover. Of course, we were not under attack, and I had to sit back up in my pew again. I looked to my right at my wife, and she was just staring straight ahead while the three elderly ladies nervously edged away. It's a good thing I at least looked respectable in my nice, new white shirt.

Hirsch's Clothing Store

Fiddlin' Ole Hanson
By Wendy Larson

My father's age equals that of a century, and with a little coaxing his memories are excavated--time capsules opened to reveal his life's stories. He remembers ancient anecdotes passed on to him through his father, tales of the old ones from generations long ago. The heritage of his family has been interwoven with fiddle tunes and strains of melodies that came from the mountains, fjords and valleys of the old country, songs so old that the original titles have long been forgotten and replaced with the name of old fiddlers in this region who brought them forward to the 20th Century and are still remembered through Ole's fingers.

The paternal side of Ole's family, kickers and scrappers as some described them, were from the Hallingdal area in Norway. Andreas Hanson, Ole's grandfather, brought his fiddle and the old tunes from Norway when he immigrated to this country. He played the springdans, hallings, Rhinelanders, mazurkas, schottisches, waltzes, and square dances for people in this area—entertaining them the same way he had in Norway. He taught the tunes to his son Gilbert, and he passed them on to his sons and daughters. But Gilbert's children didn't have the luxury of a violin to learn on. Gilbert made them one from a wooden cigar box, and this was their primary instrument for many years until their granddad's fiddle was handed down after his passing. The second generation born in America trained on the crude instrument without benefit of sheet music. Gilbert and his children couldn't read music—they learned by memorizing.

Ole Hanson was the tenth child born to Gilbert and Lukris (Wangen) Hanson. When Ole was about the ripe old age of 8, he provided music at barn dances and neighborhood parties with one or two of his brothers. The stills that produced the bootleg liquor in the hollows of the countryside meant even more opportunities for Ole and his family. After a full day of hard labor farming, out came the bottles and jars filled with home brew and distilled liquor followed by fiddles and dancing. They passed the hat at parties to pay the musicians. Before the brothers earned the kingly sum of five dollars to buy their first mail order guitar, one of them played lead fiddle while the others used a second fiddle or a pump organ to chord along.

Sliding in on the backside of the country's Depression and the end of Prohibition, Ole married Maxine Stern in 1933 and began working at Hormel's for 32 cents an hour. He supplemented that income by doing various odd jobs. He turned a necessity into one of those odd jobs that took up increasingly more time—violin repair. He couldn't afford to pay anyone to fix his violin so he learned how to do it himself. Word spread, and from the early 1940s until the late 1990s, he repaired string instruments for the community, including schools around the area and music stores. Rarely did he turn down work on stringed instruments.

Ole used the tunes he had learned from his granddad, father, brothers, sisters, and fiddlers from the area like Bennie and Thomas Peterson and Halve Halvorson, to keep up steady part-time employment as a musician. Groups of musicians used horns, accordions, and double fiddles to produce the big band sounds needed for swing music. Smaller groups of two, three, and four individuals playing country, bluegrass, and old time replaced the band of brothers. The Eddie True Band, Eddy Ralph Band, Red Walsh, Leo Thiele, Vern Huntington, Lloyd Roeske, Milton and Gloria Kopet, Cousin Merle, Roy Lilly and the Little Green Valley Boys, Rich and the Country Poor Folk, The Melody Makers, Wes Crowder and Jake Balk, Kenny Alm, Bill and Vern Keyser, Cy Christopherson and The Old Timers (including Harry Herplink), Palmer and Anna Benson, Alvin Lerum, Punk Krull, Darrell Anderson, Dean Hovland, Don Moldenhauer, Ray Johnson, Ray Stoltzenberg, and Elijah Duren entertained county folks by making music.

At any given time it wasn't unusual to see at least one of Ole's children playing alongside him. Later, he was able to draw on the manpower, or rather girl power of his family when he formed his own group, Sweet Country, using his daughters to supply the percussion, rhythm guitar, and string bass that supported his fiddle playing. The Sweet Country girls learned fiddle first through Ole's instruction and later picked up the other instruments; they were interchangeable on each, just like Dad. If things got a little dull during a dance job, well, not to fret—just switch with a sister to another instrument. Ole and his wife Maxine raised nine children, and all of them played at least one instrument.

The music venues were as broad as the styles. The Terp Ballroom, Rainbow, and the Oasis gave way to smaller establishments like the Twin Oaks, as trios or quartets replaced big bands. The downtown liquor establishments changed owners and names, and many burned or were torn down as the city changed. East side counterparts were popular places for live music on weekends: Smith's Royal Bar, Purity Inn, Wonder Bar, Blue Bar, Maple Bar, Mitchell's, Alibi Inn, Packing House Bar, Log Cabin Inn, Smitty's, Red's Hiawatha, Lefty's, and Charlie's.

Service clubs and small diners such as The Plant Café, Cottage Inn, and Lloyd's provided food and the occasional music to dine by. The village of Mapleview got in on the fun; their small bar didn't have much room so the entertainers squeezed into a space between two booths. The Isaac Walton and Conservation Club on the edge of Austin were also reserved for wedding and anniversary dances—circle two step, bunny hop, waltz quadrille, chicken dance, schottische, and the butterfly were bound to get dancers out on the floor and acquainted with each other when they learned the simple dance steps to these crowd pleasers.

Live music in Austin hasn't been replaced, but DJ's are usually spinning the popular tunes at wedding dances. VCR and DVD players and expanded cable have led to a shift away from live entertainment of big bands, fiddlers, and old time music at a plethora of popular hangouts. Ole's daughters still play music in the symphony, holiday programs, church, and family parties. A third generation also entertains and has stepped up to the plate to provide entertainment at local public scenes.

Fiddlin' Ole hasn't faded from sight. These days he commandeers his wheelchair down the hallways of St. Mark's Lutheran Home in Austin. With his fiddle tucked under his chin he plays, to the amazement of many, the old time waltzes, polkas, and two steps that his generation grew up with. Ole Hanson is a name synonymous with fiddle and a by gone era of music.

Ole Hanson

Ole's daughter, Wendy Larson, works for Austin Public Schools.

The Swimming Holes of Austin
By John P. Lembrick

Growing up in Austin in the 1950s was a special time for my friends and me because there were so many places to go swimming instead of at the Municipal Pool. Most of the rivers and creeks had reasonably clean water compared to today.

The first place was the river east of Lansing. Just below the bridge and about one block north was a sandy area that made a great beach. The water was not really deep, but deep enough to swim in and play some games like chicken fight, where one person would sit on the shoulders of another and another couple would do the same. The object was to pull the person from the shoulders of the other team. Another game was shoot the moon, where two people (usually strong boys) would grab their own wrist and with the other hand take hold of the wrist of the other person, forming a solid launching pad. A third person would place his feet on the launching pad, crouching down with knees bent. The two launchers would crouch down in the water, and on the count of three, they would rise up, throw their hands and arms up, while at the same time the launchee would straighten out his legs and be hurled up to eight feet in the air before landing in deeper water. I spent two summers driving out to Lansing and swimming in this hole.

The next hole was on the Cedar River north of Austin, just west of the current power plant north of Todd Park. This hole also had a sandy beach on the east bank, but the west bank was about six to eight feet above the river and was a good spot to jump from. There was a trail that started just north of the Hormel Institute that went through the woods about two miles to reach this swimming hole.

Also on the north side of Austin was Seven Springs out on 8th Avenue NW. There really were seven springs at this hole that one could actually drink out of in those days. The springs were in an indent in the side of the bank and flowed out into the creek. This hole was on Turtle Creek. Swimming here was a challenge as the water close to the springs was quite cold, but it felt good on a hot summer day.

On the south side of Austin was one of my favorite spots just south of the old Hormel Experimental Farm on 4th Street SE, about four miles outside of town. This hole was on the bend of the creek after one walked on the trail about one mile through the woods. This hole was quite secluded and was used mostly by boys, who did a lot of skinny-dipping. One day when we were skinny-dipping, some girls came upon us on the south bank, and our clothes were on the north bank. We waited in the water for about ten minutes, but the girls did not leave. We finally decided to run across the beach on the north side, grab our clothes and head for the woods to get dressed. We were all very embarrassed.

This hole was where I almost drowned. I broke the golden rule of swimming I had learned in Boy Scouts--always swim in pairs. This day none of my friends could go, so I went by myself thinking someone was always there. When I arrived there was no one in sight, but I went swimming anyway. On the east side of this hole in late summer there were weeds. I somehow got tangled with my legs in these weeds and could not swim out of them. The more I struggled, the tighter the weeds hung on. The water was about ten feet deep so I could not touch bottom. My head was under the water, and I could not reach the surface. I began to see only bright lights in my head, and I believe I passed out. The moment I quit struggling, the weeds released their grip on me, and I floated to the surface gasping for air. That was the last time I swam there.

My favorite hole was a wide spot in Turtle Creek at the end of 11th Avenue SW in the 1200 block. This hole was only four blocks from where I grew up. I spent many hours here because it was an easy walk ,and it was where most of my neighborhood friends went to swim. Here the city had put in a concrete slab with steps leading up to 11th Avenue. There were several trees that hung out over the water. Some of the older boys would shinny up the tree and tie a large diameter rope that would hang out over the water. We would grab hold of the rope, move far back on the concrete slab, and swing out over the water, let go of the rope and drop in about six to seven feet deep.

When I was 12 or 13, this hole was where one day two friends and I decided to see how far the creek went on our inner tubes. We started at the end of 11th Avenue and drifted downstream until we came to where Turtle Creek meets the Cedar River just east of the Catholic cemetery. We continued floating down the Cedar River for several hours until we came to the bridge over the river about two miles Northwest of Lyle. It was here we got out of the river and started to walk home. We were smart enough to wear tennis shoes, knowing we would have to walk on blacktop roads to get home.

John Lembrick, a third generation Hormel employee, worked in the Hormel Corporate Office for more than forty-seven years.

Addie's Soup
By John Lenway II

"Grandma Addie's here," yells Lisa. Immediately, my three brothers, my sister and I scurry to the door in anticipation of what tasty treat she may have in hand. Grandma, dressed in her soiled work clothes that consist of a white blouse and white pants, walks into the house with two plastic one-gallon cottage cheese containers in her arms. As she sets the containers on the kitchen counter, we all know without even popping the lids off that it is not cottage cheese in them, but something far more joyous, her homemade soup. The time is approximately 9:45 p.m., and my siblings and I are promptly redirected to our rooms without even getting a peek, as we have school in the morning. Reluctantly we jump into our beds with thoughts of chicken dumplings dancing through our heads.

While Grandma Adeline has mastered many skills including cooking, crocheting, and cake decorating, her soup making ability stands above them all. Her simple country style upbringing taught her to be frugal and ingenious.

My mom says, "Grandma can create a feast out of an empty cupboard." Her unrivaled, instinctive creativity makes it impossible to duplicate her succulent soups, for it's all just a matter of feel, Grandma will say. Since I hate peas, I am flabbergasted by her ability to transform such a despicable vegetable into such a divine treat, split pea soup.

Addie's soups, in addition to being homemade, generally are quite healthful and hearty. Understanding the value of good nutrition, she emphasizes the need to include vegetables in her masterpieces, including carrots, celery, and rutabagas. Unless requested otherwise, Grandma fills her soups to abundance with large chunks of veggies, beef or chicken. She doesn't believe in a "watered down version." When ingredients are lacking she simply mixes eggs and flour, thus creating delicate, soft noodles or plump, airy dumplings. Fortunately, the one skill I have acquired is the knack for making homemade noodles.

Most likely Grandma's soup making abilities took root as a child observing her mother. She moved on and learned more as she worked for numerous cafes and restaurants like The Oak Leaf, The Main Event, Watts Cookin', The American Legion, and many more in the Austin area. But I believe her goal of becoming a great soup maker came to fruition in the early 1970s, on the east side of Austin at the Railway Café.

The Railway was an establishment that she owned, thus her livelihood depended on the food she served.

While the Railway Café has a history all its own, the thing I recall the most was the clientele. Railroad workers from the Milwaukee Railroad frequently made a beeline over from just across the street, and employees from the nearby Hormel plant would wearily amble in after a hard day's work. By far, the most interesting customers had to be the patrons who regularly stumbled in from the adjoining Lefty's Bar, but families looking for an inexpensive place to eat out also added to the diversity of the café.

It was at the Railway that Grandma started being addressed as Addie, and it was there that her legacy began. While Grandma Adeline no longer resides in this earthly world, for those who experienced her heavenly soups, she will always be present.

The Railway Cafe

The Lot
By John Lenway II

Most adults can recollect a time or place that stirs memories of their youth. As I advance further into adulthood, I can quite vividly recall such a place in my neighborhood, where I frequently hung out in the mid 1970s. While many people may reminisce about their past time spent in the schoolyard or at summer camp, my recollection pertains to a field of dreams that lay just down the hill, at a place that simply became known as "the lot."

The lot was so named, for that's exactly what it was, a plain old grassy field in Austin, located just beyond the dead end road of 2nd Street SW. Within eyesight and approximately 300 yards to the south sat the historic band shell. It should be noted that this self-imposed playground was directly behind old Miss Weber's house.

Local boys, in their early and mid teens, primarily used this plot of land for pick-up baseball and football games. When baseball was the game of choice, home plate sat but 30 or 40 feet from Miss Weber's back picture window. While Miss Weber never really came out to watch the games, she would occasionally appear after a close call with the window. Quite often she would adamantly ask us to move our game elsewhere, with nary an ear listening. Since I was her longtime paperboy, she would insist that I talk to my friends about changing the venue of our games. At the same time she would pleasantly comment, "I wish you boys would be more careful."

Admittedly, I did not push the issue with my cohorts. At one time, we did actually discuss the idea with Park and Rec. about the possibility of putting a backstop up. Surprisingly, Miss Weber's glass bull's eye went unscathed.

In the field of play there were obstacles to deal with other than your opponent. In deep left center field sat an enormous weeping willow. Behind second base stood a wooden birdhouse that was perched atop a 15-foot metal pole (this suspiciously was found cut down one day). The deep sinkhole that laid between third base and home plate required the utmost respect, for it caused many a strain or sprain as one inadvertently stepped into it. For bases, any flat rather portable object could be used: paper plates, garbage bags, and later on someone even invested in some plastic bases. Eerily, the grass was always neatly mowed, and supposedly, no one ever actually witnessed this being done.

Neighborhood boys gathered together for ball games at this field all year long. Spring and summer were the seasons for baseball, with games called off only on a rare occasion, due to a downpour of rain. In the fall and winter, football prevailed, with only the hint of frostbite being a legitimate reason to stop the game. Days rarely went by when a game wasn't played. If you elected not to play due to weather, you could become labeled a wimp. Brief intermissions were allowed to walk to the nearby Clark station to pick up a bag of chocolate M&Ms and a cool refreshing Coca-Cola, my snacks of choice. We sometimes used this short recess to go swimming, or to pop in at home to let our parents know that we were still alive.

In the summer of 1978, the lot was victim to two massive floods, and its function as a place of leisure came to a grinding halt. The lot was reduced to a smelly, damp marshland. Coincidentally, the flooding occurred during a time when many of us had reached puberty and were beginning to expand our narrow view of the world. As each of us moved on and made new friendships, none of those relationships would compare with those established at the lot. The commonality of the shared experience cannot be recreated by any others. As my children grow, I only hope that they, in turn, may also find a place that sparks such fond memories.

A life-long Austin resident, John Lenway works at Owatonna Hospital.

The Tower
By Linda Lenz and Donna Nybo

Those of us lucky enough to be in high school during the late 1950s through early '70s remember all the great times we had at the Tower. It seems whenever we run into former classmates, the conversation eventually turns to the Tower and how we were so lucky to have a place like that to dance and spend time with our friends.

Friday nights after the football or basketball games we'd head up to the Tower. After climbing the long flight of stairs we had to wait in line to pay our quarter and get our hand stamped. Of course Clarence Nybo, also known to me as Dad, Gar Nash, or Dick Cassem would be there to check the breath of anyone who looked like he or she might have been drinking. They played no favorites, not even if it was a daughter's boyfriend. Once in, it was straight to the dance floor. We don't know if Austin was unique in this, but it was mostly girls dancing together. We didn't stay in one spot. We'd dance while moving in a counter-clockwise circle doing the Tower trot, with the guys sitting on the benches watching us dance by. We did have some guys who danced. We remember Dale Gates and Keith Unruh as two of the best dancers. The center of the circle was reserved for these brave couples.

It didn't take a lot to keep us happy. We didn't need bands; the jukebox was good enough, and it didn't cost us anything. When we wanted to pick some songs, we just went and asked for a quarter from whoever was working the door. When we hear "Venus," "Rockin' Robin," or "Johnny Angel," we have a Tower flashback. we can see the aluminum Christmas tree and hear "Rockin' Around the Christmas Tree" or remember those hot summer nights, being on the second floor of an old brick building with no air conditioning. When we couldn't take it any more, we'd go and stand in front of one of the big box fans propped in the windows.

Of course, we did have rules that we had to follow. The big one was no alcohol. If someone got caught, they were kicked out for three months, and the second time they were out for good. We had forgotten about the dress code until we ran into a Tower alumna last week. She told me about the time she decided to wear a certain top up to the Tower, even though she knew she shouldn't. It only came to her waist, so when she raised her arm when she was dancing, her bare middle showed. It didn't take long before Clarence called her over, and she went home and changed her top.

All of us who have these wonderful Tower memories are so thankful that Mr. Nybo came along just at the right time for the right reason, to give the youth of Austin an unforgettable time of their lives. Many of us have said, "If only our children could have had a place like the Tower." It was a once in a lifetime experience we will never forget.

Yup, if we could go back in time and relive one moment in our lives, we would be back at the Tower with our friend Nancy, just dancing and dancing and dancing. How we miss that! So from your daughters and a whole lot of other folks...thanks Dad.

A typical Tower crowd in the 1960s

Linda Lenz teaches at South Central Technical College in Faribault. Donna, her big sister, lives in Austin and teaches art for Southland Schools in Adams.

Riverland Community College Athletics 1940-2005
By David A. Lillemon

Austin Junior College began its inaugural season in athletics with football in the fall of 1940 when twenty-five players coached by Domonic Krezowski played their first season and won their opening contest, 19-0 over Waldorf Junior College and finished the season with a 2-2-1 record. The second season they went 3-3 under Krezowski. There was no football during World War II, but it resumed in 1946 under the direction of Mark Dean. Dean led the Blue Devils to their best football season ever, a 5-1-1 record. In the next season the Blue Devils won their first and only football conference championship. Dick Jewett took over for the next three years. In 1950 they finished 4-1-1. There was no football for the next twenty years, until the fall of 1970, when Earl Perkins, who was there for fourteen years, was hired to coach the team. There was no football in 1984 and 1985, and it resumed for five more seasons. Kevin Swank guided ACC for two seasons, and David Lillemon coached the team for the final three years. The Blue Devils' final season of football was in 1989.

Men's basketball also began in 1940 under the direction of Domonic Krezowski. In their opening contest, they defeated Bethany of Mankato 42-13 and finished the year 10-4. Krezowski coached the team one more season (8-5), and then there were four years of no basketball during the war. Mark Dean coached basketball in 1946-'47, and the team went 12-6. Dick Jewett coached basketball for four seasons, winning two Southern Minnesota Junior College Conference (SMJCC) championships. In 1948-'49 his team had a 13-1 record.

Harold (Hal) Cuff took over the basketball duties in 1951-'52 and went on to coach the Blue Devils for fifteen years. His teams enjoyed nothing but success. In only four seasons did his teams finish under .500, and his Blue Devils won or shared six SMJCC championships. His best season was in 1962-'63 when the team went 19-3 losing in the regional tournament. For the next nineteen years, Jim Mittun was the head coach. His best season was in 1972-'73 when the Blue Devils won the Southern Division and finished 13-11. Mark Weiss took over for two seasons (9-13 and 7-15), and then David Lillemon was hired to coach football, basketball, and baseball. Lillemon coached the Blue Devil basketball team from 1987-2003. His best year was in 1997-'98 when the team went 14-8 and lost its opening game to Brainerd in overtime in the state tournament. Darin Johnson has been the coach for the last three years.

The college has produced many outstanding athletes including: Larry Rensink (1958-'59), Larry Scheid (1959-'60), Dean Turner (1960-'61), Wayne LeRud (1965-'66), John Taylor (1968-'69), Dan Ball (1972-'73), Jim Riles (1973-'74), Charles Curren (1979-'80) and John Van Beek (1994-'95). LeRud led the nation in scoring (36.9) and was named second team All-American while Van Beek earned first team All-American honors, averaging a double-double in points and rebounds.

Records indicate men's golf began at the college in 1947. The Blue Devils were SMJCC conference champions the first three seasons of existence. William (Bill) Evans coached for thirteen seasons. His last season was 1960. Athletic Director Red Hastings took over as golf coach the following year and directed the program for six seasons. In that span, Austin Junior College won five conference championships, two Region XIII titles, and sent numerous golfers to the NJCAA national tournament. In 1966, Jim Mittun was hired as Athletic Director, head basketball and golf coach. He served as golf coach for twenty-four years (no golf in 1982-'83) and finished out his career in 1991. Mittun coached two conference championships, one state championship team, five Region XIII runner-ups and seven Region XIII championships.

Phil Bundy took over and coached the team four years. He guided his squads to one state championship and one Region XIII runner-up. While serving as athletic director and head men's basketball coach, David Lillemon was assigned the golf duties in 1995 and has been the golf coach since. On three occasions, the team's best finishes in team competition have been third place in the state and Region XIII tourney. Lillemon has coached seven individuals who have qualified for the NJCAA national tournament, and for eight consecutive years they participated in the event. Justin Bennett, Jeff Clark, and Dan Breuer competed in the tournament two consecutive years. Clark (2001) and Breuer (2004 *The Austin Bakery*) finished sixth and eighth respectively in the national tournament. Dan Breuer earned a 4.0 grade point average in his two years and Distinguished Academic All-American honors, the first in the college's history.

Tennis first hit the court in the spring of 1948 when Bill Evans served as head coach. His teams won two conference championships and one Region XIII title (1963) in his fourteen years. When Evans retired in 1963, Eugene Auringer took over for three seasons, winning two conference titles and one Region XIII championship. Paul Swanson had the team for one season, then Bill Blobirsch coached AJC for eight of the next nine seasons (1967-'76). Dick Organ was in charge during the 1968-'69 school year. Dave Dickinson and Terry Dilley co-coached the Blue Devils for seventeen years, guiding their teams to two state championships and two Region XIII titles. Their final season was 1993, when their team won a region title. Ken Larson coached the team for the next three seasons, winning two state championships and one Region XIII title. Tim Kjar was then hired to coach women's basketball and tennis, and he guided the team to one state title (1998-99) in his third and final season. Suzy Hebrink coached the men's team its final five seasons (1999-2004). These teams won four Region XIII championships, the last in 2004. Tennis then was terminated as a varsity sport due to declining participation in the state and region.

Baseball was introduced as a conference sport to AJC in 1958-'59 when Hal Bergeson was hired to coach the team. In his first season, the team was 8-1 and crowned Southern Division champions. Bergerson coached the team for seven seasons, winning four conference titles. George Hillberg guided the team for the next two seasons, and Arlan Burmeister coached his only team (1968) to a 14-5 record, Southern Division champions and a Region XIII runner-up. Earl Perkins was hired to coach the baseball team in 1968, and he was at the helm for seventeen years. His teams won or shared four division titles, one state championship (1972), one Region XIII runner-up, and two Region XIII titles (1973 and 1981). Mark Weiss was in charge for two seasons, and David Lillemon took over in 1987. He guided his teams to back to back state appearances in 1990 and 1991. In that second state appearance, the Blue Devils finished state runner-up with a 21-13 record. Lillemon resigned from his baseball duties in 1995 after eight seasons.

Dwight Kotila was hired, and he coached for three seasons. In his final season, his team won the Region XIII championship and participated in the NJCAA Division III championships. Herb Hofer (1999), Lee Brand (1999-2001), and Dave Meyer (2002) followed in the footsteps of Kotila. Scott Koenigs was hired in February of 2003 to take over the program and guided his first team to a 13-17 mark and a state appearance. Koenigs is in his third season as the head coach of the baseball program.

Wrestling and track were varsity sports at various stages in the college history. The inaugural season for wrestling was 1960 when Kay Hompe was hired. Eight individuals earned letters and finished 4-4 in their inaugural season. Hompe coached for two seasons, and after a two year absence the college hired Fred Kinney to guide the program. Eight wrestlers competed and finished 2-5-1 in Kinney's first season.

Ed Bakke wrestling at 123 pounds finished runner-up in the NJCAA national championships held in Worthington. The following season Bakke returned to the championships and took third overall in the 123 pound division. Wrestling existed for five consecutive seasons at Austin Junior College. Kinney coached the wrestlers for three years (1964-65, 65-66 and 68-69). Orville Moran had the squad from '66 until '68.

In the spring of 1970, four young men expressed interest in track, and Dave Dickinson served as their coach competing in five meets that spring. Dickinson continued to serve as the coach for five seasons. Track was no longer a sport after the spring of 1973. In 1980, Tom Krieger attended Austin Community College and was an outstanding high hurdler. Coach Larry Gilbertson, Austin High track coach where Krieger attended, accompanied Tom to many meets including the Region XIII championships. Krieger competed in the high jump and 110 high hurdles. His best effort in the high jump was 6-4 at the Waseca Invitational. At the Region XIII championships held in Cottage Grove, Krieger finished first in the 110 high hurdles and earned a trip to the NJCAA national track championships. He won the event with his best time of the season. Krieger's first place earned ACC 10 points and 19th place in the team event. Krieger advanced to the national tournament but did not qualify for the semifinal heats.

The first record of women's varsity sports was in basketball in 1972-'73 when the college hired Vel Moen. Her team posted a 6-2 record their first season. Her team finished 7-5 the second season and won third place in the state tournament. Moen finished her basketball coaching career after fifteen years in 1987, leaving with a 203-78 record or a winning percentage of .730. She guided her team to state-runner-up three times. In 1976-'77, ACC finished 16-1 in the regular season and then lost in the state championship to arch-rival Worthington. The Blue Devils earned a trip to the regional tournament where once again Worthington beat ACC in the championship. The team was invited to the NJCAA national tournament in Vincences, Indiana, as an at-large entry. They lost two games and finished 19-5, the best year ever in the college's history.

Oscar Haddorff coached one year in 1986-'87 before Moen came back for one more season. Denise Martin was hired as the AD, volleyball and basketball coach, and she remained for four seasons. In 1992 Sherri Stageberg was hired from Willmar to guide the Lady Blue Devils' basketball program, and she coached the team for two seasons.

Lee Koll, an outstanding coach from Austin Pacelli High School, agreed to come out of retirement and coach the team for one season. Tim Kjar took over in 1996-'97 and guided his teams for four seasons. He had the privilege of coaching Laura Chaffee (third team pre-season All-American) and Mary Kuiters, who was named second team All-American in 1998-'99. Kuiters led the nation in scoring in 1998-'99 and completed her career as all-time leading scorer (993 points). Suzy Hebrink was hired to coach the tennis program along with the women's basketball program. She has been at the helm for the past seven seasons (1999-2005), with the team's best year in 2000-'01 when they had a 13-11 season.

Tennis became the second women's sport on record, and it has been a huge success. Vel Moen served as the coach for nine seasons. During her first season with seven members, she finished 2-3. Her best year was 1977, when the Lady Blue Devils finished third in the state tournament. There was no tennis in 1983 due to lack of funds, and during this season, men's tennis coaches Dave Dickinson and Terry Dilley accepted the responsibilities of coaching the women's team. They guided their teams to one state championship and four Region XIII titles. Their final season was in 1993.

Ken Larson coached the next three seasons, including a state runner-up and Region XIII runner-up in 1995. Tim Kjar, the women's basketball coach took over the tennis reigns for three seasons, guiding them to a state championship, two Region XIII titles, and a third place finish in the NJCAA national championships in spring of 1999. Suzy Hebrink coached the team for five seasons from 2000-'04. She guided the ladies to three Region XIII championships and a second place in the NJCAA tourney in 2003. Tennis was terminated as a varsity sport due to declining participation in the state and region.

Track was the next sport to go on record, and in 1975 Theresa Parlin put ACC on the map as she won two state individual championships in the 100 low hurdles and the 200 meter hurdles. She returned the following season and broke two records at the state tournament, winning the 100 meter low hurdles and the 200 meter hurdles. Those were the only two seasons that records indicate women's track results.

In 1975, Vel Moen coached the first volleyball team. The Lady Blue Devils won the Southern Division championship their first season and posted a 12-10 record. Her team's best finish was third place in the state tournament in 1979. She coached the volleyball team for ten seasons. Donna Judsen directed the team in 1977-'78, and Nancy Carroll in 1985-'86. There was no volleyball in 1986-'87. Moen came back for her final season in 1987. Denise Martin was hired in 1988-'89, and she coached four years with her best season in her first year as the Lady Blue Devils went 23-14-1. Sherri Stageberg coached volleyball for two seasons before Helen Jahr was hired. Jahr guided her teams to nine consecutive state appearances and one Region XIII appearance between 1994-2005 as their head coach.

Softball was introduced to Austin Community College in 1979. Dan Ball was the first coach, and he guided his team to an 11-8 season. In his second and final year, his team won the Southern Division Championship, the State Championship, the Region XIII Championship and finished fourth in the country at the NJCAA national softball tournament. Lori Bergstrom won 22 games on the mound that year (22-2), and Ball's team finished 28-5, the best in softball history at the college. Softball quickly developed into a rich tradition in Austin. Sue Nelson (1981) and Marilyn Classen (1982) each guided their teams to third place finishes in the state tournament in their one year coaching stints. Coach Jim Mittun's team (1983) won the Southern Division and the Region XIII title.

Rolf Synogrond was hired in 1983 and coached the team for eight seasons, consistently finishing over .500 and having his best season in 1984-'85 going 20-9-1. After a one-year absence (1992), Pat Cornelius was hired as women's athletic director and softball coach. She guided the Lady Blue Devils for four seasons, and her final season led them to a state runner-up finish. Paula Carlsen followed Cornelius for three seasons, and in 1999 Lisa Quednow-Bickler was hired as the women's athletic director and softball coach. She immediately guided the team to a consolation championship in the state tournament and then shared or won the conference title the following three seasons. In those final three years, the Blue Devils were state runners-up. Darin Johnson took over in 2003 for one season. There was no softball in 2004-'05.

The first competition in women's golf was in the spring of 1984, when Jodi Borris competed under the coaching of Jim Mittun and finished second in the state and Region XIII championships. Mittun guided the women golfers until his retirement in 1991. Phil Bundy coached the women the following four seasons, and then David Lillemon was hired to coach the men and women's golf teams. In his tenure, the women finished runner-up in the state in 1998, 1999, and 2003. They also finished in third place twice in the Region, and Lillemon coached two ladies to the NJCAA national tournament. In 2004, Carissa Gabrielson and Alison Stutzman qualified for the national tournament. Gabrielson also earned Distinguished Academic All-American honors. Stutzman finished fourth in the Region XIII tournament the following year and qualified again for the NJCAA tournament in Florida.

In 1997 ten charter members were inducted in the Athletic Hall of Fame at Riverland Community College. These five men and five women played or coached for the college that has had four different names: Austin Junior College, Austin State Junior College, Austin Community College, and Riverland Community College. The 1997 Hall of Fame inductees were Vel Moen, Nancy Haddorff, Cynthia Dimmel-Shiffer, Patti Foss, Lori K. Bergstom, Hal Cuff, Wayne LeRud, Jim Mittun, David Dickinson, and Jay Schroeder. Every odd-numbered year since 1997 there have been six inductees.

The 1999 class included Rick Knutson, Jim Riles, Jon Stephenson, Wendy (Dickinson) Eickhoff, Sue Johnson, and Jane Synogrond. The 2001 class included Earl Perkins, Denise (Stalker) Peterson, Laurie (Vigum) Hendrickson, Christy (Arnold) Harris, Cory Hanson, and John Van Beek. The 2003 class included Julie Anderson, Richard Anderson, Kim Bass, Fred Budde, Linda Tapp and Kelly Tritz. The 2005 class included Dan Ball, Terry Dilley, Karol Hansen, Mary Kuiters, Don Leathers, and Laura (Lukes) Probst.

Austin Junior College, 1955

The House That Jack Built
By Elaine Little

We moved from South Dakota to Austin in August of 1956. My husband Jack had accepted a job with the Austin Public Schools teaching high school math and business subjects. We rented a house on Park Avenue from a couple who had just retired and opted to rent their house to us for a year. They planned to travel and decide if they wanted to remain in Austin or move south.

After we moved into their house, we made our first major purchase, a washing machine and a dryer from Sally Usem. The house had an unfinished attic that we thought would make a good play area for our 4-year-old daughter and 2-year-old son. So we asked our landlord for permission to finish the attic. He replied that it would be fine with him so Jack completed the job for our two happy children.

In the spring of 1957, we bought land on Nob Hill and planned to build our first house that summer. At about that same time the IRS notified us that due to an error, we owed them $90. That was A LOT of money for us. Where would we get it, and how could we build our home?

We were very unhappy as we opened a letter from our landlord. Now what? He thanked us for finishing his attic and told us that since we had asked for nothing for this job, we owed him no rent for the month of May. How much was our monthly rent? That's right - $90! This is indicative of the fine people we've come to know in our fifty years that we've lived in Austin. Yes, we still live in that same house, and our daughter calls it "The House that Jack Built."

January and February 1986
By MaryAnne Lynch

A cold night, a low roaring hum, and a steady stream of dim lights entering a parking lot signaled a change to the neighborhood and city. At the command of the governor, the National Guard had now arrived in Austin. The call up was in response to the ongoing strike at the meat packing plant. Tensions ran high.

In the bitterly cold days that followed, the sight of guardsmen patrolling the streets, and the low throaty hum of vehicles that ran twenty-four hours a day became part of the routine. But it never felt quite normal. The sight of soldiers walking around their temporary quarters, and the eerie night noises of radios and trucks cast a long and worrisome shadow over a residential section of the town. Sometimes on cold days so brittle sun dogs could be seen, there would be heavily jacketed men who patrolled, keeping a watchful eye on their encampment.

I never grew accustomed to their presence. Like many others in the town, I observed news reports of the labor discord. A strange unease settled over the town.

One night my college age son was walking home from his part-time job when a guardsman stopped him and asked what he was doing there. When my son explained, he was tersely told to go to his home and not to be on the streets.

When the guards were leaving I caught a glimpse of what seemed, oddly, to be old metal bedsprings. It was a sobering realization that what I had seen were gun racks. In this quiet neighborhood, we had a military presence. That memory lingers. You never know.

P9 supporters at a rally in 1986

MaryAnne Lynch is a member of the Austin writers' group.

Austin Bakery Memories
By Sarah Lysne

When I was growing up, my mom would take my sister and brother and me to buy bread at the Austin Bakery. Just the name stirs up memories of wonderful smells that I will never forget. The owner of the bakery, Mrs. Waldee, used to make sure we all got cookies before we left. I have never tasted a better cherry chip cookie.

The bakery goods became part of many childhood memories. Sometimes on Saturdays, my mom would purchase one of their delicious coffee cakes: blueberry, raspberry, apricot, pineapple, or my dad's favorite, apple. At Christmas time, Mom would order Christmas breads to have on Christmas morning.

In the fall of 1981 Irene Waldee called to see if I would like to work at the bakery on Saturdays. I was thrilled! I reported to work that Saturday morning wearing one of the blue and white checked aprons my Grandma Weber made for my new job. When I entered the back door, I was consumed by the wonderful smells of donuts frying and bread baking in the oven. Irene's husband Ordene and their son Maurice greeted me.

Ordene and Maurice took big batches of dough and kneaded it into breads, coffee cakes and rolls. Sometimes they would work in silence. Other times they would laugh and talk. Younger brother Rick often stopped in after work to visit with his brother and dad, but the days were long. They arrived each day around 3 a.m. and left around 5 p.m.

I was always in awe of their work ethic. The Waldees raised six children, two sons and four daughters. Irene Waldee was a nurse. When the kids were growing up, Irene worked at St. Olaf Hospital. Her nursing career must have left an impression on her daughters because they all became nurses too. After the kids were grown, Irene retired from the hospital and worked with her husband and son Maurice at the bakery.

My employers, the Waldees, became lifetime friends. I worked at the bakery all through high school, and the Waldees made me feel like one of the family. I learned so much from them. I learned how to be a good listener from watching Irene while she listened to the many stories the customers wanted to tell her about their lives.

Ordene taught me how to look on the bright side of things. When I complained that I was going to have to drive an extra forty miles to Winona for some of the college classes I needed he said, "Good thinking time." Maurice taught me how important family is. He and his wife had three children, and he was proud of all of them.

Irene and her husband Ordene owned and operated the Austin Bakery for forty years. They are both gone now, and I miss them. But the memories of those days at the Austin Bakery will live with me forever.

The Austin Bakery, the Waldees

Sarah Lysne is a freelance writer who lives in Austin with her husband and three children.

Lost in Austin High School
By Eileen Lysne

In 1942, when I was 11 years old, my parents, my two brothers, my sister and I left our farm near Preston, Minnesota and moved to Austin. Those were the years of World War II. My parents felt fortunate to find a home to rent. It was located on Bridge Street, one block west of the center doors of Austin High School.

We moved in October when I was in seventh grade. My older brother was in eighth grade, and my sister was in tenth grade. Throughout our prior education, my siblings and I had attended a one-room country school, although my sister had gone to one year of high school in Preston.

On the first day of school my mother went with us to register at the principal's office. After registration we were taken to our respective classes, which for me happened to be a geography class. The teacher of that class chose another student to stay with me for the next classes; that worked out well until the noon hour came. After the noon hour bell rang, I found myself all alone in a hall with my books and a locker key. I had no idea where I was in that huge building, and I didn't really know what a locker was.

In country school, a locker was a coat hook on the wall. I walked up and down that hall looking for a number that matched the number on the locker key. Fortunately, a maintenance person came by and explained to me that the third floor keys started with a three, and second floor keys started with two. I was on the second floor looking for my locker, which was on the third floor.

Many years later, I was talking to my siblings about how frightened I was that day, and I found out that they were equally frightened. We had been let loose in the largest building we had ever been in by ourselves. I have often wondered about how many other children had difficulty finding the hidden band room. It was an experience that has stayed with me always, and I hope that no children today enter school with as little experience as we had back in 1942.

Eileen and her husband Harlan have three children, five grandchildren, and are very active in Fellowship Methodist Church.

Learning to Deal With a Tough Issue
By Allan Mayotte

In 1987, I attended my first conference on AIDS: five days of epidemiology, legal statutes, educational approaches, and attempts to broaden participant awareness of the psycho-social issues of this pandemic. One of the goals of the conference was to help communities in Minnesota get out ahead of the disease's progression through a combined approach on educational, medical, legal and social action levels. In the same year, with the help of Mower County Chapter of the American Red Cross, the Mower County AIDS Task Force was initiated and developed the following set of goals:

1. Preventing the spread of HIV/AIDS infection by focusing on abstaining from IV drug use and making responsible decisions about sexual encounters.

2. Presenting facts in a calm, reasonable manner, separating facts from rumor and fear.

3. Serving as a community education, support and service forum with trained educators who offer responsible, rational information. Educators will strive to be honest and direct, and will promote understanding about HIV/AIDS and quality sexuality education.

4. Protecting each person's dignity and right to privacy by being compassionate and nonjudgmental.

Many years later we are still having trouble coming to grips with the complexity of a disease that touches on topics most of us have difficulty thinking and talking about, including: sex, homosexuality, IV drugs and death. And yet, the Mower County AIDS Task Force developed a plan and found people to carry it out.

I gave more than 160 HIV/AIDS presentations, mostly in southeastern Minnesota. The most touching of my presentations came in January, 1993. I got a phone call from Dr. Doug Myers, Superintendent of the Austin Public Schools. Dr. Myers reported to the Task Force that a teacher in Austin's Banfield School had given him permission to let the public know that he was hospitalized in Rochester with AIDS. HIV/AIDS had hit our hometown. It was now an issue that became more than just a topic on paper.

The immediate plan was to have Dr. Myers, Margene Gunderson of the Mower County Public Health, Rich Danilla of the Minnesota Department of Health and myself meet with the Banfield Elementary

School staff and parents. The following day an announcement would be made to all Austin Public School staff, community leaders and the Austin Community College students. Also, I was to be interviewed on the local radio station. The next week, the task force met with concerned parents and interested community leaders for a questions and concerns forum.

With compassion, preservation of dignity and calmness, the Task Force and Dr. Myers managed to present this hot topic in a non-judgmental and reasonable way. It took dedicated people, courage and planning to work together to make this AIDS presentation acceptable to a community that, until now, had not had to deal with AIDS awareness locally. A week later, Dr. Myers again met with the Task Force to address comments, revise and add to the plan and answer questions.

The Mower County Task Force was applauded for its swift and tactful handling of this situation. I was proud to be part of the process and to live in a community of people who were willing to open their hearts and minds to a family that was forced to deal with this devastating disease.

Allan Mayotte is a retired teacher and AIDS educator.

Dutchtown Forever
By Bob McAlister

From Sutton Park to Brownsdale Avenue, railroad yard to East Side Lake was and is Dutchtown. When the call came out, the west-enders would meet on the railroad bridge. Every kid raced to the bridge to chase the unwanted and nosy people back to the other side of the bridge. I never knew why; it was just the Dutchtown law.

Growing up we stayed pretty much on our own side of town. We did not have a baseball diamond, so when we were young we played by the wall on East Side Lake. A foul ball usually ended up in the lake, and someone had to swim out to get the ball back. As we got older, we outgrew our little ball field. Someone discovered a field north of Brownsdale Avenue, between what is now Interstate 90 and East Side Lake.

We all got together with old push mowers and spent three or four days carving out a ball field. On opening day of our new field the Hormel guard force came by to inform us we were on Hormel property and had to get off the land! We were heartbroken and didn't think it was fair.

Someone came up with a bright idea that we should go to the Hormel office and talk to Mr. Hormel. We drew straws to form our committee of four, and I was one of the four who lost and had to go see Mr. Hormel. We jumped on our bikes and blew into Hormel's and threw our bikes on the lawn in front of the office. We had started up the stairs when the guards from the guard shack nabbed us and wanted to know what we were up to. When we told them we wanted to talk to Mr. Hormel about the ball field that the guards had just chased us off of, they took us up to the guard shack and made a phone call to the office. At this point I thought we might be in big trouble, and maybe my dad's job might be in jeopardy.

We were taken into a conference room and were pretty wide-eyed. Mr. Bob Gray, the company president, came in to listen to our plight, and he said to wait until he came back from talking to Mr. Hormel. Mr. Jay Hormel said we could go back and play all the baseball we wanted on his field. He stuck his head into the conference room and told us to have fun.

The joy we experienced biking back to our waiting friends with our good news is still with me nearly sixty years later. Three days later, the Hormel yard truck pulled into the ball field with the grandest backstop and installed it for us! In the late 1980s or early 1990s I was telling the story at work at Hormel's, so during my noon hour I drove to the field, and the backstop was still standing. I think it is now gone, but the memory of Mr. Hormel's kindness is still with me.

Dutchtown

Bob McAlister worked at Hormel's for 40 years and retired in Grand Marais.

Dutchtown Memories
By Gloria Michels

I was born in Austin and still live one block from our homestead in Dutchtown. I used to go mushroom picking with my grandmother. I also went dandelion picking, for a lot of people made their own dandelion wine. Almost everyone had a garden. There was Ollma's, Krob's Grocery, and Bednar's Meat Market all within two blocks. We had neighborhood grocery stores long before we had supermarkets. We had iceboxes to keep our food in, and it didn't keep too long in there because the ice would melt. An iceman would deliver us large chunks of lake ice, which was harvested in the winter and stored in an icehouse. It always had sawdust on it.

All of our streets were dirt roads. We even raised chickens. My family had a Model T Ford, and after that a 1939 Pontiac – then no car, so we had to walk. My two brothers had bikes. Sometimes I would ride theirs out to the trail before the nature center.

Webster School was located near us. In winter it was really cold, and there was a lot of snow. Our sixth grade went to Lincoln School, and we would walk over the overhead bridge across the Milwaukee Railway yard. Only shovels cleared the walks then, and in summer we only had push lawn mowers.

There was only a little stream where the man-made East Side Lake is. They made East Side Lake and had a swimming area on the northwest corner and a raft for divers. I never did learn to swim because almost every day the firemen would come to the lake and drag it looking for someone who was missing. They also used that area for ice skating in the wintertime, and they had a warming house too. WPA built the wall by the Lake.

We had air raids at night during the war. We had to keep our curtains closed and show no lights at all in the evening. It was scary when babysitting. We also had food and gas rationing. I was fishing off the north bridge when World War II ended. Haven't fished since. Both my brothers were in the service.

There were three dance halls in Austin at one time: the Rainbow, Oasis and the Terp. Each one was crowded with dancers and people looking to have a good time. We went dancing when we were old enough, but when we were young, we would play games outside like hide-and-seek, kick the can and softball. Many times we would walk to the Paramount or Roxy. We could stay and see more than one show if we had time.

Coloring, puzzles, playing games, embroidering and crocheting were our favorite things to do when not working. Almost every day we would walk to Klagge's for an ice cream cone. A & W was the first fast-food place, and roller-skating was a nice thing to do at Sargeant's Roller Rink. On North Main there were monkeys in cages, and we also had tent shows there. Our family always enjoyed board games and cards. We didn't have a phone until 1948, and we got a TV in 1954.

When I was younger, my grandma would always have a Halloween party for the neighbor kids. We would play button button or Bunco (dice). There were always candy and cookies. The city would have Fourth of July fireworks over East Side Lake. Treats for the Fourth were ice cream and pop. Other celebrations included reunions, which would be held in Todd Park. In August it was a long way to walk to the county fair, but we did, and we walked home again too.

While in high school we sometimes would walk to the Tendermaid for a hamburger and malt; otherwise we would walk home for dinner by East Side Lake and take the bus back to school.

We did have bus service in Austin. Sometimes we would ride the whole route. We had a lot of passenger trains going through here too, and sometimes I rode them, which was fun. I would take the Great Western to Hayfield and back when I was a teen. My friend went to school here and then moved to Hayfield. We could also take a train south to Manly, Iowa, and transfer to Rock Island and travel to Winton to visit my sister.

The employment office would take workers from here to Hollandale to work in the fields (hard work). For fifty-two years my dad walked to and from Hormel Foods, and I walked there for one week. I worked ten hours a day and made $27 clear for pay.

The old library was nice and quiet, and the new one is really nice, but the "quiet" is gone.

Jam & Spam
By Dawn Midje

Note: This is a story about a visit to Grandmother Velma Wuertz's home at 808 5th Avenue NW in the 1970s. My sisters, Heather and Ann Midje, were visiting, too. Scott and Tom Wuertz are my cousins who lived in Austin and came to Grandmother's to play.

I entered the back door of the house and climbed the four stairs to the brightly colored small kitchen. There was my grandma in a flowered dress, which clashed with the yellow and orange flowered wallpaper. To a little girl, my grandma looked tall and plump. She had gray, curly hair and wrinkled skin like most grandmas. She almost always wore dresses, which were pastel and patterned, and she wore glasses sometimes described as "cat eye glasses." The frames formed sharp points by the outer corners of the eyes.

My mom, dad, two sisters and I had come to my grandparents' house in Austin. My grandparents were going to take care of me and my sisters, Heather and Ann, for a week because my mother had to attend a training session on education for the gifted, and my dad had to work. My grandpa still worked at the Hormel meat packing plant, so it would be just Grandma and us kids most of the time. I was only 4 years old, yet I still remember some things about that week.

My grandma was a great cook. She was a master at making pickles, sauces, sugar cookies and apple pies. The shelves of the fruit cellar were always filled with her homemade delicacies. The week we stayed at my grandparents' house, my grandma had bought several tiny jars of jam. Every day my sisters and I each got to pick a different flavor of jam to put on our breakfast toast. For dinner we had many good things to eat, but I can only remember eating Hormel brand meat. For some reason SPAM stands out in my mind. At home we were used to a dishwasher. My grandma would get out the sponges, towels, stools to stand on, and plenty of bubbly dishwashing soap. No wonder we thought washing dishes was fun.

We spent most of our time playing. Grandma had her usual tasks to tend to, such as cooking, cleaning, and washing clothes, but she took time to play with us. There were many toys in the house. There were dolls in particular that I remember named Penny and Lulu. Penny was a pretty doll with dark brown hair. Lulu was one of the strangest looking dolls I have ever seen. She had bright red hair that would not lie down. Lulu had eyes that were so disproportionate to her body that it made her look ridiculous. Neither of these dolls had clothes, so my grandma got out her Singer sewing machine and made tiny doll dresses out of blue and white checked cloth.

One event that week that I will never forget was when my two Austin cousins, Scott and Tom, came over to play. When Grandma was busy with her household duties, one of us must have gotten the bright idea to have a tea party in the attic. Tom found a flashlight, and someone filled the play teapot with water. Climbing over boxes and bags containing Christmas decorations, photographs, camping equipment, and other treasures, Scott, Tom, Heather, Ann and I all went into the attic. We were having a super time drinking water out of the blue plastic teacups with only the light of the flashlight and the small amount of light coming through the attic doorway from an upstairs window. All of a sudden, we heard the familiar sound of pantyhose rubbing together as my grandma walked up the stairs. We knew we were in for it. With a stern look and a disgusted tone, my grandma told us to get out of the attic. We did as she said, and luckily no punishment followed. My grandma had never scolded us before, but we now knew we couldn't get away with just anything.

My grandma took my sisters and me many places around Austin. We went to Woolworth's, Ankeny's grocery store, the park and Klagge's Ice Cream Parlor. Only three blocks away from my grandparent's house, was the most special place. I don't know what the name of it was, but we referred to it as The Little Store. The outside was white with a round barn-like roof, and the inside had a hardwood floor. Every other afternoon, my grandma would walk with us to The Little Store. While we walked along the sidewalk looking at the different houses along the way, Grandma would tell us interesting stories about herself, my mom, aunt, uncle, or people who lived in the houses we were passing. As soon as we got to the store, she would let us pick out the kind of candy we wanted, usually licorice or Bazooka Gum. She would give us nickels and dimes so we could buy the candy ourselves. We would then go home and on the way listen to more stories.

I wonder if my grandma knew how much those little things meant? It didn't seem as though she was trying to do these things, so it must have been the way she was. Whether it was little jars of jam or walking to the store, they were all important to us kids. She was one special lady!

Horses to Horseless Carriages
By Louise Wuertz Midje

Austin was very young when my grandparents, Maria and Hermann Brinkman, were married in 1890. The wedding took place at the Trinity Lutheran Church in Red Rock Township, a few miles east of Austin. Their gift from the community was a young cow adorned with a wild flower wreath around its neck. My grandparents owned a farm about a mile west of the church and worked the fields together, sharing the toil of farm labor, acquiring several more farms with no extended family support. Maria and Hermann were both German immigrants, and each of them made several trips back to Germany. Either Maria or Hermann would go, and the other person would care for the farm and the children, who spoke both German and English. These trips were long because first the traveler would take a train to New York City and then board a ship to cross the Atlantic to Hamburg, Germany.

Maria was a wonderful homemaker. She was a great cook and always made fresh bread and rolls. Every housewife in those days had 100 pounds of flour on hand as a staple. The vegetable garden was critical to the family sustenance. Maria would prepare the garden produce for winter use by canning and pickling vegetables and fruits. Meat was also dried, canned or placed in salt brine in large Red Wing crocks for future use. Maria was handy with mechanical things too. Maria kept her Singer sewing machine humming as she sewed the children's wardrobe. Wallpapering and painting freshened the appearance of a home, and Maria had good taste in furniture and furnishings to enhance the comfort of a 1900s home.

Hermann was a hard worker, an excellent farmer, and was extremely knowledgeable about the care of animals. Well cared for animals were important for the early farmers, not only for horsepower in the fields and transportation, but also for protein for a large, growing family. Grandpa's team of horses appeared in many of Austin's Fourth of July parades pulling floats of red, white and blue.

When Maria and Hermann's son John wanted to begin farming, they bought a brand new house in Austin that had a yard half the size of a city block. The house was located on Baldwin Street, kitty-corner from the southeast corner of Sumner school. The new house had many amenities not found on the farm such as electricity, running water, and indoor plumbing. On their large lot my grandparents had their driving horses, two cows and many chickens.

Maria liked her new house but couldn't help but have her eye on the beautiful Victorian house across the street at 611 North 2nd Street. This house had come up for sale and had not sold because of a rumor that it was haunted. The rumor was based on the fact that at night, lights and movement could be seen through the curtains in the attic. Maria was not superstitious and found out the lights were a result of someone playing card games in the attic of the vacant house. They bought the house, and Maria now lived in the big, white, Victorian house adorned with bric-a-brac, two fireplaces, a bay window in the dining room and an open, winding staircase to the second floor.

In the back of the white house, on the corner of Baldwin and 2nd Street, was a large white carriage house with large double doors. When Hermann first moved here from across the street, he brought his driving horse and carriage. Hermann's daughter Rose was one of the first women in Austin to own an automobile, a Ford Model T coupe. Hermann watched Rose with her car and enjoyed riding with her.

Hermann Jr. loved to back the shiny Model T out of the carriage house for Rose. Hermann decided to purchase a new auto, but he wanted a larger car than a coupe. A Dodge touring auto with a canvas top seemed similar to a carriage, and this was his choice. Driving was going well, but there were times he forgot about the mechanization of his automobile. One day Hermann was driving into the carriage house, and he shouted "Whoa." Needless to say, the auto did not respond to his command, and the car went through the back wall of the carriage house and into the neighbor's garden. As embarrassing as the incident was, it became one of the family stories that generated laughs.

Another time the family was out for a ride in the Dodge touring car when a sudden thunderstorm appeared. As there were no windows in a touring car, the family hurried to put up the side curtains. The rain and wind blew through the opening, and my teenage mother's beautiful, red silk dress was in ruins.

Hermann's oldest son John was mechanically inclined. He worked at Stallman's Carpenter Shop and learned a great deal about building. John decided he would rather farm, so Hermann moved off the farm to facilitate John's career choice. Hermann would leave Austin at daybreak and walk to the farm, six or seven miles each way. John had one son, Lorn, who began to farm when John retired from farming and moved to Austin. John was a well-liked individual with many life experiences that made him a wonderful clerk at Decker Hardware in Austin.

Emma was Maria and Hermann's oldest daughter, and she graduated from the Southern Minnesota Normal College that was located in the southwest part of Austin. After graduation, Emma married Harry Feeley, a handsome Irishman. Harry and Emma owned and operated several neighborhood grocery stores in northwest Austin. Harry had the finest meat counter in town and made grocery deliveries in his Model T Ford. It was said that the car leaned considerably because of all the years of taking the same corners on his delivery route. Emma ran the store and did the bookkeeping. Emma's philosophy was that the customer was always right, and she treated the customer with respect. Harry and Emma built a thriving business. With the advent of the supermarket, Harry and Emma decided to retire to an acreage on the exact location where the Sacred Heart Care Center is located. They raised ponies and goats as pets. The St. Olaf Lutheran Church honored Emma in 1957 for over 35 years of dedicated choir membership.

Rose, the second oldest of the Brinkman daughters, was an accomplished musician and stenographer. Rose was a secretary at Hormel and soon was promoted to secretary of the Vice President, Cy Thompson. When Rose learned that he had embezzled money from Hormel, she was shocked and felt betrayed. Rose moved to Waseca as a legal secretary. There she met and married Ambrose Breen. They moved to Austin, and they built several gas stations in Austin and Mapleview. One of the stations was located on Oakland Avenue. During World War II, Ambrose was called back into service. He served in the Navy, and when the war was over, they moved to Cleveland, Ohio. Am was a fireman on the railroad, and Rose continued to be a secretary.

Hermann Jr. was the second oldest son of Maria and Hermann. Hermann Jr. was full of life and adventures. He was 8 years old when he convinced his 3-year-old sister Velma, that he was like William Tell and he could use a slingshot and shoot an apple off her head. Unfortunately he missed the apple and hit Velma on the head with a rock. Hermann told his son he would "William Tell" him, and Velma became less trusting of her brother's antics.

When Hermann Jr. became older, he was on the AHS football team. During his high school years, especially during the summers, he served as an errand boy for George A. Hormel. Hermann Jr. would ride his bike from the 1st National Bank in downtown to the Hormel office with the payroll cash. At age 102, Hermann Jr. still marvels at the trust George A. Hormel had in him.

Hermann was well liked in Austin, but he had bigger ideas in mind. He graduated from the University of Nebraska Medical School and practiced medicine in Omaha. He served as chief of staff of Clarkson Hospital for years. After World War II, until their retirement in the 1970s, Hermann and his wife traveled extensively in Europe, Africa, the Middle East and Asia. They loved to go to Japan and shared their experiences with the people of Austin by showing films of their travels.

Walter was the youngest son in the family. He became a mechanic. His life was far too short. He died of a heart attack at the age of 23.

Velma, my mother, was the youngest child of Maria and Hermann. Velma graduated from Austin High School in 1928. The stock market crashed, and as the Depression set in, jobs were hard to find. Velma found a job as a secretary to Peter Carpretz. The Capretz Agency sold insurance and real estate. Velma had lots of contact with people in the Mower County Courthouse because of real estate transactions. The courthouse was directly across Main Street from their second story office. Mom told the story about how she decided to buy a life insurance policy for her dad, Hermann, while working at the insurance agency. Hermann was extremely upset with my mother. He believed it was not right to insure one's life because God was in charge of such things. In 1937, Velma married Lorenz Wert, originally from the Waltham area. They had three children: Louise, Ruth and Richard (Dick). Velma was a stay-at-home mother and caretaker for her mother Maria, who lived seventeen years with chronic leukemia. Velma was active in the YWCA and directed many plays for the Walther League of St. John's Church. During her parenting years, she was involved with the Sumner School PTA.

As one sat in a room with the children of Hermann and Maria, a listener could get a vision of early Austin. There were stories of early settlers, the power brokers of Mower County and Austin, the wealthy people of Austin, the scandals, the treasures, the civic contributors, the history of the community and the surrounding area. How interesting it is to know people who helped make Austin what it is today!

Summer Days of the 1940s
By Louise Wuertz Midje

I fondly remember the wonderful summer days in Austin during the 1940s. My dad, Lorenz, worked for Hormel, and my mother, Velma, was a stay-at-home mother. I never remember being bored; there was always something to do. Our family had a car that Dad drove to work. This meant the rest of the family walked to wherever we wanted to go. My family lived at 808 Lyndale, so downtown, the swimming pool, and the library, even our church were all within walking distance. Sometimes the walk was over a mile each way.

The first two weeks of summer were usually devoted to Vacation Bible School at the church of your choice. Bible School was only held in the morning so the afternoons were free for play. There was no air conditioning so by noon the classes not held in the church basement could become rather hot and stuffy. At Bible School we learned the Bible stories and songs that gave us a chance to learn more about God. Our volunteer teachers made our study enjoyable, and we felt good about ourselves. Our walk to St. John's Bible School, on Kenwood Avenue, was over a mile each way and was considered good exercise.

Sumner School was only two blocks from our house. We walked rain or shine. During the summer, throughout Austin, playground activities were held. One summer the playground leaders organized a parade. My sister Ruth decorated her trike, and I decorated my wagon with red, white and blue crepe paper. In the wagon, I placed a little wooden chair my dad had made for me. On this special "throne," I set my favorite doll, Susie. Susie sat in her white wedding dress, and I swelled with pride as I pulled my doll in that parade. During World War II, the scarcity of toys was prevalent. My aunt, Emma Feeley, sewed an entire doll wardrobe including a rose-colored hat and coat that she made from old wool underwear that she had dyed. This was my Christmas gift from Santa the Christmas before the "big parade." The parade was on the sidewalk around Sumner School, but in my mind, Ruth, Susie, and I were in the biggest, best parade ever.

When I was a child, my mother would take us to the wonderful library. Up a few steps sat the stately librarian surrounded by a large, high counter. Around her was an aura of silence and stacks of books. We would enter the main door and take a right down the stairs to a wonderful room of children's books. How I would love to go there and find those magical books that activated a child's imagination. I would check out so many books to carry home that my grandmother, Maria Binkman, decided to sew me a fabric bag with strong fabric handles so I could get the books home easily.

Swimming lessons were given at the outdoor pool after school was out for the summer. When we were very small, Mother would take us to the wading pool. We'd put our hands on the bottom of the pool, and the buoyancy would support our legs. We thought that we were swimming. Once we were old enough for group lessons, we would have lessons whether the temperature was hot or cold. Usually in the morning, when lessons were given, we would sit shivering by the side of the pool waiting for instructions to be over so we could get into the water, as the water was often warmer than the air temperature. We would walk home for lunch and then back to the pool for afternoon recreational swimming.

Once swimming was over, in our swimsuits and towels we would walk north of the pool to the Clay House. To me this was a great stop! There were many wood tables in two straight lines with benches full of children in bathing suits. Each child received a ball of clay and a mold with an imprint of some kind of fruit. The clay was carefully placed into the mold. One had to remember that the bottom of the mold would be the front side once the clay was dry and the form loosened from the mold. We carefully carved our initials into the clay with a wood stick so the attendants could identify our work of art once it was dry and knocked free from the mold. A couple of days later, my plaque was ready for painting. After the paint had dried, I carried it home, and I was so proud to see it adorning my mother's kitchen. Mother treasured each project as if it were a Picasso.

Sidewalks in Austin were our paths to adventure. Tricycles, bikes, scooters, pedal cars, and clamp-on ball-bearing roller skates took us around the block many times a day. Roller-skating on sidewalks was challenging, especially when some of the walks were the early 18"x 18" squares. These squares created a myriad of cracks to avoid, and we had lots of bruised chins, knees and arms. My brother, Dick Wuertz, had a swell red and white steel pedal car that he would ride around the block an unending number of times each day. One of our retired neighbors always sat in front of his house, on the other side of our block, watching the cute little boy expertly driving his car. Dick wore out several sets of the hard rubber tires. After several days of not seeing Dick driving his car, the neighbor came over to ask Mother why Dick no longer drove the car. Mother explained that the axle was broken, and Dad had not had time to repair it. The neighbor volunteered to repair the axle, and in a couple of days Dick was on his trips around the block once again.

In between all the aforementioned activities, my sister and I would intersperse playing house in our front porch or in the yard. Often we would make a tent out of two large blankets hung on the clothesline with clothespins. Each blanket was stretched to the sides and secured with a brick or other heavy objects. My uncle, Harry Feeley, made me a cute wood cupboard, and we had Mom's childhood table and toy pots and pans. I had a rocking chair, tin stove, lawn bench, and chair. We were ready for imagination to take hold. Last, but not least, we had a large cardboard box filled with Mom's clothing from her youthful "thin years," and some high-heeled shoes and discarded costume jewelry. You can bet that two little girls, with their neighborhood friends, established a magical kingdom in which we were the queens.

Sometimes it was scary in Austin. During World War II, Austin would hold air-raid drills. All the streetlights would be shut off, and people in houses would pull all the shades, even though all the lights were off. Boy, was it ever dark! Polio also made a change in our lives. Some activities were cancelled because of the fear that crowds might spread the dreaded disease. Once a neighboring family member had polio, and the family had to be in quarantine. When the Salk vaccine became available, Mom made sure her children had the series of shots. Austin had large trucks that would spray the city for mosquitoes. On warm summer evenings, when our windows were wide open, the trucks would come down the streets dispersing a foggy spray into the neighborhoods. We would run fast and slam shut all the windows.

Some afternoons my sister Ruth and I would walk about a mile to downtown to shop with a little money. We only had a quarter so we had to be very thoughtful how we would spend our treasure. There were two dime stores on Main Street, and Woolworth's usually got our business. Each of us had a dollhouse. My dad made my house, and my sister's was a modern tin-litho house. Our houses were furnished with the colorful plastic Renwal dollhouse furniture. Our shopping trips usually involved the purchase of a new addition to our dollhouse, perhaps a radio, clock, chair or lamp. This time the lamp, next time we'll buy the radio. It cost 29 cents, and there was no sales tax then.

On summer evenings, when the Austin Packers played at Marcusen Park, our family went to the baseball games. The three Wuertz kids were members of the Knot-hole Gang. At the edge of and in back of the third-base line was an area set aside for kids to watch their favorite team. Best of all, admission was free. Many of the neighboring cities had baseball teams that played each other and would compete in the Southern Minne League. Austin had Moose Skowron, who later played for the Yankees, and we had a super team. What fun the kids would have cheering for the home team.

Summers were full of activities that included picnics at the many parks and swinging and sliding as much as you wanted. There was no air-conditioning so on hot days the kitchen table was merely moved to the porch or outdoors. Mondays would find the housewives hanging the colorful family clothing on the lines in each yard. Bright white sheets denoted that the family had a mother who was a great laundress. Paperboys, milkmen, and the mailman were our daily visitors. Almost every day a walk was taken to the neighborhood grocery store, mostly for the staples like meat, bread, and milk. Sometimes the trip was for a Popsicle or ice cream treat. The grocer knew his customers so he kept a ledger, and the bill was paid on payday.

Our country was coming out of a bad Depression. World War II was over in 1945, and hope was strong in almost everyone. Austin was growing, the baby boom had begun. Sterling addition was being built, and schools were expanding. Austin was a great city to grow up in. Life was good!

My sister Ruth and I participated in a doll buggy parade.

Buffy the Cow
By Jack Miller

One of my favorite Austin landmarks is Buffy the Cow. Buffy the Cow has been around all my life. It has even been around for most of my dad's. I see it every day when my bus drives by it on the way to Ellis Middle School. This fiberglass Guernsey cow has stood on top of the dairy building since 1965. The city of Austin was built around agriculture, and back in the 1960s when Buffy was built, it seemed like every farmer had cows. My grandpa said that back in his day, people said that if you didn't have cows, you weren't a farmer. Shortly after the cow was mounted on the building, 5,000 entries were submitted to a "name the cow" contest. Buffy was the winner.

Buffy is located at 111 5th Place SE, but most people in Austin don't need directions to find it. I have even heard people give directions using Buffy the Cow. When Buffy blew over in the 1998 storm, they had to put her back up because she is such an important landmark. The building that Buffy the Cow was made to sit on was Ankeny's. Ankeny's was a milk distribution center. It closed many years ago, but the building is still used as a repair shop.

When Buffy the Cow was first mounted on top of the dairy building, she was a symbol of the dairy industry. Though today there are far fewer dairy farms than there were in the 1960s, Buffy the Cow is still a symbol of the dairy industry.

I feel Buffy is an important part of Austin. I think that when the building deteriorates, Buffy will be moved to the Mower County Fairgrounds to sit alongside all the other historic buildings and landmarks. Long live Buffy the Cow.

Buffy-looking good at age 41

Jack Miller will be a high school freshman in September, 2006.

Unexpected Delivery
By Evie Mohrfeld

In 1961 my husband Jerry and I and 16-month-old son moved to Faribault. We were expecting another child in mid-November. Jerry and I are from northern Iowa, and because we had relatives in Austin, we were happy to be living only a short distance away, and we visited frequently.

It was one of those dreaded phone calls you never want to receive. Jerry's sister, Marlys Clark, and her husband Kenny operated the Dixie Creme Donut Shop, along with Mom's Kitchen, located on 2nd Avenue NE, across the street from the original Usem's Chevrolet. Marlys, as calmly as she could, told us that her husband Kenny had been killed in a car accident early in the morning. Kenny loved to hunt and grabbed every chance to go out after frying donuts all night and then delivering to the Catholic schools of Saint Augustine and Queen of Angels after their morning school masses. He was road hunting early in the morning and perhaps dozed off after a night of work. His car hit a farmer's end drive and nose-dived across, landing in the ditch and crushing Kenny's chest on impact.

Kenny and Marlys had four small children, and losing their daddy who was only 29 years old was an unbelievable tragedy. Her phone call caused us to immediately make plans to be with Marlys and her family. A call to my doctor in Faribault gave us assurance that we were only an hour's drive away in the unlikely event that I would go into labor early, and since I had just been checked by the doctor, we packed some things and drove in our 1957 Ford Fairlane to Austin.

Also living in Austin then were my uncle and aunt, Harold and Cleta Stupka. Harold worked in accounting for Meier Wolf Furniture, which is now Brick's Furniture. Uncle Harold and Aunt Cleta were accomplished pianists, and they played organ at Queen Of Angels Church. After we made a quick call to them, they welcomed our family and said they would care for Michael so we could spend time with Marlys' family and friends as they arrived.

It was 10:30 p.m. when we got back to Stupkas' house and had some birthday cake and ice cream, to celebrate Uncle Harold's birthday. About midnight, we decided to turn in, and I had a very restless night. At first I thought the late night snacks and anxiety perhaps were the cause, but the nagging backache led us to believe that perhaps we should call my doctor in Faribault. When we did, he again assured us that we were only an hour's drive away, and he said we should head for Faribault, where he would be waiting at the hospital to meet us.

My aunt suggested that perhaps it would be a good idea to call her doctor here and make a quick hospital stop in Austin to check on my progress. Luckily, Dr. Ray Van Cleve was on call. After driving through town to get to St. Olaf, I was very glad to see the hospital doors as we pulled up right in front. The hospital was then located on the same site on Lansing Avenue. A nurse was there to greet us with a wheelchair.

All mothers will relate to how hard it is to move out of the car and onto a chair during that time. Jerry was quickly parking our car and rushed in following us down the hall. "Oh, I'm not leaving her. We just brought her by to check on her pains. We're leaving for Faribault."

"Oh! Sure, just stop by the window and fill out some papers."

"No! Really—we are going to Faribault." They acted like they thought we didn't know what was happening—well, maybe we didn't! By the time Jerry got to the maternity ward, I had been wheeled off to the delivery room. Joseph Kenneth was born at 6:31 a.m. the day of Kenny's funeral. Dr Van Cleve stayed at the hospital by my side during this labor and for a few hours after, checking on me constantly. I never had a chance to be scared this whole time. He was such a warm, caring and comforting doctor and new friend for me. That's for sure.

It was 1964 when we actually did move to Austin. Jerry accepted a position with Sterling State Bank. Our daughter Jan joined us in February, and we made our move here in June. It was 1967 and 1968 when Doctor Van Cleve delivered our daughter Susan and son Charles. Dr. Ray Van Cleve moved to Winston Salem, North Carolina, where he became a professor at Bowman Gray Medical School of Wake Forest University. He left behind a host of friends and grateful patients who will always remember him and his many acts of kindness.

What a wonderful experience it was that night in November to deliver our son in Austin and later deliver a daughter and another son. Later we made Austin our permanent home. When Joseph Kenneth registered for school in Austin, the story got repeated time and again. "No, I wasn't living here when he was born, but was dropped off along the way."

Burdette Haldorson, Two-time Olympic Gold Medalist
By Wayne Nemitz

I was working for Hormel in Fort Dodge, Iowa in 1956. I drove to Austin to attend a tune-up for the Olympic basketball team at the Austin High School gym. The team was playing in various gyms in the USA while getting ready for the Olympic games that were later held in Melbourne, Australia. One reason they came to Austin was that Colorado All-American Burdette Haldorson of Austin was on the squad.

I attended the game with my father-in-law, Fayette Sherman, who later was mayor of Austin. At half-time, Moose Skowron, an Austin Packers player who later became a famous Yankee All-Star and World Series first baseman, drew my name out of the hat. We had to sign in at the door for a drawing. I won a basketball that was signed by the whole team. Legendary Bill Russell's name was on the ball, and after he became famous, Bill did not give out signatures over the years.

K.C. Jones was another big name on the ball, along with Austin's own Burdie Haldorson. In those days memorabilia was not a big thing like it is today. I actually played with the basketball at the Y. I don't know what happened to it, but I know I should have put it up on a shelf.

Back in those days, only amateurs could play in the Olympics. Haldorson played in all eight games, scoring a total of 69 points, and the U.S. team defeated the Soviet Union in the final game and brought home Olympic gold medals. On a USA basketball history website roster, they list Burdette's height as 6'7" and his hometown as Austin, Texas. At least they got his height right.

Burdie also played on the 1960 United States Olympic team that featured Jerry West, Jerry Lucas and Oscar Robertson. That team, which many believe was the best basketball team of all time, defeated all eight of their Olympic opponents by an average of 42 points, defeating Italy in the finals in front of their home crowd in Rome by more than 30 points. Burdie only scored 23 points in that series, but Lucas, West and Robertson scored 382 points among the three of them.

I watched Burdie play his senior and my sophomore year at AHS in 1951. Austin was unbeaten until they got to the state tournament. In 1999, *Sports Illustrated* listed the top fifty athletes of all time from each state. Topping Minnesota's list were Bronco Nagurski, Kent Hrbek, and Kevin McHale. Austin's Burdette Haldorson was number 33.

Austin Boys' Basketball
By Wayne Nemitz

I remember basketball games in the late 1940s and early 1950s when overflow fans sat out in the auditorium. Students would get in line as soon as school got out. The doors opened at 6. At one game against Albert Lea, my friend Fred Swenson, Pastor Swenson's son, lost his loafers when the doors opened. He got pulled right out of his shoes when the crowd surged forward. Fred had to go home to get different shoes. When he returned, he had to sit in the balcony of the auditorium.

Austin had an amazing run of good teams and good players from 1942 until 1960, winning the state title in 1946 behind the skills of Harper Richardson and in 1958 behind the marksmanship of Tom Kezar. Austin was state champ runner up in 1955 to Minneapolis Washburn and in 1960 to Edgerton. Burdette Haldorson, a 6'8" center, took Austin to the state in 1951, and the 1954 team featured 6'6" Jerry Olson and 6'5" Hugh Hall. There was no shortage of skyscrapers on those teams.

Those were dynamite teams. I graduated in 1953 so there were many good years when I was in school and many after I left. The team I really liked had three skilled players: 6'6" Tom Kezar, 6'2" Clayton Reed, and 5'11" Mike Marineau. That team nailed unbeaten Hawley in the first round only to get upset by Wayzata in the semi finals of the state tournament.

I visited Millie Berven, Ove's wife, at St. Mary's a few years ago. Millie told me she rooted for the New York Yankees. She said no one liked Austin because they won all the time. She could identify with the Yankees for that reason. Austin didn't win all the time, but it sure seemed like they won a good share of the time.

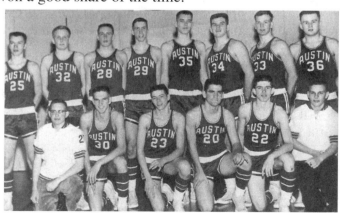

1958 AHS team

J.C. Hormel Nature Center
By Allie Neumann

Imagine you're standing in a lush garden of sensual fragrance, the pure scent of nature. Maple trees, restored prairie, pine forests, and Dobbins Creek surround you. The Austin Jay C. Hormel Nature Center has many attractions, along with fun activities that would keep any age from child to adult busy as a bee!

I don't know about you, but I am a regular Nature Center visitor. I visit the Nature Center at least thirty times a year. On nice summer mornings, my mother takes her daycare kids out there, and they have fun crossing the bridges, making believe trolls are underneath or visiting Dobbins Creek to look at the tiny minnows. The joy on their faces when they spot a deer is the best part.

My favorite part of the Nature Center is the giant rock. As you get to the top you feel like you're the king of the world! Many people attend the spooky/scary Halloween Warm-Up presented by the Matchbox Children's Theatre, which is always a great amount of fun. Blizzards and below zero temperatures better not scare you away from the Nature Center. You can strap on some cross-country skis and take a tour around the 278 acres of wildlife, and more. When summer rolls along, you may enjoy a peaceful canoe trip single or with a friend. Many people don't realize what nature is until they come to the Jay C. Hormel Nature Center.

Some people probably don't know much about this wonderful place. Free activities include storytellers, dancers, the winter haven dog sled program and more. If you're just in for an autumn walk, you'll enjoy the beautiful paths of changing leaf colors and birdcalls. During the day if you're bored, come on out to the interpretive buildings to see many textures of furs, antlers, bones and fungi. A live display of snakes, toads and an indoor beehive can keep children entertained for hours.

The Jay C. Hormel Nature Center is not only the most well known meeting place, park and recreation area in Austin, but it's also a place for peaceful getaways. Maybe next time you have nothing to do, you'll consider taking a hike to the Austin Jay C. Hormel Nature Center for a full day of fun-filled adventures.

Allie will be a freshman at AHS in the fall of 2006.

How I Came to Call Austin My Home
By Gloria Nordin

It was 1954, and I had graduated from the University of Minnesota with a Bachelor of Science degree in elementary education. I had spent the summer in Europe on a tour of twelve countries, a reward to myself for reaching my goal of becoming an elementary school teacher. Earlier I had visited Austin and the school where I would teach and had also visited the Rochester School District. I decided to teach fifth grade at Neveln School on the second floor of the new wing, which was not finished. Little did I know that my children would attend this school years later.

The teacher orientation week started on Monday, August 30. I was not scheduled to disembark from my ship in Montreal until August 31, so the soonest I could arrive in Austin was September 1. Therefore, the principal of Neveln, Fran Baxter, knew I would arrive a bit late.

When I arrived in Montreal, Hurricane Carol was attacking the East Coast. In fact, the steeple of North Church in Boston was blown down, and there was much damage elsewhere. It rained horizontally in Montreal, and there was no air transportation available. Therefore, my plane from Montreal to Chicago to Minneapolis was delayed. Because I needed to get home as soon as possible, I had booked a plane to arrive in Minneapolis at 2 a.m., but the plane was rescheduled to land at 9 a.m.

My sister Barbara met me, and we went directly home. As soon as I arrived I called the Austin school superintendent's office to inform them that I would be arriving Wednesday, September 1 in the afternoon instead of the morning as planned. The secretary to the school superintendent told me that I should not hurry as the whole town had closed down because Jay C. Hormel had passed away, and most everything in town was closing in his honor.

I arrived in Austin that afternoon of September 1 and was taken to my residence, where I met my roommates, Arlys Leach, Marnie Strand, and Cecily Spaulding. I will always remember coming to Austin just as the great leader and businessman of the Hormel Company had passed away and all the services that were held in his honor.

I changed my name from Gloria Erickson to Gloria Nordin when I married Dr. Richard Nordin four years later. But that's another story. So, here it is!

In 1956 I was teaching fifth grade at Sumner School. This was my second year of teaching, and I had transferred from Neveln to Sumner. At the year-end teacher coffee party someone asked where I was going for the summer. I had plans to spend the whole summer in Hawaii. A second grade teacher, Doris Walker, mentioned there was an Austin boy in the Navy stationed on Oahu.

I visited a friend and Austin High School graduate, Barbara Burton, in Seattle on my way to Hawaii. Barbara informed me that there was an Austin guy in Hawaii. He had played piccolo and flute in the AHS band when Barbara was a student and member of the band. She encouraged me to look him up when I was on the islands, but I wondered how I could manage to do that. Impossible, I thought.

I arrived at the Honolulu airport on a Monday in June. I stayed one night at the Reef Hotel on Waikiki Beach and the next day moved to a women's residence called Fernhurst, which was affiliated with the YWCA. Of course, my mother was happy to know that! When I went down to the dining room for dinner, I joined three girls sitting at a table for four people. We got to visiting, and the girls mentioned that there was a dance at the Pearl Harbor Officer's Club Wednesday night. They invited me to go along with them, and they decided that they should take the first seating for dinner in order to leave on time.

We arrived at the Officer's Club and started to visit with Naval officers who were not in uniform, as this was not a military function. In the process of mingling, I was introduced to Ensign Richard Nordin. I asked him to repeat his last name, and when he said, "Nordin," I couldn't believe it as I'd had two Austin people tell me about him and encourage me to meet him.

Richard and I dated until August, when I had to get back to Austin for my teaching job at Sumner School. Richard came home on a month's leave at Christmas as a Lieutenant JG, and then was assigned to the National Security Agency in Washington, D.C. for the last half of his Navy tour of duty. He was discharged from the Navy in January of 1958, and we were married June 28, 1958. We were both from Austin, but we met 4,000 miles away in Hawaii. Richard contends that I chased him halfway around the world so he married me. I still can't believe the time and place of our meeting, so perhaps it was supposed to be!

Since her arrival in 1954, Gloria Nordin has been a community leader. She serves on the Austin City Council.

Here We Go Again! History Repeats Itself
By Richard E. Nordin

The Nordin family history in Austin began in 1928 when Dr. Walter H. Nordin Sr. came to this city to open up an Optometric practice. After serving in the Navy in the First World War, he graduated from optometry school in 1921 and then worked with another doctor in Faribault. After eight years he decided to open up his own practice, and Austin was his choice. That very first year a tornado struck the town. His office was somewhat damaged in the Farmers and Merchants Bank Building, but not as badly as some that were practically destroyed.

The same Rochester architect who designed the Jay C. Hormel Home, Harold Crawford, designed one of their homes on Oakland Place NE. They sold that home to local dentist Dr. Bill Lebens, in 1958. That home was purchased by another Nordin generation, Richard and Gloria Nordin, in 1966, and we are still residing there.

Dr. Nordin became very active in a number of community activities, including the American Legion, Kiwanis, Toastmasters, Masons, Park and Recreation Board, and the First Methodist Church. He was also active in his profession, serving as president of the Minnesota Optometric Association, and he served on the Minnesota Board of Examiners in Optometry for over twenty years. Dr. Walter H. Nordin, Jr. joined the practice in 1949 after serving in the Army in the Second World War and graduating from Illinois College of Optometry. He became active in music and theatre for many years. He died in 1989. I am his second son.

After military service I returned and became active in the community, serving in the Jaycees, Kiwanis, Chamber of Commerce, Park and Recreation Board and Our Saviors Lutheran Church. I was also active in my profession, serving as president of the Minnesota Optometric Association. My wife Gloria was active in many community organizations and served on the city council as representative of the third ward. She was active in optometry also, serving as national president of the Auxiliary to the American Optometric Association.

The Nordins have always believed in serving their community, and it is interesting that often things don't change that much. We ran across the following article written by Dr. Walter H. Nordin Sr. in 1935. It is as pertinent today as it was over seventy years ago. At the end of it he asked folks to sign a pledge to shop in Austin.

Give That Extra Service to Help Create 100 Jobs (1935 Article)

This matter of creating "100 Jobs in 100 days" has great merit. I have given some thought to this the past few weeks, and have come to realize what a wonderful city Austin would be if everyone did their shopping in the Austin trade area. This would create thousands of jobs because of a "shot in the arm stimulus." When business increases we are forced to hire additional help.

How to accomplish this is the big problem. We do not have to broaden our trade territory, but we need to take care of and serve our own people. Therein lies our greatest potential.

Where do we start? With ourselves. If every businessman who operates a store or office would resolve to do his shopping in the Austin trade area, it would create many hundreds of new jobs. If every businessman asked himself this question, "How much shopping do I do out of the Austin area," it would surprise us all. How can we expect patronage when we do not patronize our own neighbor?

It is going to take more than loyalty to our community to make the people of Austin shop in the Austin area. It is going to require a concerted continuous effort to accomplish this. Here are some suggestions:

• Make your place of business a pleasant place to shop, and to come in for service. How to do this?

• Lift your place of business, store or service out of the average class. If you are average, you have a lot of competition. That little extra effort puts you above the average, and you are in a class of your own. You become distinctive. How to lift yourself above the average?

• Give that little extra service. Train personnel to give this extra service. Insist on clean, pleasant and convenient surroundings. Each business concern needs to burn midnight oil to develop ways and means to accomplish this end. The successful businessman today is giving a superior service. He is not average.

Richard Nordin is an Austin native who returned to Austin after serving in the Navy to practice optometry with his father and brother.

Losing Grandpa, Huebert "Butch" Barclay
By Donald Barclay Palmer

When I was in seventh grade, my grandfather, Huebert (Butch) Barclay, was diagnosed at age 57 with pancreatic cancer. My family was devastated by the news. The man I had grown to know and love was slowly fading away.

He resembled a linebacker gone completely to seed, with broad shoulders and a childish face. Sure, he was rather large, but he had compassion, a sense of humor, creativity, and kindness that matched or surpassed his size.

With his hobby of carpentry and mechanics, Butch helped his friends and family repair their machines, never asking anything in return. For those who would not accept his assistance without payment, he kept a notebook of his favors he earned, and either accepted their services or maintained a long line of barter and trade of tools or services. Because he would accept no money, tools were the established currency.

He also was Austin Library's handyman and bookmobile driver before retiring in 2000, after thirteen years of service. He would still spontaneously pop in to say hi or to tell the librarians a new joke.

On September 23, I had just come home from school and was starting to do my homework when the phone rang; no one else was home yet so I answered the phone. "Donny?" a woman's voice asked.

"Hi Rita," I answered realizing that it was the voice of my aunt. "Is your father home yet?" There was a tremor in her voice I didn't understand.

"No, he's on his way home. Is there anything you wanted to tell him?" She was silent. The lack of sound was unusual as she is a sociable person who enjoys talking to her nephews and niece.

With a sense of foreboding I asked, "He's gone, isn't he?"

She replied, "Yes." The rest of that day and the days following blurred together in disbelief, shock, anger and numbness. He was gone. I couldn't believe it, I didn't want to believe it, and I wanted to scream at the world to go to hell and take me with it.

The days after the funeral were the worst; the sickening finality of burying your grandfather is the most dreadful kind of pain imaginable. I felt that as he died, a part of me died with him; my soul was gone.

For a week I stayed with my grandmother. Constantly being reminded of my pain, I sat in my room most of the time, barely eating, sleeping or thinking, until I eventually realized that this was not the way it should be. A man shouldn't be remembered by his death, but by his life. The pain was real, the hurt was real, but the joy of it was so much more important. The greatest man I knew had ascended to the heavens to live among the angels and departed souls of the past, to live free. Free of the pain, free of the hurt, and free to spend his time floating among the heavens celebrating the joys of his life, and the lives of his grandchildren.

Butch Barclay, Nancy Gerber and Judy Callies... and the Bookmobile

Donald and his twin Corey are the oldest grandchildren of Butch Barclay. Donald remembers riding in the bookmobile with his grandfather in Austin parades.

Hitchhikers
By Steve Price Jr.

I was driving down I-90, just north of Hayward, on Memorial weekend in 2002 when I saw two hitchhikers. Normally, I would just drive by. But this was a young male and female in what I thought to be late teens, early twenties, and then I saw the clincher...they had a dog. I was on my cell phone, so I finished the conversation with, "I'm picking up a couple hitchhikers. Nan, don't worry. They have a dog; it's all good. Later."

I hung up the phone and rolled down the window as my Jeep came rolling to a stop. "Where you guys heading?"

"East...you?" Imagine that, I thought. Standing on the side of eastbound I-90, and they're heading east. Duh!

"Well, I'm heading to Austin. It's only fifteen miles, but east is east. Hop in." I was a little nervous. I had never picked up a single hitchhiker in my life, let alone two hitchhikers and a dog, but they graciously accepted.

A very genuine, "Thanks, man. We really appreciate it," came floating over the Jeep as I walked around to open the back hatch. "Sheba, hop up." So the dog's name is Sheba, I thought as I walked back to the driver's door.

"What kind of dog is she?"

The guy spoke up, "Pit crossed with Chihuahua. Actually, she's Staffordshire terrier, not a real pit."

"No kidding! I have a pit. She's a real sweetie. Her name's Breeze. Your Sheba reminds me a lot of Breezer." And my new friends and I were off. It turns out that they were from the East Coast. He had been in the steelworkers' union in Boston, but he got laid off so the two decided to head west. They had been as far west as San Francisco, but they had just left Portland a week before I met them. They hopped a train bound for Chicago, but around Cheyenne they were running low on water, and the dog looked thirsty, so they got off the train. After that, they got a ride with a gentleman in a motor home. He took them as far east as he was heading. That was three days' riding, sleeping and eating in a motor home. "We got really lucky there," the guy added.

Apparently the union this guy belonged to put away two dollars for every hour he worked for vacation time. But if you got laid off before you used your vacation time, you simply got a check six months later. So they were just on their way back to Boston to pick up the check.

"You know what," I started, "I have this big can of chow mein and some rice in back. I was gonna cook dinner for some friends, but they're at a pizza place. I was gonna ask them if I could cook it at their place, and it's way too much food for just me. Would you two eat some if my friends let me cook there?"

"Are you sure? We don't want to impose. If you're cooking anyway, it's not a problem..." They finally agreed. Again, very graciously. I stopped at Steve's Pizza in Austin. My new friends stayed in the Jeep, and I ran in to ask my buddy if I could have access to his apartment.

"Who's that with you?" his girlfriend asked.

I simply replied, "They're the hitchhikers I picked up."

"You're kidding!" she said. "Is that your dog?"

"Nope. That's their dog. Anyway, I brought some food with me," I explained. "I was going to cook dinner for the two of you, but you already ate. So I was wondering if I could make dinner for my new friends at your place."

My buddy said, "Sure, go right ahead." Then he asked, "What are their names?"

"Wow," I said. "I've been riding with them for twenty minutes. I know where they're from, but not their names. I know the dog's name is Sheba, and they're on their way from Portland to Boston..." I proceeded to tell my buddy and his girlfriend what I knew about them, which, admittedly, wasn't much. But my buddy gave me his keys, and I was off to make dinner. It wasn't until I was serving dinner that I finally introduced myself. Their names turned out to be Rusty and Megan. I could've just as easily never known their names, because I knew they were good people.

After dinner, I drove them to Hy-Vee. I bought two cans of food because that was all they wanted. "We should have enough to get us to

Chicago. We have friends there," Rusty told me. I then bought a liter of Windsor Canadian and a twelve-pack of Labatt Blue. I presented the whiskey and the beer and said, "Take your pick." They picked the beer.

I dropped them off in a wooded area near a campground five miles east of Austin, just off I-90. I explained the location, "There's running water at the campground a quarter mile back through these woods, and a gas station/restaurant three miles ahead. There should be a pay phone at either place if you need one." I knew that my time with my new friends was coming to an end. "You got everything?" I asked.

"Yup, that looks like all of it. Thanks again," Rusty said, extending his hand. I grabbed it. Megan chimed in very graciously.

I shook both their hands. "Thank you guys for restoring my faith in humanity. Good luck." I drove away, and they walked off into the woods. I had only spent a short time with my new friends, and I do mean friends. I had given them a ride, let them make a few phone calls on my cell phone, prepared a square meal, and bought them some groceries and beer. I gave Rusty the bead from my earring (because he lost his quite some time ago), the last dollar I had in my pocket, and I got them about twenty miles farther east. I felt better than I had in months.

Is it a good idea to pick up hitchhikers? Not always. In fact, I've had more people than not say, "Are you NUTS?" But I helped two people. I gave them everything I could think to give them, and it felt great! To quote Ted, from *Bill and Ted's Excellent Adventure*, "Be excellent to each other!"

Steve Price lives in Mankato. This story is from an e-mail he sent to his favorite Riverland teacher, retired writing instructor Paul Goodnature.

Karsrud Family History
By Judy Arett Pryor

Eighteen-year-old Mabel Karsrud sat at the 50-year-old oak kitchen table, writing a post card to her cousin, Paula Larson in 1918. Candlelight gave a shadowy look to the big kitchen as a clock ticked in the parlor. Wind whistled through the trees outside, and there was a scent of wood burning in the old iron cook stove. As Mabel signed the card and attached a penny stamp, she wondered what it must have been like for her grandparents when they came to this country fifty-one years earlier.

Mabel's grandparents, Berte "Olina" Tollerud and Johannes Karsrud, were born and raised near Gjovick, Vardal, Norway. Olina's father was a "Husman," a man who operated another man's farm and in return was given two acres of land from which he was expected to make a living. The work on these two acres was done in his spare time. He and three of his children worked at Rodfo's *Tanstik* (match) factory.

Railroads, which were expanding in the United States, ran ads in Europe, encouraging immigration to the United States, where industrial development offered opportunities. Johannes was 32, and Olina was 18 when they married on April 26, 1867. They were among thousands of European immigrants to sail for America, hoping to find farming more profitable here. It was a bittersweet farewell, as they hoped for a bright future but knew they may never see friends and family members again. Olina and Johannes boarded a small ship, which was far from comfortable. The trip was long, and many people got seasick. The weaker ones died and were buried at sea.

When they finally arrived at Ellis Island, they were met by hundreds of strangers who spoke English, a language they didn't understand. Olina was becoming uncomfortable with the weight of the baby she expected soon. The money they expected to help them get to Albert Lea was late, so they had to pawn some of their belongings. Finally they boarded a train in New York and traveled to Minnesota Territory. They went to a relative of Johannes Karsrud north of Albert Lea to stay. On February 6, 1868, a son, Henry Karsrud, was born. When he was a few weeks old, they moved to Lansing Township, where they took a homestead three miles northwest of Austin. Johannes and his cousin built a sod hut to use as a temporary home. The weather was still cold, but they began cutting down trees to build the house. In a few weeks the weather improved, and the house was finished. Olina was very happy to finally have a home of her own. Johannes built a cradle for the baby, a bed, table, chairs and a cabinet to hold dishes.

When the frost was out of the ground, they plowed up land to plant corn, oats and hay to feed and bed the animals. In summer the oxen and cow grazed on the grass. Hay was planted, and three crops were cut and stored for winter. In August oats were separated from the straw to provide bedding for the animals and insulation around the foundation of the house. Johannes ground oats into flour so Olina could bake bread. Olina was a strong, hardworking woman, and she took pride in her home. She carefully skimmed cream from the top of milk and churned it into butter. She raised a few chickens, which provided eggs. Before winter set in, Johannes cut more trees and built a stable. Gradually the Karsrud place was becoming more comfortable.

Julia, was born December 9, 1872, and a son, Bernard, in 1874. Bernard lived only a few days and was buried at Oakwood Cemetery in Austin. By this time Henry was 6 and growing big enough to help his father with small tasks, gradually learning to milk the cow, feed the oxen and cattle, gather eggs and chop wood for the stove and for heat.

In March of 1883, Olina's father, Johannes Tollerud, came to America to live with his daughter and her family. What a joyous reunion. Julia was 11 and thrilled to meet *Bestefar* (grandfather). His wife, Berte, and two of their children, Caroline and Otto, joined them in July of 1884. During the next few years several relatives followed and settled northwest of Austin. On February 25, 1892, Julia died at age 19 and was buried at Oakwood Cemetery. Henry had turned 24 less than three weeks before his sister passed away. He still lived at home, but the house felt so empty with only the three of them.

Henry helped his father farm, but his real love was engines and motors. Richard Dudgeon of New York City invented the first automobile, developed with a steam engine, in 1866. Henry spent every spare minute working on engines and inventing new ways to use them. He began courting Emma Mathilda Peterson, a pretty, Lutheran girl. Henry was 32 when they married in 1899. As was the custom, the bride moved in with her husband's family. She worked hard to please her mother-in-law by helping with the work. Having a young woman's help was a welcome change for Olina. Carrying in water from the cistern pump, baking bread, pies, and cakes, canning fruits and vegetables grown in the garden, spinning wool to sew their clothing and emptying chamber pots were just a few of the things they did.

It had been twenty-five years since a baby lived in the house, and the family was thrilled when Emma became pregnant. On November 13, 1900, Emma gave birth to Mabel Olina. Mabel was the fourth baby born in this house. She was baptized at St. Olaf Lutheran Church in Austin, three miles away. Loved by everyone, Mabel grew to enjoy a leisurely life as the only child with not only parents, but also grandparents giving her undivided attention. Mabel learned both Norwegian and English because *Bestemor* and *Bestefar* spoke only Norwegian. She was the apple of her father's eye, and Mabel stood and watched her father work on engines. She listened intently as he told her about them. When Henry Ford's Model T rolled off the assembly line in 1908, Henry Karsrud was determined to buy one. Mabel often heard her father repeat Henry Ford's words, "You can paint it any color as long as it's black." Mabel's father gave her a ride to Peerless School District 122, less than a mile north of her home in Lansing Township.

When she was 10, Mabel experienced the first death in her immediate family. Olina died, and Emma dyed one of Mabel's good dresses black, the color everyone wore to the funeral as they buried Olina at Oakwood Cemetery Mabel began two years of confirmation classes at St. Olaf Lutheran Church when she was 12. A few weeks before classes ended, Mabel's parents took her to a photography studio in Austin for her confirmation pictures. She was confirmed with several other people her age. Getting confirmed was the first step to growing into a young lady. On the day of confirmation, grandparents, aunts, uncles and cousins came from Lansing, Hayward, and Faribault to celebrate.

When World War I broke out, many people went to fight for their country. In 1917, Minnesota sent wheat and iron ore to help soldiers. One of Mabel's admirers was among them, and he sent her postcards. Mabel wrote postcards a couple of times a week to friends and relatives and received many in return. During the summer she sometimes spent a week with one of her cousins, and other times they would stay a week with her, leaving on Sunday after church.

Shortly before Mabel turned 17, Emma told her that she was expecting a baby. Mabel envisioned having a sister to share her life. Verna Marie was born on March 16, 1918. Gradually, Mabel noticed that there wasn't much time with her mother alone anymore. There were diapers to wash and hang on the line to dry, clothes to sew for the baby, and of course, all the usual cooking, cleaning, laundry and gardening. All the attention seemed to be centered on the baby. Mabel loved Verna, but my, what a change.

Peter Arett drove his buggy over from Moscow on Sunday afternoons if the weather was nice and the fieldwork was done. Soon Mabel's mother sent him a postcard, inviting him for Sunday dinner. His visits became more frequent, and Mabel began to look forward to Sundays. She learned that Pete was born near Postville, Iowa. The country was in a depression at that time. Pete went to school through fourth grade and then went to work. They moved to Minnesota, and Pete and his brother, Henry, bought a farm near Moscow in 1919. They went to barn dances for miles around, some as far away as Glenville. Pete loved to dance the jig. Sometimes the dances lasted late into the night, but when the sun rose in the morning, these two brothers were out milking cows and working in the fields.

In November, 1920, Pete and Mabel got married at the Lutheran Church in Blooming Prairie. Mabel moved into Pete and Henry's house. She turned 20 a week after the wedding, and Pete was 30. It didn't take long for the house to turn from a very plain, bachelors' house to a home with a feminine touch. Mabel was a good cook, making lefse, lutefisk, rosettes and other Norwegian dishes that Pete enjoyed. She wrote postcards to her mother weekly, sometimes sitting on Pete's lap at the dining room table while she wrote. During the day she wore her black hair braided and coiled with combs. At night she brushed out the braids, and her beautiful hair fell below her waist.

Pete and Mabel lived a long and happy life together, raising two children. Emma and Henry remained on the home place with Verna and her family. After Emma's death, Mabel's son and his wife, Glenn and Shirley Arett, purchased the farm. Later his daughter Nancy and her husband, David Finley, bought it, and they own it to this day. It is a home full of happiness, laughter and good food. Nancy uses recipes that have been passed down through the generations, and she often sends food home with her guests. She would make her great, great *bestemor* proud with the lefse she makes and the flower gardens she grows.

Judy is a secretary for the Worlien Funeral home of Austin. She loves to write family history.

The Life of a Farm Girl in the 1950s
By Judy Arett Pryor

"Judy, it's time to get up." Hearing my mother's gentle voice from downstairs, I rolled over in bed and sighed. "Six o'clock already?" Sitting up in bed, I placed a bookmark in *The Secret in the Old Clock,* a mystery featuring Nancy Drew. Late the night before I had been reading with a flashlight so as not to disturb my sisters in the adjoining room. They weren't as devoted to reading as I was. My parents often chided me for always having my "nose in a book." Living and working on a farm in the 1950s didn't leave too much leisure time. I dreamed of the day I could live in town, work 8 to 5, and read all evening. It wasn't that I minded the work; I just wanted more time to read.

A warm breeze was blowing in the open window as I got out of bed and dressed in old jeans and a shirt. I walked down the stairs, put on my tennis shoes and walked out into the sunny morning. The screen door closed behind me as I walked down the steps and out to the barn to begin my day by helping my dad milk cows. My favorite time of year was summer. I loved the smell of clover hay in our old red barn with the cupola topped by a rooster-shaped weather vane. Hollyhocks bloomed next to Grandpa and Grandma's house 100 feet from ours.

Daddy was letting cows into the barn as I walked in. I sometimes wondered how each of those twenty-five cows knew which stanchion to enter, almost like people in church on Sundays. You always knew where each would be. We washed the cows' udders and put milking machines on to begin the twice-daily process of milking. Grandpa came into the barn to spread straw for bedding and do other light work. After about ten minutes, as the first of three milking machines was full, three cats and an assortment of kittens ran to a dish next to the milk cans, knowing they would get a sample of this warm, steamy milk. This was one of the things that made summer mornings enjoyable. I knew that my dad liked the way I worked. I was a ninety-eight pound, five-foot-two 14-year-old, and my younger sisters said I was too skinny, so I took pride in handling 20-25 pound milk buckets. When feeding cows, I simply made more trips. I wanted to please my father and grandfather. They didn't talk much, but there was a feeling of closeness. Daddy had a dry sense of humor, and once in awhile he would say something to make me smile, such as when Marilyn Monroe died. With a somber look on his face, he said, "Did you hear that my girlfriend died? I won't even get to the funeral."

Milking was a leisurely time. Harder work would come later in the day. After the cows were milked and let out of the barn, we got the big forks and shovel out to clean the barn and put ground corn in front of each stanchion for evening. There was also time for reminiscing.

Austin and the area within a twenty-mile radius had been home to my family for five generations. My grandfather, Pete Arett, bought the 100-acre farm near Moscow in June of 1919, and married my grandmother, Mabel Karsrud, in November. They had a son, Glenn. He grew up learning agriculture, and when he was 18, he met 16-year-old Shirley Corson at a Fourth of July parade in Lyle. They had both grown up on farms during the Depression, conservative people with good morals. Mom went to work as a hired girl when she was 14. She had seen the best of both worlds, sometimes taking care of a large family when a new baby arrived and other times serving as cleaning help for a wealthier family. Glenn was very handsome with black hair and the bluest eyes you've ever seen. Shirley was full of spunk, and this quiet young man fell in love with the petite redhead with green eyes. Pastor Henry Noss married them at the Lutheran parsonage on May 9, 1943. Shirley wore a turquoise suit with a white corsage of sweet peas from her mother's garden. Glenn wore his blue suit. After a small reception with cake and coffee, they moved into a house a half-mile from his parents' so Glenn could go to work on the farm with his dad.

When I was born on a cold winter day in December, 1945, World War II had just ended. My uncle had returned home safely in July in time for the birth of his little sister's first baby. What a joyous Christmas that was. When I was a year and a half old, my sister Beverly was born. A year later I remember going to St. Olaf Hospital with my dad, Bev and my maternal grandmother to pick up Mom and our new little sister Nancy. By this time, we lived in the creamery house at Moscow. Grandpa was building a new granary, but after Nancy was born we decided to make the granary our house. Neighbors came and helped finish building it, and my parents painted, varnished and laid linoleum evenings when farm work was completed. Our farm supported two families. My grandparents and my dad's sister Mary lived in the big house, and we lived in the smaller house. I enjoyed living next door to my aunt who was nine years older.

Grade School

When I was 5, I started first grade at Moscow School District 29, which my dad and Aunt Mary attended before they went to Austin High

School. The one-room country school provided education for grades one through eight, totaling 25-30 students with one teacher. She taught one grade at a time with students gathered around her on chairs in a semi-circle in the front part of the room while the other students worked at their desks on lessons. She taught all courses -- arithmetic, spelling, grammar, reading, geography and singing.

During winter months, the school was heated with a fuel oil stove in back of the room, and it was common for children to put potatoes wrapped in aluminum foil to bake on the stove. Placed on the stove at 9 a.m., the potato would be cooked in time for lunch at noon. Other entrees included hot dogs cut in half and put in small jars with water to heat and casserole in a jar. These things didn't have to go on the stove until morning recess.

Water for drinking was pumped from the well outside into a white enamel pail with red trim and carried in by the older boys, who put it on a table near the basement stairway. A metal dipper with a long handle was kept in the pail, and everyone drank from the same dipper. That water must not have been very cold and dirty by the end of the day, but we didn't know any better. Most of us had one just like it at home.

After I had been in school for a few weeks, the first graders were given a primer. It was a book about Dick, Jane, Sally, Mother and Father, and the dog and cat, Spot and Puff. I discovered a whole new world in books. Small for my age, I was extremely shy. I read everything I could get my hands on, slowly sounding out words until they made sense. I considered myself the heroine in each story. My favorite part of school was the library, located on the west side of the main schoolroom.

Winter

We had a lot of snow. The wind whipped it into drifts about four feet high that curled over like ocean waves. We bundled up in warm clothes and walked to the barn, where there were thirty cows to milk and about seven little calves in a pen. It was cold and snowy outside, but when you walked into the barn, it felt warm with all the animals inside.

Our house was never warm in winter, but it was very cold upstairs. The only heat in the house was an oil-burning stove in the living room, so we had electric mattress pads on our beds that were like electric blankets. In the morning, my two younger sisters and I would take our clothes downstairs and get dressed next to the stove. You had to be careful not to get too close, or the stove would burn your -- well, whatever part of you that touched the stove. We didn't have chores to do before school except make our beds and keep our rooms picked up. Mom always made breakfast and visited with us before we left for school.

Summer

My sisters' bedroom faced north out onto our back yard. The shade of trees kept the north rooms cool in summer. You could hear birds singing, and the green lawn made a pleasant spot for picnics. There were clotheslines on the east side of the lawn and beyond that, the outhouse. All buildings were painted except the toilet. Inside, nailed to the wall, there was a picture of a cocker spaniel. I'm sure my Aunt Mary put it there. And of course there was last year's Sears Roebuck catalog.

To the west was the chicken house, where we raised chickens for eggs and eating. We got baby chicks from the hatchery each winter and put them in a brooder house heated with heat lamps. During warmer months, the chickens were allowed to run freely in the yard. We gathered eggs every afternoon, washed and crated them and took them to Blooming Prairie to sell on Saturday night. My mother caught roosters with the use of a long stick with a hook on the end and prepared them for the freezer. She called them spring fryers. As a child, I was always taking that chicken catcher off the hook and trying to catch a chicken with no success. Finally, one day when I was about 6 years old, I caught a chicken. I had been working at this since I was about 5 years old, so I was very excited and surprised. But now, what do I do with it? I hated to let it go. Here I am, a little skinny 6-year-old girl, holding this stick with a chicken attached to it. The chicken was squawking and flapping its wings, trying to get away. Well, the only place I could think of to keep it from running away was down the toilet hole. I dropped that chicken down the toilet hole, and the next person who went out there was my mom. I don't remember how she got it out, but I do know I had to listen to a little lecture on the use of the outdoor toilet.

Indoor Plumbing

When I was 13 or 14, my dad put a bathroom in the house. He put up pink and black tile-design linoleum on the walls. You would have thought we'd won the lottery. We had hot water in the house, no more running out to the well for a pail of water or drinking out of the dipper. When the bathroom was installed, we finished the attic into bedrooms.

My sisters and I had slept together in a three-quarter-size bed. With the remodeling, my sisters got twin beds in the north room, and I had my dad's old bed that he slept in when he was growing up and took with him when he got married. Mom made curtains and bedspreads. I loved my new room. The moon cast light into my room on clear nights, and in summer, the breeze coming in the window was wonderful. I had a view of cows grazing in the pasture, pretty and green in summer.

Meals at Home

Growing up in the 1950s meant that every meal was family time. Conversation was polite and in good taste. Manners were very important. Our parents talked a lot about right and wrong, so we knew what was expected of us. They set a good example. They had a certain look if we misbehaved. They didn't have to speak to us about it; we knew the rules. Food was prepared from scratch. Bread was made at home; potatoes were grown in our own garden and peeled before cooking. Cakes were made from eggs, milk, flour, salt, baking soda, shortening and vanilla. We didn't use box mixes, although they were being introduced on the movie newscasts and television. A typical evening meal was beef or pork roast, boiled potatoes, gravy, corn, peas or carrots, bread and butter, milk, coffee and dessert of cake, pie, cookies and sauce. "Sauce" meant peaches, pears, apricots or cherries that we canned in the summer. We went to town and bought a crate of fruit, sterilized jars with boiling water, peeled the fruit, cut it, and put it in quart jars with water and sugar. The jars were put in a huge kettle that covered two burners of the stove. This canner with a gauge on the cover was heated to boil.

The jars were placed on the cupboard to cool. You could hear each lid pop, one by one. This meant that they were sealed and safe to put in the basement for up to a year or more. If one didn't pop, you used it within a couple of days, because it would spoil. We raised vegetables in the garden and canned them, as well as chickens and various kinds of pickles. The table was set with a tablecloth – older ones for weekdays, and a special one called the "good tablecloth" for Sundays -- one of the many things we ironed. The evening meal leftovers were used the next day at noon. Leftover potatoes were fried or heated up with meat and vegetables in a pan on the stove. Microwaves hadn't been invented yet.

On Saturdays we cleaned house and baked. We made our beds every morning and kept things neat, but on Saturday Bev cleaned house, and I baked. Nancy was the youngest, and she enjoyed working outdoors. From the time I was 9 years old, I baked bread every Saturday to last the week. I also made pies, cake, cinnamon rolls and cookies. We all learned to cook, clean and bake. My dad liked Mom to keep him company, so she worked with him in the field, in the barn or wherever he happened to be, even if it was just to hand him tools. On rainy days he worked in a section of the barn used for storing machinery and doing repairs. After dinner dishes were done and the floor swept, we often spent time out there with him. Those were happy times. Sometimes farm work can be frustrating if it rains too much or too little, and you worry about the crops, but Daddy enjoyed working on machines and equipment, so he was relaxed and seemed to enjoy the light work.

Our life on the farm included a lot of hard work, and my parents were strict by today's standards, but we were a close, happy family. We learned to work hard and live by the Golden Rule, which meant my mom reprimanding us when we broke a rule. "Shame on you! How would you like it if somebody did that to you?"

I live in town now and have my 8 to 5 job. It is definitely as good as I dreamed it would be. I still love pretty bathrooms, and I enjoy going home to the farm every week for my mom's good cooking. I'm glad I learned to cook and clean. It has come in handy over the years while raising three children, and the grandchildren seem to enjoy my pies. My Uncle Stub still remembers my birthday every year because of his association with the war. I have a furnace now, so I can keep an even temperature, and the best part is that I can walk to the library to check books out and read every evening. I'm still addicted to mysteries.

Judy, Bev and Nancy on their farm with their dad, Glenn Arett

Worms
By Marsha Richardson Qualey

Not long ago I read a book by John O'Hara, *A Rage to Live*. The story takes place in the early years of the 20th Century, and it peels back the proper public veils from a number of lives in a small Pennsylvania town that's dominated by a single employer. Not surprisingly, I thought about Austin quite a lot while reading the novel. A number of times I let it drop onto my lap and wondered, did stuff like *this* go on in Austin? I was fascinated by the idea that a whole lot more happened in my hometown than I ever knew about. So when I heard of the sesquicentennial memory project, I was delighted. One town, many lives, a million memories – a perfect premise for a book. And I wanted to be part of it.

Writing my own piece for the compilation, however, has been a struggle. While I welcomed the invitation to contribute and loved the idea of being part of this collective, I was stumped as to what I should write about. I've been writing novels for over fifteen years, and that's sort of ruined my ability to be casual about writing. Everything looms like a 200-page project filled with multiple characters and life-shaping conflict, which is an awful handicap when you sit down to reminisce for a few hundred words about your safe and (mostly) pleasant childhood.

As the deadline approached for submitting an essay, I got desperate and started reaching out to friends and family, encouraging them to submit something to the project. Certain I wouldn't get over this block, I felt better about failing when I knew I had personally kicked others in the butt and got them going on contributing their stories.

One of the first people I contacted was one of my older brothers. I told him I was stumped. He didn't seem to have much sympathy with my writer's block because in an immediate e-mail reply this very busy lawyer ran off a long list of potential subjects; in other words, "What's the problem, sister?"

One of his suggestions had to do with the death of our oldest brother in 1969 in Vietnam. Well, that remains perhaps the defining and most complex memory of my childhood in Austin, one that instantly conjures up images of his military burial in beautiful Oakwood Cemetery as well as the May 1970 anti-war protests on Main Street and at the band shell that I was involved in. Yes, there's plenty of material there, but I'd dealt with the subject directly and indirectly in at least two of my novels and didn't feel like opening it up again.

Scott also suggested that I write about working on the *Sentinel* with Rosie Seltz, legendary AHS journalism advisor. This was a logical suggestion. I was on the paper's staff for two years, editor-in-chief my senior year, and hanging out in that wonderful hideaway classroom at the high school was one of the few things that kept me interested in school during those two long final years. Good material there too, no doubt, but it's not a subject I care to dig around in because the truth is, during my tenure on the *Sentinel,* I spent two years under the watchful and caring eye of the best writing teacher I was ever going to have, and I didn't take advantage of it, choosing instead to cultivate a tendency to take it easy and delegate the real work to others who were smart enough to want to learn something. No, better leave all that alone.

A friend suggested that since my novels often are about teenagers muddling through the consequences of their bad decision-making, I should be honest about some of my own at age 17. In other words, memories of misbehaving in Austin. No way! My husband and I have four children, and the youngest is not 20. I'm happy to say that all four got through their teen years without doing any apparent harm to anyone or calling us from the police station. I'd like to believe our good example had something to do with that, helped by, no doubt, a selective and conveniently foggy memory and even one or two outright lies. I'm not going to blow my cover now.

I often speak to teens and adults about writing. Inevitably I get the question, "Where do you get your ideas?" Well, obviously not from my brothers and friends, I can now say. No, most often the ideas that move me to quit taking it easy, quit delegating the project to others and instead inspire me to flip open the laptop and start writing – those ideas usually come out of the day-dreamy blue. This time the necessary idea was right under my feet on a recent rainy day when I walked out of the nearby campus library and looked down.

I left Austin in 1971 to go to college in St. Paul. Since then I've lived in a lot of places. There were stints in Texas, Arkansas, and Pennsylvania, a couple of pleasant stretches in the north country, and nine barely tolerable years in suburban Minneapolis, where we managed to stay put until the last of our kids finished high school. My husband and I are now living in Wisconsin. Eau Claire and Austin might have dissimilar chamber of commerce profiles and wildly different physical environments, but right away my new town reminded me of Austin. And the weird thing, for the first time in years of resettling, I immediately felt at home.

We left a large and congested metropolitan area, but it's not just Eau Claire's smaller population or lack of traffic that reminds me of Austin. Nor is it the neighborhood grocery store that's so much like the Piggly Wiggly I'd run to on errands for my mother. Or the big old houses on our street that resemble my childhood home.

It's the sidewalks. For the first time in years we're living in a place that's pedestrian-friendly. We've ditched the second car, and I'm walking everywhere. And that's what I remember about Austin – the sheer liberty of living in a place where almost every destination was within walking distance.

From the time I was 6 we lived at 308 6th Place NW, a few blocks from downtown, and I could walk anywhere I cared to go: friends' homes, the swimming pool, downtown to buy Nancy Drews at Nemitz's, the A & W and my beloved public library. And, of course, I walked to school. Sumner School. There weren't a lot of kids in our neighborhood who went to Sumner. By some odd quirk of fate, however, there *were* three other girls my age, Janet Lane, Mary Johnson, and Ann Catherwood. One or the other was my usual companion for that long walk coming or going to school, four times a day.

Mary was my best friend, a perfect friend for someone like me who, given the choice, would never have left the comfort and safety of a favorite chair and stack of books, unless it was to go to the library to replenish that stack of books. Mary got me out of the house, got me moving, and helped me shake off an often-paralyzing shyness. Thanks to her, I learned to water ski (sort of), snow ski (sort of), and I once even car-hopped at her family's A & W.

Like the stories I write, Mary's and my ideas for having fun usually came out of nowhere. But we knew a good one when we saw one. And one rainy day – I suppose we were about 7 or 8 – we were on that long walk home for lunch from Sumner. I don't know which of us looked down first and noticed all the worms writhing on the concrete, and I don't know who first thought of what to do with those worms. Probably neither of us. Like most of our fun together, I suspect this new project was the result of simultaneous inspiration.

We started picking up worms and putting them in our coat pockets. I referred to that day in my memory as "when we saved the worms." But now I'm not so sure that's what we were doing.

Even at that young age we'd know to just toss them onto the grass, right? Not stash them in our pockets? I sure hope so. I now think that it's just as likely that we were supplying ourselves with worms for fishing. Spotting all that fresh bait on the wet concrete, we no doubt decided then and there to scoop up all we needed for the next trip down to the Red Cedar or to her family's cabin on Lake Pepin. Whether we intended to be worm saviors or crucifiers, we'd hit pay dirt. The sidewalks were covered, and we pocketed worms all the way home.

This, of course, slowed us down. By the time we got to Mary's, we were really late, and kids were already heading back to school. She ran into her house, I ran a half block farther to mine. Coats were shed, lunch consumed.

Meanwhile, the sun came out. We ran back to school coat-free. What's more, the weather stayed fine all the way to summer vacation, which meant that those raincoats with the loaded pockets hung unused until the fall rains. And that's when Mary and I discovered the amazing transformation worms undergo when they die and dehydrate. To this day I cannot reach into a sweater or coat pocket, encounter a bit of fluff or torn paper, without shivering a bit in recollection of the treasure Mary and I scooped up on that long-ago rainy day; a day when Austin's sidewalks weren't just the path home to lunch, but the canvas and palette, stage and scenery, paper and pen for the shared imagination of two best friends.

Marsha Qualey's books for young adults include **Hometown,** *Everybody's Daughter, and* **Revolutions of the Heart.**

Basic or Deluxe?
By Becky Repinski

As a relative newcomer to Austin, having moved here just a few years ago, my historical contributions and recollections are somewhat limited. However, I do have significant recall regarding the kindness and compassion offered by one of our local business persons on a particularly stressful day in September, 2001.

Keeping things in perspective, this day had nothing at all to do with the events of 9/11, but for me, the panic level certainly exceeded the "red alert" stage on the blood pressure scale. I had just received word the night before that my mother had died in the Adams Care Center. While her health had been deteriorating for a number of years, the finality of hearing my brother's voice on the phone had left me in a peculiar state of numbness. I managed to drive here safely from Buffalo, Minnesota, where I was living at the time, and was even able to deal with the mortuary issues surprisingly well that morning. As the day progressed, my steady nerves and clear thinking continually encouraged me. However, this soon ended with one small, regrettable decision.

Walking out of Jerry's Other Place after devouring a delicious bowl of bean soup, I noticed that my black Ford SUV was not only low on gas, but was covered with a heavy layer of dust. I assumed it might be necessary to drive it in the funeral procession, and since the Shell gas station was close at hand, I decided to fill up the tank and take advantage of their car wash, since it included a generous discount. No problem.

The fill-up went smoothly, and I was pleased to see that no one was using the car wash at the time. The gods were looking out for me. As I drove my SUV onto the slowly moving tracks of the car wash and was being pulled into the area where the "bottom blast" and the trickle of soap would soon begin, I glanced into my side mirror and noticed that the tiny door to my gas cap was wide open. Horrors! What if it would be ripped off by the massive, swiftly spinning brushes?

I responded quickly by opening my door, scampering back to flip it shut, and attempting to leap back into the driver's seat before the first cycle kicked in. Marveling at my own speed and agility, I turned to jump back into the car just as the huge vertical brush on my left caught the edge of the open car door, and began to slowly crush it forward into the left front side of my vehicle. By this time, generous amounts of soap began to ooze all over my car and onto my head.

In sheer panic, I grabbed the doorframe of my two thousand pound vehicle and hung on, desperately trying to pull it back while screaming at the top of my lungs. To this day, I can still hear the hideous sound of heavy metal being crushed and bent against the side of my car. I also recall seeing one lone woman standing near the entryway to the car wash. Her eyes were the size of saucers, and her mouth had dropped open, resembling the famous Edvard Munch painting entitled *The Scream*.

While I continued to pit my puny strength against the monstrous moving equipment, which was slowly chewing up my vehicle, the entire operation miraculously came to a halt. I hung there dazed and full of soap, still clinging to the side of my SUV as if it would be taken from me and flung over Niagara Falls.

A very calm and efficient gas station worker then slowly moved the track forward, releasing my vehicle onto the parking lot in front of the car wash. He quickly hooked up a hose, washed the embarrassing soapsuds from my SUV, and completely ignored the gawking onlookers who kept asking him what had happened. Then he attempted to close my damaged door the best that he could, and he kindly gave me directions for the shortest route to the Ford Body Shop. At that point, I realized it is often the quiet, understated efforts of persons in ordinary jobs that have the most impact on a person's daily life. I still think of this man from time to time, and would like to take this opportunity to thank a marvelous human being. It is obvious that angels do exist, and they are right here in Austin.

Becky Repinski moved to Austin five years ago after retiring from General Mills. She has been a high school teacher, freelance writer, computer training coordinator and corporate librarian.

The Flood of 2004
By Bonnie Besse Rietz

The evening of September 14, 2004 Roger Boughton came rushing into our home all soaked and called out to everyone, "It sure is pouring rain out there!" Similar expressions came from all the people coming and going. It was the day of Austin's primary election, and we were having an open house in our home to thank all the people who had helped with my campaign for mayor.

I no longer had a funny feeling in the pit of my stomach every time we received a heavy rain. It had taken over a year for me not to have that strange feeling after our 100-year flood of 2000.

The next morning was going to be one of celebration and thanking the many people who had helped with the campaign. I was going to put my up my feet, drink coffee and make calls. I went to bed very tired as I heard the continual patter of rain on our roof.

In an instant how life can change! Early in the morning I received a call from Chief of Police, Paul Philipp. "Mayor Rietz," he said, "Blooming Prairie has received 12 inches of rain, and it's heading our way. The Cedar River is rising rapidly." Visions of our 2000 flood filled my mind as I quickly dressed and headed out to what was going to become a devastating time for our community.

As I look back now from a vantage point of one year and seven months later, visions of the flood of 2004 are still vivid. When I think about the flood, I cannot get the picture of a cap floating on the Mill Pond out of my mind. We did not know for a couple of days that it belonged to Bradley Symmonds, age 20, a young man who died after being caught up in the strong current of the Cedar River. This was the first time someone had died because of flooding in our community, and it still haunts me. Visiting their home and talking with his mom, Kelly Nystel, and other family members was one of the hardest things I did throughout our flooding time.

James Darling, who lived south of Austin along the Cedar River and who was a chemistry teacher at Riverland Community College, also died because of a heart attack while sandbagging. Businesses and homes can be replaced, but the lives of these two men cannot. They and their families continue to be in our thoughts and prayers.

Another vision I have is that of the many smiling faces of people handing out sandwiches and drinks from the Salvation Army trucks and the Red Cross vehicles. I was working with Benny Thompson's daughter and several others in the northeast filling bags of sand to help protect the homes located near Wildwood Park. Along came the Salvation Army truck with bottles of water. We were so thirsty, and I actually got tears in my eyes as the volunteers handed them out.

These generous people worked all around the community for many days bringing food, drinks and a friendly smile to everyone impacted by the flood. I remember a saying I heard once at a volunteer function, "No act of kindness, no matter how small, is ever wasted."

The very first afternoon, government officials arrived in a helicopter to view the situation in Austin. What an incredible feeling of sadness I felt as I saw Jerry's Other Place from the air and saw the water from the Cedar River rushing into the north side of their building and shooting out the south side. We were viewing what was to become the worst flood in our history.

Turtle Creek was overflowing, and water was rushing into homes in the southwest part of Austin. The Cedar River was overflowing all along its pathway throughout the city. From the air you could see businesses, buildings, homes and vehicles being deluged with water. It was devastating.

Friday afternoon I received a call from John Clark at Johnny's Restaurant on Main Street. His business was one that had been flooded. He was calling from a cell phone and was very upset. He left a message and wanted me to call him, but he did not leave a telephone number.

I looked up the number of the restaurant, and their phone was out of order so I decided to go and see him. I drove north on Main Street but could get no farther than Community Bank. I drove up 4th Street NW and turned down 12th Place NW, but the street in front of the SPAM Museum was covered with water. I backed up and went out on I-90, took the 6th Street exit and tried to reach his restaurant from the north. It was flooded also. I could not get close. It was such a strange feeling to physically not be able to get to a place in Austin. When the water receded the next day, I drove to his restaurant and visited with him about his situation.

Everywhere we went in the aftermath of the flood, people were helping people. Neighbors, friends, young people, co-workers, church members, city workers, utility staff, people from other communities-- the list goes on and on. Working with students from our schools in the parking lot of Jim's Super Valu helping them wash all of their muddy shelves was quite an experience. To see the young people helping others was an inspiration. Matt Day, a senior at AHS in 2004, was one of the people who spoke about our flood at my State of the City address the following January. Matt told of his experience of working in the aftermath of the flood with his football buddies, and he said, "The flood of 2004 didn't just teach me how to sandbag; it also showed me how much the people of Austin care about each other."

Throughout the flood and its aftermath several government officials continued to visit our city to see what they could do to help. I felt that the closer they could get to the situation, the more helpful it would be when they were making budgetary decisions about flood relief. Governor Pawlenty came about a month after the flood to review the situation. We took him on a tour, and one of the places we stopped was at Lois and Ron Peter's home. After we saw their basement and the destruction from the flood, Lois asked the governor if he would like a piece of apple pie. The last thing he did on his tour of Austin was have a piece of apple pie and a cup of coffee at their kitchen table. And as he left, they handed him a jar of homemade dill pickles. What great memories he has of the hospitality of the people in Austin!

That strange feeling in the pit of my stomach still comes every time as I look out and see the rain drops falling and the river rising. The memories are still vivid. Even though the flood was devastating for our community, it also brought out the kindness and generosity of many. I think of Martin Luther King's words, "Everybody can be great, because everybody can serve." Our community certainly experienced a time when everybody was great during the flood of 2004.

A statue watches the waters rise.

Bonnie Rietz served as Austin's mayor for five terms.

Big 9 Basketball in the 1940s
(First published in *Red Wing Today* magazine)
By Bob Richardson

Austin High School basketball was hot stuff sixty years ago. On game day folks would start lining up for tickets an hour before the B-squad game. By eight o'clock our fans were at a fever pitch for the main event. When the scarlet and white A-squad came out to warm up, "Pop" Sperati's high school band would rip into the fight song, and the place would go wild.

In high school gymnasiums across the state, basketball meant excitement, noise and competition. For schools in the far-flung Big Nine Conference, out-state Minnesota's premier high school league, it also meant a lot of travel. If you played on a Big Nine team, you got around, because the league ranged from Red Wing and Winona on the Mississippi River, to Mankato on the Minnesota River. Two packinghouse towns on old Highway 16, Austin and Albert Lea, were included. So were Owatonna, Faribault and Northfield, three towns on Highway 65 going into the Twin Cities. Rochester, situated on Highway 14 between the hills and the flat country, completed the make-up of the league as it was back then. It's a little different today.

From the early 1930s to the mid-1960s, from the time Hitler came to power in Germany until the rise of the miniskirt, Austin was "the class" of the league. At every school in the state, large or small, the team's goal was not only to win its conference, but also to get to the state tournament, which was first held at Carleton College in Northfield.

Austin hoped to get to the state in 1915, but got distracted. In the 1915 AHS yearbook, the school's second-ever publication, a writer noted that, "In all probability, we would have been represented at the state tournament, had it not been for the fact that some of the boys did not buckle down to their studies enough to be eligible to play until near the end of the season."

Red Wing and Austin sent a number of teams to those early meets at Carleton, and to later ones held in various Twin Cities locations, most notably Williams Arena at the University of Minnesota. For many years, the Big Nine was actually the Big Eight. Owatonna came into the league as the ninth member in about 1941. In recent years, the Rochester schools, John Marshall, Mayo and Century, have ruled the roost in the Big Nine, which no longer includes Northfield and Red Wing.

In 1946, a year after the end of World War II, Austin won the state tournament by overpowering tiny Lynd, a village way out near the South Dakota border. What a David and Goliath story this was for the media. Austin, which had a population of 21,000 and was the 1935 state champion, versus Lynd, with a population of 218, where it was said the farm boys learned to play by shooting at baskets in their barns. Each team had won the playoffs at the district and regional levels. Each had won its first two state tournament games. Who would win the championship?

Every kid at the time dreamed of playing at Williams Arena. From Iowa to the Canadian border, from Wisconsin to the Dakotas, every Minnesotan who put on basketball shoes dreamed of hitting the winning shot at a tournament game in the grand old fieldhouse. On our big night in March of 1946, my Austin Scarlets were there because we had beaten Hayfield, Albert Lea and Blooming Prairie, regional foes Faribault and Rochester, and state contestants, Roseau and Mountain Lake. Look out, Lynd! Here we come!

On the big night, about fifteen of the sixteen thousand or more fans were pulling for David to slay Goliath, for tiny Lynd to take down mighty Austin. Lynd was the sentimental favorite all across the state. "Clobber those Austin pig-stickers!" was a common battle cry.

WCCO Radio reached every nook and cranny in Minnesota. In April of the year before, we had listened as CBS broke into the WCCO programming to announce the death of President Franklin Roosevelt. In May we heard the wonderful news of the fall of Germany, and in September, news of the surrender of Japan and the war's end. Now, on this wintry night in 1946, six months after V-J Day, Austin folks turned their radios on once again, this time hoping to celebrate victory in a sports arena. WCCO, KATE and KROC were all beaming the play-by-play accounts to their audiences. WCCO had real competition that night.

I vividly remember that weekend. In the family life of the Drs. Richardson and their three children, Harper, Robert and Margaret, this was a very happy chapter. Doyle and Lois Richardson were doctors of osteopathy who had graduated from Still College in 1925. In 1929, the year of the great stock market crash, they returned to Doyle's hometown and settled in as family doctors. Their first years of practice in Austin were lean; they had to watch their spending. Their sole indulgence was a weekend trip to the Twin Cities at the end of each March to take in the state basketball tournament.

On Thursday morning, they would see a couple of patients and then close up shop. A little over two hours later ("Remember, Medford's a speed trap"), they would drop their suitcases at the Curtis Hotel and race to Williams Arena for the day's quarterfinal games. On Friday, they would go to the two semifinals, and on Saturday night, they would take in the grand finale.

Their Thursday to Sunday "coat rack," the Curtis, was the hub of state tournament activity. "Need a ticket? See Harold "Red" Hastings, the Austin athletic director. He's around here someplace." "Just saw him down at the coffee shop!" "Need a ride? Someone will be going to the fieldhouse pretty soon. Hang around here in the lobby. You'll get there."

"Want to go out to eat? Let's go to the Forum Cafeteria. They sure don't have anything like that in Austin!" "Have you heard the orchestra in the ballroom? Pretty neat, huh?" "Hey, somebody said they saw Dean Martin in the lobby! Wow!" "Come on. The game is going to start. We gotta go!"

As the Scarlets bounded up onto the raised floor of Williams Arena, "Pops" Sperati started up the fight song, and we all went bonkers! "Toss it up! Let's get going!"

From the opening tap, I knew we'd control the boards, for 6'5" Dick Ravenhorst and 6'3" Harp Richardson (my brother!), towered over the small Lynd boys, who hoped to grab the ball and run their fast-break style of basketball. There was one slight problem. You can't play fire wagon style basketball if you can't get the ball. Raven and Harp saw to it that the Lynd players did not grab many rebounds.

Without boring you with all the silly details about how Austin crushed Lynd by thirty-two points, how Harp looked at me just before he took a long shot and how I winked and told him, "Go for it!" and – well, you don't want to hear about all of that. Only after the final horn sounded did Mom and Dad unclench their fists. Harp looked up and waved to us (mainly to me, of course). Mom, Dad, Marg and I all whooped and hollered and slapped each other on the back. Dad broke into an ear-to-ear grin that he wore for six months. Mom beamed, as only my mom could. Margie's pigtails went flying around the arena, carrying my little sister with them.

On Sunday, a triumphant caravan of cars tooted their horns and blinked their lights most of the way home from Minneapolis. In each of the Big Nine towns along the way, Northfield, Faribault and Owatonna, cheering crowds greeted us, and I gallantly acknowledged their applause. Austin's state championship gave every school in the Big Nine a little more prestige.

At Lansing Corners, five miles north of Austin, a police car and a fire truck met and escorted us to Austin's Milwaukee Road station, where a huge crowd awaited the arrival of the team's train. What a great time for me, when the team star, my brother Harper, stepped off the train carrying our trophy! What a great time for our whole family. We all giggled like fools through the entire ceremony. Then, it was time to go home and begin the rest of our lives.

Epilogue: In September of that year, Harp went to Carleton College and discovered that college basketball was a wee bit more difficult than high school basketball. Mr. Ove Berven, the man who coached Austin to the 1946 title, continued his fine career by leading another Austin team to a state title in the late 1950s. Austin's gymnasium is now named the Ove Berven Gym.

There were some golden years in Austin, not just for the high school, but also for George A. Hormel and Company. SPAM had gone big-time during the war years. We were all living "high off the hog." In 1948 Mom and Dad started watching their second son play basketball at AHS. In 1949 our team made it to the Region One finals as Rochester, led by Ray Lee and Jim Larson, topped us 47 to 41 to gain a trip to the state tournament. In 1950 Albert Lea beat us in the district after we had defeated them twice during regular season play. We did win the Big Nine conference title that year, which was some consolation, but getting beat by Albert Lea in the district playoffs was a shock.

Following in Harp's footsteps, I enrolled at Carleton in the fall of 1950. From 1951 to 1954, I played in Carleton's austere Sayles-Hill gymnasium, where my older brother and idol played from 1946 to 1948. Sayles-Hill was built in 1910, two years before the *Titanic* went down. Austin's 1915 team might have played in Sayles-Hill, if some of its athletes had buckled down and studied harder.

A Wonderful Town to Grow Up in Back in the 1960s
By Scott Richardson

When I was in tenth grade in 1963, Norm Westby, the youth director of the YMCA, whose office was upstairs over what is now Mi Tienda restaurant, recommended me to George and Edith Dugan, who were looking for a high school boy to work for them in their sporting goods store. I was hired and worked there about four years. They were terrific people. I was paid $1.69 per hour, and I worked two and a half hours on school days and from 3:30 to 9 on Fridays. Saturdays and during summer vacation I worked 9 to 5.

George Dugan had just founded the Lion's Eye Bank. He would have calls with the Minnesota Highway Patrol to arrange emergency transport of enucleated eyes from local mortuaries to the University of Minnesota Hospital for corneal transplanting.

LeRoy Schultz was their full-time hired man. Lee was a friendly, older man who maybe was not older than I am now. He would engrave trophy plates, put line on reels, repair shotguns and rifles, string tennis racquets, and talk about the merchandise as though he were an expert. He was a Jack-of-all-trades. The irony was that I think he never hunted, shot guns, or played sports. But he was a good person, and I learned a lot from him.

John Hastings worked there too. He was two years older than I was, had a gift of gab and was terrific in sales. I heard all about the numerous crushes he had on girls. He was fun to work with, and he was a good mentor.

Red Hastings was the high school's athletic director. A preferred customer, once a year he would come in to order team uniforms. Even though I was small and uncoordinated, he always gave me Bs for gym class, and I never got smacked on the butt with his famous "board of education."

Bowling league was a huge deal. Austin had two bowling alleys, and bowling was very popular. The town had more people than it does now. In the fall, bowling shirts would be ordered. In the spring, trophies would be ordered and prepared. Jean Quednow and I were the engravers. Jean is a dear person, so patient and almost always upbeat and pleasant. She could sell guns and sporting goods as well as John or LeRoy or even George.

The engraving station was in the front window area. Across the street was Synder's Texaco station. Dugan's store was on the southwest corner of the intersection of 1st Street NE and 3rd Avenue NE. It's a city parking lot now. Across the street and next to the gas station was Nate's Clothing. Farther to the west was Art's Barber Shop. Lane's Rexall Drug store was on the corner of Main and Mill Street (now 3rd Avenue NE). On the south side of the block was Dugan's, Fox Candy (a candy and tobacco distributor run by Fred Creighton), the Turf Bar, Robinson Office Supply, and Simonson Paint Store. On the corner at the west end of the block was Wallace's Department Store.

Mr. Pearl Elam ran a jewelry store on Main Street, where the vision shop is now. He would bring over pewter baby cups for me to engrave the kid's name on. I botched a few, and Mr. Elam sold the ruined cups to me cheap. I liked him. When I was 20 years old, I bought my wife's engagement ring from him on credit, and I drove down from the University to pick it out.

Once at Dugan's there came word that the fire department was dragging the Cedar River for a suicide corpse. So at quitting time, I walked down to the bridge by Klagge's ice cream store and watched. The men were in a rowboat tossing a large treble hook device attached to a long rope. The man would haul it in and toss it out again. There was a crowd, but it was quiet and somber. Then we heard him say to his partner in the boat, "I've got him." Sure enough, he hauled in the body. He held it in the water next to the boat as they rowed over to the shore. The back of that man was gray like the skin of minnow that had been dead in the bucket for days. It was interesting, but I shouldn't have watched that. I recall watching the destruction by fire of Botsford Lumber Yard, located next to Klagge's. It was a huge fire, and it was over quickly.

George Dugan used to have me walk over to the Fox Hotel to pick up special deliveries transported to Austin by bus. I'd walk up the front steps and go inside to the counter to the left of the doors and get the package, usually ammunition. Otherwise, I was never in that hotel.

Right behind the hotel was the Zesto Stand. I lived only three blocks away on Nassau (Third Place NW), so the Zesto Stand was a big deal in my junior high school years. My best friend, Fred Robinson, and I were regulars. Each summer when school let out, we would register our bike license plate numbers for the weekly drawing. A couple of times each summer my number would appear along with the five or six other weekly winners of the drawing. The prize was a sundae or some other ice cream treat. Occasionally, I could come up with a quarter to buy the large Zesto. What a treat! The *Austin Daily Herald* was on that block as well as a Mobil station.

Fridays were hectic. I'd go home at 5:30 for dinner and get back to work in about forty-five minutes. We'd work until 9, and usually it was pretty busy. What was exciting was the anticipation of going to the Tower after work. I'd go home and clean up and change clothes and watch Emma Peale on "The Avengers" and then walk to the Tower. I'd go up the long stairs, pay the entrance fee to Gar Nash or Clarence Nybo, go in and play pinball (a dime for five balls), and stand around waiting for some girl to ask me to dance. They never did. I just couldn't figure it out, but it was exciting and tense. A couple of times I got my nerve up to ask a girl to dance. She would give me one dance and then come up with a lame excuse to leave me standing out on the dance floor. I am not sure why that place holds such fond memories for me.

Saturday morning at 9 I'd start the long day at Dugan's. Christmas season was tough. School would be out, and I would be putting in twelve-hour days. It must have been a hard life for George and Edith, although I never heard them complain.

I continued to work for Dugan's during my first year at Austin Junior College. The campus was on the third floor of the high school in the south and west corridors, and the college had a very big enrollment. It seemed like most of the classes of '65 (Central-525 graduates, Pacelli-170 graduates) went to JC so some of our classes were in the basement rooms of the Methodist Church and the 100 Building.

Loren Bellrichard gave a stirring campaign speech that won him the student body presidency. We had a welcome and informational assembly in the auditorium, and the lower level was nearly filled. I spied across the auditorium a cute girl, and it was an instant crush. I got my nerve up to talk to her, and one thing led to another. Forty years later we're still a number, and I still think she is good looking.

She went to Pacelli and lived out by the airport, and I had never seen her before. I think most of us didn't know the Pacelli kids. I sure didn't. When I started dating Cathy, Jean Quednow from Dugan's, a devout Catholic, told me that the Pope's plan was to have Catholic girls marry us Protestant boys in order to expand the realm of the Church.

The only contact I had with Pacelli kids during junior and senior high was at Shaw Gym, next to the north side of Brick Furniture. It had a basketball court, and downstairs there were some pool tables, two racquetball courts, three ping pong tables, a boxing ring, a small concession stand and a shower/locker room. It was the place to go after school and after dinner for those who could go out on a school night, but it was for boys only.

For my sophomore year we moved to the brand new junior college building where Riverland College is now. I have had seven years of post high school education, and I enjoyed the two at Austin JC the most. I met my wife there, most of my high school friends were there, the instructors were excellent, and it was great.

While in junior college, it was no longer appropriate to go to the Tower. That place was for high school kids. Jim Watkins (Class of '65 Central) and John Falconer (Class of '64 Central) established the Brig Coffee House in the basement of the old Armory Building, located where the firehouse is now. Every Friday night the place jumped. Occasionally there was live music. There were booths and a dance floor and a concession stand, and "California Dreamin" played constantly. The place had great atmosphere, and it was a big success.

I recall a debate at the Brig with a moderator and several students seated on a little stage. The topic was the Vietnam War, and it got a bit out of hand with people yelling and threatening each other. I am surprised by how little the war was discussed elsewhere. Most of us guys lived under the threat of the draft, so we all carried at least twelve credits to maintain our student deferment. There was no war protesting at JC that I can recall.

Those were the days when the Hormel Company hired college kids to work during summer. Thanks to the strong union, the college workers were paid the same wage as the permanent workers. It was hard to get into the plant. I applied and got an interview with Mr. Ployhart at the Minnesota Employment Office. He said I was too small, but that Dr. Barber, one of the two Hormel staff physicians, had put in a good word for me. I was hired! The good doctor's son Skip and I were best buddies. I was elated, and I worked there for three summers.

The summer of 1969 I worked up in Dairy Pak, packaging bacon with all the ladies. I had been warned how dreadful working there was, but they were so nice and considerate. I got three collections from them that summer: one when I got married, one when my oldest brother died in Vietnam, and one when I left the department.

I took my physical for the draft that summer. About fifty of us loaded onto the bus at 6 a.m. for the drive up to the military's recruitment center near Third Avenue and Washington in downtown Minneapolis. On the trip home, half of the bus was joyful, as they had flunked the physical - mostly big guys who messed up their knees in football. We skinny guys passed, and we were pretty depressed.

In late summer they held the first lottery for the draft. I drew 125, and that number was on the bubble. It was predicted that anyone with a number lower than 125 would be drafted for sure. So I enlisted for two years. I left for the Army in December and basically didn't come back to live in Austin until after law school five years later.

Dugan's Store staff, Jean Quednow and Edith Dugan

My Favorite Experience at Austin Public Library
By Lauren Rosenberg

My favorite experience at Austin Public Library was when I was 8 years old. I was there with my Grandma Jane. My grandma and I went to the catalog computer and looked for a book on dogs. When the catalog computer was done loading, I found a book called *Shiloh,* and when I was looking for *Shiloh* I found a book called *Confidence*. I thought both looked interesting but before I checked the books out, I went to a desk to read because my grandma wanted to go and get a book.

So I was reading, and I looked outside. It was spring, and I saw kids running around and laughing and just having fun. When I was done reading two chapters, my grandma came up to me with two novels in her arms. "I want to show you something," said my grandma. We walked over to another side of the library, and my grandma showed me two model boats. I thought they were amazing. I wonder how long it took to make the boats and who made them. It probably took more than two years to make those boats.

I asked my grandma if we could sit and read for a few minutes, and we did. Yeah, it wasn't really a few minutes. It was exactly an hour until my grandma and I noticed it wasn't a few minutes. When my grandma and I got up to check out our books we passed the computer lab. "Do you want to go into the computer lab?"

"Sure," I said, "but the computer lab is full."

"Well, we can go to the kids' computer," said my grandma. I played on the computer all day long, and I had so much fun. Then it was almost closing time so my grandma and I went to check out our books. We had spent a long time there, and that was my favorite experience at the Austin Public Library.

Minneapolis resident Lauren Rosenberg visits her grandparents in Austin.

The Millennium Maple
By Michael Ruzek

It was the fall of 1999, and in Austin, as throughout the USA, there was much discussion about the upcoming change of the century and millennium. Unique events like this can be opportunities to do the unexpected and the unusual.

Spruce Up Austin, an organization started in 1990 and dedicated to the improvement of the Austin landscape, was interested in doing something special for the coming year. For many common sense people, spring would be the earliest to plant trees, but for Spruce Up Austin, the challenge was to plant the first tree of the new millennium in Minnesota and maybe even the first in America.

At precisely 12:01 a.m. (CST) on January 1, 2000, the first tree of the new millennium was planted in the winter wonderland of Horace Austin Park in Austin, Minnesota. The weather was very mild, and there was not much snow. Around forty-two people showed up – some with party hats – and everyone helped cover the ball and burlapped portion of the tree with dirt that had been in a warm place all day. The maple tree was given the title "The Millennium Maple," and at the time of planting was already 15 ½ feet high and had a 4-inch diameter trunk.

That beautiful tree was already ten years old and could very well be alive in three different centuries. Many people that evening felt that this tree was not only a symbol to care for our environment, but also of a renewed spirit to carry on the values most represented by a generation who began their lives in the early part of the past century.

As of 2006, no one else we know of in Minnesota or the USA has claimed to have planted the first tree of the new millennium. That early morning gathering in 2000 was unexpected and unusual, and it was a gathering we won't forget.

Walkers notice the Millennium Maple

Two Grand Teams
By Mike Ruzek

Most people who have been in Austin a long time remember the 1958 Minnesota state high school basketball tournaments in which both Austin High School and Pacelli High School won their respective state championships. It was quite an exciting time in our community, especially for a sixth grader like me who dreamed of representing Austin some day on an athletic team.

In the fall of 1961, the undefeated AHS football team was recognized as the *Minneapolis Tribune* Consensus State Champion. The Pacelli football team also went undefeated that year, but the parochial school system was not involved in a polling process to determine rank. Had there been one, they would have been ranked number one also. These two undefeated football teams attracted statewide attention for their outstanding seasons just as the two basketball teams did.

Soon after the season ended, there was considerable discussion about the two teams playing one more game. My dad, who worked at the Hormel plant, told me about some rather heated debates as to who the better team was. It was pretty much divided along religious lines with Catholics and Protestants expressing their opinions.

As a player on the AHS team, I would have been excited if there would have been a game, but hindsight has convinced me that the leadership of the two schools made a good decision. Over the years I've met players from both teams, and they all seem to have much fun talking about a game that never happened, and who might have won. We each have eternal bragging rights.

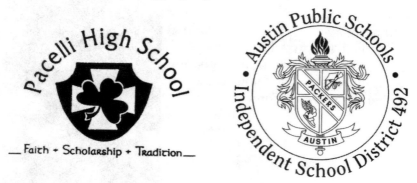

Mike has been an Austinite all his life. He finds Austin a good place to raise a family, work and do community service.

Moving From L.A. to A.L... and Finally to Austin
By Carolina Salazar

Four years ago I moved to Albert Lea, Minnesota from Los Angeles, California. We got there in March, and the trees were bare, the grass was dry and the dirty snow was melting. The town did not look very nice, and I was not very happy. The first weeks I got depressed and lonely. It was difficult because I didn't know anybody or have anyone to talk to or visit with, and it was very expensive to call my family and friends in California very often.

After a few weeks, the town started to change. Everywhere I looked was green, and the trees were blooming. The town was getting beautiful. As the summer went on, I loved to see the cornfields and eat corn on the cob. I am from a small town in Jalisco, Mexico, and I do not like to live in a big city.

The first two years were hard. I did not speak the language, so I could not communicate, and I could not drive either. One year later I started to drive, and that is when my life started to change a little. By that time, I started to attend an English as a Second Language program, where I learned English and had the opportunity to meet very nice teachers and Spanish speaking students. Life was getting easier when another change came to my life.

One year ago, I moved to Austin because of my husband's job. At first, I was a little afraid because I had heard people saying that the people of Austin were not friendly and that they did not like foreigners. However, my experience has been somewhat different. My neighbors are really nice and helpful, and I believe I am a good neighbor also. My children are in school now, and their teachers are nice.

Now I am happy because my kids are happy. They are growing in a good environment and getting a good education. My life is busy now, and I have a job that I enjoy a lot. I have friends also, and with my three kids, I do not have time to get sad and depressed.

Reminiscing
By Joanne Upcraft Sass

My family moved from Albert Lea to Austin when I was 7 in 1940 and rented a house in Dutchtown on the corner of Clark Street and Center. There were lots of kids in the neighborhood, some only-child families and some notably larger families, like eleven kids or so. There were three neighborhood grocery stores in a couple of blocks, the most familiar –probably having the best selection of penny candy was on what is now the corner of 13th Street and 5th Avenue NE. One block south was a small, square, two-story brick grocery called Ollman's.

The third grocery store, across the street from the popular one, is largely unremembered, probably because kids rarely frequented that side of the street. Next door to the grocery was an old man, "Pinky," who lived alone and had many lovely lilacs, which he most definitely did not wish to share with the neighborhood. He would exit the house yelling, chasing, and cursing anyone who dared to covet or get near his bushes in lilac time.

We kids went to Webster School. Some of us early grade school girls used to walk around the lake, to the east side of the lake, to visit classmates – probably boys – in what was then a few scattered houses in the area known as Decker Acres. In the summertime, we found our fun at the swimming beach at East Side Lake. The roped off beach was at the northwest corner, and there was a changing house, which in winter became a warming house for our ice skating amusement at the same spot.

The old overhead bridge began near Webster School on the east, and it led to Mrs. McCormack's little grocery store, the location now occupied by Fox Electric. I don't recall that Mrs. McCormack dealt in anything other than penny candy.

Clark, Division and Center Streets made up an interesting neighborhood with some prestigious career men including Austin fire chief John Tobar and Martin Hanson, head of Austin's street department. There were no career women in those days. Remnants of most of these families are still scattered around Austin.

My dad Charlie worked for the Anhorn cousins at a little Pure Oil service station on Brownsdale Avenue, just next to the railroad tracks. What fun for this tomboy to occasionally visit there, go up and down the ladder into the grease pit, and then go in the back where they sold tires and, in an old cooler that had (gasp!) 5-cent glass bottles of pop. Orange Crush was good, but grape was my favorite!

We moved to the high school area into a duplex on what was then First Street, now 5th Street NW, the block now full of the high school annex. In addition to the high school, the building then contained elementary grades in the south end and the junior college.

I remember going with friends after school in winter to ski down Skinner's Hill with big wooden skis, then going home with them, listening to scary radio programs like "The Whistler," and "The Shadow," and then having to walk home alone in the dark.

All of us old timers remember Austin's four movie theatres. The Roxy was on the east side, the Paramount in its present location, The State Theatre was across the street, and on Main Street, next to the Pure Oil service station on Main and Oakland, was the Austin Theatre. I don't recall whether they all had inexpensive Saturday matinees, but I do know for sure the Austin Theatre did! I saw lots of "oaters" and adventures of Henry Aldrich.

I particularly remember Pearl Harbor, which I didn't understand at the time, but which certainly had a great impact on all the grown-ups. My family left Austin in March, 1944, when Dad went into the service, and returned to Austin from living with grandparents in Blooming Prairie in 1949. The rest, I guess, is fairly modern history.

I married my husband in 1958, and we lived in a newly built house on the east end of a then dead-end Ellis Avenue, soon to become 4th Avenue SE under the new street naming system. My husband walked across the street to empty fields to hunt, but the fields didn't stay empty long. Our quiet dead end street didn't stay that way. Austin has been a good town to me, and I enjoy reminiscing.

Joanne and Kevin Sass have been married 48 years. They have one daughter and five grandchildren, and they enjoy reading and tennis.

My Story
By Phyllis Schaumann

I was born in Monmouth, Illinois on August 9, 1946. I weighed 8 pounds, 14 ounces and was 19 ½ inches long. I had chicken pox before I was a year old. On April 6, 1947, I took my first steps. I had whooping cough in1947, and while I was whooping, I swallowed my tongue and could not breathe. The doctor didn't think I would live, but I pulled out of it. If it wasn't for my Grandma Nyberg, I would not be alive today.

On July 10, 1953, I was put in Dixon State Hospital, as my mother could no longer take care of me. I didn't like it when the staff would pinch me in the shoulder, and they also hit me with a cane because I had an accident in bed. We had to scrub the floor on our hands and knees and wax the floor until you could see your face in it. We had no privacy. We took showers together and twenty-four people slept in the same room.

We had good times and bad times, and I went to school. In the school I was in Girl Scouts and many plays. I rode horses and worked. I got out on January 3, 1967, and I went to Sterling, Illinois for a trial period. The trial took place in a home and in the community as provided in Article X, section 10-6 of the Mental Health Code.

I went to live with my sister Betty. I looked for a job and got one working at the Pump Handle Motel, cleaning rooms. I also worked in several restaurants and at Girls Enterprise doing towel racks, counting screws, and packing boxes.

In 1970, I had a son and named him Richard. I also had a daughter, Nancy Josten, in 1977. On June 3, 1999, I moved to Austin to live with Bob, my boyfriend. I joined ARC in Mower County. They have activities such as nutrition class, bowling, diners' club, dances, and all different things. We all have a lot of fun. I learned to take care of myself, to cook, and pay my bills, and ARC helps me a lot with these kinds of things. I was at ARC to write my story.

Here in Austin I keep myself busy with friends, family, and hobbies. I go to the Senior Center. We eat there, and I help in the kitchen and wash dishes and help them clear the tables. I also do volunteer work for ARC, the Senior Center and at the Paramount Theatre. Austin is a good place to live.

Leslie Will Always Be Remembered
By Lois Potter Schmidt

The year we turned 17, the parents of one of my friends presented her with a car--an old, black, shabby fifth or sixth-hand car of long forgotten, if ever known, origin. We immediately christened the car Leslie and thought of it as "him."

I am not sure why Leslie was a he. Perhaps it was because we made his acquaintance in 1950, when the world was still mostly male-oriented. Or maybe he reminded us of a tattered derelict needing to be loved and cared for by us girls. The usual order of events was to pool our nickels, dimes and quarters, then pull into the service station with the best looking attendant and order, "One dollar's worth, please." Back in 1950 this was enough gas to keep Leslie cruising up and down Austin's Main Street for an entire evening.

From Oakland Avenue on the south, up to a turnaround in Horace Austin State Park on the north, then back, we drove Leslie, all the while scanning the street for boys in a Tin Lizzie (they drove girl cars). Passing one another, Leslie and Lizzie would greet with raucous horns. After a few passes, by some remote intuition, the cars would detour and rendezvous a few blocks off Main Street at the A&W root beer stand. The boys in Lizzie and the girls in Leslie chatted as if we just happened to meet there.

But this was small potatoes compared with the best place Leslie took us – to the drive-in theatre, where else? Spending so much of our money on Leslie's supper, we didn't have quite enough left over for the admission. No problem. Pooling our resources, we figured just how many could remain visible and pay for a ticket.

The rest? You guessed it. We lay on the floor under blankets or in Leslie's trunk. The trouble was, when we all emerged, there were more of us than could sit in Leslie and watch the movie. We had to take turns sitting on the bumpers, slapping mosquitoes and just waiting to get back inside, even though inside was stifling.

We left long before the movie was over, unanimous in our opinion that the movie was nowhere worth the discomfort. Actually, the best part of the evening had been getting into the drive-in undetected. I wonder if anyone noticed Leslie leaving with twice as many girls as he had brought.

I don't know what eventually became of Leslie, who took departure while I was away at college. Likely he moved on to new owners who I hope loved him even half as much as we did. Who knows? Maybe they even fed him a full meal once in awhile.

The turnaround point by the entrance to Horace State Austin Park.

We Girls "Knew" About the Roxy
By Lois Potter Schmidt

When I was a young girl growing up in Austin, the Roxy Theatre was off-limits, not so much by direct parental order as by implication--the pursed parental lips and hooded eyes whenever the Roxy was mentioned. We girls "knew" about the Roxy, raising our eyebrows and snickering at what we guessed went on inside. Now, don't get me wrong. We were nice girls--so nice we were known as the Ice Cream Gang, but we did have a normal, healthy curiosity.

It was in the summer of 1950, just before our senior year in high school, when we heard the news. The Roxy would be running a one-night movie showing the birth of a baby. (Remember, it hadn't been too many years since babies were presumed to have popped out of cabbage patches). Were we excited! Here had to be the answers to all the questions we were too embarrassed to ask our mothers. We absolutely had to see that movie. Fanning the flames of our desire were rumors that people got sick or even fainted from the shock of seeing it.

Determined to attend the Roxy Theatre just that once, we set about making plans to do so discreetly. We weren't sure just what our parents or other important people might think, so we decided it would be best to go incognito. To ensure our anonymity, we devised what we thought were foolproof disguises.

As I recall, it all happened during August's hot, humid dog days, but nevertheless we covered our heads with turbans and babushkas, encased our bodies in the standard baggy jeans and long-tailed men's shirts and our feet in triple-rolled sweat socks and saddle shoes. Applying much makeup bought at Kresge's just for the occasion (ordinarily we wore lipstick—period), we topped it of with sunglasses to be removed after the lights went out in the murky Roxy.

We were all set, and off we went. Arriving at the theatre and pretending not to know anyone, we found seats all in one row. There evidently weren't many curiosity seekers around that evening. The movie? It was nothing to write about after all these years. No one fainted or even screamed, and the Roxy wasn't steamy or murky or even mysterious. But the intrigue was well worth the elaborate preparations.

As we walked out after the movie, sunglasses on in the near dark, we came face to face with "the boys" from our class. We ignored their greetings, even though they called us by name. After all, even if we hadn't been trying to sneak off, we weren't looking our glamorous best.

Trying to walk, not run, to our car, we piled in and began to laugh and laugh until we were so weak we could barely sit up. Soon, as you might guess, all of Austin High School knew what we thought was our secret, but we never publicly admitted we'd been at that movie. The incident has become one of our longstanding, all-time favorite reminiscences to be rehashed at reunions and passed on to children asking about the "old days." But only in private, of course.

The Roxy girls, also known as the Ice Cream Gang

Memories
By Thomas M. Seery

My memories of life in Austin began in 1948 when I joined the Austin Clinic. With my wife Elizabeth, son Mike and baby daughter Kathy, we moved here on a beautiful day in September, and knew from the first that this was the place for us. I had been very happy with the doctors I had met, and driving around on that lovely day, we fell in love with the town itself. We were impressed with the schools, churches, parks, playgrounds, the well-kept neighborhoods, the bustling business district, and the general sense of well being of the people. Clearly this was a thriving and happy town.

I grew up in Michigan but came to Minnesota for my medical training. I received my M.D. and also an M.S. in pharmacology at the University of Minnesota. I did my internship at the Minneapolis General Hospital (now Hennepin General). In 1943, with the war on, I went directly into the Army Medical Corps.

On being released from active duty in 1946, I continued my specialty training in Internal Medicine at Milwaukee County General Hospital. After a year, I transferred to the University of Minnesota Hospitals to finish my residency, which I completed in early 1948. I began interviewing at many clinics in the Midwest, trying to decide where I could practice medicine in the way I wanted and where we could settle down and raise our family. On the short list of places that I was most impressed with, I felt especially drawn to the Austin Clinic, as it was called until the clinic and hospital formally united in 1992. At the time I joined, it was a five-doctor clinic composed of a general surgeon, an eye, ear, nose and throat specialist and three family practitioners. I would be the sixth, and my specialty was internal medicine.

The clinic was established in 1919 by four local, forward thinking, private practitioners doing what we would now call family practice. These founders were Dr. E. C. Rebman, general practice, Dr. C. Allen, general practice/surgery, Dr. W. Grise, general practice/obstetrics, and Dr. C.F. Lewis, general practice/optometry. Dr. Lewis also became known as the father of the Austin Rotary Club.

At that time, clinics were not at all common (the Mayo Clinic was a pioneer in this and may have been an inspiration). Since three of the four founders had developed areas of particular interest, a desire to form a local "specialty clinic" was a part of their motivation. Austin was a growing community, and the immediate World War I social ferment made it an auspicious time. In the coming dark days of the 1930s, the people of Austin would rejoice in such slogans as, "The world takes what Austin makes," and, "Austin, the little town that the Depression forgot."

It is fair to note that the Austin Clinic, now an anchor of the Austin Medical Center Mayo, was the true initiator of specialty medicine in this community. As Austin celebrates its sesquicentennial in this year of 2006, it is fitting that special note be taken of the importance of this organization in the city's history. A building for the clinic was constructed in northwest Austin on the corner of Greenwich (2nd Street NW) and Mill (3rd Ave. NW) in 1929 and was the clinic's home until March of 1953.

Of the original founding members, only Dr. Grise remained when I joined. He was a classic early 20th Century family doctor, very dignified, attentive and kind. He was an inspiration to me. The others were Dr. David P. Anderson, a brilliant general surgeon and our first boarded surgeon, Dr. Leonard "Stub" Flanagan, formally trained in eye, ear, nose and throat, certainly among the last of those designates because ophthalmology had separated into its own specialty in the early 1930s. Dr. Robert Wright specialized in family practice and anal and rectal surgery. He had come back with David Anderson from the Air Force after the war. Dr. Harold Rosenthal (family practice) came after release from three years active duty in the Army in the South Pacific.

At this point in the third millennium, it is fascinating to look back to my early years here. It was indeed a different world. At that time the optimism and stability of the post war years spoke of a time of great promise. The Korean "Police Action" was three years off, and the full impact of the Cold War, with threats of imminent nuclear annihilation, was still in the future. There was prosperity, an unquestioned national confidence from our victory in World War II, and thoughts of the creation of a new and peaceful world as we were entering our own golden age.

The Hormel Company was hiring, ultimately peaking at over 3,000, and the city population was at or nearing 27,000. Local general prosperity was very good. A large number of homes were supported by one or more Hormel paychecks, and early winter profit sharing checks gave a boost to holiday spending. Paychecks of the time look small compared to inflated incomes of the well paid today, but there was little poverty, and there was an exuberant sense of worry-free good times.

An illustration of this from the perspective of a beginning professional person's experience is probably worth noting. My starting salary was $600 a month, increased in three months to $750. Office calls were $3, house calls were $5, with country calls a bit more. Office hours were Monday through Friday, and Saturday morning was for acute problems. Emergency hours were held on Sunday at the clinic for two hours "after church".

House calls in town and the country in those days were frequent, and some account of these long-gone services deserves mention. Most of us who made house calls, and probably grumbled about it on being pressed, would have to admit that at the time they were essential. With limited emergency and laboratory services and the absence of monitored beds and trained critical care nurses, they made good sense. There was also a particular value and satisfaction in seeing the patient in his/her home with the family. This created a bond between the doctor and the patient that could have a very positive effect in many ways, not the least of which was knowing what made the most sense for that person and where certain limitations might lie.

Then there was the adventure of the call itself. Before Austin streets and avenues were designated by number and by cardinal directions, this could be complicated. Austin is divided geographically into segments by East Side Lake, the railroad tracks, the serpentine Red Cedar River, and Turtle Creek. The streets are grid-like only in part, and in Austin Acres almost all are in curves and mazes. The old street names were charming but of limited help. A doctor, starting on a call, was well advised to get more useful coordinates established. This was true when going on country calls, especially at night. How well I remember the fun of those house calls. The landmarks given were often obscure in the dark, and there was the challenge of just getting into the general area, of differentiating dwelling in-drives from field in-drives, and then picking the right farm. It was interesting how often the residents didn't know their "fire number," the one thing that assured that you were at the right place. One thanked The Almighty for rural electrification and yard lights.

During the late 1940s and early '50s, the increase in patients required more doctors and the following were added: Wallace Anderson (pediatrics), Ray Van Cleve (family practice/dermatology), and Ed Sargent (obstetrics/gynecology) joined in 1949; Harold Anderson (general surgery/orthopedics) joined in 1950; Inman Hesla (family practice) joined in 1952;,and John Hagen (internal medicine/cardiology/pulmanology) joined in 1955. During the '50s the need for a larger building progressively made itself felt, and in 1958 serious planning for a new building was started. Where should it be located? What should it be like? What will it cost? How will it be financed?

Many serious questions and many serious meetings took place, always with the staff as a whole. The Austin Clinic was, and remained (until its purchase by the Mayo Clinic) a model of direct or Athenian democracy with rare attempts at pulling rank. An architect and a building contractor were engaged, and a large site purchased on the southwest corner of Oakland Avenue and 14th Street SW, as no site was available adjacent to the hospital or in the downtown area. Here, a handsome two-story building of blond brick with a central blue facade emerged with service and administrative areas on the first floor and clinical offices on the second floor. We occupied it on a snowy March day, and all were dazzled and euphoric in our new quarters. There were generous areas for lab and x-ray. The lobbies were large and attractively appointed, the offices were of an ideal size, and the main corridor was broad, similar to the Mayo Clinic. Regarding the corridor, one of the nurses excitedly exclaimed, "Why you could drive a truck down here!" We felt that we had provided for a remote future, but enlarged it within twelve years.

Over the next three years an additional four doctors joined the clinic: John Patten (surgeon), Gene Muchow (family practice/obstetrics), Reginald Harned Isele (internal medicine) and William (Bill) O'Rouke (family practice). At this point the clinic stabilized at twelve to fourteen doctors, which prevailed with some comings and goings for the next twenty-five years, with major additions occurring over the years just before the move into the hospital offices in 1989.

Back in 1948, our family quickly found Austin to be all we had hoped for. As my practice grew in those early years, so did our family. Over the next nine years we had three more delightful girls, Susan, Ann, and Elizabeth (Beth). Our life was busy indeed, with my wife Elizabeth doing the "heavy lifting" at home and I at the clinic, working 60+ hours a week. We were active in the church and school and in some recreational social activities such as the Cotillion, a group that met for dancing monthly. Elizabeth joined several women's groups including the Medical Auxiliary, Girl Scouts, and the Red Cross Blood Bank. She put much energy into establishing Meals on Wheels and then served this organization for many years. When the kids were in high school, Elizabeth returned to her profession as a laboratory technician when this group was in short supply. I served a number of medical and other organizations including the Mower County Medical Society, hospital and clinic meetings, Mower County Board, medical advisor at St. Marks and Sacred Heart Nursing Homes, Austin Rotary Club, and Boy Scouts at the local and regional levels. With all of this, we made an effort to put primary emphasis on activities related to our children.

During the time our kids were growing up, we lived in a big old house. We felt lucky and were happy to get it when we came to Austin. Growing up in a house like this, with all its rooms, closets, attic space and miscellaneous crannies, was an adventure in itself, great for rainy days! The corner lot location with its long sidewalks gave all of us plenty of work with a shovel, and there was also plenty of lawn to mow.

I look back with particular warmth on the chance to be active in the Boy Scout program when Mike was a scout. It was great to share special times and projects with Mike, especially considering the early years of his life missed when I was overseas and had other military separations, as well as the intrinsic time requirements of medical practice. In 1957 we went to the annual Boy Scout Jamboree at Valley Forge, Pennsylvania. There we shared many of the sights and excitement of this large, colorful celebration.

There, as a special clinical bestowal, I became a very early victim of the 1957 Asian flu pandemic. This flu emerged there as one of the earliest U.S. sites. Mike and Walter, a Bolivian exchange student who lived with us for a year, escaped it, and by the time I got home I must have been non-infectious, since no one here got it then. I was involved a great deal with Mike's troop and camp and "camporee" outings and also the Area Council and was one of twelve people to receive The Order of The Arrow in this area that year. This was an honor that I felt proud to receive. At the Austin centennial, Mike was one of the boy scouts who laid flowers on the grave of Chauncey Leverick, one of the founders of Austin. Elizabeth did a lot of work with our daughters in the Girl Scout programs. We tried to be present at all athletic events that Mike, Ann, and Beth were in. Unfortunately, competitive athletics were not available to girls when Kathy and Susan were in high school.

While we did not play golf or tennis, we belonged to the Country Club for many years and all enjoyed the pool in the summer and the fine dining room the year around. One of the town's attractions, dear to the kids, was the annual Mower County Fair. After leaving home and having their own children, it wasn't unusual for them to show up at fair time, kids in tow, to enjoy it again... who said you couldn't come home?

I retired in 1985 but continued to work at the hospital doing chart reviewal into the late 1990s. After I retired, Elizabeth and I traveled a lot seeing different parts of the country, We enjoyed music and the theatre and regularly went up to Orchestra Hall and the Guthrie Theatre. During retirement, I also had much more time to spend on woodworking and taking part in a woodworker's club of local enthusiasts.

Elizabeth developed heart disease in the late '80s and had increasing heart problems over the last few years of her life. She had great tenacity and courage, which she attributed to her iron range roots, and she was always proud of being a "ranger." We were able to celebrate our sixtieth wedding anniversary at a favorite spot on the Boundary Waters, and we continued our trips to the Cities up to a few months before her death in the spring of 2004.

Since I retired more than twenty years ago, I did not practice with the many doctors who joined the clinic after that, but my job in the hospital enabled me to get to know many of them, and I was happy with the continuing fine quality of the men and women who joined the staff. The tradition of excellence continues.

Dr. Seery worked at the Austin Medical Clinic from 1948-1985.

The Austin Clinic

Seven Springs
By Beatrice Furtney Sheedy

Grandmother Jessie Simpson Griffith and grandfather Edward Griffith lived on the farm they called Silver Spring Farm—later to be known as Seven Springs. In 1912 Edward died, and my mother inherited part of the farm. When she and my father married in 1913, Dad bought the remainder of the farm, but Jessie continued to live with them the rest of her life. Although Dad and Mother were the owners, Grandmother always insisted it was her home.

We never knew how the name got changed to Seven Springs, but it may have been because my father and the hired man used a team of horses and a big scoop to clean out the spring area. It did open up other springs, so it really was a lovely spot.

Dad allowed the public to use the area for picnics and for swimming in Turtle Creek. I think any kid born during the time Dad lived knew where Seven Springs was. During the summer months there wasn't a day when the river didn't ring with happy kids swimming, diving off the diving board, swinging out over the water on a rope swing, and dropping off into the river. Some of the time we had a raft. We would all get on one side of it so then it would tip over, such fun.

Seven Springs

One summer in the mid-30s it was particularly hot, and young people from farms would flock to the river after working in the evening. One evening twenty-six cars were lined up along the road, while all of the occupants enjoyed the swimming hole.

While my father lived, we had very little trouble with vandalism or beer parties at night. I guess it was understood he wouldn't put up with that sort of thing. However, my father died in 1964, and soon Mother had to deal with loud parties at night and people who would not clean up after themselves, so she had to get the sheriff to put up signs to keep the general public out.

The river has been dredged a couple of times now so it looks more like just a ditch, and the spring which was so lovely has dwindled down to just one spot. We used to lie on our bellies and drink the wonderful cold water, but the last I saw of the spring, it would take a mighty long neck to keep from going headlong into the water.

I have wonderful memories of growing up at Seven Springs, and I am grateful our five daughters were able to enjoy it too.

Ray "Bud" Furtney, Bernard Eide, Ray Furtney Sr. at Silver Springs, 1910

Bea Sheedy's family has been in the Austin area since the town began in the mid-1800s, and Bea has lived here all her life.

Austin, My Hometown
By Kathleen Sherman

My father was Fayette Sherman, who died in May, 1968. My mother was Etta Peterson Sherman, the youngest child of George Peterson, the first employee of George A. Hormel. Mother passed away at the Adams Care Center on June 4, 2006, and would have been 105 years old in November of 2006.

The Shermans adopted me in the fall of 1938 when I was 2 years old from the State Public School for Dependent and Neglected Children in Owatonna, Minnesota. I was at the Owatonna facility only a few weeks before coming to Austin. When Mother and Daddy realized I was getting entirely too much attention and hadn't a hope of being a normal child, I was joined by my sister Sally when I was 5 and she was 4. Sally (originally Ida Mae) was also a ward of the Owatonna facility.

My first Austin memory is being taken to see Grandma and Grandpa Sherman. Their house was across from the Methodist Church on what was then Maple Street. After I was shown off and passed from lap to lap, mention was made of going home. Apparently I thought I was already home and went into a complete meltdown fit at the thought of going anywhere else. Daddy's version of this always was that they finally settled me down enough to get me home, where I wouldn't go even as far as the front steps until a new black patent leather shoe expedition was organized with the promise to come right back home. I still have the shoes.

Mother and Daddy were temporarily caring for a female Springer spaniel named Wally. Daddy wasn't particularly impressed with the Duchess of Windsor, so he named the dog after her. I progressed to sitting on the front steps with Wally and then to trailing Daddy everywhere. He took me to work with him at the employment office of the Hormel Company and later even on business trips. I remember sitting in the reception area of a radio station in Omaha, Nebraska while he was interviewed about the purchase of a meat packing plant in Fremont, Nebraska. The best part of the trip was when the radio station receptionist gave me a book to read while I waited, and she let me keep the book!

Apparently I had Grandpa Sherman well trained before I started school and before Sally arrived because he would walk me up and down Main Street visiting his friends, and he also took me to his work at

the Mower County Courthouse, where he was clerk of district court.
The Main Street tour always included a stop at Nemitz Cigar Store for
peanuts for the monkeys at Horace Austin Park. I didn't like the thin
brown skins on the peanuts but tried to eat them because Grandpa did. I
remember being very impressed with the transom windows in the very
tall doors at the old courthouse.

Another memory is of a lady who had a studio upstairs somewhere
on Main Street where she cut paper silhouettes. I remember my Austin
up through high school as having everything within walking or biking
distance for kids – school, the swimming pool, the Clay House, sledding
on Skinner's Hill and going to Klagge's for frosted malts on our way
home from the swimming pool, even though it was in the opposite
direction.

Fayette and Etta Sherman. He served as mayor in the 1960s.

Garnet Keogh came to our house as Santa Claus with his sleigh
with horses. I remember watching high school athletics in sports crazy
Austin. I remember bunking parties at our house in late September, when
my birthday coincided with homecoming. We had three bathrooms, and
Daddy directed traffic when all the girls came to our house to change
clothes between the football game and the dance at the high school. I
never had the slightest understanding of football, but it was so much fun
anyway. With basketball I was a bit better because if the ball went into
the basket it was good. The state basketball tournament was a big event,
and we could go to Dayton's while we were in Minneapolis.

I remember walking a route with Daddy when he was an air raid warden during World War II – in the dark! I think I remember Nelson's grocery store on West Oakland Avenue, where the dog would go with us and she would hustle straight to the meat department for a wiener. In Austin we ate wieners, not hot dogs. Hot dogs came later. I remember the swimming beach at East Side Lake as being rather an expedition, since Mother probably drove us there. I remember picnics at Todd Park and biking to the Girl Scout cabin for sleepovers. I know we never found time for television.

I remember picking out Christmas trees at the A&W root beer stand and at Burr Oaks Market, where once the dog was left behind while she was supervising the selection. I remember the Ruth Fox Dance Studio in the basement of the present 100 Building location. We had little girl dance classes with recitals at the Paramount Theatre with silver sparkles on our soft dance shoes. Most of all, I remember being happy and being loved. I have no doubts about that, but whenever I am in Owatonna I can't help but think – with other parents, another town, I'd be an entirely different person.

Kathleen Sherman has lived in Austin since she was 2 years old. She worked in the Hormel Corporate Office.

Paramount Memories
By Bev Smith

It seems to me most people went to the movies more often back in my high school years and shortly thereafter. Of course, we had no TV, and for some of those years (1941-1945) we had little gas for just driving around. I think entrance prices were ten cents most of those years. I can remember that it seemed like a lot to pay then.

It was not only fun to go to the movies, but it was the place to go to see friends, see who was dating whom, and what everyone was wearing. The balcony was the date place most often. It seemed all movies were good then. There were no X or PG ratings. We all assumed that all movies were suitable and good, and they were. We didn't care if they were comedies, Westerns, or whatever. We just wanted to be there. We attended the other theatres too, but it was never like being at the Paramount.

During the war years we saw lots of war movies that brought the war closer to us. Many of our classmates were already in the service, as were a lot of brothers. In the fall of 1944 and into the spring of 1945, I spent a lot of time there. Karl Lindsteadt asked some of us girls to help at the theatre.

After the ads, March of Time, and cartoons, the movie would be stopped, and we would take a collection from the audience. We'd pass baskets up and down the rows. The collections most often went to the Red Cross or the United Service Organizations (USO) that provided recreational and other kinds of services to military personnel at ports and bases. Since we had to be there for each showing of the feature film, we'd just hang out in the beautiful ladies' lounge between features. Especially on Sundays we would have a long day. I think at that time movies were at shown at 1, 3, 5, 7 and 9 o'clock. I remember that when *Meet Me In St. Louis* was playing, I saw it – or a portion of it – thirty-four times.

I don't recall that we collected great sums of money because no one had much, but every little bit helped. I remember some people dropping ration tokens in the baskets. We had to have ration tokens for sugar, meat, gas, and other items during the war because ensuring that our troops had enough goods that were manufactured in our country was a priority.

I can give an example of the fact that most every young person went to many movies. When I was in high school, the movie with Cary Grant, *Arsenic and Old Lace,* was showing at the Paramount. If you are familiar with the movie, you'll remember that a man thinks he is Teddy Roosevelt. Every time he went up the stairs, he'd yell "charge" and go up the stairs thinking it was San Juan Hill. At school during this time you could see boys, particularly, standing at the bottom of a flight of stairs saying "charge" and leaping up the steps. Everyone thought it was hilarious; and it was. We all knew exactly what was going on because we'd all been to the movie.

Opening day at the Paramount in 1929--before Bev's time.

Bev Smith is a retired elementary school teacher living in Austin.

Austin High School During the 1940s and War Years
By Bev Smith

In the early 1940s Austin High School contained grades 7-12, with the three lower grades designated junior high. After Pearl Harbor in 1941 and through to the end of the war, students and faculty were active in the war effort.

The Class of 1945 published the *Austinian* with Porky Pig as the theme, very apt for a meatpacking town. The inscription on the front page shows the patriotism everyone felt during those war years. "Porky is most thankful that he is an American for whom men are fighting to make the future secure. He knows that he can plan his life the way he wants it, that he can speak and write the way he likes, that he can attend the church of his choice on Sunday, and that he can go about his school activities gaining knowledge and having fun."

Wartime projects were visible everywhere at school. Slippers and afghans were made and collected by the home economics department and sent to servicemen and women to make them more comfortable. Everyone was urged to buy Defense Stamps and Defense Bonds to fund the war effort. A contest was held. A "thermometer" was erected in the second floor corridor to record the "temperature" of each class's efforts. The main goal in 1945 was to fly the Treasury Flag, and it was flown from March on.

Over $2,000 worth of Defense Stamps were sold each week in the Austin Public Schools, and over $70,000 by the end of the year – a grand showing! Many senior high students enlisted in the services after Pearl Harbor, even before graduation. Each service person's name, including recent alumni, was listed on large framed posters called the "Rolls of Honor." A large flag with a star representing each service person was hung in the auditorium. Unfortunately, there were also gold stars, which represented a death.

The student council and several other student organizations published a paper called *The Scarlet Letter*, which was sent to every member of the armed forces from the last three graduating classes and students who had left school to go. They also started a service center room for anyone home on furlough to visit. Teachers and students welcomed returning service people home on leave. They often came to visit classes and speak at meetings. These same young people came home from the war, went to college or got a job, married (or not), built a home, and raised a family and generally became good citizens. They are among ones Tom Brokow wrote about in his book, *The Greatest Generation.*

Austin High School students have always excelled in academics, but also in sports and musical activities. The years in the 1940s were no exception. There was a war on, but that didn't dim the enthusiasm of faculty and students for those activities. There were not as many sports to participate in. Girls' sports had not come into their own as yet, but that didn't diminish the enthusiasm for sports!

The stadium was often filled at football games. Basketball games were so well attended that the high school auditorium was often filled as well as the gymnasium! Homecoming was as important as it is now. The night before the game a "snake dance" was held on Main Street. It ended at the north end of Main Street, where a huge bonfire burned and crackled. A pep rally was held, and students yelled so much they almost lost their voices and had to make a quick recovery to support the team at the homecoming game. The 1943 homecoming game had to be postponed because of a huge snowfall. The 1944 homecoming game was a smash! Austin beat Rochester.

In 1945 the swimming team won the state championship. And I think the basketball team was district champion in 1945. Ove Berven was the basketball coach. He had a little son named Tom who never missed a game and often "conducted" the pep band – probably the youngest conductor in the history of Austin.

Spring brought tests, the prom and field day. Field Day was one long day of sports activities with competition between the junior and senior classes. Races, relays, softball and other activities were great, and teams were separated by gender. It was all on the up and up, and teachers kept the scores of each activity. Late in the afternoon everyone went to Turtle Creek. The "tug of war" was the climax of the day with junior boys on one side of the creek and senior boys on the other side. The girls had a tug of war too. The tug of war continued until one side was pulled into the creek.

I mentioned earlier that Austin has been very good at promoting good music education and activities. Several orchestras, bands, and choral groups were busy even way back then, with fine music instructors. Most people would agree that one of the most outstanding directors was Mr. C. V. Sperati. For many years he taught almost all the bands and orchestras, plus senior high chorus. In 1944 he became strictly the bandmaster. As a result, the band had its own separate concerts for the first time, and for the first time ever, swing or jazz numbers were played at concerts and games and at the district band festival.

Since it was wartime, many extra activities were added to the band's agenda in the form of parades, rallies, etc. In fact, the band was awarded the War Council Distinguished Service Citation in recognition of its outstanding contributions to the war effort through participation in special wartime musical activities. Mr. Sperati taught in Austin from 1930 to 1964. Recent band directors credit him for starting the tradition of strong music in Austin, and they are following his fine example. In his honor the band room in the Annex, Room 1128, has been named the "Sperati Music Room."

Truly the sports, scholastic and music programs that were strong in the 1940s have continued to this day.

Austin High School

Austin in the 1950s
By Evelyn Smith

In December of 1950, my husband Vern and I and our two children, David and Roxann, moved to Austin from Forest City, Iowa. When we first came we stayed with Vern's sister and her husband, Erwin and Dorothy Berry, until we found an apartment at Oakland and 11th Street NE called Parkview Apartments. On the north end of this complex was a row of apartments, and on the west side were two rows of small houses. The Super Valu now sits where those apartments once stood. On the east side facing 11th Street was Al and Vi's Bar, and on the east side of the street was Smitty's Bar and Eckert's Implements. On the south side was a small café. With all those businesses and people coming and going, it was a merry place to live.

On the west end of the complex, up a hill, were the railroad yards. At that time the railroad was a very busy place. When our kids went out to play, I always had to watch that they didn't go up to the tracks and get in the way of a train. When I washed clothes and hung them out, it seemed like that old steam engine always sat up there puffing out its black soot that would come down on my clothes. They would get black specks on them from that old engine's soot, and it was almost impossible to get it out. One day I was so upset I shook my fists at the engineer. All he did was smile and wave at me. I knew he couldn't help it. We lived there two years.

A half block north of us there was an overhead railroad bridge so people didn't have to walk across the tracks. Our kids really liked to go there and watch the trains come and go. We had a grocery store across the tracks on Railway Street (now 10th). I would cross the tracks and go there to get groceries. Also, across Oakland Avenue was Sutton Park, and we often took the kids there to play on the swings and slide.

While we were living here our son Vance was born. Vern was working at Holland Furnace Company on South River Street (now 6th). In 1953 we moved to South River Street. There our daughter Pam was born. That was a very snowy winter. Vern was working for the Austin Dairy, and the snow was so deep he got stuck many times and came home very tired. This was when we still had milkmen delivering milk in town.

We moved to 7th Street NW across from Sumner School, where David and Roxann started school. They went there two years before we moved to the Austin Acres area, and the kids went to a country school. They really liked it there. I had a garden, and we had two wonderful, close neighbors, Mr. and Mrs. Schlicter and Mr. & Mrs. Johnson. Mr. Schlicter and his son came over to plow my garden, which I greatly appreciated. Mr. Johnson had horses in a pasture by our house, and when we weren't looking, our 4-year old Greg went out in the pasture, picked up a stick and hit the horse's back leg. Naturally it kicked back at what hit him, and hit Greg in the chin. Thank goodness it was a slight kick, but it put a gash through his chin, and he bled a lot. We rushed him to the emergency room and they sewed him up and he was okay. Mr. Johnson felt so bad, but it wasn't his fault.

The house was very small, and by now we had five children with one on the way, so we needed to find something larger. By then Vern was working for Wagner Construction. We bought a house on 13th Street NE in 1958 and lived there for forty-four years. I remember there were a lot of kids on that block. We had eight, Durbens had seven, Deyos had three, and Johnsons had two so it was a lively, busy neighborhood.

The railroad pedestrian overpass

In those days the Fourth of July parade went east on 4th Street to 10th, and the fireworks were held at the East Side Lake. In the wintertime the kids would all go skating on the ice at the lake, where the city put up a warming house. In the summer the boys went fishing there. What I didn't know was that when the water was low, the boys would walk across the dam. That was very dangerous, and I would have scolded them soundly if I had known.

The old Post Office

The post office was on the corner of 1st Street and 3rd Avenue NW, and the library was kitty-corner across the street from it. I used to go there and look at the census films, looking for my lost relatives. I remember when the Hormel plant was imploded in order to build the new plant. Now there is a new Hormel SPAM Museum, which is extraordinary – a lot of fun to go and see. Austin has changed a lot over the years, and I hope it will continue to do so.

Evelyn Smith worked at St. Olaf Hospital for fifteen years. She enjoys volunteering at the Austin Public Library.

FACTS: Floodway Action Citizens Task Force
By Alice Snater

In the summer of 1978, Austin suffered two record-breaking floods in the span of ten days. The first flood, on July 6 and 7, crested at over 19 feet, the highest watermark in the city's recorded history. Then on July 17, torrential rains caused the Cedar River to crest at a mark exceeding 21 feet. The result was massive destruction.

The two floods resulted in damages amounting to a total of $12 million. Three hundred and ten city homes and another hundred homes in the county were either damaged or destroyed. Fifty Austin business firms were damaged, and some closed permanently. Friends, neighbors and local disaster assistance groups quickly aided flood victims.

It is significant to note that it was the flood victims themselves who banded together to create the Floodway Action Citizens Task Force, called FACTS. Most had no previous experience in citizen action organizations, but they officially organized FACTS in September of 1978, with the election of officers who included Marie Casey, Orv Snater and Alice Snater. The new group coordinated citizen participation in city council meetings and at hearings before other local and state government organizations. They were in pursuit of immediate flood relief and coordinated efforts to initiate planning to prevent future flood disasters. FACTS numbered more than one hundred citizens. They were persistent, attending city council meetings on a weekly basis for the balance of 1978. FACTS represented 450 city and county households. Of the total membership, 154 people attended meetings with local, state and regional officials.

As a direct result of the committee's extensive research, compilation of data and total commitment to working with city officials, Austin was awarded a $1.7 million HUD grant for relocation, the first of many such grants to come after suffering through several more disastrous floods. Austin was also granted $14,000 from the Department of Natural Resources for Cedar River cleanup and a CETA labor grant of $31,700 after the 1978 floods.

The police department, at the request of FACTS, implemented a special siren for use as an early warning system. Changes were made in the county flood plain map regarding floodway-flood fringe lines. Each year on July 17, for five years following the floods, FACTS sponsored a potluck picnic, which was open to the public. The event, held in

Lafayette Park, was a reminder to the community that Austin remains in a serious flood hazard situation.

The work, successes, and the cooperation put forth by the citizens and city government have laid the groundwork, credibility and excellent track record for the city to continue the work of applying for and receiving numerous federal and state grants that have nearly cleared the flood plain of family households. This is an important part of Austin history.

The 1978 flood

Alice Snater recently retired after twenty-three years with the Austin Catholic Schools. She volunteers for Birthright and is a child advocate for the court system.

Barnstorming Provided a Glimpse of Major League Talent
By Paul Spyhalski

The *Austin Daily Herald* noted with civic pride when the downtown businesses closed to support the opening of Austin's baseball season in the 1910s. It was with great pride that Austin claimed the state championship in 1912 with the assistance of future Hall of Fame member Buleigh Grimes' curves.

One way that a community ball team measured its talent was to play against the most talented teams. From 1912 to 1917, one of the most dominating traveling teams was the All Nations Team, founded by J.L. Wilkinson. The team may not have had members from all nations, but it did feature players who were Chinese, Japanese, Hawaiian, Cuban, Mexican, Norwegian, Swedish, Bohemian, Irish and American. The featured players were Jose Mendez and John Donaldson.

Jose Mendez, called "The Black Diamond" in his Cuban homeland for his efforts against American major leaguers, pitched or played short. His efforts in Cuba included a one-hit shutout of the Cincinnati Reds and a total of 25 innings of shutout baseball against major league hitters in 1908.

Mendez continued to develop a name by traveling with Cuban teams in the United States and dominating the Cuban leagues. In 1911, he blanked the world champion Philadelphia Phillies following the World Series and defeated the great Christy Mathewson 4-0.

John Donaldson was the other half of the marquee pitching tandem. Donaldson was one of the elite left handed pitchers of this era. He was regularly known to strike out as many as eighteen batters in a game and was capable of throwing a no-hit game if not a shutout. When he didn't pitch, he played in the outfield.

The only thing that kept these two wonders from the major leagues was the color of their skin. New York Giants manager John McGraw said that either one of them would have been worth $50,000 if their skin had been white.

The issue of segregation caused J. L. Wilkinson to innovate by having his All Nations travel in their own Pullman rail car with their own cook. With their own sleeping quarters and place to eat, the players were able to sidestep the race issue while entertaining on and off fields throughout the country. The All Nations visited Austin twice in 1913 and four times in 1914. Jose Mendez, advertised by Wilkinson as the "Cuban Wonder," demonstrated his craft and class while showing off his fancy wind-ups and deliveries in a 6-1 win in 1913.

Demonstrating their all-around ability to entertain, the All Nations often provided a concert following their games. Indeed, players on the All Nations had to be solid ball players and able to entertain off the field. Mendez played clarinet and the guitar. Following their 1913 game, the All Nations Ball Team Band and Orchestra performed a concert at the Austin armory.

John Donaldson demonstrated his mound skills for the Austin locals in 1914. Extra seats were erected so that as many fans as wanted to see the "colored left handed phenomena" could attend. With Donaldson on the mound, 627 more people came to the park on Sunday than on Saturday. Donaldson threw a nine-inning no-hit game, despite losing 1-0 when a misplay in the field allowed a runner to come home.

The All Nations, again innovating, added electric arc lights to their traveling gear. The lights allowed the All Nations to play two games or more in one day. In what may well be the first night game in Austin history, the All Nations played at Austin at 3 p.m. and 8 p.m. on August 28, 1914. Without Mendez or Donaldson on the mound, the Austinites were able to win both games.

The greatness of this traveling team is borne out by the inclusion of both Mendez and Donaldson on a special ballot of the Baseball Hall of Fame for players who were unable to play in the major leagues due only to their skin color. Of the thirty-nine players, managers and owners on the special ballot, Mendez and team owner J.L. Wilkinson were elected to the Hall of Fame. Donaldson's amazing career continues to be documented, and more wins and strikeouts continue to be found.

Paul Spyhalski is an Austin attorney. He enjoys baseball and trains.

Where I'm From
By Victoria Spyhalski

Ask me where I was born, and I'll say I was born in Albert Lea, Minnesota, where I-90 and I-35 cross. Albert Lea is also home to the Tigers. Growing up as a Tiger, the Austin Packers were our most hated rival in the Big Nine Conference. Tiger fans deplored the red and white of the Packers' uniforms. Packer students would occasionally come to Albert Lea and cause trouble during our football games, especially if it was homecoming. This was a thorn in our sides, especially after sitting in our marching band uniforms during a damp, cold football game that didn't turn out as we had hoped. As a loyal Tiger fan, I recall thinking how superior Albert Lea's school colors were because they are blue, white and red, the same colors as the American flag.

The rivalry between the two towns was not limited to the schools. Albert Leans viewed Hormel with jealous eyes because it was a superior competitor to our frequently struggling Wilson packing plant, which changed ownership several times during the course of my childhood. Eventually the Wilson packing plant closed, and later burned in a spectacular fire that forever changed the landscape of Albert Lea.

Despite the rivalry, we did eat SPAM as children, which my father would fry up in a pan with a generous dose of ketchup and onions on the evenings when my mother worked at the hospital. I usually ate what I could wash down with milk, and plotted to get a larger than usual portion of Dad's evening popcorn before bedtime.

What a strange irony it is that I would end up working and living in Austin. In search of a better paying job, my husband and I drove to Austin for his first job interview in this town. We saw Oakland Avenue lined with banners that said, "Welcome to SPAMTown, USA!" and I thought back to the salty concoction that Dad used to make. I couldn't help but wonder what kind of place were we coming to.

Now, having been an Austinite for the last ten years, I realize this place is much bigger than a corporation, a food product, rivalries or school colors. Ask me now where I am from, and I will say Austin, Minnesota. Where do I work? You guessed it – Hormel's. And where do I live? Two blocks from Austin High School, which

I can see from several of our windows. What are the colors of my Columbia jacket? Red and white.

Austin is a small town, home to many things I love dearly like Marcusen Park and its rich baseball history and Piggy Blues, a delicious barbecue restaurant that often features live music. A favorite pastime of mine is to drive down 4th Avenue NE, a flag-lined boulevard that features the Austin Public Library, the Tendermaid, the Paramount, the Hormel Historic Home, and finally, St. Augustine's Catholic Church. The spires of the church are visible from various parts of town, and the bells toll regularly, a comforting sound that calls us in for dinner whether we are working in the garden or shoveling snow.

Austin is a town with a rich, diverse history. Although St. Patrick's Day parades are only pictures in a book, and a street once named Hope now bears the moniker of 5th Avenue NE, the city holds the promise of a rich and diverse future. What becomes of that future is my responsibility, and yours, too. Austin is home -- my home and our home.

Victoria and Paul Spyhalski moved to Austin in 1996. She enjoys writing, baseball, and communing with Mother Nature.

Remembering Ernest
By Jeanne M. Steinbrink

I remember the first time I met Ernest "Ernie" P. Wilson. It was just after Christmas in 1995, and I was working in my little office hidden away in the book stacks of a remote corner upstairs in the old Austin Carnegie Library. Unless you ventured upstairs to look for dog books, cookbooks or car manuals, you seldom saw me. I was the library secretary/bookkeeper, and at that time, I was also in charge of receiving donations from our successful $1.8 million dollar fund drive to help build the new Austin Public Library in 1996.

Ernest, roughly shaven and dressed in his trademark blue denim overalls with buckle straps, flannel shirt, quilted winter jacket and lined farmer's seed cap with earflaps, walked up to my desk and asked if I was the person in charge of the money for the new library fund drive. I replied, "Yes, I am. How can I help you?" At that point he reached into his pocket, pulled out his checkbook, tossed it on my desk and said curtly, "Here. You write it out." As I started to write, I asked him what amount he wished to donate. When he matter-of-factly stated the four-digit figure, I was a little taken aback – his humble appearance belied the size of his generous donation.

After he signed his check "Ernest P. Wilson," I asked him if he was a retired Hormel employee. He looked me straight in the eye and in the same curt manner, replied abruptly, "Yes. Why?" I told him that the Hormel Foods Corporation was matching any donation given by current or retired employees, and I asked him if he'd be interested in having his gift matched dollar for dollar. He said, "OK. Sure." Again, he asked me to fill out the form, and then he signed it and left.

I didn't run into Ernest again until he showed up at my office in the new library shortly after Christmas the following year. He came with his checkbook in tow and again tossed it to me to make another donation to our building fund, signed the check and left. Since my new office was a little more centrally located near the front entrance of the new library, I was able to see Ernest on occasion after this as he quietly made his way to the back of the library to read the *Wall Street Journal* and our other investment publications. He was a quiet man who had lived simply, but had invested wisely. Ernest went about his business discreetly and seldom spoke unless spoken to.

I learned from him that he had been retired from the Hormel plant for many, many years. He was a common site in northeast Austin walking his small dog Peanut. Peanut was his constant companion, as Ernest had never been married and had no desire to be, as he told me in no uncertain terms. I later learned how Ernest had acquired Peanut. In addition to his generosity to the library, in his retirement, Ernest enjoyed helping other people and thought everyone should help others in need. He told me that he had helped care for a woman who was dying, and he promised to take care of her dog. When the woman died, Ernest kept his promise.

In addition to helping this woman, Ernest also had a severely ill brother who was hospitalized for a lengthy stay in Albert Lea. Ernest sacrificed his time to spend most of a month staying with his brother in the hospital and caring for him. He had also helped a neighbor lady. Later, when he hurt his foot and was housebound for a short time, he asked her one day if she would mind running to the store to get a loaf of bread for him. She replied that she was too busy that day because she had a meeting to go to at church. He was hurt and disappointed and felt it would have been better for her to skip the church meeting and help someone instead.

Throughout the past ten years, I would visit with Ernest in the library whenever I had the chance. A few years ago, I gave him a box of Girl Scout cookies. After that, he would occasionally meander to my office for a quick visit, always being a gentleman and never overstaying his welcome. Each time, he would give me a small thread of the tapestry of his life.

It became an annual event to save a box of cookies for him, and I would warn him ahead of time that they would be coming soon. Then at Christmas time, I began ordering homemade Amish chocolate candies and inviting Ernest to stop by my office for a sample to take home.

About a year ago, I noticed Ernest walking around town without his dog. The next time I saw him in the library I asked him about it. He said his dog had died and that he missed it, but he wasn't sure if he would get another dog. He went on to tell me that his dog would only eat steak and that it had various health problems (related to the poor diet, as I found out from my daughter who worked at the veterinary clinic at the time). The dog had run up a few expensive veterinary bills. Though Ernest always complained about the cost, he would have done anything for his dog. After Peanut died, Ernest mentioned that a stray cat had begun hanging around his neighborhood, so he started feeding it. He sounded disappointed when he told me the cat didn't like steak!

This past Christmas I had my small package of Amish candy ready for Ernest's visit to my office, along with an invitation to my home for dinner on New Year's Eve to celebrate a late Christmas with me and my husband. We had invited Ernest and several other people whom I knew lived alone, hoping they might enjoy a big home-cooked meal and fellowship with us.

Our six guests started arriving late morning, and at noon we sat together at my round oak table extended with five leaves and ate a turkey dinner with all the fixin's and homemade pie, and we enjoyed interesting conversation. Afterwards, we moved to our small living room where we continued visiting while we munched on various Christmas goodies. I learned more about Ernest that afternoon than I had in the previous ten years. As he was walking out the door to leave, I asked him about his family. He told me he was the last of seven brothers and that he had just one sister, who was the youngest and still living, along with about ten nieces and nephews.

About a month later, I read in the paper that Ernest had died in his home, alone. He was 94 years old. The paper did not list a date of death, which led me to believe he had not been found right away. The funeral was on a day I had off from work, so I was able to attend the simple service at the funeral home—a few friends, his few remaining relatives, a short service, a closed casket topped by a framed photo of him holding Peanut, his dog and companion.

It is often too easy to forget the quiet, lonely people we see every day, and unfortunately we sometimes tend to look past or ignore folks without bothering to say hello. But I just wanted Ernest to know someone remembers him and misses him. His box of Girl Scout cookies is still at my desk.

Ernest Wilson and Peanut

Jeanne Steinbrink has worked at the library since 1984. She was project manager for this book.

Highway 218 South
By Jeanne M. Steinbrink

It was an April morning, and I was leaving my home in Lyle and heading north on Highway 218 to my job in Austin. Springtime roads in southern Minnesota are notorious for appearing to be in fine condition, only to surprise you moments later with a stretch of ice or slush where the warm air and the sub-freezing ground make a deadly connection. Often these conditions occur in early spring on windy days when the late winter snow blows across the road and clings to the highway, protected by a farmyard or clump of trees near the side of the road. As the April roads had twice tricked me and my car into the ditch several years ago with the unexpected slush, I had grown older and wiser. Or so I thought. Each damp spring morning I check the road and adjust my speed accordingly. Highway 218 can sometimes be unforgiving and has taken many lives in the past thirty years I've driven it. Little did I know that morning that I was its next intended victim.

This particular April day was heavy with dew and a bit overcast, so as soon as I left Lyle and hit Highway 218, I did my familiar tap, tap, tap on the brakes of my Dodge Caravan to check to see if the road was slippery. Though it appeared fine, I had been surprised before, so I slowed my speed to 50 miles per hour and headed north. About a half mile south of Austin, I was following a car that stopped ahead of me signaling to turn left on Mower County Road 28, the last turn before Austin. The driver was waiting for a southbound car to go past so he could complete his turn. Checking my rearview mirror, I noticed there were a couple cars behind me, so I began braking and tapped my brakes to warn the driver behind me that I was slowing down. Nothing happened! It was as if I had no brakes.

The startling realization hit me; what I thought had been a dry road was actually covered with the dreaded black ice that you hear horror stories about, but that no one is ever quite able to actually describe for you. My stopping distance had suddenly become too short. I knew at that instant that I couldn't stop in time and that if I didn't get off the road, I would rear-end the car in front of me. I could envision my car then veering off into the other lane and hitting the southbound vehicle head-on, causing a pile-up with the cars behind me.

When I realized this, I was angry with myself, knowing I had misjudged the road condition and that my mistake would probably be fatal. But I also knew I did not want to cause any deaths besides my own. With an unexpected calmness, I knew what I had to do; I had to hit my brakes and hope to end up in the ditch. I also knew that by taking the ditch at that speed, I would probably die. At that moment I prayed, "God, please take me and don't take anyone else," and I hit my brakes. Hard.

The next few seconds rushed together in a blur, with little recollection yet of what actually happened. I do remember my vehicle spinning wildly out of control while I desperately jerked the steering wheel back and forth. The van was doing 360s, or whatever fancy term it is that teenagers use to describe what happens when they purposely set their car into a skid to go around in circles. But just as quickly as I had spun out of control, the van stopped…in an instant.

I sat dazed, with my hands still on the steering wheel. My van was stopped dead in its tracks in a driveway a few feet from where the car ahead had been seconds earlier waiting to turn. I cannot explain how, but my van was well off Highway 218, backed into the last driveway before the corner, having miraculously avoided the deep ditches on either side and missing a mailbox at the end of the indrive.

My first thought was to thank God that I hadn't killed anyone. My second thought was, "I'm alive!" Next I marveled at the fact that my van wasn't wrecked lying in a ditch or field and that I wasn't even hurt. And last, I was incredulous when I realized that my van was backed perfectly into the center of the driveway and that I would just be able to drive out as if nothing had happened.

I waited in my car while the cars that were behind me headed north, most likely with their mouths gaping wide in wonder, shaken by the woman driver in the car they had just seen spinning wildly out of control. I am also sure they later reflected on their good fortune, realizing how lucky they were to avoid a deadly collision that day. After they had all safely passed, I pulled back into the northbound lane. But as I did so, I could hear a quiet but frantic "tapping" sound, and it took a moment to realize it was my foot on the gas pedal shaking!

Though I had just missed my brush with death on Highway 218 South that day with a certain calmness, the reality of what had nearly happened that April morning still makes me pause for a moment each time I drive by and give a slight shudder at what could have been.

It Takes a Village
By Susan Stevenson

It was 1997, and as a single mom I was looking for a home to raise two boys, one in elementary and one in middle school. Raised in a rural area, I looked for a home that would provide the essentials for raising little boys into men. I wanted a place where family means more than money, where religious education is expected and where my children could find minorities who were leaders both at school and in the community. I chose Austin.

After living their entire lives in one location, it was a difficult move for my boys and certainly no easier for me. We were leaving behind all that we knew for a future 800 miles away. We knew no one in our new location. As we drove away with our past in the rear view mirror, I wondered if my children were feeling the empty, anxious and sad feeling that goes with such a change. When asked, they said they were feeling the same. I said, "But you know, we are Stevensons, and we make friends easily, and it will be fun to get to know new friends."

While moving into our new house, I felt like a spider that had spent a long time weaving a perfect web for my family after the forces of life tore apart my plans, and I had to start all over again. One week Louise Davis and later Carol Holmen stopped by to welcome me to the neighborhood with FOOD! What had been a sad day was transformed into a happy one. I felt like I was home. I still love Minnesota nice!

Middle school is a difficult period for parents as well as kids. I faced my own challenges with my oldest. It was concert time. Owen played the saxophone, and the students especially enjoyed Amy Chalmer's band. In an effort to make the best of the event, Owen and his friends concocted a plan to purchase some "threads" appropriate for the occasion at the Salvation Army store. Owen was the only one who followed through. The other parents were probably smart enough to put the kibosh on this plan.

I sat toward the back of the auditorium and was mortified to see my son, sax in hand, hair "froed" to the max, chest out as if he was king of the world. He strutted across the stage dressed in his rust polyester leisure suit and gaudy wide tie. He gave a "thumbs up" to a covey of girls in the front row. Suddenly the girls began to chanting, "O-wen, O-wen!" It took the gentle but commanding voice of Principal Jean McDermott to quiet the fans. There is no doubt that Owen had easily made the friends that I had predicted on our move to Austin and so had Noah. Not only did Noah have new friends, but for the first time he had two male teachers, Mr. Brown and Mr. Orcutt, two of the best.

When they got a little older, I decided to devise an aversion therapy technique to prevent them from ever smoking. I explained that I did not want them to smoke, and it was time for them to find out about this disgusting temptation. After getting both boys in the car, I stopped and purchased a package of little cigars. It was difficult to even light the cigar, but after a few tries I got it started, making certain not to inhale, a technique I learned from President Clinton.

Owen took the first puff, complaining every step of the way. This reluctance made it hard to convince Noah that he should follow suit. One puff is all it took, and the coughing and sputtering that followed confirmed that I had achieved my objective.

Many years later the boys were trying to figure out what to get me for Mother's Day. They had me buy a package of cigars. Owen, who then had his license, drove. Noah sat in the back seat, and we all puffed on cigars enacting the family joke that we had talked about when the boys were little. It has become a family tradition.

Single parent is a misnomer. Single indicates that a person is one whole person, and I would argue that as a single parent, you are no more than maybe 50%. As I see it, on our best days, it takes two adults who support each other to maintain the intellect and energy to parent. Probably because both parents work, children today seem to demand even more of us. Divorce leaves a deficit. A single parent is no longer a one, but more like a one half. Without a life partner you have no one to fill in the gaps during fatigue, illness, decisions or the everyday stresses of life. As a single parent, I often feel as if I am operating at about 25% or less. I never feel more than about 50%.

Austin has helped make up that deficit. Friends, teachers, school counselors, clergy, coaches and many others in the community have been the village I needed to raise my boys. I am fortunate to have such wonderful children that have learned to fit into the world and respect my decisions. Thank you, Austin, not only for what you have done to help my children, but also for the contribution each of you makes in the development of all children in Austin. I am home.

Susan Stevenson came from North Dakora to teach at AHS in 1997.

The Hormel Strike
By Jenny Subra

Travel back through time to the 1980s, and imagine all of the events going on. On a hot August day in 1985, Local P 9 workers went on strike for their low wages of $8.25 per hour, more or less, depending on how long they had been with the plant.

This strike was important to me because it changed families' lives dramatically. Hormel Foods lost many workers who did not come back after the strike. On August 16, just thirty minutes before midnight, a man named Guyette walked into the Austin plant and handed plant manager Deryl A. Arnold a letter that stated the local P 9 was going on strike. Minutes later Guyette emerged from the plant leading a procession of night shift workers. They marched to the gate, chanting and cheering under the glare of television cameras. They were protesting wages and plant safety problems. More than 1,000 workers piled out of the plant that day just waiting to be a part of the strike. It affected my family's life when my dad had to go through all the angry men and women just to enter the building. He told me it was just like a bad dream hearing all the people shouting and chanting, "Strike, Strike!"

The Hormel strike lasted thirteen months, and by the end of those long months, the whole town was changed. Incidents of name-calling, vandalism, and violence occurred frequently. Bodyguards shadowed key managers from Hormel, and the safety of their families was at stake. The strike soon made the headlines of national newspapers and commanded almost daily broadcast coverage in Minnesota. Militant union supporters were attracted to Austin and joined the fight against Hormel.

Twenty years after the strike at Hormel divided the town of Austin, some parts of the community are still angry. The Hormel strike of 1985-1986 is not only one of the most important labor conflicts in Minnesota history, but it was also one of the key national struggles of the 1980s. This is one of the biggest events that has happened throughout Austin's history, and it is one that I will never forget. Some still remember that hot summer day as if it were yesterday, when everything they knew changed.

Jenny Subra and her family have an animal farm. She enjoys competitive swimming.

It's A Wonderful Life in Austin
By James Gerhardt Sucha

Austin to me is not SPAMTown USA, but it's a place just like Grover's Corners in *Our Town* or Bedford Falls in the annual Jimmy Stewart movie, *It's a Wonderful Life*. When I watch that movie, I get homesick, as my dad was just like George Bailey in that movie when he grew up in Austin.

Many generations of the Sucha and Hoeper families have lived in Austin or Mower County since the 1880s. My great-great grandpa Josef Sucha and his wife Anna came over from Vatinka, Bohemia in 1880. They brought with them four daughters and one son named Joseph, my great-grandpa. They lived out by Glenville and Hayward, and eventually young Joseph moved to Austin and worked for the Milwaukee Road in the shops. He married Mary Rous of Austin and produced a large family, which lived across the street from Lincoln School. His son, my Grandpa William Joseph Sucha, followed in his footsteps and was promoted to locomotive engineer in 1916 for the Milwaukee Road. William J. met a beautiful, raven-haired German woman from Brownsdale on a blind date in 1916. Her name was Rocena K. Hoeper, born of Heinrich and Katherina Hoeper, who were German Lutherans and had emigrated from Hanover, Germany. They farmed outside Austin in Brownsdale with its rich, black soil.

Before she married Grandpa, her father died from typhoid fever, which caused a financial hardship for the whole family since there was no insurance back then. Rocena and her family sold the farm and moved to Austin. She enrolled in the Austin Normal College, which was then located in what is now Galloway Park. After obtaining the equivalent of an associate's degree in business, Rocena took a job at the Austin Telephone Company as a telephone operator. Her job was to manually plug in and pull out the phone connections that had to be made to connect people to the party they wished to speak to. In those days, an operator did the calling for you. Her supervisor had to wear roller skates in the room in order to keep up with the operators on their phones. Grandma had fun listening in to conversations of Austin people on the phone. In 1914, she even posed for an advertisement for Austin Telephone Company and wore a headset that resembled a football helmet!

She and Grandpa had to wait to be married until after World War I, because if you got married during the war, and were not "over there" fighting, you were considered yellow. William and Rocena were married in 1919 by the justice of the peace because Rocena's pastor at St. John's Lutheran on 4th Street would not perform the marriage because my grandpa was a member of the Masonic Lodge, and the Missouri Synod still doesn't recognize people who are members of such organizations.

Grandpa came home from a long train run in 1920 and found my grandma had been liberated with the right to vote, and she also bobbed her long raven hair! He nearly divorced her for that, but soon forgave her. They bought a house at 507 Park Avenue (4th Street SW) in 1921, and Grandpa planted a maple tree in the backyard to honor the birth of my father, William D. Sucha, in 1922. That tree grew to be huge.

Dad had a great time growing up in that neighborhood. He attended Shaw Elementary School and loved to go to the movies down at the Park Theatre or the Paramount, which was built on the same site. On a hot, muggy August day in 1928, he was at a matinee when the projector broke and the theatre staff sent the children home. After a friend's mother brought him home, the sky turned still, green and dark; a twister dropped from the sky and started tearing up Winona Street. Grandma was out getting the wash off the line, and could not figure out why straw was raining out of the sky. It was in the days before tornado warnings. The damage was great. St. Olaf Lutheran Church was wrecked, along with several homes and businesses. The spire on the courthouse had been bent, and the Park Theatre, where the kids had just been watching a movie, was destroyed. The damage path included the Austin Utilities, Lincoln School, (my great-grandparents' house was a near miss right across the street), and several boxcars were overturned in the Milwaukee yards.

The ruins of the Park Theatre after the tornado of 1928.

Dad was confirmed at the rebuilt St. Olaf Lutheran Church in the late 1930s when his family joined that church after a dispute with Rev. Millbrath at St. John's over my grandpa being a Mason. However, Grandma went to both churches. Dad graduated from AHS in 1940 and worked at Paul and Louie's (Knauer) Market, Montgomery Ward, and helping his dad, Uncle Art and his grandpa in the Milwaukee yards.

Dad was drafted in 1942 for World War II, and he served in the Army medics with administrative duties. He saw England, Germany, Africa, and France. His folks would send V-mail to him every week. The War Department would take letters sent to GIs and shrink them to make it easier to send overseas to GI's. After being held up in France with a bout of diphtheria after the war, Dad returned to Austin in January 1946 to a whole different world. Many of his childhood friends had been killed in the war, and he had to adjust to civilian life.

He started working for the Milwaukee Road because he was bitten by the railroad bug, and he loved every minute of it. However, Grandpa encouraged him to take advantage of the GI Bill and finish college at St. Olaf in Northfield, which he did. After graduation, Dad taught school in Amboy and Upsala, Minnesota. He even joined the Masonic Hall in Austin like his father.

He met my mom, Bernice Eklund, while he was boarding at her father's house in 1949 in Upsala. Mom's father was a Swedish Mission Covenant pastor, and Dad boarded at the parsonage when they met. They were both teachers, and she didn't like him at first. On my grandparents' anniversary September 29, 1950, my folks got married in Chatfield, where Mom was teaching. She even had Jim Wheeler as a student there, who would later become the AHS band director in the 1960s. Would you believe they had to ask both school boards if they could marry? It was that controlled back then. They eventually moved back to Austin in 1951, where Dad became a guard at Hormel's, and Mom substitute taught in Austin Public Schools. He later became a juvenile probation officer in Austin and helped many troubled teenagers.

In 1958, Dad ran for the position of Mower County clerk of court and campaigned all over the county. Everyone knew my dad after much campaigning; his blue Plymouth had a big yellow sign on it with his picture reading "Elect William 'Bill' Sucha" plastered on it. After he won the election, Dad worked in the old domed courthouse, kept great records, and even signed birth records. He helped out many people in Austin who needed help through his efforts with the Salvation Army,

March of Dimes, and Masonic duties. A regular "George Bailey" is how you could describe my dad and his concern for other people. If you look at the park benches on the courthouse square, Dad got those for old folks to sit on under the elm trees.

His biggest effort was helping save locomotive 1004 at the fairgrounds. He and a group of friends got the Milwaukee Road to donate their last steam engine to Austin. It was moved in the summer of 1957 down Winona Street (1st Avenue) and 12th Street. Other equipment was donated by the Milwaukee, thanks to the efforts of Harold Davison, my dad, and others.

Mom and Dad bought a house in 1957 at 818 Miller Road, which is now 18th Street SW. They had the typical 1950s suburban lifestyle with wonderful neighbors like Russ and Lorraine Hegge, Dave and Mary Christensen and others. Once, a small F-1 tornado dropped down in our backyard there and ripped up the swing set and hammock before jumping over the house. Dad got everyone down into the basement while the house was shaking, and the dishes fell out of the cupboards in the kitchen. The small twister picked up Terri Hegemier across the street, and then jumped over to 17th Street, blew up a garage, then took the roof off the grandstand at the fairgrounds. With the family outgrowing the house, my folks moved over to 404 21st Street NW after I was born in 1964.

My earliest recollections of Austin are sublime. I remember going to Austin Clinic and seeing Dr. Inman Hesla, who was a marvelous doctor, but I hated getting shots. I marveled at the tall blue water tower at a young age, loved being carted around with Mom at Piggly Wiggly or Trowbridge's Red Owl. I loved going to Nemitz's downtown for popcorn balls, and eating hamburgers at Robby's Drive-In on 4th Street and Oakland Avenue, and going to Wold's Drug Store or Sterling Drugstore for red licorice or wax lips with my sister was a delight. Len Astrup there was always nice to my family.

I remember when the grocery store burned down where McDonalds is located now on Oakland Avenue and the construction of the McDonalds in 1969. I saw all my Disney movies at the Paramount, and remember looking at the awesome storybook interior while sipping on an orange drink in a container shaped like an orange, which my sister Julie would buy me. Saturdays were spent with Dad and Grandpa going down to the Hiawatha Bar and Café for pancakes, where the railroad yards were. Dad or Grandpa would walk me over the pedestrian bridge that spanned the railroad yards. And I was enthralled with the orange and black Milwaukee Road diesel locomotives and shops where three generations of my family had worked.

The Mower County Fair would just make me jump out of my skin with excitement every August, as Dad would get us free passes. You could always tell when the fair was coming because they put up stars on the grandstand every July. My sister Julie would take me, and we would hang out on 1004 with Grandpa, then leave him behind to keep his watch on the train, and take in the rides. Summers also meant having a hot dog at one of the two A&W Root Beer stands in Austin.

In December, we would get our Christmas tree at the A&W location by First United Methodist Church downtown. Christmas was very special in Austin then. The huge lit Christmas trees that were strung over the intersections excited me. Streetlights had big red bells that lit up at night. Downtown was decked out, and Santa Claus had his little house on the corner of the courthouse square where you could tell him what you wanted for Christmas. It was enchanting to a kid, I tell you!

Sometimes my family would take our toboggan and go sledding at Skinner's Hill, which was like Mount Everest to a little kid. Our church was Our Savior's Lutheran on Oakland Avenue, where our pastor was Glennys Knutson. On Christmas Eve, there would be a live manger scene, and every family would bring home a lit candle to bring the light of Christ into our homes. Our street after church with our neighbors getting out of their cars with their lit candles going into their houses, was a wonderful scene. My newborn brother Jordan and my parents were in the live manger scene in 1966, and I remember clapping because I was so proud of my brother. My older brother backhanded me for that one!

I had great childhood friends like Johnny Emholz, Billy Fleiner, and Danny Kraft, and we would always be in some mischief there on 21St Street. Billy's dad was Al Fleiner, who inspected and signed his name to Cure 81 hams at Hormel. I remember going with Billy Fleiner to his Catholic church's picnic at Todd Park. We fell into the creek while playing, and a mortified Sister Cree pulled us out and dried us off. Once a mallard duck followed me home from Turtle Creek. I was sad when he had to be brought back because I wanted to keep him as a pet. I attended preschool at First Congregational Church and started kindergarten at Banfield in 1969, and then all of a sudden, I experienced a change that would affect me for the rest of my life.

In 1970, my dad took a job in Denver, Colorado as a court administrator, and my wonderful life in Austin came to an end when we moved away. It was hard for my family to leave, and many dinners were held for us to say goodbye. My godparents, Dick and Bernice Baudler, never forgot me or my birthday after that. It was most difficult for my grandparents, who wept as we pulled away on our journey west. That is something a 6-year-old doesn't forget.

Since moving away from Austin, I never forgot where I came from with all the generations of my family who lived and died there. I came back a few times to visit my grandparents, and even spent the summer of 1979 painting the locomotive at the fairgrounds. However, I have never felt like I belonged anywhere else in all the moves I experienced while growing up all over the country. I was in seven different schools from the time I started Banfield to high school in Green Bay, and never fit in. I am lucky here in Denver because my cousin from Austin, Joe Samon, lives nearby in Lakewood. However, I occasionally return home to Austin to visit my grandparents' graves in Oakwood Cemetery, and someone in a store can still recognize me as one of Bill or Bernice's kids after thirty years. That is what makes Austin so special after living in a nation of strangers. It's a place where people know my name and where I have roots, a place that gave me a solid beginning. It is true, just as it was in fictitious Bedford Falls or any hometown, if you keep *home* in your *heart*, you can always return to it. Happy 150th birthday, my beloved hometown!

Workers moved old 1004 down Winona Street as spectators watched.

Still Dancing After Fifty Years
By Jane Taylor and Natalie Taylor

Jane Wanous Taylor began her dance training in the 1950s as a child in Austin under the direction of Ruth Bucklin. Jane's sister, Margaret Tverberg, attended classes with her. Jane has many fond memories of classes with "Miss Ruth," including performing a solo on the Eagles Cancer Telethon when she was a teenager. She performed a ballet to "Spectre de la Rose." She also has fond memories of performing at the 1956 centennial celebration.

After high school, Jane attended the University of Minnesota and continued training. She began teaching in Austin after moving her studio out of her Brownsdale home more than thirty years ago. Her studio has been located in different locations throughout the years. Jane's sister teaches dance in the Minneapolis area.

Jane is included in *Who's Who Among America's Teachers*, and has studied under the direction of many professional dancers, including an instructor who was a member of the Bolshoi Ballet. Her studio holds classes in ballet, tap, jazz, hip-hop, pointe, and lyrical, and she teaches liturgical dance at her church. Many who grew up in Austin have memories associated with these classes, recitals and programs. She has also choreographed pieces for the Miss Austin Pageant, Miss Minnesota Pageant and numerous musicals. Jane's students perform an annual recital, and they participate in many other performances during the year including Austin's "Christmas In The City," many city festivals, parades, competitions, and cancer fundraising benefits.

Margaret Wanous Tverberg, Meridee LeBarron Levy, and Jane Wanous Taylor performed a can-can for Austin's 1956 centennial celebration under Ruth Bucklin's instruction. All three went on to become dance instructors. The teacher who started it all, Ruth Bucklin, visited Jane's students recently and shared many memories.

Margaret, Meridee, and Jane at Austin's centennial

1956, What a Year!   Hello St. Augustine--Good Bye Columbus!
By Yvonne M. Thiele-Bell

Sister Giovanni's piano lesson studio was way up on the top floor of the 1909 school. There were many steps to climb every week for the half hour lesson. Because I lived so close to the school, I had mine at the end of the day, so that I meant I left my third grade class in the basement just before the final bell rang and climbed the four flights of stairs to the music room. I counted those steps and usually ended up forgetting what number I was at, 50, or 70, by the end of the third story. Even for 9-year-old-legs, that was a slow and tiring climb. It was my first year of piano lessons. I learned quickly from Sister, and with my grandmother's extra help, I practiced and learned fast from my red Thompson music books.

Sister Giovanni had the most beautiful ebony parlor grand piano. It filled the room that was already crowded with music-filled bookshelves and a west window for light. There was a closet size room next to the studio with an old upright piano for students to practice on. I never used it since I can't be in small spaces.

It was my last lesson for the school year, and Sister gave me my three summer months of lessons to do until she returned in September. Her studio was in for a big change. It would not be on the top floor of this old school because this was the last year our school building was to be used for teaching.

What used to be the Columbus School yard and church parking area was now a brand new three-story red brick school building. The $435,000 construction was started the previous summer in 1955. The 48-year-old Columbus was bursting at the seams, and there were safety issues. The last three classes consisted of the first baby boomers, and the numbers were up. The basement, which had been an auditorium and at times a makeshift church, had been partitioned into three third grade schoolrooms. The teachers were Mrs. Leighton, Mrs. Krebsbach and Mrs. Weaver. I was in Mrs. Weaver's class.

All three stories were made of wood that creaked when walked on by hundreds of feet that had trod the half-century-old halls. Pete Merten, the janitor, was daily sweeping those floors with his special dusting compound and his two-foot wide push broom. When we saw him coming down the hall, we got out of the way fast. And if one were not so lucky, he would find himself being swept out with the dirt. Pete was a no nonsense kind of man, but his gruff bark was worse than his bite. When we entered the front door in the morning, the whiff of that tangy compound was so strong it made your nose itch and eyes water.

The basement was a dull color with windows near the ceiling for light. We had old fashioned wood desks with flip-up seats and open storage spaces under the desktop. Each top had an old inkwell hole and many etched scars and designs from years of students. Both sides of the hall were lined with wood railings full of wire hooks for coats and hats. Boots and lunch pails were set on the floor under designated hooks.

School came to a close the first week of June. Students helped teachers with boxing up the contents of storage shelves and classroom cupboards so that the custodians and summer helpers could move the heavy furniture into the new building during summer vacation. In early summer, Mr. Merten gathered a group of strong young men from the high school, and one day they wrapped up Sister Giovanni's beautiful piano with old blankets and hauled it down all the flights of stairs, out the door, and into its new home, Throughout the following school year, workers prepared for the sad day when the old school would be demolished. Total demolition had to wait until the spring of 1957.

As the summer grew warmer, my anticipation for the new school grew. I would peek in and check it out every day. There were shining steel railings going all the way to the third floor. Every room had enough space for more than forty students, and the teachers would have plenty of bookshelves and storage. The new, smooth blackboards were hung on two full walls of each room. There was an office and reception area for the principal, and Sister Giovanni had a new piano studio right on the first floor.

I was to enter fourth grade, and I ventured to find out who my teacher was. The policy was that all students would find out the first day when it was posted on the classroom doors. I went daily to help the sisters get their rooms ready. I loved being in the new school because there was room to move. There was natural light from both ends of the halls, and new full-length metal lockers lined the walls. Bathrooms for boys and girls and water fountains were centrally located on each floor. The newly buffed floors shone like silk, and it was glorious to be in the new school. The complete basement cafeteria had new tables with swivel-out seats, and the cooks had a complete kitchen to prepare hot lunches for both grade school and high school students.

The sisters' faces beamed with enthusiasm because they appreciated the new building. School started the Tuesday after Labor Day. I was dressed for the day in a brand new dress, and I even wore a hat and carried a matching purse. No Levi blue jeans were allowed in school. Girls wore dresses and even full crinoline slips to make the skirts flare out. Boys could only wear dress pants and shirts. All women wore something on their heads when they entered church, and the men always took off their hats.

Our nuns were dressed in the regular habits of the Franciscan Sisters from Rochester, with long, flowing brown habits with paneled scapulars hanging full length that hid their arms and hands when they were standing around watching the children. The first day started with parents and children going to mass at 8:15. Monsignor Robert Jennings gave a warm invocation to the new school year.

It was a good time to be 9 years old and going to a new school. Students ran ahead of their parents in exuberance to find out who was to be their new teacher. To my great delight, I was in Sr. Nadine's (Ellis) Class. My room was on the second floor to the front of the building facing north. There were two fourth grade classes with about fifty students in each.

In 1956 a new foundation of learning for Austin's parochial students began, and our parents were proud to be able to send their children to such a school. The rooms were full, even on the first day. The only rooms that didn't have a student in them were the piano studio, the library and the teachers' lounge in the basement. My first piano lesson did take place the first week of school, and as usual, it was the last one of the school day at 3 p.m. Sister was so proud of her first floor studio. She had room to bring in all her favorite music and be ready to teach any and all of it to her students, and the place was brightened with a wall of windows. I noticed that the piano was set up in the new studio, and the ebony finish shone in the sunlight. Sister said that she couldn't go to watch them move it for fear it would get damaged. We shared her joy that all went well.

The week of July 8, 1957, Wehner Construction Company commenced the demolition of the vacant old building. Among them were many who had gone to the school, and I heard their stories of years gone by every day as I came to watch my old school grow smaller piece by piece. Some found items lost years ago, things that had fallen through spaces in walls and mopboards and between the heaters. Old mittens, books, a few old coins, and some rosaries were collected, held in awe, and taken home for keepsakes.

Being so close to the school, I daily rode my bicycle around the site to see what was happening. I parked it in front of the home where the sisters who taught at the high school lived on Moscow Street as I stood and watched men and the heavy equipment outside the school's arched front door. Brick by brick, the mortar crumbled to the ground, and as the workmen continued to tear the old walls down, I heard that some bricks were sold to benefit the church and school. I wonder if those bricks are still in Austin.

Monsignor Jennings spoke a tribute to Columbus the week before the razing. "No history of St. Augustine Parish would be complete without a tribute to the educational advantages that have been offered here in these old walls."

By the end of summer, a new blacktop playground and parking lot sat where the old school had been. The newness of the school did help take away the sadness of losing old Columbus and soften the hurt that the older generation felt. Many St. Augustine High School students watched with mixed emotions from across the street as their beloved grade school building and all its memories was being torn down. It was for the good of the students of Austin, and that's what schools are all about--to move ahead to newer and better adventures in life.

Columbus School

Oh Brother!
By Yvonne M. Thiele-Bell

Grandma had just laid my dinner plate down on the table as I walked onto the front porch. I daily walked home the two blocks from Columbus School for lunch break. It was May 24, and I knew that my mother wasn't gong to be home as she had gone to see her doctor that morning, so Grandma was the cook.

The phone rang, and Grandma told me to go and answer it for her. I picked up the receiver. "Well, Yvonne, what do you think of your new baby brother?" It was my dad on the other end, but what he said made no sense at all. I had no brother!

"Dad, what are you talking about?" With a surprised and puzzled look, I stared at Grandma Swenson, who was smiling a big grin with a twinkle in her eyes. Then it came to me. Mom was going to have a baby, but I didn't know when. Throughout the past years my parents were wishing for more children, and this time the doctor had high hopes that it would happen, but with some special help. Mom had great faith in him, and she believed her prayers would be answered if she, the doctor, and God would work together.

She had been the subject of many prayers by her friends and family, especially the Sisters that I saw every day at school. There was much speculation and hopefulness during her pregnancy because she had trouble in her past times carrying a full term baby. Now my father was telling me, his 9-year-old daughter, that I was finally a big sister to a baby brother. I had waited all my life for a sister or brother, and now today I had a new little brother!

I was so excited I could hardly eat my lunch. Grandma and I talked about the events of the morning and how happy she was for her daughter Evelyn to finally have another child in her life. I just gobbled down what food I could and ran off to school. I was yelling to all the neighbors who could hear me. I told the Ellises, the Chaffees and the Hansens and whoever was outside as I ran down the blocks to school.

Running around the construction site of the new grade school, I ran up the old stone stairway through the back door of Columbus School and down the hallway to the principal's office and told Sister Lonan about my new baby brother. Then I ran outside to the playground and went to all of the sisters with the exciting news. Sister Imogene was more than delighted and said, "Yvonne, our prayers for your family have been answered." And she gave me a big hug.

The afternoon just couldn't go fast enough for me. I wiggled and whispered to anyone who would listen about my news. Mrs. Weaver, the third grade teacher, knew how I felt and was very grateful to see 3 o'clock arrive. I ran home so fast I felt like I would burst with excitement.

Dad finally came home, and we tried to eat supper, but I couldn't wait another minute. We all climbed into the dark olive green '49 Chevy and drove over to St. Olaf Hospital for me to get a sneak peek at Jerome. In the 1950s a visitor to the hospital had to be over 12 years old, and I wasn't. Dad snuck me up the back stairs. The nurses looked the other way as I stood, glued to the floor, looking through the window into the nursery at my very small but real new baby brother in a clear glass box with all the apparatus to keep my brother content and safe.

My new baby brother was born on this chosen day about 10 a.m. via Cesarean. It was the best medical procedure for both mother and child if they were to have a chance to save his life at 28 to 30 week gestation period. Jerome Joseph was baptized by our dear friend, RN Dorothy (Mrs. Joe) Flanagan in the delivery room. The little guy weighed in at 3 pounds 1 ounce. He was small enough to fit in a cigar box. Diapers had to be cut in half with a special folding to fit his tiny body, and then the diaper covered him up to his armpits. Little guy that he was, he lived in an incubator for almost one month until he grew to weigh five pounds. Mom often compared his size to my Tiny Tears doll that I had received at Christmas. It was a great miracle for our family and those who knew us.

Jerome came home to a very warm welcome. His big sister got to hold him for the first time while sitting on the davenport with my arms propped up with pillows. I was so excited and proud. The first time I had to change his diaper, mother stood over me and talked me through it. I was so scared that I might hurt him.

This was late June, and there was much talk about the upcoming July Fourth celebration as Austin was going to celebrate its centennial year. I had joined in a few of the children's activities, but the big parade was going to be on the Fourth, and our family was going to go.

What a proud day that was for me. I carefully pushed the new steel blue/gray baby buggy with some help from both Grandma and Mother all the way downtown. My new brother was inside the buggy for everyone to see. We found a place with a good view and plenty of space on the curb for me to sit. There was a drugstore awning to give shade over the sidewalk on the SE corner of Main and Water Street. I looked across the street to Fantles' Fashions and also kitty corner to the Fox Hotel. All sidewalks were full with spectators who were celebrating the city of Austin's one-hundredth birthday.

As the parade progressed, I could hear the "ooh and aahs" over my brother as people walked by and talked with Mother and Grandma. I saw the shiny new '56 Chevrolet and Ford cars with the fancy new tailfins and a lot of shiny chrome drive by with officials and honored guests. My father, Joe, was in the parade too. He was driving a brand new John Deere tractor pulling a hay wagon with a local farmers' organization and promoting Fossey Implement. Many great school bands from all over the area brought out cheers from the crowds. But with all the excitement of the parade, the best was that my new baby brother was here to stay, and I was his big sister.

The following late autumn my parents informed me that I was to become a big sister again in the spring. As the Christmas holiday season started, Mom decided that it was time to send out special cards with our family photo of a proud father and mother with me and little Jerome, and of course, our dog Tippy.

As time would tell, someone else was in the picture, but we couldn't see him yet. Sure enough, with the help of Mom's "miracle team," on May 23, one year after Jerome's birth, my new baby brother Galen Lee was born. He weighed 5 pounds, as his delivery date was prolonged a couple of weeks more than Jerome's. He stayed in the incubator for two weeks before coming home. Our home was full of unbelievable joy because he wasn't planned or expected to be. Mom always said God just wanted those two boys to have each other as pals. Being the proud sister, I always stayed the "big" sister with nine to ten years' difference in ages, and I was a natural born baby sitter too.

The brothers grew up confusing everyone who thought they were twins. They almost always received the same gifts for their birthdays. One of the best birthdays was in 1960, when they received two pedal-mobile black and white Dragnet police cars with speakers.

They went to St. Augustine and Pacelli and continued their education at Austin Community College. Jerome graduated from Grand Forks University of North Dakota, and Galen from Saint Cloud State. In 1973 both earned their Eagle Scout Award in BSA Troop 233. Today, both have beautiful wives and the families, adding six grandchildren.

Medical miracles were happening during the 1950s and 1960s with heart machines, cancer research, prescription drugs that helped with arthritis, stomach ulcers, pregnancy and so much more. Jerome was one of the smallest babies born in Austin's hospital who survived. With increased knowledge by the doctors, my family was able to grow and multiply. Years later, through genetic testing, we learned that what caused my mother to lose her babies was a familial genetic dysfunction that can be controlled. My daughter Maria, Evelyn's oldest granddaughter, has had the same inherited problem, and with pre-natal medical support, she has three wonderful children.

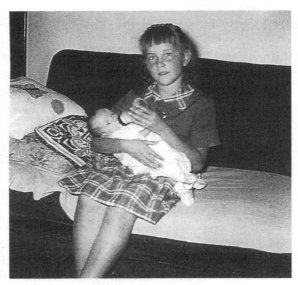

Yvonne and Jerome

Austin native Yvonne Thiel-Bell and her husband Ken live next to Seven Springs on Turtle Creek. They were on the committee for the Mower County Veterans' Memorial.

Tendermaid
By Alice Tomaschko

I started my working days at the Tendermaid. At that time it was located about a half mile from the Hormel Packinghouse. When my brothers were still single and living on the Hormel Pine Crest farm with my folks, they worked at "the plant." When they got out of work, they walked to the Tendermaid, and used the pay phone to call my mother to come pick them up. Of course to save the nickel they would let the phone ring once and hang up. That was my mother's signal to come into town and pick them up. It was during this time that I met the owners, Jerry and Mildred Thatcher.

We moved into town when I was 15, after my brothers were married and living elsewhere. That summer Jerry Thatcher decided he would try curb service and asked if I wanted to work there. Curb service wasn't very successful, but I had the opportunity to stay on to work part time while going to school. This couple, Jerry and Mildred Thatcher, were from Iowa. They were hard-working, honest people. The shop was a favorite hangout for the high school crowd, and I liked being around them as well as the adult customers. Jerry always cautioned his men customers to be careful with their language around the young help.

I learned about customer service, to be dependable and loyal as well as to "do it right the first time." I learned that you could work hard and still have fun. I received my first post-graduation job offer from a banker who regularly ate at the Tendermaid with his wife.

My admiration and respect for Jerry and Mildred have never lessened. They were excellent role models, not just as employers but also as human beings. Their work ethic and personal principles were heady stuff for a 15-year-old's first job experience.

The Tendermaid,
open since 1938

Alice Tomaschko has lived in Austin since 1931. She is a volunteer for the Red Cross. She and her husband Frank have two children.

The Alley
By John Tribbett

I remember clearly the lilac bushes bending over the cracked and decaying asphalt, the sticky heat of summer that rose in wavy lines. When it rained, the decaying alley formed small oceans for long summer days. At night the alley became a long cavern formed by soon to be dead elm trees, a canyon of garage backsides and dented garbage cans. By the time our mothers called to come in for the night, the streetlights had begun to throw weird shadows, and we had to run fearfully home through the menacing corridor. Our lungs would scream under the spell of dark fantasy, our bare feet peeling back gravel. Then the alley was pure terror—unfiltered.

Out in front, Fourth Street was strictly off limits by day or night. Cars were dangerous. The front yards were no-go zones only to be enjoyed under the police-state eyes and quick grabs of diligent parents. As we watched safely from behind locked porches, longhaired high school kids with cigarettes dangling from their mouths strolled past. This was the early '70s, and although we didn't know it, the last days, the death rattle of the Vietnam War were at hand. These sullen creatures sauntered past in the morning and after we woke from our afternoon naps, hiding their fear of draft boards and machine guns behind ragged bell-bottom jeans and an aura of fearlessness.

We stayed in the backyards, away from hippies and machines speeding past. The backyards meant safety, a world unto itself, all connected by the alley that was the fast track to a best friend's house. And it was in the alley that "M" and I became blood brothers. It was hot, and the sky was blue like a robin's egg. We stood silent in the cool shade of the garage. We could hear the cicadas buzzing loudly. His older sister held the needle out to us watching, waiting, and wondering if we would really do this. I don't know if he went first or I did, but I remember the needle, snuck out by his sister from their mom's sewing kit.

I had to jam it in. I closed my eyes. Nothing. I did it again. Still nothing. I was trying to be brave to prove I wasn't afraid of blood. And I was afraid of the blood and afraid of sticking the needle into my finger. But I needed to say to "M" that I would be by his side forever. We would be like pirates or bandits or kung fu warriors. Just like Indians or cowboys…forever. We would rescue one another, and never back down from the world.

"M" just showed up in my world. One day, early in the morning, my mother announced that he had arrived. I walked down the alley and stepped into his backyard. There was "M" and his older sister, his new mom and dad. He was just standing there with all these people looking at him. And then he caught my eye, and we just stood and stared at each other. He was looking back and forth at the people. He looked like he had lost something. I couldn't figure it out. We looked at each other for a long time. He seemed kind of scared. Then we smiled.

He was from Korea. I knew the word but didn't know the place. I knew my father had been there a long time ago. I knew he was a soldier and he'd had to go there to fight. He had shot a big gun—a sort of cannon. But Mom didn't like to talk about it. And she didn't like it when we played war. Mom told me he came to Austin because of the war. I thought that sounded pretty cool. After all, I could always use another partner to raid pirate ships or take the other side in army man wars. So we smiled at each other, and we became friends. Just like that…

"M" squeezed his finger, and a little drop of blood appeared. I poked again. This time I went deep, and it hurt. I pulled the needle out and squeezed. A tiny red drop rose up. We looked at each other and smiled. Then we pressed our fingers together, and our blood smeared against each other. Now we were brothers. We were doing something important and secret. Well…his sister knew. But that was important too because somebody else besides us had to know or it wouldn't count. We sucked the leftover blood off our fingers and looked at each other for a second or two. Then we smiled. We had done it. We were brave, and we had claimed something important. We ran back into the alley, chasing each other. We played army. We splashed in puddles. We ran separate ways when our moms came out. We hid behind lilac bushes when the older kids came looking for us. It didn't matter that I was from Austin and he was from Korea. Later that year I moved to another part of town. I don't remember if I ever saw "M" again.

A few years back I was home visiting my parents. After they had gone to sleep, I took my father's bike out for a late-night ride. I found myself in the alley dodging potholes as I peddled. The moon was up and the shadows wound themselves around garages and garbage cans in weird shapes. But instead of terror, there was a quiet so pure I felt I would evaporate into the night if I held my breath too long. I stopped when I came to "M"'s old backyard and stood for a moment next to the garage. I am older, and things have changed, but for a few seconds I was 5, hiding in the garage with "M" and his sister. We were doing something important. Something permanent. Something worth remembering.

Construction of the New Library
By Kenneth Tribbett

A real highlight of my life after retirement was being appointed to the Austin Public Library Board. The city of Austin was in the planning stages of building a new 26,000 square foot public library to replace the Carnegie Library built in 1904. It was decided the location would be on the south side of our Mill Pond, just east of downtown. The architecture firm of Meyer, Scherer and Rockcastle of Minneapolis was hired.

After the drawings and specifications were submitted, the board members and Robert Hays, the librarian, reviewed the building layout and location with regard to accessibility for the public, and the current site was approved. I attended meetings with the architect and the builder, who was a local contractor, Joseph Construction Company. Early meetings were held weekly. We always had donuts and coffee in a construction trailer that was parked on the site. My grandson, Scott Lessman, still remembers attending some of those meetings with me.

Bonnie Rietz and I climbed up the ladder to reach the roof so that we could get an overall view of the building while checking the roofing project. The next year, Melissa Sibley, our new librarian, and I made a further inspection of the roof looking for the cause of various leaks. Flat roofs are notorious for having leaks! Eventually that problem was solved.

An anonymous donor donated a fireplace for the reading room. The architect suggested that we install a natural vented fireplace in the northwest corner of the reading area. Once the building was complete, we found that a natural wood-burning fireplace was not very functional. It was then decided that we should replace the grate material with a gas log type fireplace that could be turned on by the staff.

The aluminum columns supporting the trellis were to provide shade along the southwest walkway. When we found that the vines could not cling to the shiny aluminum support columns, we added wood to the columns to give the vines a real chance to climb. This met with very limited success until the Mower County Horticultural Society began to tend them. The ladies of the Austin Floral Club donated the beautiful circular mosaic granite floor for the entryway.

The library cost around $3.6 million, of which the city was to pay half. The estate of Alice and Karl Lindstaedt was left to the public library to help pay for building a new library. The board and staff mailed thousands of brochures asking for public support. They were overwhelmed by the generous response from the community. They achieved their goal of $1.8 million and raised an additional $600,000. The library was paid for immediately and opened in the summer of 1996.

The library is a modern focal point of downtown Austin. It has received several bequests that support its work, including the Walter Wienke bequest that was, in part, used for the statues of children placed outside near the entrance. It is often shown off to out of town visitors. Even the architect has had prospective clients inspect our library as a good example of his firm's work. Best of all has been the wonderful acceptance and use of our library by the people of Mower County. We all love our library!

The new library opened in 1996.

Illinois native Ken Tribbett has been retired from Hormel Engineering Department since 1994. He is a serious bicycling enthusiast. His wife Carmen, a former nurse and teacher, retired from Riverland after 18 years in the nursing lab. Their son, John Tribbett, who wrote the previous story, has been traveling in much of Asia.

P 9   Cookies
By Kenneth Tribbett

A really dark period in the life of Austin occurred during the strike between the P9 workers and the Hormel Corporation. Even the National Guard was called to Austin to maintain law and order. Feelings ran high, and many friendships were stressed.

Early one morning I tried to go to work at the Hormel Corporate Office, but I was not allowed to enter the complex because of the P9 picket line. I then turned the car around and drove out to what was called the Corporate Annex, which processed spices and other ingredients going into the Hormel foods.

Since I had my briefcase, which included my business telephone address book, I proceeded to use their telephone system to make business calls and calls to other plants where I had projects going on. Later when I sat down in the annex lunch room to have a cup of coffee, one of the office ladies came over and said, "You can have one of our cookies if you don't mind having a P9 cookie, as these cookies were meant to be given out to workers who were on the picket line."

My response was, "I would love to have a P9 cookie, and as a matter of fact, some of our best friends are members of the P9 Union, and we continue to go out for dinner with them on Friday nights. Sometimes we have even waited until they got off the picket line."

Some years later, on my last day of employment at the Hormel office, I went to the Hy-Vee Supermarket and purchased several dozen cookies decorated with smiling faces, which I took to the break room. I treated our office staff, including the lady from the Corporate Annex. To my surprise, she had a sack of cookies for me. Inside the sack was a note that read:

Roses are red,
Violets are blue,
These P9 cookies
Are just for you.

This remembrance points out that many people in our small town of Austin managed to maintain their good will toward each other during and after those trying times.

School Tour
By Carmen Tribbett

It has been a long time since I was 8 years old and in third grade at Lincoln School. But the memory of that day in Austin lives with me yet. It was a beautiful spring day as we children walked two by two down what was then Oak Street on our way to tour the Hormel plant. I grew more and more excited as we walked under the railway bridge and up to the office.

Like most of the children in my class, my daddy worked for the Hormel Company, and I was excited that I might actually see where he worked. I don't remember much about our tour except that at one point we were taken up some stairs to a platform with glass windows and allowed to watch the animals being led to the slaughter. There were black and white cows. I can hear them now, but I am not certain how much of this is imagination and how much is real. At any rate, this was pretty upsetting to a sensitive 8-year-old!

Later, we were back in the classroom, and our teacher was discussing what we had seen on our tour and I, not knowing how to give expression to my feelings, stated, "George A. Hormel is a crook!" The teacher was horrified. The class was horrified.

The teacher reminded me that my daddy worked in the plant and that I should be very grateful to Mr. Hormel. She sent me out to the hall where we hung our coats. I cried and cried. Mrs. Marble's second grade class walked by the coatroom and saw me crying in my disgrace and embarrassment. Many years later I became a teacher. None of my children were ever shamed in front of the class or sent out into the hall.

The Band Shell
By Carmen Tribbett

When I think about growing up in Austin, I remember how important the band shell was to the city of Austin and to me. I don't know when it was built. It just seems like it has always been there.

Famous Hollywood stars went from city to city in an effort to sell War Bonds during World War II. Imagine our excitement when we heard that Abbott and Costello were coming to Austin and would be at the band shell! We had heard them many times on the radio and had seen them in movies. Mother and Dad said that of course we would go. My brother and I could hardly wait.

The big day came, and I remember that there were so many people there that the park benches were filled. People were everywhere. They were on blankets and parked in cars along the road. They milled about greeting each other. Abbott and Costello were introduced, and they did their famous "Who's on first?" routine as the crowd roared with approval. The dome of the band shell turned red, white and blue as the city band played our national anthem. It was a great patriotic occasion.

The Austin Municipal Band had splendid black and white uniforms that they also wore when they marched in the city parades. Two of our neighbors, Jack and Roy Tedrow, played in the band. My cousin, Ken Carlson, played the clarinet.

We would brave the mosquitoes almost weekly to attend the Austin Municipal Band concerts at the band shell. To a child the most wonderful thing in the world was seeing the band shell light up with rainbow colors and change over and over again while the city band played all the wonderful marches and the crowd clapped its pleasure.

The band shell is still there and used on some occasions. There is no longer a band, nor are there weekly concerts. Times are different. We are not so simple in our interests. We are so busy that time no longer exists for long nights filled with the sounds of Sousa and King amid the changing of colored rainbows.

Bringing the World to Austin
By Josh Verges
First published in the *Austin Daily Herald*

A new student from Korea came into Miguel Garate's office on a Tuesday afternoon hoping he could find her a friend. Next came a Somali man stopping by to show off his straight A's. Another from Togo followed and received a warning about his low grades and a threat to call his father on the other side of the world. And then there was the phone call from a student who didn't know where to find a truck that could move his furniture.

"I become like a parent for these kids," Garate said.

He is in his sixth year as the multicultural and minority student advisor at Riverland Community College's three locations. He helps students pick classes, get financial aid, take tests and get oriented to the campus. He serves people of color from the United Sates as well as every student from another country. The number of international students has grown from two when Garate started to sixty-five students now.

"This guy is known everywhere in the world," said Ahmad Abdirahman, the straight A Somali student.

Riverland's website draws international students, who are lured by an inexpensive quality education. Garate helps bring in the regional students, traveling to college fairs in Minnesota, Wisconsin and Iowa. It helps, he said, that RCC has a bilingual representative. Spanish-speaking parents especially like to visit with someone who knows the language they are more comfortable with.

"Every year there are more and more people of color interested in Riverland," he said.

Scattered in Garate's Austin office are a Canadian teddy bear, a sign that reads "Parking is for Mexicans Only," and a bulletin board of photographs. Some are family members or friends, others current or past students. There are also apples and candy bars, to which the Togolese student helped himself.

"Every year I see my kids going through the graduation lines is a reward," he said.

Garate was born in Mexico and began his romance with the United States on a trip with friends to a baseball game at the Houston Astrodome. Three friends returned home, but he and two others stayed and found work within the week. He attended college in Mexico and still visits there, but it is no longer home. He told of a friend so awed by his new country that he said, "Even the garbage looks beautiful in the United States."

He moved to Austin in June, 1997. Now when he returns to see family in Texas, he shows off pictures of the Minnesota snow. A sign of Garate's recruiting talent, two of Owatonna's newest residents are his nephews.

Miguel Garate

*Josh Verges grew up in Milwaukee. After graduating from the University of Minnesota, he came to Austin to work as a reporter for the **Austin Daily Herald**.*

My Grandpa Phillips
By Inez Vietor

William M. and Inez Phillips were my grandparents. My grandfather staked his 80 acres near Brownsdale, coming from Oxford, Wisconsin. When he was a young man, he built his house and farm buildings and even had a schoolhouse built across the road. It was called Phillips District 139. He tilled the land, was a schoolteacher and had telephone lines put through that area.

But my tale to tell is how one very early morning he had a load of butchering hogs in a wagon and his two big bay horses hitched to pull them to Austin. Since there were no fences to hinder them, he could go straight to the Hormel butchering shed. That shed is shown at the Mower County Fairgrounds.

When he approached the area, George A. Hormel left the butchering area, shook hands as they introduced each other, and told my grandpa to stay under the shade tree until the hogs could be unloaded. When that happened and he was paid, he turned to go back home. He told us that it was dark when he arrived to put two tired horses to their stalls.

I loved many of my grandparents' stories because I was born and raised on that farm. I attended eight grades of school at the Phillips District 129. Then I rode a bus to attend high school in Austin for four years.

The last year of high school, Inez married a Coast Guard man. After the war, they returned to Austin and raised six children. She now lives in St. Mark's.

Coming of Age
By Robert J. Vilt

As young boys growing up along Turtle Creek with neighborhood peers across the creek and up on Bauman, we kept busy in the summer. We had woods on the south side of our house where we built a foxhole to hold our meetings, and further along the woods we tried to launch our rafts that usually sank. We had better luck finding rafts that made their way downstream with high waters that usually flowed every spring.

Turtle Creek ran just a few feet away from the back of our house, and there was about a ten-foot drop down to the creek below. It was shallow directly behind the house, and you could hear the water passing by in what I guess you would have to call rapids. It was in the shallows by shore where we hunted crawdads, and where one crawdad pinched a hole in my boot and drew blood from my toe and tears from my eyes.

Upstream toward Clay Hill there was a small rock island flooded with rocks and many of them "skippers." Not far from there was a row of aging willows, where we smoked cigarettes at the ripe age of 10, not all the time, but enough of the time.

We played baseball in one way or another almost daily. We would either hit flies or else my brother and a few of his neighborhood friends would pitch to us, and sometimes someone would cheat-kick a ball foul into the weeds that had gone over Feely's fence. I would go into the house crying, where my mother would "there-there" me and send me back out after my tears had dried.

Of course we played Army regularly. One of the two acres we had north of the house was like a pasture, and we spent days crawling through tall grass on it looking for "the other side" with our toy guns. We advanced farther north toward Clay Hill behind Feely's house. We usually had about four on each side. We created our own sound effects –"POW, POW, A-A-A-T-T, A-A-A-T-T, A-A-A-T-T! You're dead. I got you." Sometimes the fallen enemy wouldn't fall, and we might argue, but not fight over it.

On Saturday we would go to the Austin Theatre, pay our 12 cents, and take our seats. There would be clips of war on the newsreel, I suppose from Korea, and there were often war movies we watched with great intensity. Admission cost 12 cents until you reached 13, and then the price went up.

Sometimes I would go with my mother to the Paramount Theatre just off of Main Street on Water Street. This was the finest theatre in town and one of the town's first. Its predecessor, the Park, was destroyed in 1927 when a tornado hit. My father used to talk about it. He said that straw was stuck in light posts. He hid under a pool table at Nemitz's Cigar Store on Main Street. They rebuilt the Paramount, and it was beautiful, like something you would expect to find in California. Beautiful brick surrounded the building with a Broadway-like marquee.

When I went to the Paramount as a child, I would count rows when I went to the bathroom and then count the rows back down to where my mother would be waiting. I remember thinking that going to the bathroom by myself was a true act of courage.

One of the first movies I remember seeing there was *Shane*. I was about the same age as the young boy in the movie with Gary Cooper, and I cried. I went with my sister to see *The Flying Trapeze* starring Gary Cooper. I cried in that one too when someone plunged to their death after missing the trapeze.

Sometime later I watched *From Here to Eternity* there. This was filmed in Hawaii, much of it at Schofield Barracks, and of course there was the love scene on the beach with Burt Lancaster and Ava Gardner madly "making out" with the Pacific Ocean rolling in trying to remind them where they were. Not so long after that I watched *South Pacific*, again at the Paramount with friends and decided that someday I would go to Hawaii.

Those were days when we used the phrase "puppy love," at the beginning of seventh grade. My older brother had graduated from high school and was beginning to speak to me again like older brothers do. He and his date invited me and my date to the movies. My date was an eighth grader, an older woman, but we were pretty evenly matched in height. Her father was a high school teacher. That first time going to the door to pick up a date is still etched in my aging memory--I was terrified. This is something I would not recommend to seventh graders. My brother and his date held hands so Cindy and I held hands.

Later that year, my cousin and his date, who were sophomores, took me and my "new date" to *The King and I*, again at the Paramount, on a bone-chilling night. We sat near the back of the theatre. My cousin, a country boy, I think was quite a bit further along or more advanced in his ways with women. He and his date were soon "making out" with fury right there in front of Yul Brynner and Deborah Kerr so...monkey see monkey do... soon Suzanne and I were locking lips to beat hell. Suddenly I recognized a voice from the row behind saying, "Maybe we should trade places with these kids in front of us."

I asked Sue to sneak a look back and describe the person. Her description matched the voice. It was the minister of our church with his wife and children. I stopped dead in my tracks, the kissing that is. For the remainder of the movie, making sure not to turn so he could see my face, I devoted my attention to Yul and Deborah while wondering if he had recognized me. When the movie ended, I pulled up my jacket hood in such a fashion that it shielded me from recognition by Pastor Knutson as we slipped out of the theatre into the cold winter night, shouldering some tenuous guilt.

Eventually I graduated from my coming-of-age classes. The Paramount closed down, and I found my way to Schofield Barracks in Oahu, where we trained to go to Vietnam. In November of 1967, we took a sea cruise on *USS Gordon*, a troop ship that landed us two weeks later in Vietnam.

Ten years later I returned to Hawaii looking for a woman who resembled the woman who married Lieutenant Cable, who died in *South Pacific*. When I wasn't looking for her, I was busy writing poetry and substitute teaching. One Sunday I carried an old fighting cock into the ring down by "Long Bridge" for his last fight.

A few years ago my guitar-playing friend Ben and I, with a few other local poets, shared the stage at the Paramount's first Chautauqua, and last summer our daughter spent some time on the Big Island, where we fought the "Oahu Cong" thirty-seven years ago and supposedly won before being deployed to Vietnam with the rest of the 11th Infantry Brigade, where we eventually lost the war and justifiably so...

Robert is a semi-retired counselor working with adults in the Austin community. He and his wife Jeanne have three children.

The Public Library
By Julia Wagner

When I look back on my childhood memories, the place I remember spending a lot of my time is the public library. It is a great place to check out books, attend the programs they offer, or just sit and read. Children can go there after school to be in an educational environment, and adults can go when they need a break. It has played a great role in Austin's community.

The new library was built when I was about 4 or 5 years old. I remember seeing the finished library for the first time. It is really a beautiful building, inside and out. There are flowers all around it, trees, and a great path leading up to the front doors. What I will always remember as the most beautiful thing about the new library are the statues. There are two statues of a boy and a girl reading on the rocks outside, and they look so real to me that on the way in or out I sometimes stop and look at them awhile. The place where some of my fondest memories at the library took place and where I still love to go is the area in the back. I remember we called it the "home sweet home" area because it makes me feel at home with its view of the pond, comfortable chairs, couches, and a fireplace.

Even though the new public library is beautiful, a lot of my childhood memories are of the original Austin Public Library. It was torn down when I was a young child, but was located a block from St. Olaf Church. When they tore it down, the property where it used to sit was made into a parking lot. I remember a big set of stone steps leading up to the front doors. I also remember loving to go to the children's area, which was separated from the other places. It had all the children's books I could ever want and a little checkout desk of our own.

The library expansion in 1964

My absolute favorite place in the original library was the upstairs. On both sides there were steps leading up to it, and I would go up with my sister for storytelling hour, which was my favorite time of the week. An adult would choose a book and read it to us while we all gathered around. I also recall that there were paintings and artwork that you could check out and take home for a couple weeks. Every few weeks my grandma would check out a painting to hang on her wall.

The Austin Public Library, old and new, is definitely worth remembering. It has been the source of fond memories for all citizens of Austin, everyone from toddlers to senior citizens. It played a large role in Austin's history. As Norman Cousins has said, "A library should be the delivery room for the birth of ideas – a place where history comes to live."

LIBRARY, AUSTIN, MINN.—1

The original Carnegie library, before the addition in the 1960s.

The Farmer's Store
By Sidney Wakefield

We recently took some guests to lunch at the Chatham Street Café, a great little café at the corner of 1st Avenue NE and 1st Street NE here in Austin. It used to be Maple Street and Chatham Street until the streets were all renamed.

The Farmer's Store was located here in the 1920s and 1930s, and I worked there in 1930 and 1931. I worked on Saturday from 9 a.m. until closing time, usually about 11 p.m. Sometimes I just worked in the afternoon, because my job was mostly candling and sorting or grading eggs.

Farmers would bring in fifteen to thirty dozen cases to be traded for groceries and other merchandise. The eggs would be candled and graded before they could have credit for them. We graded out the small eggs, the extra large, the dark brown, the dirty, the cracked, and stained eggs. All had different prices. Candling determined if the eggs were fresh. The bad eggs were rejected and returned.

As we were eating lunch, I told my guests about the store. I am surprised at how much I can recall. The floor is the same as it was many years ago. It has been cleaned, but it is the same floor. The ceiling is also the same as it was, except for a wall at the rear, which separates the kitchen area. The building has remained much the same as it was years ago. The front door opened onto Chatham Street, and the back door onto Maple Street. Sometimes, if it was crowded inside, which it was much of the time, merchandise was put on the sidewalk outside on the Maple Street side of the building.

The main counter for serving customers was on the right as you came in the front door. There was a display shelf along the front windows. Fresh fruit such as oranges and apples were stacked in pyramids with the prices displayed here. On the main counter were two scales, one towards the front and the other to the back.

The coffee grinder sat on the main counter, and there were several varieties of coffee available. The customer could blend coffee to suit her taste. The grinder had a large wheel that was turned, and the coffee was poured in. One good spin of the large wheel would grind it, and there was a fresh coffee aroma in the whole store much of the time.

Wrapping paper dispensers were also on the main counter. One had brown paper and the other had white paper for wrapping meat and cheese. They had a variety of fresh meat and fish in season. Cheese was cut in wedges and put on the scale and wrapped. This was excellent cheese, and there were various kinds of cheeses to choose from.

They sold several kinds of chewing tobacco--Spark Plug, Peachy Scrapes, and Cut Plug, which was cut from a large plug in the amount desired. They also sold cigars, pipe tobaccos, cigarettes, and Copenhagen snuff.

A complete line of groceries was in stock all the time. Crackers and cookies were kept in bulk and sold by the pound. Flour was sold by 49-pound sacks, sugar in 25 and 50 pound bags. One of my jobs was putting sugar in 2, 5, and 10-pound bags.

The wall behind the counter had shelves full of canned goods and other grocery items. The shelves went almost to the ceiling and had a ladder that moved along them. There was also a pole with a clamp on it to get cans from the shelves.

There were two telephones for taking orders. One was beside the fold down cabinet that had all the customers' sale books. When an order was called in, it was written in the sales book and given to a clerk to fill. Many grocery orders were delivered. Many of the orders were charged and paid for weekly or monthly. They had a lot of money on the books. Some customers called every day for fresh meat and other items that needed refrigeration. The eggs were candled and graded at the rear of the store.

On the left of the front door and along that side were many items, including clothing such as gloves, overalls, jackets, and caps. Hardware was kept along here, along with pails, washtubs, boilers, forks, shovels and garden tools.

I remember the people who worked here. Mr. C.C. Loomer, the owner, was the boss. Kato Ide, his son, Bill Ide, Mr. Hart, Glen and Gert Hase all worked full-time. When Mr. Loomer retired and closed the store about 1940, Bill Ide bought a neighborhood store in the northeast part of town. Glen and Gart Hase bought the Cashman West Side Market, which they operated for a long time.

Cleaning up after the day was over was another of my jobs. I put sweeping compound on the floor and swept it. I think that is why I remember the hardwood floors. Sometimes the farmers would still be standing around and visiting. Mostly they would take the hint that it was closing time, but some would just stand there. I swept around them. This was a good general store. Too bad it had to close, but the supermarkets were taking over.

FARMER'S STORE

MAPLE AND CHATHAM

WE DELIVER — 2 PHONES—2358 - 2359

MISS MINNEAPOLIS FLOUR . 49 lbs. $1.35
VICTOR FLOUR . . . . . . 49 pounds $1.14
SUGAR . . . . 10 pounds 49c
CHRISTMAS CANDY . . lb. 10c - 12c - 15c
MIXED NUTS - - - - - Pound 19c
APPLES . . . . . . Ganos, bushel $1.49
APPLES . . . . . Jonathans, lug 95c
BLISS COFFEE . . . . 2 pounds 39c
Choc. Covered CHERRIES 19c, 23c
PITTED DATES - - - - - 2 Pounds 27c

Meat Department

BEEF ROAST—Pound	16c – 18c
BRISKET BACON—Pound	20c
SLICED BACON—Pound	23c
FRESH SIDE PORK—Pound	17c
SPARE RIBS—Small, pound	16c
DAIRY PICNIC HAMS—Pound	17c
PURE LARD—Pound	10c

CHICKENS – OYSTERS – LUTEFISK

Sidney Wakefield died shortly after submitting this story.

The Big Old Barn Still Stands
By Anne Waldman

There have been three barns in my life. The first was the white barn of my grandfather. It housed his work team and a line of milk cows all with Hungarian names. I lived on his farm in Ohio till I was five. The second barn was on a farm Dick and I moved to in Glen Rock, Pennsylvania. A bunk barn built to last forever, it had cattle underneath and hay stacked to the rafters above. We dropped the bales directly down to the bunks below.

The barn I want to tell you about for this remembrance is one we live with now. We came to it in the fall of 1982, and it was so much larger than the one we left behind. We found the harsh winters of Minnesota had aged the exterior especially since it no longer housed the livestock. The demise of most of the big barns here followed as farmers became less diversified and chose to raise only crops.

This barn, hit by a bad storm, leaned to the east and south, and the east side had a crumbling foundation. We had to make a decision. You can't borrow the money to renovate a barn if it won't work for you when it is finished. Dick was more determined than I, and he decided we would bring it back if we could, and we would use it to finish hogs. Gordon Bonzer came from Nashua, Iowa to straighten it using rods and turnbuckles to bring it in line again and make it square. The rods are still there, and it stands true twenty-two years later.

Evelyn Jorgenson, who lived on the farm as a child, gave us a photo of the new barn when her grandfather, Lorenzo Mott, built it in 1896. He built it 100' long, 36' wide and 45' high. There is no one living now who knew him. I truly regret not asking Evelyn more about the barn and the home place before she died. Why do we always think there is time yet to have those conversations?

Lorenzo and Sarah Mott had seven children. When you see the size of their home, you may wonder if the creatures didn't enjoy more room than the people. As Evelyn was growing older, and after the death of her grandfather, dad and mother, Frank and Minnie Mott Bushman ran the farm. Their household included a hired man who slept in the tiny bedroom upstairs, and the schoolteacher, who was given the bigger bedroom. Evelyn and Aunt Bertie slept in the attic over the kitchen with the only heat coming from the chimney of the cook stove.

Dale Rugg is a nephew who recalls that Frank Bushman raised purebred sorrel Belgians and also slender gaited horses for driving and riding, some of which would go to the J.C. Hormel estate not far away. The far end of the barn housed the dairy cows in stanchions facing the center. Jerseys were on the left and shorthorns on the right. We don't know if he sold their milk separately, but they always stood Jerseys on the left and shorthorns on the right. As you entered the big front doors and to the left, there was a small room where the milk went through the separator. The skim milk was given to the hogs, and the cream taken to the milk house, where the windmill kept cold water in a shallow cement basin to cool the milk cans. We keep garden equipment in there now.

Hay was stored in the huge expanse above. It was stored loose in those days. They used a grapple hook and pulley to lift it up to the loft. Horses provided the power to the ropes. A grain bin towered from the hayloft floor, clear to the rafters, to hold oats for the horses.

It took almost six months for Dick to tear out the main floor and another six months to finish the work. It was successful in that we were able to make the barn work again. We put a new metal skin over the old wood but tried our best to preserve the original appearance. Paul Schulz and his father Laurence supplied us with young pigs, and because Paul had farrowed all our hogs, they carried "the same bugs" so to speak. We could market around 1,400 hogs each year with fewer problems than most barns. Each week we would load a trailer of 25 or so for market. It has become very difficult to run a small but profitable livestock business.

In 1991 there was a terrible ice storm on Halloween. Our whole area was without power. What do you do? Our neighbor, John Jax, had dairy cows and owned a portable generator and was able to pump water. Dick happened to have a large plastic tank he hauled to John's for water. Dave Andree, our neighbor to the east, brought his four children, helped to fashion a holding tank in the hay loft, and lined up the kids to make a bucket brigade to carry water up so that gravity could let it flow down to all of the hog nipples.

The weather was fierce and terribly, terribly cold. We were fall lambing and lost a nice set of ram lambs that simply froze as newborns. It was all we could do to keep going without heat and each day carrying the water up for the hogs and feeding the sheep also. Other areas were getting power one by one, but not us; it was now two and a half weeks.

Dick and I stood out in the dark where we could see the lights in Austin. The night was completely still, but we could hear a tractor coming, coming, and coming closer. I remember the lights far off made him appear as a silhouette. It was John Jax towing his generator.

His power was on now, and he was coming to us. I bawled like a baby. Harry Mentel, bless his heart, with his face covered with frost, climbed the pole in the wind to connect our wires. We had power at last.

We no longer own the pigs in the barn. Jack Akkerman comes each day to care for his hogs that call it home. The wood roof has new green shingles. The silo, empty for years, has a tree growing right in the middle of it. The pigeons call it home. Fans keep the air currents moving inside the barn, and temperatures are constant as the pigs sleep, eat and grow.

I wish I could have known this barn as it was years ago. I can just imagine it. We wonder from time to time what's to become of it when we are gone. Lorenzo Mott probably wondered the same.

This photo or the Dobbins Run Farm includes Sarah and Lorenzo Mott.

Ann and Dick plan to remain on the Dobbins Run Farm as long as possible.

The History of District 14 School
By Nettie Trowbridge Warrington, Written in 1930

In 1870, sixty years ago this spring, District 14 appeared on the map with a new frame schoolhouse lathed and plastered and whitewashed inside and out. A real slate blackboard and "homemade" wooden desks, made of white pine, strained every temptation for the boy with a sharp jack knife. The Grange held its meetings in the new schoolhouse. There were spelling bees, debates and school entertainments almost every week all winter and the minister from Oakland conducted services Sunday.

The schoolhouse stood on the southeast corner of the Monnahan farm, where the road from Cedar City comes down to our east and west road, and it was squarely in the center of the district, which at that time included the Orcutt, Heledebrandt and Long farms. After the Eppler school district built a new schoolhouse farther south, a part of the Orcutt and Heldebrandt farms were set off into that district. Several farms had been built up to the west, such as the Wynns, Peachys, Watkins and Morelands, so it was decided they should move the schoolhouse one-half mile to its present location in mid-summer of 1882, when the sloughs were driest. They had to construct a pontoon bridge before they could cross the bottomless quagmire at the foot of this hill. There was no road across these sloughs for years. How the mothers dared send their children to school through these rattlesnake infested cow paths passes understanding. Every child of school age kept an ear tuned for the rattlesnake whirs, and every man and woman was duty bound to kill them.

The entire flat east of here and south to County Road E, and also the slough east of Wynns' farm had never been broken, and was a mass of wild flowers from early spring to fall. Cowslips, buttercups, violets, lady slippers, yellow and spotted anemones grew abundantly. There were wild phlox, cornflowers, tiger lilies, butter daisies, goldenrods and a moist gum weed that we used to break in the morning and gather the most delicious gum from coming home from school. The fall rains filled the sloughs, and after it froze we could skate from Monnahan's hill to John Magee's on the most beautiful glare ice you ever saw.

They say the best neighborhoods are found when people own their homes for more than one generation. If so, our neighborhood has a claim to that distinction. Magees, Wynns, Moshiers, Monnahans, Campbells, Hotsons, Trowbridges and Warringtons have lived here into the third and fourth generation.

For sixty years this little old schoolhouse has given its best to the girls and boys in the neighborhood. Some have made good and some have failed. Superintendent Belden years ago told my father that there was only one school in the county that ranked higher than District 14 in scholarship. Years later, Mrs. Rice said that District 14 had more children graduate from Austin High School than any other district in the county, and we hope that our school will always be the banner school.

It is always refreshing to trace the history of a neighborhood. Babies are born; children grow to be men and women. A new house goes up here and a better barn there. Death comes too, that mysterious change we must all pass through, and sorrow, and still a little more joy. A radio, a new car become topics of conversation. Our friends and neighbors and children come and go. We meet with other mothers, and keep in touch with our friends. The memories of the school and the teachers, to whom we entrusted those precious little souls who represent all, we can take with us to the next world.

A typical country school

The Austin Pedestrian/Bike Trail
By Emily Weiss

There are lots of neat things and places in Austin. One of the many is the Austin bike trail. It's a great place to spend a nice, sunny day while also getting some exercise. Another benefit is that it is a public place. Anyone can use it whenever they want, and it's free.

I like the trail and everything it has to offer. Using it is like taking a free mini-tour of Austin. It goes all over, from downtown to the Cedar River, through the town, around Mill Pond, through Todd Park, and to the J.C. Hormel Nature Center –you really see it all. It's perfect for a nice day in spring, summer, or fall, and a great way to get exercise while viewing the beautiful scenery that Austin has to offer.

My experience with the Austin pedestrian/bike trail has been very enjoyable. One sunny Saturday last summer, my whole family was just sitting around bored. My mom suggested we all go for a bike ride together, as a family. We all agreed (my brother and I reluctantly). We went on the trail, not really knowing what to expect, and we were really impressed. We got to see lots of neat things, including flowers, the river, animals, the downtown area, a bridge, some parks, the Mill Pond, a skate park, and many other people who were also enjoying the wonderful weather and the bike trail.

The trail is important to the community for many reasons. People can learn about different places in Austin that they've never been to before. Biking, walking, jogging, or rollerblading on the trail are excellent ways to get some fresh air and exercise. Sometimes that's what you really need after a week of being at work or school.

The city of Austin is thinking of adding on to the trail. I think it would be a really good idea for it to be expanded because I believe expansion will encourage more people to use it more. Having a longer trail would also bring people from the surrounding areas to come and see our delightful city while enjoying the bike trail.

Emily, an Ellis eighth grader, plays volleyball and dances on the AHS Varsity Dance Team.

Considering Austin Home
By Effie Lou Willson

My story about Austin started some fifty years ago, when the town was only a hundred years old. I was planning to come to Austin to marry a young Marine. I was a little leery about coming here, however, because as a child I read history books about Indians on the warpath in the Midwest. I also was afraid Austin would not have indoor plumbing. I was very naïve and a little stupid.

As it turned out, I was happy to see the indoor plumbing, and no Indians were to be seen on the warpath. It was a culture shock coming to Austin as I was from the Washington, D.C. area. I had a job out there, and I could visit all the beautiful buildings, as well as the Library of Congress, the Smithsonian and other cultural places.

Austin has culturally changed for the better since I arrived, which is wonderful! It has been a wonderful city to raise children. At the time our children were in school, the Austin schools were great. I don't know too much about the schools today. Austin has been a friendly city to me. I have lots of good friends and neighbors. Unfortunately my young Marine is gone, but I consider Austin my home.